Textiles of the

WIENER
WERKSTÄTTE
1910–1932

Textiles of the
WIENER
WERKSTÄTTE
1910–1932

ANGELA VÖLKER
with the collaboration of
RUPERTA PICHLER

417 illustrations, 306 in colour

THAMES AND HUDSON

ACKNOWLEDGMENTS

The present publication, devoted to the textiles of the Wiener Werkstätte now in the collection of the Öster-reichisches Museum für angewandte Kunst, Vienna, was made possible by generous financial support from the following textile firms in the Austrian province of Vorarlberg: Hermann Fend KG; J. M. Fussenegger; Getzner Textil A.G.; F. M. Hämmerle Textilwerke A.G.; Huber Tricot; Textilwerke Josef Otten; Rhomberg Textil GmbH; Textildruckerei Rueff, Weber GmbH; and Wolford A.G. The author wishes to express her sincere thanks to all the above companies and to Ruperta Pichler, whose collaboration was essential to the realization of the project. Grateful thanks are also extended to Dr Elisabeth Längle for her tireless liaison efforts between the museum and industrial firms, and to Eva Limberg, whose preparatory work in the Wiener Werkstätte archive was an essential preliminary to the detailed analysis of the material.

SOURCES OF ILLUSTRATIONS

Unless otherwise stated, all illustrations are of items in the Österreichisches Museum für angewandte Kunst, Vienna. Copyright in works by Carl Krenek, Arnold Nechansky and Dagobert Peche is vested in the Verein Bildender Künstler (VBK), Vienna. Supplementary photographs were supplied by the following: The Art Institute of Chicago (gift of Robert Allerton) 388, 392; Bildarchiv Christian Brandstätter, Vienna 5, 35, 39, 46, 51 (inset), 66, 72, 89, 133, 171, 180 (main photo); Bildarchiv Christian Brandstätter Verlag, Vienna 29–34, 59, 92, 253, 256–259, 262, 275, 188, 386; Historisches Museum der Stadt Wien, Vienna 239; Archiv der Hochschule für angewandte Kunst, Vienna 56, 61; Musée de l'Impression sur Etoffes et du Papier Peint, Mulhouse 325; Österreichische Galerie, Vienna 263

ILLUSTRATIONS ON PAGES 1 AND 2:
1 *Poster designed by Maria Likarz in 1919 for the Wiener Werkstätte showroom at 32 Kärntnerstraße, Vienna*

2 *'Erna', an ensemble designed by E. J. Wimmer-Wisgrill featuring the use of the pattern 'Grünfink' (1910/11) by Lotte Frömel-Fochler; cf. fig. 393*

Translated and adapted from the German edition, *Die Stoffe der Wiener Werkstätte 1910–1932*, first published in 1990

This edition first published in Great Britain in 1994 by Thames and Hudson Ltd, London

British Library Cataloguing-in-Publication Data. A catalogue record for this book is available from the British Library.

ISBN 0 500 23681 X

Printed and bound in Austria

CONTENTS

3   *Blouse featuring* APOLLO *(1910/11) by*
Josef Hoffmann. Fashion photograph album, 1911

AN OUTLINE OF ITS BACKGROUND HISTORY AND ARCHIVAL AND OTHER EVIDENCE OF ITS ARTISTIC AND BUSINESS ACTIVITIES

4 Josef Hoffmann. APOLLO (1910/11). Fabric sample

In 1903, when Art Nouveau was at its peak in Vienna, the architect Josef Hoffmann, the painter Koloman Moser and the industrialist Fritz Waerndorfer founded the Wiener Werkstätte, an association of artist-craftsmen working with various materials; its members included gold- and silversmiths, jewelry makers, leather workers and bronze founders, and there were also workshops for painters, varnishers and cabinetmakers.[1] Designers and craftsmen with specialist skills worked as equals, producing hand-crafted objects to meet the needs of everyday living in all its aspects. Wiener Werkstätte products were intended to stand out from the general run of aesthetically unsatisfying, badly finished factory-produced merchandise and conventional handicrafts then available, and in this way the association would become the purveyor of good taste to its customers. In Vienna this meant the abandonment of the typical stylized floral and vegetal motifs associated with international Art Nouveau, and the substitution of simple, practical objects, the special character of which was derived from a combination of artistic design and sympathetic treatment of the materials em-

5 Blouse featuring APOLLO (1910/11) by Josef Hoffmann. Artist's postcard by Mela Köhler, 1911

ployed. The models known to have influenced design in Vienna were contemporary English and Scottish artists, especially Charles Rennie Mackintosh, and the work of Dutch architects and graphic artists was also an important source of inspiraton.[2] Recent research has demonstrated clearly the comparatively late, but significant interest of Viennese artists in Japanese art.[3]

With Josef Hoffmann as architect, the Wiener Werkstätte was responsible for the design of two major buildings: the Sanatorium at Purkersdorf near Vienna (1904) and the Palais Stoclet in Brussels (1905–11). In both of these buildings not only the structure but the interior decoration, the furnishings and the entire range of household objects formed part of the total concept. Whilst the Sanatorium represents the early 'severe' stylistic phase, the interior of the Palais Stoclet reflected the more ornamental tendencies which were gaining ground again shortly before 1910.

These trends were activated not least through Carl Otto Czeschka, who was with the Wiener Werkstätte only between 1905 and 1907, but continued to contribute designs after he left.

As a result of financial disagreements Koloman Moser also left in 1907, but he too supplied designs subsequently.[4] In the autumn of 1906 Hoffmann's pupil Eduard Josef Wimmer-Wisgrill began working for the Wiener Werkstätte, taking over as head of the fashion department between 1910 and 1922; he was succeeded by Max Snischek, who had worked in various departments from *c.* 1914. Dagobert Peche, one of the most influential of the Wiener Werkstätte artists, began working with the association after 1911, but this collaboration came to an abrupt end with his premature death in 1923. Maria Likarz, Mathilde Flögl and Felice Rix, the designers who were most important in respect of the textile department, first made a significant impact in the years after the First World War.

Around 1910, when the departments of fashion and textiles were being formally established, the Wiener Werkstätte had ceased to be the idealistic association of artists as originally conceived by its founders. In Moser's eyes it had distanced itself all too soon from its stated aims: 'In my opin-ion the work became too diversified and altogether too dependent on the taste of the client',[5] was the frank assessment he offered later in his memoirs. With the founding of new departments, the Wiener Werkstätte pursued an overtly commercial course, offering as wide a spectrum of hand-crafted merchandise as possible, all displaying a uniform and easily recognizable style and available to the public from the Wiener Werkstätte's own elegant showrooms.

The first such showroom was opened on the Graben in the centre of Vienna in 1907, followed in 1916 by shops stocking the products of the fashion and textile departments respectively. In 1918 a new showroom for *Stoffe, Spitzen und Beleuchtungskörper* (fabrics, laces and light fittings) was opened. Branches were likewise established in other towns and cities, including Berlin, Zurich and New York, with varying degrees of success. In addition, from 1904 onwards the Wiener Werkstätte participated regularly in exhibitions, fashion shows and trade fairs, both at home and abroad.

6 *Josef Hoffmann.* REFRAIN *(1929). Final pre-print drawing*

Despite the range of its activities, the Wiener Werkstätte was often beset with financial problems, leading to internal reorganizations and a succession of financial directors. After the association ceased trading and was wound up (its assets were sold at auction in 1932), Alfred Hofmann, its last financial director and liquidator of the business, acquired the archive containing all the records of the association, and in 1939 he offered to sell the complete collection to the Österreichisches Museum für Künst und Industrie, today the Österreichisches Museum für angewandte Kunst. However, his proposal did not receive the favourable response he had hoped for, and consequently he sold off parts of the archive separately, including fabric printing blocks which were purchased by a company based near Zurich.

The then curators of the museum cannot be absolved of all blame for the resulting dispersal of what was not appreciated for its value as an essential historical record of the association's business. It was only after the Second World War, in 1947, that the archival material entered the museum's collection, and finally, in 1955, the remaining stock – still considerable in quantity – was donated in its entirety. The museum began compiling an inventory, dealing first with the 'artistically valuable' documents such as original drawings (figs. 6, 55, 56, 207, 241, 303, 342, 343), but work on it is still by no means complete.

The extensive range of archival material now owned by the Österreichisches Museum für angewandte Kunst – a collection which provides the basis for the content of this book – embraces documentary and artistic material of a rare completeness, offering challenges in the exploration of as yet uncharted aspects of the Wiener Werkstätte's history. In the last ten years of so numerous publications dealing with the Wiener Werkstätte in general have appeared, often in association with major exhibitions. They describe individual departments and their fields of activity (fashion, ceramics, cutlery, postcards, leather goods etc.)[6] or feature the work of leading designers such as Josef Hoffmann, Koloman Moser, Eduard Josef Wimmer-Wisgrill and Dagobert Peche.[7] The research involved has always relied heavily on the almost inexhaustible source material still preserved in the Wiener Werkstätte archive.

One well-known area of the Wiener Werkstätte's productions – textiles – which was probably one of the most successful, has not yet been thoroughly researched. The scope is wide, including printed silk ribbons, silk shawls, embroidery and lace (all of which undoubtedly call for detailed investigation), but in this book only the printed and woven fabrics designed and produced by the Wiener Werkstätte are featured. There are in fact some 20,000 fabric samples in a wide variety of shapes

8 Maria Likarz. RADIO (1926). Fabric samples in various colour-schemes, large card index

and sizes which provide the basis for research. About a hundred artists were responsible for designing over 1,800 patterns, which exist in a great variety of colour-schemes.[8] Printed silks predominate, but there are also examples of printed cottons, voiles and linens, as well as a group of woven fabrics. They are all still kept in the original order, as established by the Wiener Werkstätte: large folders containing the various fabric patterns are arranged in alphabetical order according to individual pattern names and stored in boxes. Although this method of storage, which was evidently useful and practical for commercial purposes, must of course be preserved as a historical document, it is irritating for the researcher and even more so for the interested member of the public, and tends to create a confusing picture. Any attempt at a systematic description of the Wiener Werkstätte's fabric production thus required a radical rearrangement of the source materials with the aid of colour slides, card indexes and, more recently, computerized records.

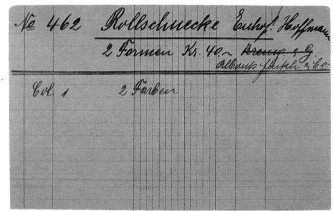

9 Josef Hoffmann. ROLLSCHNECKE (1910/12). Small card index, recto (right) and verso with sample

10

As a result of these research aids, we now have the choice of being able to review fabric patterns according to their dates of origin, so presenting a clearer perspective of stylistic developments within the Wiener Werkstätte as part of the overall production of the workshops, and at the same time gaining a comprehensive view of the association's historical development in general.

In addition to the Wiener Werkstätte archival material, the Österreichisches Museum für angewandte Kunst owns various other related items (now scattered among different departments) which were purchased directly from the Wiener Werkstätte, acquired at auction when its assets were sold in 1932 after it had closed, or which the museum acquired later (a number of items entered the collection in 1967 after the Wiener Werkstätte

exhibition held in Vienna; see figs. 7, 17, 49, 279–81, 297). The museum is not, however, the only institution in which archival material concerning the Wiener Werkstätte's textile department can be found. For example, the Historisches Museum der Stadt Wien acquired after the Second World War an extensive collection of printed silk ribbons and a number of fabric printing blocks.[9] In addition, the Cooper-Hewitt Museum in New York acquired in 1988 an important group of gouache designs with various colour-schemes – a collection which must have originated from the Wiener Werkstätte archive.[10]

While the surving patterns, along with the fabric samples in the collection of the Österreichisches Museum für angewandte Kunst, give an impressive overall view of the Wiener Werkstätte's fabric

10 Stock register, dated 1912/17

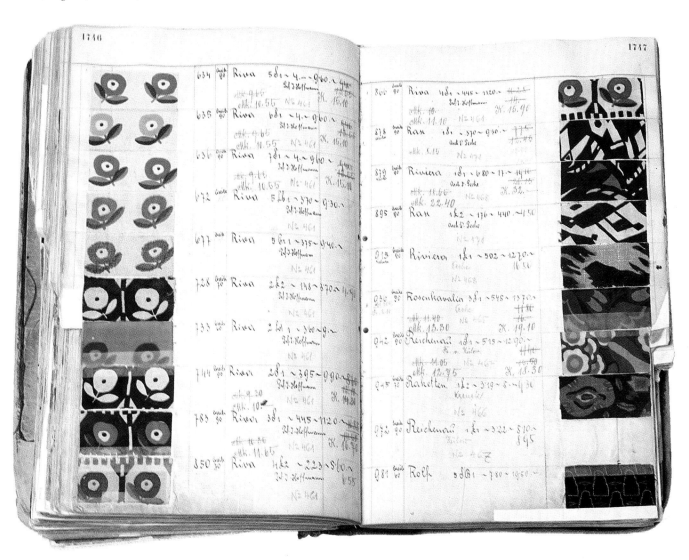

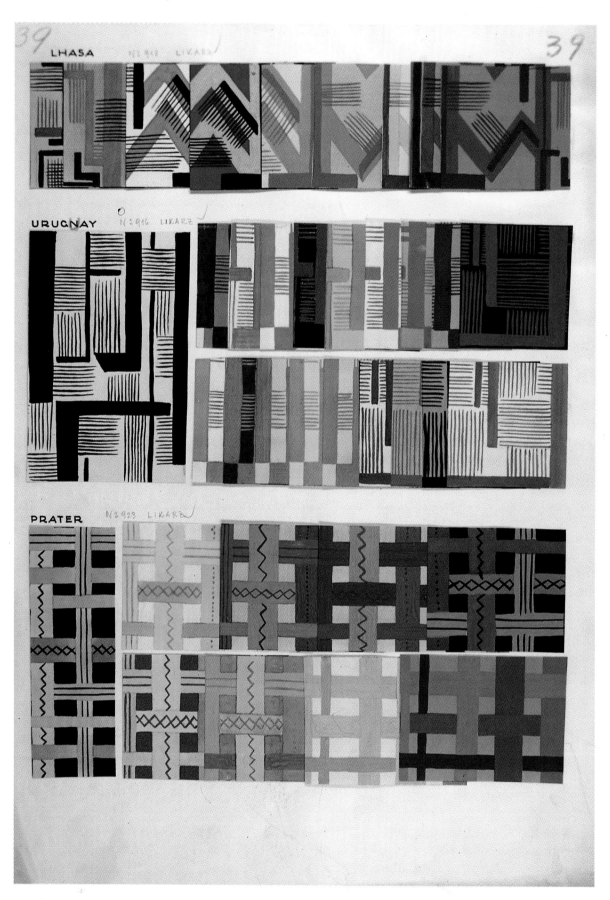

11 *Maria Likarz. LHASA (1925), URUGUAY (1925) and PRATER (1925). Trial colour-schemes; gouache on paper*

12 Annalen.
*Newspaper cuttings,
1927, including the
open letter to Adolf
Loos published in the*
Wiener Allgemeine
Zeitung *on 23 April*

Wiener Werkstätte, served to keep the association in the public eye. Although it experienced mixed fortunes, both in terms of artistic quality and of commercial success, during its three decades of active production, the Wiener Werkstätte very rapidly fell into oblivion in the 1930s, and it was only in the mid-1960s that a new interest took root. This has continued to grow in recent years, to the point at which international enthusiasm has been reflected in exhibitions held not only in Vienna, but in cities the world over, including Venice (1984), Paris (1986), Brussels and New York (1987), Tokyo (1989) and Barcelona (1993).[12]

production, the suriving archival evidence helps to establish matters of dating by reference to two different production card indexes, store registers and two stock registers which include dates of production. The final pre-print gouache drawings, kept in envelopes or pasted on to large sheets of paper (fig. 11), convey the entire range of colour-schemes for individual patterns, complementing the actual fabric samples in various colour combinations. Surviving photographs, mostly catalogued in large albums and showing objects, interiors and fashions, serve to illustrate the contexts in which fabrics were used, whil the extensive correspondence, invoices, minutes of business meetings, reports and other written records provide invaluable information about the Wiener Werkstätte's customers and sales policy.

A further important source of information is contemporary publications; thanks to the reputation created by the Wiener Werkstätte, critics, journalists and museum curators, both at home and abroad, described the impact made by new collections, focused on the contributions made by various artists or illustrated the use of fabrics in fashion and interior decoration. The Wiener Werkstätte itself collected press cuttings, which are now preserved in the archive.[11] The daily press reported on fashion shows, exhibitions and current events, such as the opening of new showrooms or the presence of prominent visitors. Even the polemical lectures delivered by Adolf Loos, the leading architect and opponent of Josef Hoffmann and the

1 For a summary of principal events in the history of the Wiener Werkstätte see Schweiger 1984, pp. 11ff.
2 Cf. Brussels 1987 (exhib. cat.), esp. p. 11.
3 The Wiener Werkstätte itself laid emphasis on Japanese handicraft techniques as ideal models, notably in its *Arbeitsprogramm* (working programme) published in 1905. Cf. *Hohe Warte* I, 1904/05, p. 268; also Brussels 1987 (exhib. cat.), p. 12; Wien 1990 Japonisme (exhib. cat.), pp. 57–64. See Schweiger 1984, pp. 42f.
4 Wien 1979 (exhib. cat.).
5 Op. cit., p. 12.
6 E.g. Schweiger 1984, Neuwirth 1985, Völker 1984 and 1990, Hansen 1982 and 1984, Pichler 1992.
7 Hoffmann: Sekler 1985; Zurich 1985 (exhib. cat.); Wien 1986/87 (exhib. and stock cat.); Wien 1987 (exhib. and stock cat.); Wien/Brtnice 1992 (exhib. cat.); New York 1992/93 (exhib. cat.). Moser: Wien 1979 (exhib. cat.); Fenz 1984. Wimmer-Wisgrill: Wien 1983 (exhib. cat.). Peche: Wien 1987 (exhib. cat.); Salzburg 1987 (exhib. cat.); Reiter 1987.
8 The present publication lists 1,335 of these patterns; those for which inadequate illustrative material is available in the museum have been omitted from the catalogue, but can be traced in the WW archive with the aid of card indexes and colour slides.
9 The ribbons and printing blocks are kept in the museum's *Modesammlung* (fashion collection), which is housed in Schloß Hetzendorf, Vienna.
10 Cooper-Hewitt Museum, inv. nos. 1988–62: 1–1494.
11 The press cuttings are preserved in the so-called *Annalen*, a series of large-format albums, inv. nos. WWAN 82–87.
12 For details of exhibition titles see the list of bibliographical sources; the Barcelona exhibition of 1993 was held at the Fundacio la Caixa.

QUESTIONS OF DATING AND THE SEQUENCE OF PATTERN NAMES AND NUMBERS

14 Blouse featuring BIENE (1910/11) by Josef Hoffmann. Fashion photograph album, 1911

Opposite
13 Josef Hoffmann. BIENE (1910/11).
Fabric sample

15 Leopold Blonder. ISPHAHAN (1912/17).
Colour proof on paper, 1912

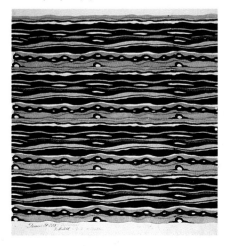

No evidence has yet been found to determine exactly when fabric production within the Wiener Werkstätte began. Since there are apparently no internal records of attempts by the Wiener Werkstätte to produce fabrics in its own workshops, the chances of ever discovering the exact date on which the designing or manufacture of textiles started appear slim. Surviving documents and the appearance of Wiener Werkstätte fabrics in source literature only serve to confirm the establishment of the textile department in 1910, or shortly before (see pp. 33 ff.). By placing its production orders with one or more outside suppliers, the Wiener Werkstätte could circumvent certain official regulations and laws which would have applied to any properly constituted commercial establishment. For example, the fashion department had to have as its director a qualified dressmaker, otherwise it could not have obtained a trading licence; thus the precise date of the official establishment of this department is on record.[1] One can assume, however, that individual artists had been working in fashion design previous to this. From the excellently documented history of the Viennese firm Backhausen & Söhne, to which we shall return, it is known that the artists involved in fabric design were active in this field before the founding of the Wiener Werkstätte's own textile department and furthermore continued to create designs for other firms after its formal establishment.

In the early years of the textile department it was extremely rare for the Wiener Werkstätte to put a date on individual pattern designs. Not until *c.* 1919, when production was registered in a card index listing not only pattern names, designers, block-cutters and manufacturers, but also the date of production, was any means of establishing exact dates available, and even after this there were frequent exceptions.[2]

At first the Wiener Werkstätte labelled fabric designs simply by name, but later each pattern had an identifying number as well, this system also being the one used by other departments. In early Wiener Werkstätte sample books (figs. 16, 17) now in the Österreichisches Museum für angewandte Kunst no numbers are given, only the name of each fabric design.

The pattern names are of little help in providing information

15

about groups of patterns which were created at about the same time. For example, designations featuring certain categories, such as animals or plants or the names of towns could have served as a basis for the grouping of designs. Hoffmann's 'Biene' ('Bee', figs. 13, 14), Moser's 'Bachstelze' ('Wagtail'), 'Apfel' ('Apple') by Czeschka (fig. 134) and Zülow's 'Lianen' (fig. 25) or Blonder's 'Isphahan' (fig. 15) and Krenek's 'Monte Carlo' (fig. 16) are instances of 'early' pattern names which, however, cannot be combined into more exactly datable groupings. Neither are the pattern names necessarily always related to the subject; thus 'Fischreiher' (literally 'Heron', fig. 132) by Czeschka features a dainty floral pattern, while 'Erlenzeisig' (literally 'Siskin', fig. 18) by Hoffmann has boldly drawn stylized flowers strewn overall. On the other hand, the name of Wimmer-Wisgrill's 'Goldblatt' (fig. 19) is descriptive of its small yellow-gold leaves arranged singly in regular rows on a black ground, and Jungnickel's 'Hochwald' (fig. 24) represents a forest landscape with animals. Other pattern names have topical associations, e.g. Frömel-Fochler's 'Sada Jacco' (fig.

20), named after a famous Japanese dancer of the day, Sada Yaco; Flögl's 'Bambi' (fig. 369) took its title from the children's book by Felix Salten published in 1923 which has become world-famous, while 'Tokio' (1924) by Rix (fig. 272) recalled the scene of a recent devastating earthquake.[3]

Occasionally one gains the impression that the use of the same letter connects a group of patterns chronologically; however, this was not done consistently or systematically. There were evidently repeated attempts to begin an alphabetical sequence: thus, the pattern names matching the numbers 1 to 16 – 'Basel' to 'Blütenzweig' all began with 'B', while those numbered 17 to 34 – 'Aussee' to 'Amur' – all began with 'A'. Following these, though not in alphabetical order, are a great variety of names; small blocks of anything from two to five patterns by the same designer are grouped consecutively; it is therefore likely that such patterns were sold to the Wiener Werkstätte not singly but in groups, as Fritzi Löw did in the case of those numbered 50 to 53, 'Klein-Zack' (fig. 21), 'Himmelschlüssel', 'Amanda' and 'Glacis'.[4]

16 Silk sample book, c. 1912

16

17 Josef Hoffmann. KERNBEISSER (1910/12). Linen sample book II, before 1914

There is a long sequence of pattern numbers – 257 to 545 – where names occur in alphabetical groupings from 'B' to 'Z', though not adhering to any strict alphabetical order within the groups with the same initial letter. These are fabrics which also appear in one of the textile department's few dated documents, a stock register with '1912 to 1917' written in pencil on the front endpaper; these dates could of course have been added later, but a glance at the fabric samples pasted into the book confirms that the years stated are probably correct. Besides this, the prices noted in this stock

18 Josef Hoffmann. ERLENZEISIG (1910/11). Silk sample book, c. 1912

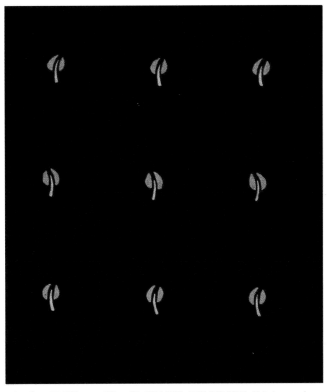

19 Eduard J. Wimmer-Wisgrill. GOLDBLATT (1910/11). Fabric sample

20 *Lotte Frömel-Fochler. SADA JACCO (1910/13). Fabric sample*

21 *Fritzi Löw. KLEIN ZACK (1910/17). Fabric sample*

register correspond to the ones listed in the catalogue of the Frühjahrsausstellung (Spring Exhibition) of 1912, as was true of Lotte Frömel-Fochler's fabrics, for instance, so providing another sound reason for accepting the date.[5]

If one attempts to deduce a logical correlation between dates and the numbering system, it seems odd, for instance, that some patterns reliably dated 1911, such as 'Ameise' by Wimmer-Wisgrill and 'Jagdfalke' or 'Erlenzeisig' by Hoffmann, are

allocated very different numbers: 33, 357, 290.[6] This may well be proof that numbering was started only after a fair number of fabrics had been designed and produced. The older patterns would thus have been introduced into the new system retrospectively. This supposition is also supported by the fact that number 1, 'Basel' by Maria Likarz, was first recorded only in 1914 in the Werkbund Exhibition held in Cologne,[7] and that 'Blumenstrauß' by Peche, which bore the number 2, could have been

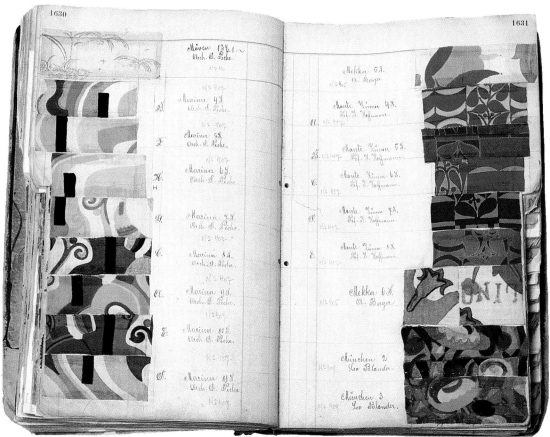

22 *Stock register, dated 1912/17*

Opposite
(from top to bottom):

23 *Ugo Zovetti. TRIPOLIS (1910/12). Length of fabric*

24 *Ludwig H. Jungnickel. HOCHWALD (1910/11). Fabric sample*

25 *Franz von Zülow. LIANEN (1910/12). Length of fabric*

18

designed at the earliest in 1911, the year he first met Hoffmann.

Model books providing a basis for exact dating – like those that existed for metal, wood or ceramics, for instance – were not kept in the textile department. Only after the fabrics had been made up into, for instance, fashion accessories or *Galanteriewaren* (fancy goods),[8] were they recorded in the relevant context. Apparently, fabric production could not be registered with the same degree of precision as was possible for hand-crafted items produced individually or in small series in other departments. There were simply too many participants involved in the whole textile production process – from the Wiener Werkstätte artist's design, via the block-cutter and the outside manufacturer – to the sale of the finished fabric, to permit the systematic recording of details relating to each pattern. It becomes clear from documents in the archives that systematic numbering did not in fact begin until 1912, and even then it was not observed with precision. Thus, many of the fabrics numbered from 1 to about 550 can hardly be dated more precisely than 'between 1910 and 1917'. Source materials or stylistic criteria often provide a more suitable basis for accurate dating.

If the suppositions outlined above are correct, it must be assumed that in the years from *c.* 1910 to 1917 about 550 fabric patterns were designed and also produced in the Wiener Werkstätte textile department, suggesting that on average over seventy fabric designs were on offer annually – an unexpectedly high number.

Some Wiener Werkstätte fabric patterns can be dated quite accurately from documented acquisitions by museums, mostly abroad, especially in the years between 1912 and 1914. Thus, apart from purchases of Wiener Werkstätte fabrics from Lotte Frömel-Fochler in 1912 (see p. 46), the textile department of the Österreichisches Museum für Kunst und Industrie bought only four Wiener Werkstätte fabrics which had been exhibited in the Winterausstellung (Winter Exhibition) of 1913/14 – 'Tripolis' (Zovetti, fig. 23), 'Wasservogel' (Krenn), 'Lianen' (Zülow, fig. 25) and 'Irland' (Likarz, figs. 99–102) – this time, however, from the Wiener Werkstätte itself. It was not until the final liquidation sale following the closure in 1932 that this major museum bought textiles in significantly larger amounts.[9]

In the pre-war years more interest was aroused elsewhere (see pp. 203f.). In 1913 Isabelle Errera, editor of the catalogue of textiles in the Museés Royaux du Cinquantenaire in Brussels, bought the following patterns from P. A. Walther in Frankfurt am Main: Hoffmann's 'Apollo' (figs. 3–5) and 'Jagdfalke' (figs. 60–63), Wimmer-Wisgrill's 'Heimchen' and 'Leopard' (fig. 16), Jungnickel's 'Hochwald' (fig. 24), as well as Nechansky's 'Pompeji' (fig. 26), Czeschka's 'Po-Ho' (fig. 135) and 'Waldidyll' (figs. 81, 133) and Rose Krenn's 'Backfisch'.

Maria Likarz's 'Irland' (figs. 99–102) was among the donations made later to the Belgian museum by the artist. Also in 1913 the municipal museum in Chemnitz acquired at least three Wiener Werkstätte fabrics.[10] In 1913 and 1914 the Musée de l'Impression sur Étoffes et du Papier Peint in Mulhouse acquired a total of about fifty samples of fabric designs, again providing a sound basis for dating. The French museum bought the patterns through a subscription arrangement with the dealer Maison Claude Frères in Paris.

If the catalogue presented in this book is arranged, as already noted, alphabetically according to the artists' names and retains the Wiener Werkstätte's system of numbering, this course has been followed because, despite all the inconsistencies, it nevertheless allows a certain chronological sys-

tematization within comprehensible periods of time. Furthermore, it corresponds roughly to the phases of development within the textile department of the Wiener Werkstätte and to its history.

1 Cf Völker 1984, p. 18; the date was 9 March 1911.
2 The so-called small card index seems to be the earlier counterpart of the large card index, the dates noted ranging from 1916 to 1919. There are, however, large gaps, and it is therefore unreliable as a guide to the production of these years.
3 Further examples are: 'Rapallo' by Anny Schröder (in 1922 the Treaty of Rapallo, normalizing Russo-German relations, was signed); and 'Lindbergh' by Maria Likarz (recalling the first solo flight across the Atlantic by Charles A. Lindbergh in 1927).
4 Some drawings of fabric patterns have 'price' and 'purchased' noted on the reverse, along with the relevant figures; see fig. 241.
5 Wien 1912 (exhib. cat.), p. 28; Lagerbuch (stock record) I.
6 Karl Walde, 'Ausstellung österreichischer Kunstgewerbe 1911–1912' in *TKI* V (1912), pp. 50 ff.; WWMB 54, p. 522.
7 *DK* XVII (1914), pp. 470 f.
8 Cf. for example WWMB 54.
9 Cf. Auktionshaus für Altertümer Glückselig Ges. m. H., Wien IV, Mühlgasse 28–30: Versteigerung des gesamten Warenlagers der Wiener Werkstätte (12–16, 19 and 20 September 1932). The Österreichisches Museum für Kunst und Industrie acquired 25 lengths of fabric.
10 'Santa Sophia' (Hoffmann, figs. 70, 296), 'Montenegro' (Zovetti) and 'Kahlenberg' (Alber, fig. 69); information kindly supplied by Frau Katharina Metz. In the minutes of the third board meeting, held on 15 April 1915, it is recorded (p. 5) that the Osthaus Museum in Hagen (whose collections were transferred to the Kaiser-Wilhelm-Museum in Krefeld in 1922) began purchasing textiles from the Wiener Werkstätte in 1915 at the latest. Cf. also Krefeld 1984 (exhib. cat.), p. 163.

26 *Arnold Nechansky. POMPEJI (1910/11). Fabric sample*

A New Interest:
Fabric Designs Before the Establishment of the Wiener Werkstätte's Own Textile Department

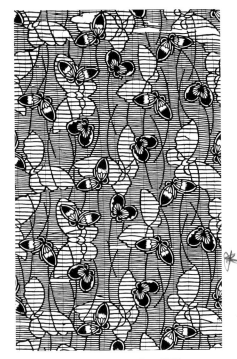

27 Japanese stencil (katagami), c. 1870

28 Kolo Moser. DIE SCHWARZEN TULPEN (woven fabric). Ver Sacrum 1899

As in many fields of the fine and applied arts in Vienna around the turn of the century, the beginnings of creative activity in textiles and fabric patterns can be traced to influences from England and Scotland. Around 1900, Viennese architects of the Secession movement were using English fabrics in their interiors and later in combination with their own designs.[1] The urge to shape the entire environment now raised even the status of textile designing to that of a recognized artistic contribution. William Morris, Walter Crane, Christopher Dresser and Charles Francis Annesley Voysey were all pioneers and models for Viennese artists as well; their ideas and solutions were among the most harmonious and convincing.[2]

The creative interest in the flat surface, in the pattern and not least in textile design derived from the general contemporary approach to style, which aimed at flatness, at stylization based on natural forms and especially at abstraction itself. The method of composition adopted was denigrated as 'only' pattern-making, which eventually led to abstract art being censured by its opponents.[3] Particularly the

Viennese artists began to break free from the use of naturalistic forms, leading eventually to a rejection even of their own stylization and of floral Art Nouveau in general. Small-scale, mainly abstract and geometric patterns were first created by Koloman Moser and Josef Hoffmann, the founders of the Wiener Werkstätte.

Kolo Moser was especially attracted to pattern designing and was able to introduce new and exotic dimensions. With his designs for Johann Backhausen & Söhne published in *Ver Sacrum* in 1899 and shown as 'woven surface decor' in the fourth Secession exhibition in the same year,[4] he created for Vienna the prototypes of the new artistic awareness. Around 1901, the well-known publishing house of Gerlach issued a compendium of Moser's patterns, in the form of a portfolio entitled *Flächenschmuck* ('surface decoration'), in the series *Die Quelle*. It contains designs for widely contrasting categories, including not only woven fabrics, floor-coverings and wall decor, but also book endpapers or wallpaper.[5] Two groups of motifs can be distinguished in Moser's textile designs: stylized animal

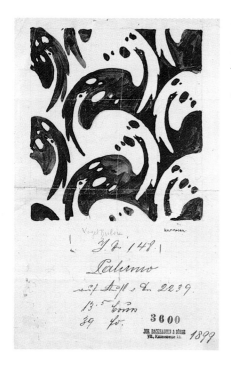

29 Kolo Moser.
VOGEL BÜLOW.
Final pre-print drawing
for Joh. Backhausen &
Söhne, Vienna, 1899;
pencil and ink on paper

Designers need receptive and open-minded manufacturers for the execution of their ideas. In Vienna the well-known firm Johann Backhausen & Söhne was the leading pioneer in this field.[7] Its production consisted exclusively of materials for interior design, mostly woven textiles, but printed fabrics also played an important part. In addition, Backhausen sold machine-woven and hand-knotted carpets. Thanks to the proprietors' appreciation of art and artists, their interest in recording the firm's history and the care they took, precise details are available today concerning those artists who were active in textile and carpet design in Vienna around 1900. Backhausen's archive has survived almost intact and provides an impressive and unusually detailed picture of this aspect of textile production during these years; it was innovative

and plant forms dominate, and there are also simpler patterns of abstract linear compositions. Forms using two colours, often applied reciprocally – a feature of many Oriental and East Asian patterns – contrast with multi-coloured designs of great lavishness. The motifs, in their strict adherence to two-dimensional design limitations, met contemporary demands for designs to be appropriate to the materials employed. At the same time Moser was to a great extent already freeing himself from the English model. He preferred a more abstract vocabulary, one of his main sources of inspiration being Japanese stencils known as *katagami* (figs. 27, 28, 30).[6]

31 Josef Hoffmann.
FLORIDA.
Fabric woven by Joh.
Backhausen & Söhne
for the Kunstschau
Wien, 1908

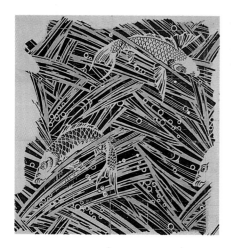

30 Kolo Moser.
SPIEL DER WELLEN.
Print proof on paper for
Joh. Backhausen &
Söhne, Vienna, 1899

and in no way subservient to the popular taste of the time.[8] Firms such as E. & S. Steiner and Philipp Haas & Söhne followed the Backhausen example.[9] Hartwig Fischel, himself an architect and art critic, noted in his review of the Ausstellung österreichischer Kunstgewerbe held at the Österreichisches Museum für Kunst und Industrie in the winter of 1911/12: 'In this exhibition great interest has been aroused by textiles, an area seemingly destined to absorb and develop new ideas and one which plays such an influential role both in interior decoration and in clothing.'[10]

Right
32 Dagobert Peche.
Fabric and carpet
pattern. Final pre-print
drawing for Joh.
Backhausen & Söhne,
Vienna, 1917

Far right
33 Kolo Moser. Woven
pile carpet. Final pre-
print drawing for Joh.
Backhausen & Söhne,
Vienna, 1902

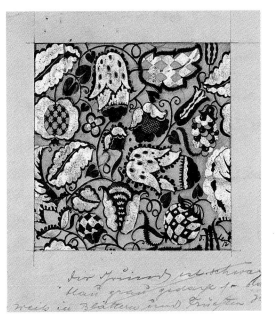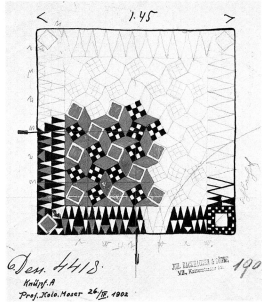

34 Otto Prutscher.
CHANTILLY. Final
pre-print drawing for
Joh. Backhausen & Söhne,
Vienna, 1905

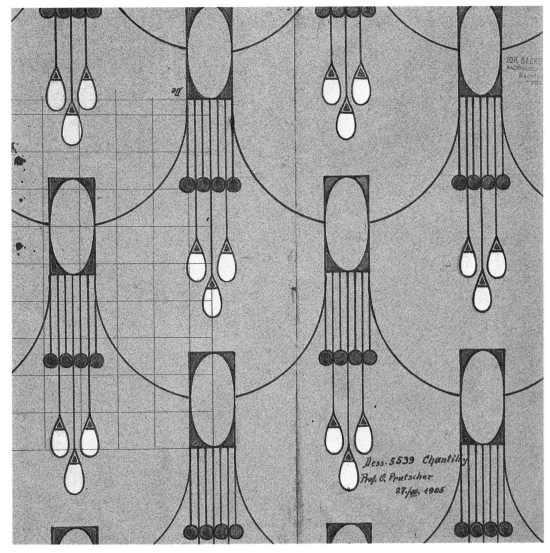

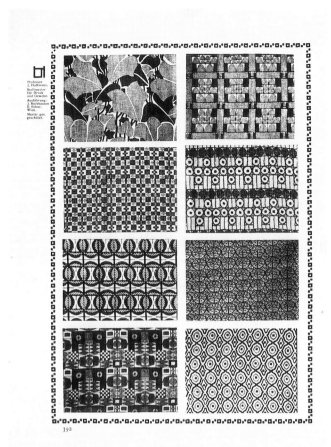 

35 Josef Hoffmann. Woven and printed fabrics, 1909, made by Joh. Backhausen & Söhne, Vienna. DKD 1909/10

Kolo Moser worked for Backhausen between 1898 and 1904; his repertoire included both textiles and carpets. In the early days of the Wiener Werkstätte it was above all Josef Hoffmann who, in addition to his using own creations for upholstery and drapery, employed fabrics designed by Kolo Moser in other contexts during the years before the founding of the Wiener Werkstätte textile department.[11] Josef Hoffmann began working for Backhausen only in 1901. From 1904 onwards, Wiener Werkstätte commissions are recorded in the Backhausen books, some of them, however, being entered also under the name of Josef Hoffmann; the record-keeping at Backhausen's does not seem to have been particularly meticulous in this respect, and Hoffmann's name was evidently identified with the association of artists. The records do not make a clear distinction between commissions for Hoffmann's own architectural practice[12] and orders he might have placed on behalf of the Wiener Werkstätte in his capacity as its director. An example of this casual approach is provided by a double page in *Deutsche Kunst und Dekoration*, which regularly carried reports about the Wiener Werkstätte from 1904 onwards. In the section of volume XXV (1909/10) devoted to it, a total of sixteen patterns based on designs by Josef Hoffmann was shown (fig. 35), but none of these was classified in the Backhausen archive as being of Wiener Werkstätte origin.[13] The printed and woven textiles published in the magazine were created between 1906 and 1908.[14] One of the printed fabric designs crops up again later in the textile department of the Wiener Werkstätte in a simplified form as the pattern 'Kernbeisser' (fig. 17). Of all the patterns in the series illustrated in black and white it is the freest and most lively. The patterns of the remaining materials are characterized by small grids which

24

regulate the abstract or stylized plant motifs used as space fillers. As far as the colours used can be determined from Backhausen's records, they can be said to conform with more rigid impression already described. In addition to simple black-and-white two-colour contrasts, there are printed and woven patterns which show a lively and versatile use of colour combinations.

There are only two fabric designs in Backhausen's archive that can be unequivocally classified as Wiener Werkstätte commissions: 'Notschrei' (figs. 36, 37)[15] and 'Sehnsucht',[16] both designed and manufactured in 1904. The finished drawings still in Backhausen's possession bear the Wiener Werkstätte monogram, either stamped on or glued to the paper.[17]

It is quite probable that Hoffmann created both textiles for use in the Purkersdorf Sanatorium near Vienna, built by the Wiener Werkstätte in the same year (figs. 37, 40). At all events, these patterns were used in upholstery fabrics for the waiting room ('Sehnsucht'), the billiard room and the table tennis room ('Notschrei') and the writing and reading room ('Sehnsucht'). Hoffmann also used a third fabric, designated Backhausen no. 5226, which was illustrated in *Deutsche Kunst und Dekoration* (fig. 39, lower left) together with 'Sehnsucht' (upper left) and 'Notschrei' and a fourth pattern, 'Streber' (fig. 38).[18] Hoffmann also used 'Notschrei' as an upholstery fabric in the first Wiener Werkstätte exhibition held in Berlin at the Hohenzollern Kunstgewerbehaus in 1904 (fig. 36).[19] In the same year 'Sehnsucht' was used by Moser for the same purpose in the dining room of Dr S.'s (Stonborough) house in Berlin.[20]

The patterns reflect contemporary trends in ornamentation, which aimed at achieving simplification and smallness of scale. Straight lines, squares and arrows are deployed by Hoffmann as basic features. Serving as decorative elements are: in 'Sehnsucht', small ovals, whose bold colour makes them stand out in relief; and, in 'Notschrei', heart-shaped ornaments. No. 5226, which follows this trend, features parallel lines and small, decorative motifs with curving outlines. With the invention of 'Streber' the artists went one step further towards abstraction. Here the pattern consists simply of fine straight lines and triangles of various sizes. The material – silk – contributes to the richness of effect. By the use of different weaving textures, the colouring acquires a subtle shading, with the colour-contrasted lines and contours appearing to stand out in relief against the ground. In the ladies' lounge at Purkersdorf, on the other hand, Hoffmann upholstered the furniture using one of Kolo Moser's designs for silk fabrics dating from 1900, 'Das Schweigen des Abends' (figs. 40, 41), which the stylized plant motifs were inspired by Japanese sources.[21]

The principal Wiener Werkstätte commissions recorded in the Backhausen archive between 1903 and 1913 are those for carpets.[22] There is a distinction to be drawn here between so-called velour carpets and Smyrna carpets. The former were machine-woven broadloom carpets which were usually laid as a fitted carpet covering the whole floor area of a room. In contrast, Smyrna carpets were hand-knotted and specially made to order.

36 Wiener Werkstätte exhibition at the Hohenzollern-Kunstgewerbehaus, Berlin. 1904. Upholstery fabric NOTSCHREI by Josef Hoffmann. DKD 1904/05

37 Purkersdorf Sanatorium near Vienna, designed by Josef Hoffmann, 1904. Upholstery fabric NOTSCHREI by Josef Hoffmann.
Wiener Werkstätte photograph album 102. Woven fabric sample (inset) made by Joh. Backhausen & Söhne, Vienna

We cannot ascertain today the original purposes for which all the carpets were intended. The velour carpets were used in a variety of interiors. The 'Sanduhr' pattern, for example, originally designed by Hoffmann for the Ausstellung österreichischer Kunstgewerbe held in 1911/12, was again used in 1916 for the floor-covering of the fashion department's showroom (fig. 169) and for the Knips apartment.[23] A further example – also a design by Hoffmann – is a runner, strikingly patterned with abstract and stylized floral forms, which was first used in the Villa Ast on the Hohe Warte in Vienna (1909/11, fig. 42),[24] and later in the Gallia family's apartment (completed in 1913) in the Wohllebengasse in Vienna's fourth district;[25] in the same year, it was also seen in Geneva in the apartment of the Swiss painter Ferdinand Hodler,[26] and again later in Gustav Klimt's studio in Vienna.[27] Hoffmann used this pattern yet again in Friederike Beer-Monti's apartment in 1914 (fig. 262).[28] The earliest velour carpet for the Wiener Werkstätte, a design by Josef Hoffmann dating from 1904, was used by Kolo Moser as a floor-covering for Dr. K.'s (Koller) apartment.[29] It is also frequently seen in the early photographs of interiors preserved in the albums in the Wiener Werkstätte archive.[30]

The destinations of the specially commissioned hand-knotted Smyrna carpets designed by Hoffmann are usually noted in the Backhausen archive. As with the velour carpets, the circumstances of other uses can be reconstructed by reference to the source literature and contemporary photographs. However, the precise purpose of some singly produced pieces and velour carpets remains a mystery,[31] for example that of the earliest hand-made carpet, reticent in pattern and measuring approximately 2 x 3 metres (6 ft 6 in. x 10 ft). The design for it, owned by the Backhausen company, shows the Hoffmann monogram as well as the Wiener Werkstätte stamp, together with an early Wiener Werkstätte number (an unusual feature in the context of textiles).[32] Two identically patterned carpets were made in 1906 for the Brauner House on the Hohe Warte and laid in the study and master bedroom.[33] A third carpet, in a different design, was used in the entrance hall.[34] Two groups of carpets more extensive in range are dated 1910 and 1913: a total of four for the Palais Stoclet in Brussels,[35] and five carpets and runners for the Gallia apartment.[36] In these designs Hoffmann adopted a new, more

pronounced ornamental-decorative approach, using colours of striking intensity, especially in the Gallia apartment. He enclosed stylized plant motifs in geometric grids and combined them to create repeating patterns.

After the foundation of its own textile department – that is, from *c.* 1910 onwards – practically the only textiles used for the Wiener Werkstätte interiors were those designed there and produced under its own name. Early examples dating from 1911 are the Marx apartment[37] in the Hinterbrühl, near Vienna, and that of Mimi Marlow, a well-known soubrette (figs. 53, 54).[38] Two houses in which especially lavish use was made of Wiener Werkstätte textiles were the Primavesi family's country house in Winkelsdorf, Moravia (1913, figs. 79–86),[39] and later (1924–25) the Villa Knips in Vienna.[40]

Some carpets manufactured independently in the early period by Backhausen in the name of the Wiener Werkstätte or using its designs are known only from illustrations published in the magazine *Textile Kunst und Industrie* in 1913 (fig. 70).[41] They originally featured in the Österreichische Adria Ausstellung, an exhibition held that year at the Österreichisches Museum für Kunst und Industrie. Familiar fabric patterns – Hoffmann's 'Santa Sophia', Wimmer-Wisgrill's 'Herbstsonne' and Riedel's 'Klatschrose' – were adapted to machine-woven carpets and exhibited alongside pile carpets with patterns that can also be traced back to fabric designs, namely 'Jagdfalke' and 'Triangel' by Hoffmann, and, again, Riedel's 'Klatschrose'. The

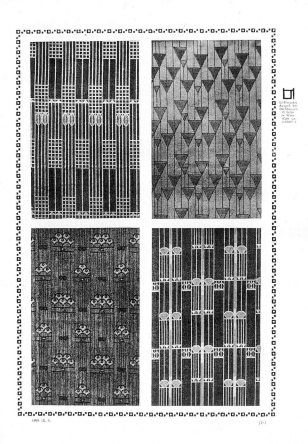

39 *Josef Hoffmann. Woven fabrics (1904), made by Joh. Backhausen & Söhne, Vienna. DKD 1905*

Opposite
38 *Josef Hoffmann.* STREBER *(1904), length of woven fabric made by Joh. Backhausen & Söhne, Vienna*

40 *Purkersdorf Sanatorium near Vienna, designed by Josef Hoffmann, 1904. Upholstery fabric* DAS SCHWEIGEN DES ABENDS *(1900) by Kolo Moser. Wiener Werkstätte photograph album 102*

41 *Kolo Moser.* DAS SCHWEIGEN DES ABENDS *(1900). Woven fabric made by Joh. Backhausen & Söhne, Vienna*

Teppichhaus Orendi, a well-known carpet manufacturer which also dealt in oriental carpets, is
listed as the maker. No traces of this production
exist either in the Wiener Werkstätte archive or in
the collections of the Österreichisches Museum für
angewandte Kunst, nor are any other examples
known to have cropped up in other collections.
It was only in the late 1920s that the Wiener Werkstätte started to place orders with the German company Vereinigte Smyrna-Teppich Fabriken AG in
Cottbus for the production of simple carpets with
patterns typical of the period. Accounts from the
years 1928 and 1929 and a portfolio of pattern cards
in the Wiener Werkstätte archive are the only
available information concerning this production
(fig. 44).[42]

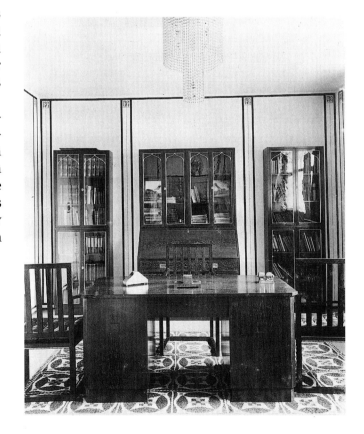

1. *Ver Sacrum* III (1900), p. 81; Sekler 1985, cat. no. 32, p. 259 (Berger-höhe); *DKD* XXIV (1909), pp. 216f. (Knips family dining room), and XXV (1909–10), pp. 400 f. (country house near Budapest).
2. Stuttgart 1979 (exhib. cat.); Parry 1983.
3. Paul Schulze, 'Der Einfluß der Futuristen auf die Textilmusterung' in *TKI* VI (1913), pp. 227ff.; Bouillon 1989, pp. 191ff.
4. *Ver Sacrum* II (1899), no. 4; *Katalog der III. Kunstausstellung der Vereinigung bildender Künstler Österreichs* (Vienna 1899), pp. 191–204; also Ludwig Hevesi in *KKHW* II (1899), pp. 160ff.
5. Cf. also Giovanni Fanelli, 'L'Infinito Ornamento' in *FMR* 8 (1982), pp. 29ff.
6. *Völker amk;* cf. also Johannes Wieninger, 'Was können wir von den Japanern lernen? Japanische Kunst und Wien um 1900' in Tokyo 1989 (exhib. cat.), pp. 450 ff.; and Wien 1990 Japonism (exhib. cat.).
7. Cf. *TKI* II (1909), no. 5, pp. 35 ff.; Wien 1992 (exhib. cat.).
8. Wien 1909/10 (exhib. cat.). For the first exhibition in the new building of the Östereichisches Museum für Kunst und Industrie, including fabrics designed by Hoffmann, Frömel-Fochler and Witzmann produced by Backhausen & Söhne; see *Die Kunst* XI, no. 6 (March 1910), pp. 261ff., esp. 278f.
9. Cf. *DKD* XXVI (1910), p. 65, and XXVIII (1911), pp. 66ff.; also *DK* XX (1912), pp. 581, 583
10. Hartwig Fischel in *KKHW* XIV (1911), p. 663.
11. Baroni/D'Auria 1981, p. 38 (fig. 87) and pp. 80f.
12. Sekler 1985, p. 236.
13. *DKD* XXV (1909/10), pp. 392f.; cf. also Wien 1992 (exhib. cat.), nos. 14, 16, 20–22.
14. Cf. Zurich 1983 (exhib. cat.).
15. Backhausen no. 5113.
16. Backhausen no. 5116; cf. Zurich 1983 (exhib. cat.), nos. 201, 202 and fig., p. 92.
17. Wien 1985 (exhib. cat.), no. 306, p. 352.
18. Backhausen no. 5147; *DKD* XVI (1905), p. 561; *ID* XVII (1906), p. 36; *DKD* XIX (1906/7), pp. 46f.; Zurich 1983 (exhib. cat.), no. 205 and fig., p. 92.
19. Sekler 1985, cat. no. 87 and fig., p. 289; *DKD* XV (1904/5), pp. 22–6.
20. *DKD* XVI (1905), p. 538.
21. Backhausen no. 4016.
22. Cf. Wien 1992 (exhib. cat.), nos. 34–36, 43.
23. Fashion department showroom: Sekler 1985, cat. no. 197, pp. 376f. Knips apartment: *DKD* XLI (1917/18), p. 120, and Sekler 1985, cat. no. 193, pp. 374f.
24. *MBF* XII (1913), pp. 11ff.; Sekler 1985, cat. no. 134, p. 334; Zurich 1983 (exhib. cat.), no. 228, fig. 8.
25. Melbourne 1984 (exhib. cat.), no. 98, p. 83.
26. Fanelli/Godoli 1981, fig. 195.
27. Fischer 1987, p. 34, fig. 29.
28. Schweiger 1984, p. 73. The runner in the Palais Stoclet is repeated in the Knips apartment of 1915/16; cf. *DKD* XLI (1917/18), p. 120.
29. Backhausen no. 5042; cf. *DKD* XVI (1905), pp. 562-4; Wien 1992 (exhib. cat.), no. 36.
30. For example, WW photo album 137.
31. Backhausen no. 5911 (pile carpet, 1906); no. 7715 (runner, 1910); no. 7721 (velour carpet, 1910); no. 7741 (velour carpet, 1910); no. 8216 (velour carpet, 1911).
32. Backhausen no. 5002 (Smyrna, 1903). Cf. Wien 1981 (exhib. cat.), p. 349, no. 299; Wien 1992 (exhib. cat.), cat. 34.
33. Backhausen no. 5733; cf. *DKD* XIX (1906/7), pp. 49f.
34. Backhausen no. 5730; cf. *DKD* XIX (1906/7), p. 47.
35. Backhausen nos. 7537 ('carpet'), 7538 ('washroom and breakfast room'), 7542 ('hall') and 7627 ('runner').
36. Backhausen nos. 8932 ('smoking room'), 8934 ('boudoir'), 8937 room'), 8938 ('salon'), 8939 ('ditto'); cf. Melbourne 1984 (exhib. cat.), pp. 81ff.

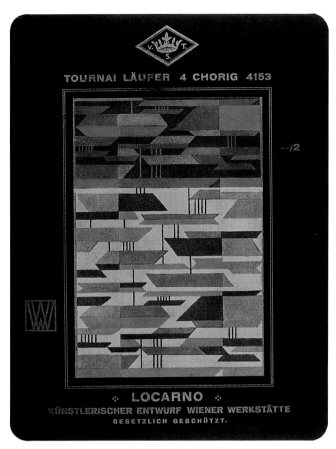

44 *Maria Likarz. LOCARNO (c. 1930). Design for a woven carpet. Vereinigte Smyrna-Teppich Fabriken AG, Cottbus*

37. Sekler 1985, cat. no. 145, pp. 342f.
38. Sekler 1985, cat. no. 152, p. 345.
39. Sekler 1985, cat. no. 179, pp. 360ff.
40. Sekler 1985, cat. no. 265, pp. 400ff.
41. *TKI* VI (1913), pp. 441ff.
42. This refers to a collection of pattern cards in a portfolio; each is marked with a crown and below it the letters V.S.T. (Vereinigte Smyrna-Teppich Fabriken), as well as the Wiener Werkstätte monogram, and the portfolio cover bears the words 'Künstler-Entwürfe Wiener Werkstätte' ('WW artists' designs'). The designers concerned could have been Maria Likarz and/or Mathilde Flögl. Cf. Neuwirth 1984, pp. 238f.

THE BEGINNINGS OF THE
WIENER WERKSTÄTTE'S OWN TEXTILE DEPARTMENT

46 *Wiener Werkstätte. Rose mark printed on silk*

Opposite
45 *Ladies' dresses. Fashion photograph album, 1911*

The textiles manufactured by Backhausen & Söhne for the Wiener Werkstätte were probably not sold in the Wiener Werkstätte itself, nor did the name or the Wiener Werkstätte monogram appear on the selvedge of fabrics, as was the case with most of the materials produced later for its own textile department (fig. 47). The successful partnership with Backhausen may in the end have been instrumental in providing the Wiener Werkstätte with an even larger range of textiles when it went into production in its own name; these were meant mainly for the workshop's own use, and only secondarily intended for retail sale. In the years around 1910 printed fabrics appear to have become more and more popular. As Hartwig Fischel noted, 'They permit such freedom of choice in colour and such flexible ornamentation.'[1] This may also have been a reason for the Wiener Werkstätte's decision not to continue the partnership with Backhausen, since the mainstay of the firm's production was woven rather than printed fabrics.

There are no official documents, personal letters or general information surviving in the Wiener Werkstätte archive or any other sources which today give any

47 *Selvedges with identifying marks*

concrete information about the organization's motives for having textiles manufactured in its own name. Hoffmann wrote on the occasion of the organization's 25th anniversary in 1928: 'There are workshops for fashion and knitwear, beading, embroidery and fabric painting … , woven and printed fabrics, carpets, wallpaper and printed silks are made in the excellent workshops associated with the Wiener Werkstätte. Lace articles, small pieces of tapestry and unusual curiosities are produced with loving care by outworkers.'[2]

Information about the start of production and sales appeared in the Viennese daily newspaper *Neue Freie Presse* of 5 October 1910, namely, a report about the exclusive availability of Wiener Werkstätte products in Berlin at the Wertheim department store: 'In addition, the German company [Wertheimer] has signed long-term contracts with the most important German textile, silk or similar firms, with a view to the production of fabrics based on designs of the Wiener Werkstätte.'[3] Corroborating this is an undated contract in the Wiener Werkstätte archive establishing the foundation of a limited company, the Wiener Werkstätte in Deutschland Gesellschaft mit

beschränkter Haftung, in which 1910 is recorded as the first year of active trading. The headquarters of this company was established in Berlin and the stated 'object of the enterprise' was described as: 'The selling agency for all handicraft creations of the Wiener Werkstätte in Vienna. The manufacture and sale of textiles and other merchandise designed by the Wiener Werkstätte or their artists. The production and trade with all the materials pertaining directly or indirectly to the advancement of relevant aims. The establishment of mercantile or industrial enterprises, which are likewise directly or indirectly advantageous to relevant aims, and the participation in same.' Other than this, no further information about the enterprise is available.[4] Indeed, the endeavours of the Wiener Werkstätte seem to indicate too that fabric designs were already in existence and were the subject of discussion with manufacturers.[5]

Thus it is not improbable that the fashion photographs in the album *Mode* (figs. 45, 48)[6] – unfortunately undated, but probably taken about 1910/11 – showing dresses and blouses made of Wiener Werkstätte fabrics represent the very first examples of their use in the fashion department. Among the newly created fabrics are: Hoffmann's 'Apollo' (fig. 3), 'Biene' (fig. 14) and 'Lerche' (fig. 142) used for blouses (figs. 3, 14); dresses featuring 'Ameise' (fig. 55) by Wimmer-Wisgrill, Moser's 'Amsel' (fig. 48) and 'Bergfalter' (fig. 50), and 'Edelmarder' by Mitzi Vogel. The characteristic mixture associated with the simplified reform or rational dress of the Wiener Werkstätte's early years and with daytime fashions has great charm, showing off materials to their best advantage.

By the spring of 1911 at the latest, textile production by the Wiener Werkstätte was a self-evident reality: in one of the pattern books, *Diverses* (miscellaneous), there are references to items made of particular Wiener Werkstätte fabrics. As suggested by its title, the pattern book documents all kinds of products, including textiles.[7] Whilst production in 1910 evidently consisted of cockades, hats or shawls using materials of one colour as well as embroidered or batik-printed fabrics, here, on 15 April 1911, mention is made of the first shawl to

48 Dress featuring AMSEL (1910/11) by Kolo Moser. Fahsion photograph album, 1911

Opposite 49 Kolo Moser. AMSEL (1910/11). Fabric sample and (inset) linen sample book I, before 1914

34

feature the use of a Wiener Werkstätte fabric – 'Erlenzeisig' by Josef Hoffmann (fig. 18). After this come shawls and cushion-covers using various designs: 'Ameise' (fig. 58), 'Mandelkrähe' (fig. 52) and 'Heimchen' by Wimmer-Wisgrill; Moser's 'Baummarder' (fig. 297); 'Apollo' (fig. 4) and 'Alpenfalter' (fig. 98) by Hoffmann; 'Edelmarder' (fig. 45) by Mitzi Vogel; and Frömel-Fochler's 'Eisfuchs' and 'Geier'. Apart from these items, 'bouquets made of our silk fabrics' are recorded, but with no mention of the names of patterns.[8] The new textiles were integrated into the production of other departments without any special advertising or marketing publicity.

An early use of one of the most popular Wiener Werkstätte fabrics, 'Ameise' by Wimmer-Wisgrill (fig. 58), and one that was certainly highly prestigious, was at the International Art Exhibition held in Rome in the spring of 1911. 'Ameise', which features a striped ground with evenly scattered floral motifs, was inspired by the idea of 'Neo-Biedermeier'. It was used as background decoration in the showcases for handicrafts displayed in the Austrian pavilion built by Hoffmann.[9]

Also in 1911, Eduard Wimmer-Wisgrill featured his own apartment in the magazine *Das Interieur*.[10] Although he complained of lack of funds, one can see here the luxuriant adaptation of a Wiener Werkstätte fabric, a concept which artists of that time may have imagined as an ideal. The main decorative element of the bedroom furnishings, for instance, was Wimmer's own fabric 'Heimchen'. Wall-coverings, window curtains and bed curtains all made of the same material reflect a taste tending towards the rococo, or at least suggest an interpretation of whatever idea Wimmer may have had of that period and its boudoirs. In the same issue of the magazine there is an illustration of a sofa designed by Wimmer, which in terms of both form and colour is entirely in keeping with the image of a classically inclined 'Neo-Rococo', the most perfect expression of which must surely be Richard Strauss's opera *Der Rosenkavalier*, first performed in Dresden in 1911, with stage sets and costumes by Alfred Roller, the Viennese stage designer.

50 Dress featuring BERGFALTER (1910/11) by Kolo Moser. Fashion photograph album, 1911

Opposite
51 Kolo Moser. BERGFALTER (1910/11). Fabric sample with (inset) artist's postcard by Mela Köhler, 1911

53 Mimi Marlow's apartment, Vienna, designed Josef Hoffmann, 1911.
Anteroom featuring upholstery fabric SAMTENTE (1910/11) by Lotte
Frömel-Fochler. Wiener Werkstätte photograph album 105

Left
52 Dining room of Mimi Marlow's apartment, Vienna.
Fabrics: MANDELKRÄHE (1910/11) by Eduard J. Wimmer-Wisgrill.
Photograph album 105. Inset: MANDELKRÄHE, colour proof on paper

54 Lotte Frömel-Fochler. SAMTENTE (1910/11). Fabric sample

55 Eduard J. Wimmer-Wisgrill. Fashion drawing 'Auge Gottes', dated 15 June 1912, showing collar, hat and cuffs featuring AMEISE (1910/11); pencil and Indian ink highlighted with white on paper

56 Eduard J. Wimmer-Wisgrill. Fashion drawing, dated 15 October 1912, showing collar featuring AMEISE (1910/11); pencil and watercolour on paper. Hochschule für angewandte Kunst, Vienna

At about the same time Wimmer, together with Josef Hoffmann, designed the apartment built in 1911/12 for the well-known Viennese soubrette Mimi Marlow. Besides 'Heimchen', which again featured in a bedroom scheme very much like that of his own, Wimmer used another of his designs, 'Mandelkrähe' (fig. 52), for lamps, upholstery, curtains and the dining-room tablecloth. In addition, a sofa in the entrance hall was upholstered with Lotte Frömel-Fochler's 'Samtente' (figs. 53, 54). Karl Riedel's 'Klatschrose' (fig. 69) was used for a seat and piano cover in the salon.[11] With its small

stylized floral elements, 'Mandelkrähe' remains within the tradition of early Hoffmann designs for Backhausen, while Frömel-Fochler's 'Samtente', Wimmer's 'Heimchen' and Riedel's 'Klatschrose' generally display a retrospective tendency, being expressions of the newly awakened interest both in 'old-fashioned' decorative ornament and in decorating. No wonder that just at this time Adolf Loos announced that ornamentation should be declared a criminal offence.[12]

Illustrations of fabrics erroneously described as having been executed by the Wiener Werkstätte are

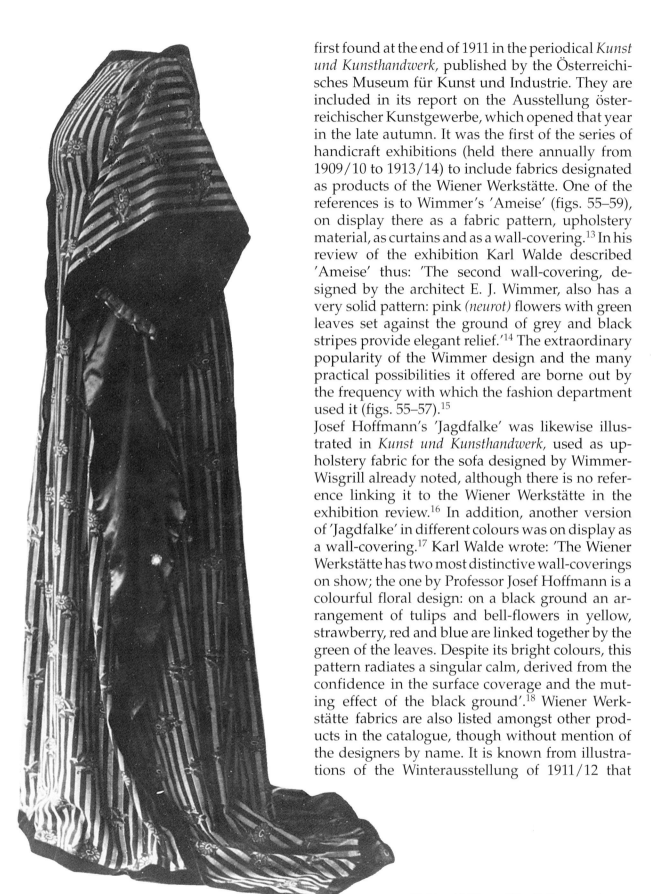

first found at the end of 1911 in the periodical *Kunst und Kunsthandwerk*, published by the Österreichisches Museum für Kunst und Industrie. They are included in its report on the Ausstellung österreichischer Kunstgewerbe, which opened that year in the late autumn. It was the first of the series of handicraft exhibitions (held there annually from 1909/10 to 1913/14) to include fabrics designated as products of the Wiener Werkstätte. One of the references is to Wimmer's 'Ameise' (figs. 55–59), on display there as a fabric pattern, upholstery material, as curtains and as a wall-covering.[13] In his review of the exhibition Karl Walde described 'Ameise' thus: 'The second wall-covering, designed by the architect E. J. Wimmer, also has a very solid pattern: pink *(neurot)* flowers with green leaves set against the ground of grey and black stripes provide elegant relief.'[14] The extraordinary popularity of the Wimmer design and the many practical possibilities it offered are borne out by the frequency with which the fashion department used it (figs. 55–57).[15]

Josef Hoffmann's 'Jagdfalke' was likewise illustrated in *Kunst und Kunsthandwerk*, used as upholstery fabric for the sofa designed by Wimmer-Wisgrill already noted, although there is no reference linking it to the Wiener Werkstätte in the exhibition review.[16] In addition, another version of 'Jagdfalke' in different colours was on display as a wall-covering.[17] Karl Walde wrote: 'The Wiener Werkstätte has two most distinctive wall-coverings on show; the one by Professor Josef Hoffmann is a colourful floral design: on a black ground an arrangement of tulips and bell-flowers in yellow, strawberry, red and blue are linked together by the green of the leaves. Despite its bright colours, this pattern radiates a singular calm, derived from the confidence in the surface coverage and the muting effect of the black ground'.[18] Wiener Werkstätte fabrics are also listed amongst other products in the catalogue, though without mention of the designers by name. It is known from illustrations of the Winterausstellung of 1911/12 that

57 Eduard J. Wimmer-Wisgrill Dress featuring AMEISE (1910/11). Fashion photograph album, 1911

59 Werkbund Exhibition, Cologne: Austrian Pavilion. The Wiener Werkstätte room, designed by E. J. Wimmer-Wisgrill, 1914.
Upholstery, curtains and floor-covering featuring AMEISE (1910/11). Wall-covering in the display cabinet: MEKKA (1911/13) by Arthur Berger

Opposite: 58 Eduard J. Wimmer-Wisgrill. AMEISE (1910/11). Fabric sample

61 *Umbrella featuring JAGDFALKE (1910/11) by Josef Hoffmann.*
Hochschule für angewandte Kunst, Vienna

Opposite
60 *Book cover (detail) featuring JAGDFALKE (1910/11) by Josef Hoffmann.*
Inset: fashion drawing 'Franziska' by E. J. Wimmer-Wisgrill, dated 21 June
1912, with jacket featuring this pattern; pencil and watercolour highlighted
with white.

Right
63 *Josef Hoffmann. JAGDFALKE (1910/11). Wallpaper, 1913*

Below
62 *Book cover featuring JAGDFALKE (1910/11), formerly owned by*
Emilie Flöge

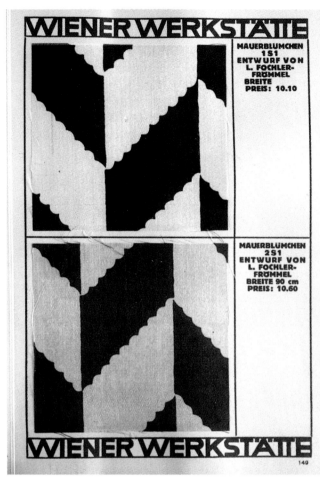

64 Lotte Frömel-Fochler. MAUERBLÜMCHEN (1910/13). Silk sample book, c. 1912

65 Villa Primavesi, Winkelsdorf, designed by Josef Hoffmann, 1913. Children's bedroom with wall-covering and lampshade featuring MAUERBLÜMCHEN by Lotte Frömel-Fochler (1910/13). DKD 1916

Hoffmann's 'Sanduhr', specially designed for the event, was on show as a velour carpet in the entrance hall.[19]

Apart from this, four printed silks by Hoffmann's pupil Lotte Frömel-Fochler were included in the exhibition, but only 'Geier' and 'Grünfink' (fig. 393) were illustrated in *Kunst und Kunsthandwerk*. The catalogue stated – incorrectly – that they were 'executed by the Wiener Werkstätte'.[20] Evidently the relationship between the Österreichisches Museum für Kunst und Industrie and the Wiener Werkstätte did not always run smoothly. In February 1912, i.e. at the end of the 1911/12 winter exhibition, and in connection with the next spring exhibition, the Frühjahrsausstellung, which was held from May to July, the museum bought a total of six fabrics from the artist personally, not from the Wiener Werkstätte.[21] All the Frömel-Fochler acquisi-

tions, together with seven other fabrics designed by her, were on show in the Frühjahrsausstellung of 1912.[22] In the first exhibition of Wiener Werkstätte fabrics in 1911/12, no specific advertising strategy was involved in presenting the items, nor – it would appear – were they deemed worthy of special attention, if we disregard the general interest in textiles that was evident from the previously mentioned articles by Fischel and Walde.[23] It seems that the fabrics were integrated seamlessly into the general Wiener Werkstätte creative programme and were not necessarily given special emphasis as new or especially innovative products.

As a final example of the early use of Wiener Werkstätte fabrics consciously adapted for their decorative effect within contemporary interiors, reference must be made to Josef Hoffmann's design for the Hugo Marx apartment. Here he chose a subtly reciprocating, serrated decor by Frömel-Fochler, 'Mauerblümchen' (fig. 64), for the living-room upholstery.[24] The abstract lines and the sharp contrast of the material when seen against the boldly striped pattern of the wallpaper can be regarded as a further variation on the theme of patterned opulence in general.

In November 1911, when Paul Poiret was in Vienna with his sensational fashion show, he took the opportunity to visit the Wiener Werkstätte. He seems to have been especially enthusiastic about the fabrics, since he bought a great number and used them for some of his own creations.[25] Besides this, they were quite evidently a source of inspiration at the Studio Martine, founded by Poiret in the same year. The successful fashion designer's enthusiastic endorsement was an affirmation of the Wiener Werkstätte fabrics' high artistic quality. Moreover, it provides further clear evidence that the Wiener Werkstätte textile department was already working on a professional basis in 1911.

It can be assumed that actual fabric production was established in the Wiener Werkstätte after an initial short experimental phase, starting at the latest at the beginning of 1910. Production must have begun in earnest in the spring of 1910, for by the following autumn the Wiener Werkstätte's output of fabrics had reached the stage at which negotiations could be held with foreign manufacturers and selling agents. The artists' fabric designs must therefore have existed by the beginning of 1910 or earlier, since they had to be transferred onto the printing blocks before production could proceed.[26] Whether the official establishment of the fashion department in March 1911 provided a compelling reason for the Wiener Werkstätte also to commission the manufacture of fabrics is impossible to prove today.[27] It is, however, clear that the fashion press commentaries always laid special emphasis on the colourful printed silks: 'The most beautiful among these compositions, where rich colours, orange, wine-red, etc., frequently recur, are the hand-printed materials from the Wiener Werkstätte, silk or voile with geometric ornaments, stylized flowers, etc.'[28] Nevertheless, although the start of the Wiener Werkstätte fabric production coincides with the experimental beginnings of the fashion department, there can be no question of any clear-cut reciprocal interdependence.

66 Poster advertising. Paul Poiret's visit to Vienna, November 1911

In fact, calls for the Wiener Werkstätte to found its own textile department apparently did not emanate only from the fashion sector. In the years up to c. 1914 there is evidence of an unusually frequent use of Wiener Werkstätte textiles in interior decorative schemes. Hoffmann's interiors in particular are conspicuous for the exploitation of lavishly patterned materials, which verges on the prodigal. Finally, Wiener Werkstätte *Galanteriewaren* (fancy goods) and fashion accessories (figs. 61, 63, 71, 255, 256) aroused great interest amongst customers; the colourful textiles were often used for coverings and linings, or combined with leather, wood or paper. The textile department thus fulfilled an integrating function within the various departments.

The trade mark, officially registered in November 1913, was valid for 'Articles of Clothing, Textiles and Millinery' and was likewise applicable to the fashion department.[29] This date thus marked the end of the experimental phase for both departments. The establishment and furnishing of the textile department's own showrooms at 4 Maysedergasse (see pp. 159 ff.), which opened on 15 August 1916, and later at 32 Kärntnerstraße in 1918,[30] represented an unambiguous expression of the commercial success of the Wiener Werkstätte textile products. A few months earlier, on 1 April 1916, the fashion department had moved to its own premises at 41 Kärntnerstraße.[31]

[1] Hartwig Fischel, 'Rezension der Ausstellung österreichischer Kunstgewerbe, Wien 1911/12' in *KKHW* XIV (1911), p. 664.

[2] *DKD* LXII (1928), 197ff.

[3] WW *Annalen* 82, p. 149.

[4] Cf. Schweiger 1984, pp. 124, 251 (note 576).

[5] Amongst the various drawings of Wiener Werkstätte designs in the Österreichisches Museum für angewandte Kunst there is a sheet with Ludwig Jungnickel's pattern 'Papageienwald' (K.I. 12.228/5) on which the date 1909 has been inscribed, though not in the artist's hand; such a dating could quite feasibly mean that this was one of these designs.

[6] Photo no. 124; Völker 1984, pp. 9–13, 23–25, 28.

[7] Pattern book no. 54.

[8] Ibid., pp. 522–1017: for 'Boukets' see pp. 571–5.

[9] *Internationale Kunstausstellung Rom 1911. Österreichischer Pavillon nach Plänen von Architekt Josef Hoffmann* (Hall VII), Vienna and Leipzig 1911, n.p.

[10] E. J. Wimmer-Wisgrill, 'Bemerkungen zu meiner Wohnung' in *DI* XII (1911), pp. 74ff.

[11] *DI* XIV (1913), pls. 1–4; Sekler 1985, cat. no. 152, p. 345.

[12] Cf. Burkhardt Rukschcio, 'Ornament und Mythos' in Pfabigan 1985, pp. 57ff.

[13] *KKHW* XIV (1911), illustrations on pp. 618, 621, 631, 682, 683, 687.

[14] Karl Walde, 'Ausstellung österreichischer Kunstgewerbe 1911–1912' in *TKI* V (1912), vol. 2, pp. 51, 53 (fig.).

[15] Schweiger 1984, p. 73 (Friederike Beer-Monti wearing housecoat); Wien 1983 (exhib. cat. p. 24, fashion drawing); Völker 1984, p. 13, fig. 6 (fashion photo album); Österreichisches Museum für angewandte Kunst, WWMO I, 83 (fashion drawing).

[16] *KKHW* XIV (1911), p. 619.

[17] The effect of the pattern when used as a wall-covering is revealed in black-and-white photographs of the interior of Karl Bräuer's apartment, where he also made use of 'Jagdfalke'; cf. *DI* XIV (1913), pls. 90, 91.

[18] Karl Walde, op. cit. (see note 14), pp. 50f.

[19] *DKD* XXIX (1911/12), p. 396; Sekler 1985, cat. no. 149, p. 343 (fig.).

[20] Wien 1911 (exhib. cat.), p. 77.

[21] This refers not only to the patterns seen in the exhibition: 'Fuchs', 'Forelle', 'Eisfuchs', 'Goldfasan', and 'Grasmücke' for the so-called *Wanderinventar* (roving inventory) of items acquired from and for exhibitions. 'Krammetsvogel', also acquired on the same day, could originally have come from the Frühjahrsausstellung of 1912; it is also illustrated in *KKHW* XV (1912), p. 344, together with a further design by Frömel-Fochler, 'Samtente', illustrated on p. 345.

[22] Wien 1912 (exhib. cat.), p. 28.

[23] See notes 1 and 14 above.

[24] Sekler 1985, cat. no. 145, p. 342. Cf. *ID* XXVII (1916), p. 131, where a photograph of an armchair upholstered with Peche's 'Schwalbenschwanz' is reproduced; this photograph was also taken in the Marx apartment. If the views of the interior as published in 1916 in fact date from the original decor of 1911, this could be the earliest example of a design by Peche associated with the year in which he first met Hoffmann.

[25] Berta Zuckerkandl, 'Bei Paul Poiret' in *Wiener Allgemeine Zeitung*, 25 November 1911 (*Annalen* 83, 606). The Wiener Werkstätte's loyal chronicler recalled the same occasion in 'Paul Poiret und die Klimt Gruppe' in the *Neues Wiener Journal* of 25 November 1923 (*Annalen* 87, 102). A coat designed by Poiret with a lining featuring Peche's 'Diomedes' was displayed in the 1920s in a fashion show held in Berlin; cf. Berlin 1977 (exhib. cat.), no. 43, fig. 20.

[26] See note 5 above.

[27] The Wiener Werkstätte had applied for a licence to establish a ladies' dressmaking business (*Damenkleidermachergewerbe*) on 1 October 1910; the permit was issued on 9 March 1911. Cf. Völker 1984, p. 8. Most of the writers dealing with the history of the organization take the view that the existence of the fashion department made the setting up of a textile department a necessity. See, for example, Schweiger 1984, p. 222; Hansen 1984, p. 139; New York 1986 (exhib. cat.), p. 99.

[28] *Berliner Lokalanzeiger*, 12 March 1913 (*Annalen* 83, 8).

[29] Völker 1984, p. 64; Neuwirth 1985, pp. 232f.

[30] Sekler 1985, cat. no. 208, p. 380.

[31] WW business report for 1916, p. 1.

STYLE AND FORMS OF THE EARLY PERIOD

67 Carl Otto Czeschka. Illustration to 'Die Nibelungen', Gerlach und Wiedling, Vienna-Leipzig, 1908

At the time of the textile department's foundation the Wiener Werkstätte was already seven years old and had not always succeeded in overcoming financial problems and personal differences unscathed. Josef Hoffmann ensured continuity and set standards of quality, both in his own work and in his untiring personal commitment to the association. Some artists – above all Kolo Moser and Carl Otto Czeschka – had ceased to be full-time members of the Wiener Werkstätte, but through their designs continued to contribute to the production of the various departments. New members joined, among them Eduard Josef Wimmer-Wisgrill, who was active in the Wiener Werkstätte from the autumn of 1906. He took charge of the fashion department from *c.* 1910, before which it had still been in an experimental phase.[1] Wimmer, moreover, designed items for production in other departments as well. In addition, Hoffmann was instrumental in getting a fair number of his pupils from the Kunstgewerbeschule to contribute work which was new and contemporary in feeling: Lotte Frömel-Fochler has already been mentioned, and likewise Mitzi Vogel; other names to be noted

68 Josef Hoffmann. MONTEZUMA (1910/12). Fabric sample

include Wilhelm Martens, Leopold Blonder, Reni Schaschl and Vally Wieselthier.[2] The first name to be considered, however, is that of Maria Likarz, who must have been supplying designs to the Wiener Werkstätte by around 1912.[3] In the course of her long and extraordinarily productive career she worked for various Wiener Werkstätte departments and became the most prolific designer of textile patterns, including many of the most beautiful examples. After 1911 Hoffmann's friendship with Dagobert Peche evidently brought a new and influential member into the textile department – one who did much innovative work in the organization as a whole.

In Vienna around 1910 the Art Nouveau style had been abandoned in both the fine and applied arts; one can search in vain amongst the Wiener Werkstätte fabrics for floral Art Nouveau patterns and traces of Viennese abstract 'Secessionism'. In 1909 it was noted in *Textile Kunst und Industrie* that 'Whilst earlier work used naturalistic motifs and then progressed to the exploration of curved lines, today it is the turn of geometric forms, which is exactly what we have come to appreciate from the Viennese. Frugality of ornament,

bareness of form, an individual aesthetic language, a superlatively disciplined colour awareness – structural nature, rejection of the fantastic, of opulence, contrived decorative whimsy and "hysterically rectangular banality" – it is this that creates the effect of beauty in the textiles.'[4] New influences caught on, and interest in children's and folk art, in stylized, decorative forms and saturated primary colours was aroused, while the abstract tendencies of Cubist, Futurist and Constructivist painting played a part in forming the constituents of patterns and colour combinations. Alongside this trend there was a sustained interest among designers and recipients in simple patterns though these are quite distinct from the later 'simple' Bauhaus fabrics, which relied on the principle of plainness and suitability of material, not on reduction. Hoffmann, renowned as a past master in this field, invented such convincing patterns as 'Miramar' (fig. 150) and 'Wasserfall' (fig. 148); sometimes, however, the effect was 'banal', as in the case of 'Riva' (fig. 140) and 'Lerche' (fig. 142).[5]

The vivid overall impression of the diverse trends in textile design in pre-First World War Vienna which is conveyed by the many surviving Wiener Werkstätte textile patterns is augmented by illustrations and articles in contemporary journals. They contain articles about the Wiener Werkstätte in general, and about individual artists, but seldom deal specifically with textiles. Thus it is possible to name approximately thirty artists working in fabric design until 1913, which was certainly the most productive year before the outbreak of war. Because of questions concerning dating, such as those already described, it is impossible to give the exact number of textile patterns available each year. It can only be presumed that in 1913 the customer could choose from more than the statistically calculable 280 designs, along with their many variable colour-schemes.[6]

That the wide range of merchandise on offer had no correlation whatever with the department's commercial success is documented in the minutes of business meetings held in 1914 and later, which survive in the Wiener Werkstätte archive. They contain complaints about the muddled state of various accounts and the book-keeping in general, which certainly helps to explain why the sorting system of the fabric patterns is so difficult to unravel.[7]

In the spring of 1912, at the Frühjahrsausstellung of the Österreichisches Museum für Kunst und In-

70 Austrian Adria Exhibition, Vienna, 1913. Runners, hand-knotted carpet and folding screen featuring KLATSCHROSE (1910/11) by Karl Riedel, SANTA SOPHIA (1910/12) by Josef Hoffmann and HERBSTSONNE (1910/12) by E. J. Wimmer-Wisgrill. Manufactured by Teppichhaus Orendi, Vienna. TKI 1913

Opposite: 69 Winter Exhibition at the Österreichisches Museum für Kunst und Industrie, 1912/13: Fabric sample of KLATSCHROSE (1910/11) by Karl Riedel (inset) and dress; and dress featuring KAHLENBERG (1910/11) by Martha Alber. DKD 1912/13

dustrie, a Wiener Werkstätte dress made from one of the organization's own fabrics was on show for the first time. Wimmer-Wisgrill's dress design was made up using Karl Riedel's only fabric, 'Klatschrose'.[8] A photograph, in which the entire showcase is seen, was published in *Deutsche Kunst und Dekoration* (fig. 69); amongst the contents is a corsage using Martha Alber's design 'Kahlenberg'. Other items illustrated, in this case from the *Galanteriewaren* (fancy goods) section, included Wiener Werkstätte boxes covered with Hoffmann's 'Apollo' and 'Rollschnecke' (fig. 71).

Hoffmann created a dining room for this Frühjahrsausstellung, using Wilhelm Jonasch's 'Vorgarten' (fig. 95) for curtains and upholstery. In his

71 *Stationery boxes made by Brüder Rosenbaum, Vienna, covered with APOLLO (1910/11) and ROLLSCHNECKE (1910/12) by Josef Hoffmann. DKD 1912/13*

Opposite
74 *Wilhelm Jonasch. KRIEAU (1910/11). Fabric sample*

72, 73 *The Grabencafe, Vienna: interior decoration by Josef Hoffmann, 1912, with upholstery featuring KRIEAU (1910/11) by Wilhelm Jonasch. Artist's postcard, and photograph from Wiener Werkstätte album 105*

furnishings for the Graben Café in Vienna in the same year he selected another Jonasch design, 'Krieau' (the name of Vienna's trotting race-course), again for upholstery and curtains (figs. 72–74).[9] Alber's 'Kahlenberg', likewise Jonasch's 'Vorgarten' and 'Krieau', are vivid examples of the adaptation and development of folk-art motifs. The use of clear and strong colours also derives from this source. In contrast, Otto Prutscher's 'Glockenblume', a pattern consisting of simple stripes with small flower-sprays used at the exhibition, is reminiscent of Wimmer-Wisgrill's 'Ameise', and is again an expression of a new-found enthusiasm for Biedermeier.

In the years 1913 and 1914, an example of the lavish and versatile uses of Wiener Werkstätte textiles in interior design occurs in an especially characteristic form in the country house of the Primavesi family at Winkelsdorf, Moravia. The co-ordination in each room of the curtains, bedspreads, upholstery, wallpaper and lampshades was particularly effective in creating the atmosphere of the bedrooms. In addition, each guest received a kaftan-like robe in the same pattern as that of the room.[10] The house was burnt down in 1922, but surviving photographs still provide impressive evidence of the effect of the designs (figs. 75–80, 82–84, 86).[11] A total of eleven different patterns can be picked out in the old photographs. The textile patterns were chosen to fit in with the more rustic aspects of the villa's architecture, in part, too, with its palladian-classical allusions: Frömel-Fochler's 'Waldkapelle' (fig. 84) 'Zülow's 'Dorfrose' (fig. 86), Czeschka's 'Bavaria' (fig. 77) and Jungnickel's 'Hochwald' (fig. 24) represent the folkloristic tendencies, while Frömel-Fochler's 'Mauerblümchen' (fig. 65) and Zovetti's 'Stichblatt' (figs. 261, 262) hint at classicism. The house demonstrated a successful synthesis of architectural design with textile decor.

In 1913 the Wiener Werkstätte presented its first wallpaper collection to the public in a special exhibition held at the Museum für Kunst und Industrie. Practically all the patterns shown there correspond to fabric designs, which were simply printed onto wallpaper.[12]

Space does not allow a listing of all the textile designs and designers documented in 1913. Of course, one repeatedly encounters Hoffmann, Czeschka, Wimmer-Wisgrill and Peche with their

Opposite and right

75–80 Villa Primavesi, Winkelsdorf, designed by Josef Hoffmann, 1913. Photographs from DKD 1916

75 Gentleman's bedroom with upholstery featuring MEKKA (1911/13) by Arthur Berger

76 Library with upholstery and curtains featuring PAPAGEIENWALD (1910/11) by Ludwig H. Jungnickel

77 Lady's boudoir with upholstery and curtains featuring BAVARIA (1910/11) by Carl Otto Czeschka

78 Anteroom with curtains and lampshades featuring PARADIES-VOGEL (1911/13) by Dagobert Peche

79 Hall with upholstery and curtains featuring ROSENGARTEN (1911/13) by Dagobert Peche

80 Dining room with curtains featuring HOCHWALD (1910/11) by Ludwig H. Jungnickel

81 Carl Otto Czeschka. WALDIDYLL
(1910/11). Fabric sample

Right
83 Gustav Klimt in the Villa Primavesi,
Winkelsdorf, wearing a houserobe featuring
Czeschka's WALDIDYLL (1910/11).
Wiener Werkstätte photograph album 137

82 Villa Primavesi, Winkelsdorf, designed by
Josef Hoffmann, 1913. Guest room with
lampshades featuring Czeschka's WALDIDYLL
(1910/11). DKD 1916

84, 86 Villa Primavesi, Winkelsdorf, designed by Josef Hoffmann, 1913. Photographs from DKD 1916

84 Governess's room with curtains, bedspread and lampshade featuring WALDKAPELLE (1910/13) by Lotte Frömel-Fochler

Below
86 Children's bedroom with lampshade featuring DORFROSE (1910/11) by Franz von Zülow. DKD 1916

85 Lotte Frömel-Fochler. WALDKAPELLE (1910/13). Fabric sample

Below
87 Franz von Zülow. DORFROSE (1910/11). Fabric sample

characteristic pattern designs; especially popular were Franz von Zülow, Ugo Zovetti and Ludwig Heinrich Jungnickel, who invented expressive, colourful patterns often with large repeats: for instance, 'Sommerabend' (fig. 125), 'Konstantinopel' (fig. 109) and 'Papageienwald' (fig. 76).

Dagobert Peche was commissioned to furnish a salon in the Ausstellung österreichischer Kunstgewerbe of 1913/14, in which he used his design 'Marina' (figs. 89–92, 169) for the curtains and upholstery. This abstract pattern, composed of flowing lines and small spirals, was printed on various

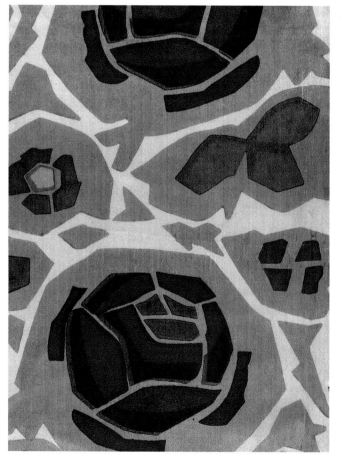

88 Winter exhibition at the Österreichisches Museum für Kunst und Industrie, 1913/14. Upholstery and curtains featuring MARINA (1911/12) by Dagobert Peche

WALL COVERINGS OF WIENER WERKSTAETTE SILK ▪ WOODWORK GRAY AND BLACK ▪ KERAMIK FIGURE BY STRNAD ▪ CANDLESTICKS BY HOFMANN ▪ PICTURES OF COLORED ENAMEL

89 Wall-coverings featuring MARINA (1911/12) by Dagobert Peche. Catalogue for the 'Wiener Werkstätte of America'

kinds of fabric in the Wiener Werkstätte over a very long period. It can be found mentioned in the production files until 1929.[13] With the simplicity of its linear composition and a variety of colour combinations, it shows a tendency to chromatic shading. 'Marina' thus contrasts strongly with the textiles of Zülow, Zovetti or Jungnickel, with their bold colours embellished with naturalistic forms.

Carl Otto Czeschka's textile designs for the Wiener Werkstätte owe much to the ornamental and stylized forms for the years before 1910, and demonstrate a subtle use of colour, e.g. 'Bavaria' (figs. 77, 138, 139), 'Apfel' (fig. 134), or "Kropftaube' (fig. 93). Alongside these he designed scaled-down patterns in two colours and featuring small design motifs, as in 'Feldlerche' (fig. 98), 'Haushund' (fig. 96) and 'Wasserorgel' (figs. 136, 137). Only at the beginning, and then for a relatively short time, was Czeschka one of the formative influences in the textile department. From 1907, when he moved to Hamburg, he designed a small group of materials there whose effectiveness and significance are evident. The influence he had on Wimmer-Wisgrill, for instance, is shown by the latter's pattern 'Maikäfer' (fig. 94), virtually a copy of Czeschka's 'Kropftaube' (fig. 93). Czeschka had an equally direct influence on Hoffmann; compare the latter's 'Montezuma' (figs. 68, 245) with Kriemhild's dress illustrated in the 1908 edition of *Die Nibelungen*, published by Gerlach. Today the impression given by Czeschka drawings for this book is similar to that conveyed by an early collection of Wiener Werkstätte textile patterns.[14]

90 Dagobert Peche. MARINA (1911/12). Colour proof on paper

92 Gustav Klimt. *Portrait of Friederike Beer-Monti, wearing a dress featuring MARINA (1911/12) by Dagobert Peche; oil on canvas, 1916. Metropolitan Museum of Art, New York*

Opposite: 91 Dagobert Peche. MARINA (1911/12). Fabric sample

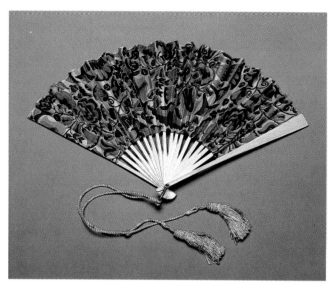

93 *Fan featuring KROPFTAUBE (1910/11) by Carl Otto Czeschka*

Czeschka designed fourteen fabric patterns for the Wiener Werkstätte. Some resemble each other, e.g. 'Bavaria' (figs. 77, 138, 139) and 'Kropftaube' (fig. 93), while others complement each other or are simply combined with one another, for instance 'Po-Ho' (fig. 135), and 'Waldidyll' (figs. 81–83). 'Löwe' ('Lion', fig. 96) has an abstract pattern with no bearing on its name. 'Wasserorgel' (figs. 136, 137) and 'Feldlerche' (fig. 98) likewise have an

94 *E. J. Wimmer-Wisgrill. MAIKÄFER (1910/11). Fabric sample*

abstract linear basis. In Czeschka's work we see the variety and range characteristic of Wiener Werkstätte artists who combined very different styles in their work, whereas other leading personalities, for example Dagobert Peche, left their mark on certain phases of development due to the homogeneous nature of their feeling for form.

Karl Walde's comments on the Ausstellung österreichischer Kunstgewerbe of 1913/14 attest to the importance of the Wiener Werkstätte and its fabric production in the eyes of the art critics: 'First and foremost to be mentioned are the works created by the Wiener Werkstätte. This enterprise has found many adherents and its influence has long since exceeded the bounds of city and empire. It is clearly traceable in the creations of German handicraft, and has even overtaken Paris, the usual trendsetter until now, which, in its search for a new French style, has ended up following in the wake of the Wiener Werkstätte. Even though the inherent taste of the Viennese may be very particular and, being more attuned to the delicate, the fine, the discreet, may occasionally be creations from this workshop, its success is fully comprehensible on account of the profusion of beautiful and significant creations which its artists produce. It may also be traced back to the fact that the original roots of the majority of Vienna's present population lie in other countries of the multinational [Austro-Hungarian] monarchy, where folk art, with all its enjoyment of colour lives on. The great significance of this enterprise for Vienna and the empire does not only lie in what it creates for itself, but much more in the fact that its endeavour always to aim for the utmost originality in its work acts as a catalyst which sustains the constant process of change in Viennese arts and crafts, and thus avoids the danger of introspection.'[15] Here Walde summarized once again the influences which the artists were subject to during these years: the great diversity of folk art within the territories of the monarchy and Expressionism in painting; their abundance of forms and brilliant colours recur repeatedly in the patterns of Zovetti and von Zülow, as well as those of Krenek or Mitzi Friedmann, and also in some of Czeschka's or Hoffmann's designs. The lavish scale of the abstract concept in the pattern 'Irland' by Maria Likarz remained an exception, and it was only after the First World War and most of all in her own later designs that it found worthy successors.

95 Josef Hoffmann.
FEIERTAG (1910/12);
Wilhelm Jonasch.
VORGARTEN
(1910/11). Silk sample
book, c. 1912

Kolo Moser's contribution to the textile depart-ment, neither particularly wide in range nor indeed very influential, has already been mentioned. When he revived three patterns that he had origi-nally designed in 1901 as subsidiary items for his portfolio,[16] he also revised one of the main items published in *Flächenschmuck* – 'Goldene Schmet-terlinge' – for the Wiener Werkstätte, now giving it a much simpler form and calling it 'Baummar-der' (fig. 297).[17] The golden butterflies, from which

the original pattern took its name, were eliminated, leaving serpentine chequered bands arranged into rhomboid forms. Moser invented one completely new pattern for the Wiener Werkstätte, 'Amsel', one instance of its use being a dress produced by the Wiener Werkstätte fashion department, as seen in a black-and-white photograph in the archives (fig. 48).[18] Moser is encountered yet again as a de-signer of abstract, small-scale patterns, which are now enhanced through the application of a single

96 Dagobert Peche.
PIERROT (1911/12);
Carl Otto Czeschka.
HAUSHUND
(1910/11) and LÖWE
(1910/11). Silk sample
book, c. 1912

colour in each case, contrasting with the grey ground of the reverse side of plates in the portfolio *Flächenschmuck*. His wallpaper design for the 1913 collection – no printed textile version of this is known – owes much to the Wiener Werkstätte's early leaning towards abstraction, but nothing as yet to the new decorative style.

Besides Moser and Czeschka, Hoffmann and Peche – a more extensive coverage of the contributions of the two last artists will be found on pp. 169 ff. – there is a singularly wide range of artists who worked in the Wiener Werkstätte textile department only during the pre-war years, mostly pupils of Hoffmann, including Wilhelm Jonasch, Arthur Scharrisch, Martha Alber and Leo Blonder. Although few in number, the patterns they designed were stimulating, among them 'Hameau' (Jonasch, fig. 129), 'Blumenwiese' (Scharrisch, fig. 126), 'Blätter' (Alber, figs. 263, 264), and 'Isphahan' (Blonder, fig. 15). These artists then disappeared from the Wiener Werkstätte scene. Rose Krenn and Wilhelm Martens likewise belong to this group. Gustav Kalhammer must also be mentioned here; his nine patterns demonstrate his interest in folk art, always displaying stylized plant forms in geometric grids (fig. 130). On the other hand, Carl Krenek drew the more interesting designs; the abstract and serrated forms of his 'Granate' (fig. 121) or 'Mosaik' (fig. 120) point to Art Déco, and their bold colour contrasts contribute greatly to their striking effect. Just as impressive are Mitzi Friedmann's designs, such as 'Aschermittwoch' (fig. 114) or 'Feldpost' (fig. 115). Like 'Granate' ('Grenade'), 'Feldpost' ('Army Postal Service') is probably a name that originated during the war years. Each of these artists has a distinctive, easily recognizable style. They contribute to the extraordinary diversity of the designs and the heterogeneous picture of the Wiener Werkstätte textile production between 1910 and 1914.

Whilst some of the organization's members, such as Zovetti, Wimmer-Wisgrill, Prutscher and Nechansky, gave up designing fabric patterns after this period – for many a superlatively productive time – there are later examples of textile designs by Franz von Zülow, Mitzi Friedmann, Arthur Berger and Lotte Frömel-Fochler; other artists, primarily Maria Likarz and Max Snischek, began the most intensive stage of their work for the department only after 1918.

[1] Hansen 1984, pp. 38 and 206, citing Hans Ankwicz-Kleehoven (not always the most reliable source in matters of dating).

[2] Cf. *Die Kunst* XI (1912), pp. 513ff.

[3] Schweiger 1984, p. 264. Errera purchased Maria Likarz's 'Irland' in Frankfurt am Main in 1913; see Brussels 1927 (stock cat.), p. 386, no. 454. The acquisitions made by the museums in Vienna and Mulhouse occurred in 1914. See also p. 20 above.

[4] F. A., 'Wiener Möbelbezugsstoffe' in *TKI* II (1909), p. 195.

[5] Cf. a comment made by Hoffmann quoted in Hansen 1984 (p. 139), but without naming a source. In a memorandum dated 18 June 1913 from the Wiener Werkstätte executive, the artists' department was requested 'As soon as possible to submit further designs for dress fabrics, which should be in keeping with new fashion trends in general and at the same time original patterns characteristic of the WW.' Hoffmann adds, in a marginal note, that '... above all they must be genuine WW patterns', i.e. corresponding to the institution's current very individual style. He goes on to note that 'in the first place only small and simple designs using two or three colours, and, secondly, large strewn flowers and sprays of flowers (especially as regards muslin) are to be considered.'

[6] See above, p. 19. Assuming that the first collection was designed in 1910, this again would suggest an average of about seventy new designs each year.

[7] Minutes dated 9 June 1914, p. 1: '... in the following report I should like to submit an anthology of the activities that have been undertaken: books, correspondence, files, buyers' requirements, stock intake, insurances etc. were found by me to be to be – to put it mildly – in the most incredible state of neglect. The main body of those officially employed, with the exception of one or two members, turned out to be ignorant and self-indulgent.'

[8] *DKD* XXXI (1912/13), p. 102.

[9] Sekler 1985, cat. no. 155, p. 346; *DI* XIV (1913), pl. 5, pp. 35 f.

[10] Gowns such as these are to be found in the collections of the Historisches Museum der Stadt Wien – cf. Tokyo 1989 (exhib. cat.), p. 354, no. 479 – and the Badisches Landesmuseum, Karlsruhe – cf. Fischer 1987, p. 91, fig. 107; the former example features Zovetti's 'Stichblatt', the latter Czeschka's 'Wasserorgel'.

[11] Sekler 1985, pp. 129 ff.; Salzburg 1987 (exhib. cat.), p. 21.

[12] Völker/Pichler 1989, vol. I.

[13] The most famous example of its use is in the dress worn by Friederike Beer-Monti, depicted in the portrait of her by Klimt painted in 1916 (reproduced here in fig. 92).

[14] Bouillon 1989, p. 42.

[15] In *TKI* VII (1914), pp. 56 ff.

[16] *Die Quelle*, pls. 5, 8, 10 (verso); cf. p. 31, note 5, above.

[17] Op. cit., pl. 2.

[18] Wiener Werkstätte photograph album 124, p. 21.

Opposite
97, 98 Silk sample book, c. 1912. The patterns illustrated are: (above) ARBE (1910/11) and ADRIANOPEL (1910/11) by Ugo Zovetti, and (below) FELDLERCHE (1910/11) by Czeschka, KANARIENVOGEL (1910/11) by Mitzi Vogel, ALPENFALTER (1910/11) by Josef Hoffmann, SCHÖNBRUNN (1910/12) by A. Pospischl and ADLER (1910/12) by Josef Hoffmann

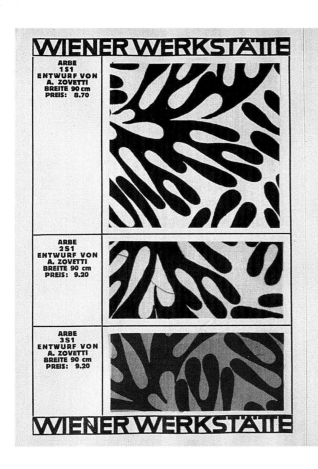

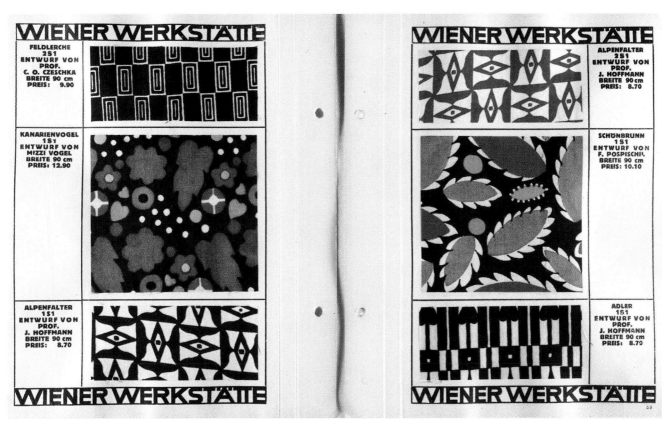

WIENER WERKSTÄTTE

ARBE 1S1 ENTWURF VON A. ZOVETTI BREITE 90 cm PREIS: 8.70

ARBE 2S1 ENTWURF VON A. ZOVETTI BREITE 90 cm PREIS: 9.20

ARBE 3S1 ENTWURF VON A. ZOVETTI BREITE 90 cm PREIS: 9.20

ADRIANOPEL 1S1 ENTWURF VON A. ZOVETTI BREITE 90 cm PREIS:

FELDLERCHE 2S1 ENTWURF VON PROF. C. O. CZESCHKA BREITE 90 cm PREIS: 9.90

KANARIENVOGEL 1S1 ENTWURF VON MIZZI VOGEL BREITE 90 cm PREIS: 12.90

ALPENFALTER 1S1 ENTWURF VON PROF. J. HOFFMANN BREITE 90 cm PREIS: 8.70

ALPENFALTER 2S1 ENTWURF VON PROF. J. HOFFMANN BREITE 90 cm PREIS: 8.70

SCHÖNBRUNN 1S1 ENTWURF VON F. POSPISCHIL BREITE 90 cm PREIS: 10.10

ADLER 1S1 ENTWURF VON PROF. J. HOFFMANN BREITE 90 cm PREIS: 8.70

99-101 Maria Likarz. IRLAND (1910/13).
Fabric samples

Opposite
102 Maria Likarz. IRLAND (1910/13).
Fabric sample (actual size)

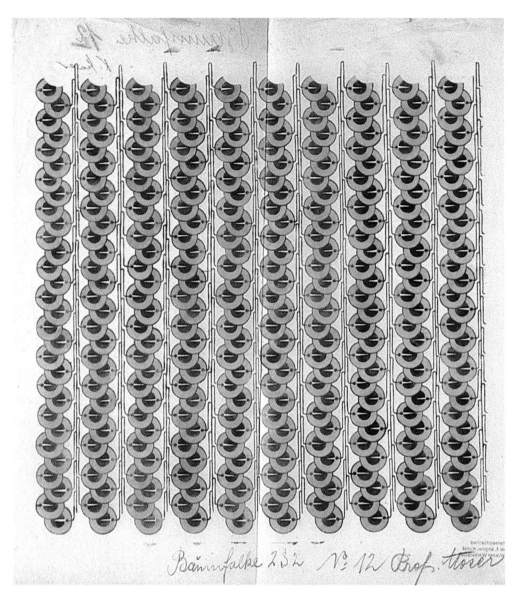

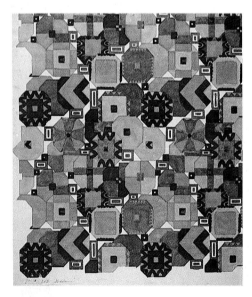

Left
103 Kolo Moser. BAUMFALKE
(1910/11). Colour proof on paper

Below left
104 Eduard J. Wimmer-Wisgrill.
HERBSTSONNE (1910/12).
Colour proof on paper

Below right
105 Lotte Frömel-Fochler.
FASCHING (1910/13).
Colour proof on paper

106-108 Fabric samples
(from top to bottom):

106 Lotte Frömel-Fochler.
KREBS (1910/11)

107 Lotte Frömel-Fochler.
SUMATRA (1910/17)

108 Marianne Perlmutter.
ZAKOPANE (1910/17)

109–111 Colour proofs on paper:

109 (top left) Ugo Zovetti. KONSTANTINOPEL (1910/12)
110 (above) Angela Piotrovska. ANASTASIUS (1914/15)
111 (right) Mela Köhler. GEISHA (1910/12)

112–115 *Designs by Mitzi Friedmann:*

112 (top left) ASTA (1910/14). Fabric sample
113 (centre left) JUNO (1910/14). Fabric sample
114 (below left) ASCHERMITTWOCH (1910/14). Fabric sample
115 (above) FELDPOST (1910/14). Colour proof on paper

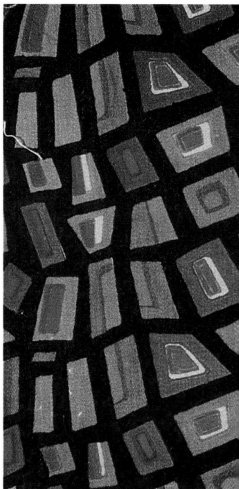

116 (top left) Luise Stoll. BISAMBERG
(1910/16). Fabric sample

117 (centre left) Mitzi Friedmann. KARST
(1910/14). Colour proof on paper

118 (below left) Maria Weissenberg. BENARES
(1919). Fabric sample

119 (above) Leopold Blonder. MAUERWERK
(1921/22). Fabric sample

120 (top right) Carl Krenek. MOSAIK (1910/12).
Linen sample book II, before 1914

121 (centre right) Carl Krenek. GRANATE
(1910/11). Fabric sample

122 (below right) Carl Krenek. BLITZ
(1910/11). Fabric sample

123 (top left) Leopold Blonder.
FLORA (1911/14). Fabric sample

124 (centre left) Angela Piotrovska.
GORLICZE (1914/15). Fabric sample

125 (bottom left) Franz von Zülow.
SOMMERABEND (1910/16). Fabric
sample

Opposite
126 (top left) Arthur Scharrisch.
BLUMENWIESE (1910/12). Fabric sample

127 (top right) Wilhelm Martens.
KRANICHGEIER (1910/12). Fabric sample

128 (centre left) Mitzi Vogel.
KANARIENVOGEL (1910/11). Fabric sample

129 (centre right) Wilhelm Jonasch.
HAMEAU (1910/11). Linen sample book I,
before 1914

130 (bottom left) Gustav Kalhammer.
SCHÖNAU (1910/12). Fabric sample

131 (bottom right) Vally Wieselthier.
SALPINX (1914/19). Fabric sample

132-134 Fabric samples by Carl Otto
Czeschka:

132 (top left) FISCHREIHER (1910/11)
133 (centre left) WALDIDYLL (1910/11)
134 (bottom left) APFEL (1910/11)

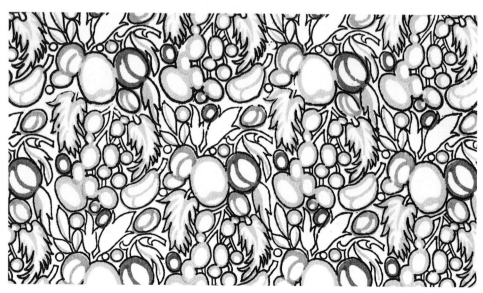

Opposite
135 Carl Otto Czeschka. PO-HO
(1910/11). Silk sample book, c. 1912

PO-HO
1 S1
ENTWURF VON
PROF.
C. O. CZESCHKA
BREITE 90 cm
PREIS: 11.10

136 Carl Otto Czeschka.
WASSERORGEL (1910/12).
Fabric sample

Opposite
137 Carl Otto Czeschka.
WASSERORGEL (1910/12).
Bookbinding for the fashion
department's 'Mode Herbst 1918'

W W
MODE
HERBST
1918

Right
139 Eduard J. Wimmer-Wisgrill.
Wiener Werkstätte coat 'Cresta', 1913,
featuring BAVARIA (1910/11) by
Carl Otto Czeschka

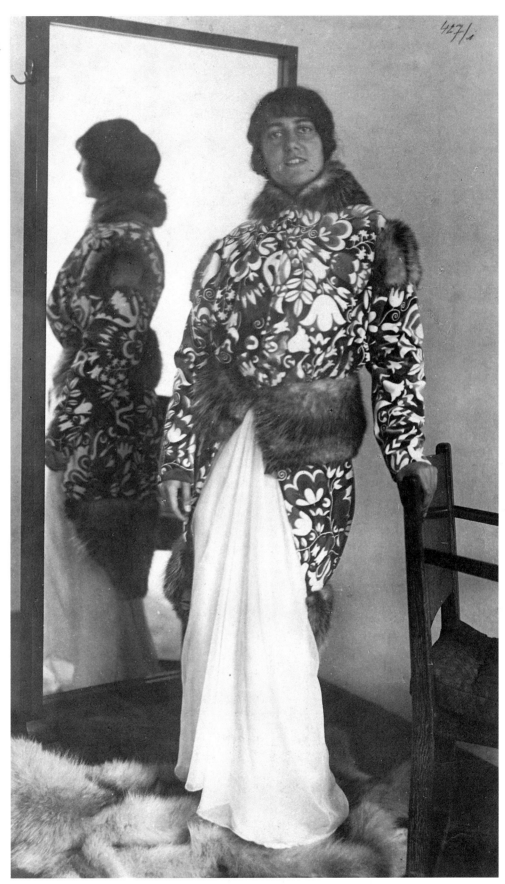

Opposite
138 G. Kottowitz House, Vienna:
music room. Upholstery, wall-
coverings and lampshade featuring
BAVARIA (1910/11) by Carl
Otto Czeschka. ID 1915.
Inset: BAVARIA (1910/11);
silk sample book, c. 1912

140 (top left) Josef Hoffmann. RIVA (1910/13). Fabric sample
141 (top right) Josef Hoffmann. KIEBITZ (1910/15). Linen sample book II, before 1914
142 (below left) Josef Hoffmann. LERCHE (1910/11). Fabric sample
143 (below right) Josef Hoffmann. HOPFEN (1910/17). Fabric sample

Opposite
144 Josef Hoffmann: LUCHS (1910/12). Fabric sample and (inset) blouse photographed in 1913

145 *Josef Hoffmann. SERPENTIN (1910/15). Fabric sample*

146 *Josef Hoffmann. TRIANGEL (1910/13). Fabric sample*

Opposite
147 *Josef Hoffmann. ADLER (1910/12). Fabric sample*

148-151 Fabric samples by Josef Hoffmann:

148 (top left) WASSERFALL (1910/12)
149 (top right) THEBEN (1910/15)
150 (below left) MIRAMAR (1910/15)
151 (below right) HIRSCHENZUNGE (1910/12)

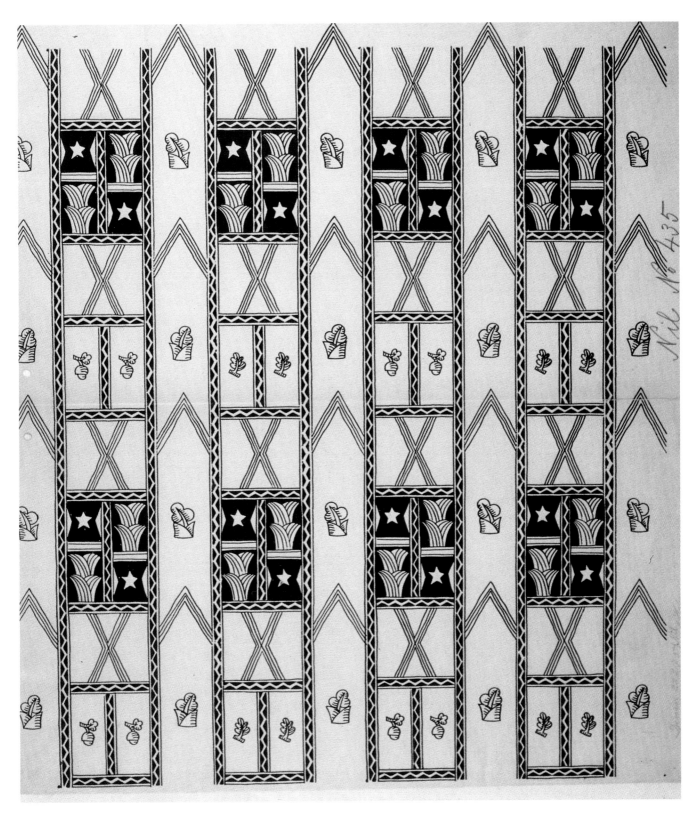

152 *Josef Hoffmann. NIL (1910/17). Proof on paper*

Opposite and above
153, 154 Dagobert Peche.
SCHWALBENSCHWANZ (1911/13).
Lengths of fabric

Right
155 Eduard J. Wimmer-Wisgrill.
Wiener Werkstätte coat 'Fürstin Metternich', 1913,
featuring SCHWALBENSCHWANZ by
Dagobert Peche

156–158 *Dagobert Peche.* WICKEN (1919), OSTEN (1911/17) *and* FLUT (1911/16). *Fabric samples*

90

159 Dagobert Peche.
ROSENGARTEN (1911/13). Colour proof on paper

Opposite: 160, 161 (top and centre left)
Dagobert Peche. SPINNE (1911/17). Fabric samples

162 *Dagobert Peche. RAX (1911/17). Drawing*   163 *Dagobert Peche. LABYRINTH (1911/17). Fabric sample*

Neuer Laden

Spitzen/Stoffe/Bänder/
Beleuchtungskörper
Wiener Werkstätte
1. Kärntnerstrasse 32

Wiener Werkstätte Textiles in the War Years 1914 to 1918

166 Dagobert Peche. Advertisement design for the first textile showroom, at 4 Maysedergasse, Vienna, c. 1916; pencil, ink, and Chinese white on tinted paper

The activities of the Wiener Werkstätte textile department during the war years can be documented from various articles in art magazines, a few exhibition catalogues, fashion and interior design photographs in the Wiener Werkstätte archive, as well as three surviving sets of minutes of Wiener Werkstätte board meetings held in 1915 and 1916. The last-mentioned documents present an ambivalent picture of the situation at that time. Slightly earlier, the minutes of 9 June 1914, concerning the state of the textile department shortly before war broke out, state: 'The reduced sales figures compared to the same period last year are to be explained by the general economic depression, under which, of course, luxury articles suffer the most; at the same time it must be pointed out that printed silks, having hitherto played a major role in sales, are no longer as fashionable as they used to be.'[1] On the next page it is stated that: 'The managing director … reports the employment of a textile industry expert already in effect and the intended employment of Herr Geo Michaelis, who is to create an English-American department on a commission basis, which is accepted by the board. In connection with this all fabric collections are to be withdrawn and new ones introduced, which means not only a great increase in costs for the textile department, but also a major growth of the work load. The urgent need for a reorganization of the textile department is best demonstrated by the fact that over 30 items of silk and other textile merchandise have been in stock for a year and a half without being catalogued [*unbemustert*], thus totally unproductive.'

These statements reflect the bureaucratic and disorganized state which apparently was typical of the Wiener Werkstätte departments. This is in contrast with the impression that was created of a particularly productive phase within the textile department in the years 1913/14, which has already been noted in the preceding chapter. The unsorted textiles may have been left in store in the early period because of the previously described surplus in production. One can imagine the difficulties involved in cataloguing the collections methodically, i.e. entering individual items into stock lists, sample books and similar records.

Regarding the first year of the war, the report states optimistically: 'The most pleasing trade devel-

Opposite

164 Lotte Frömel-Fochler. KRAMMETSVOGEL (1910/11). Fabric sample

165 (inset) Hilda Jesser. Advertisement design for the second textile showroom, situated at 32 Kärntnerstraße, Vienna, c. 1917; pencil and ink on paper

167 Façade of the Wiener Werkstätte branch in Zurich, designed by
Dagobert Peche, 1917. Photograph album 137

opments have been in the textile department, although sales of linen materials, usually accounting
for an average of 65 per cent of all fabrics sold,
have almost completely ceased, seeing that the entire interior decorating branch, which needed our
linen materials, has to all intents and purposes become redundant since the outbreak of the war. In
contrast, our printed silks, previously used for the
most part in the interior decorating branch, have
now with the help of persistent advertising, found
a wide-ranging demand in the clothing industry,
and in this category we have achieved quite significant improvement in sales figures as compared
with peacetime figures.'[2]

168 Wiener Werkstätte showroom in the Marienbad branch, designed
by Josef Hoffmann, 1916. Photograph album 137

169 Showroom of the Wiener Werkstätte fashion department, 41 Kärntnerstraße, 1916.
Photograph album 137

170, 171 MEKKA (1911/13) by Arthur Berger.
Jacket photographed in1915 and fabric sample

Opposite
172 Eduard J. Wimmer-Wisgrill. Blouse, 1915,
with collar featuring IRLAND (1910/13) by
Maria Likarz

The following year's departmental accounts also made a positive impression in comparison to other sectors: 'The growth of the textile department has been best of all; at the moment it presents the best possiblities for future development', noted the report for the financial year 1915, and furthermore: 'In spite of the first six months' reduced demand on account of the general depression, we succeeded, through large-scale advertising in the second half of the year, in reviving trade in our textile products to an extraordinary degree. Unfortunately, the available sales opportunities could not be fully exploited, since materials were in such short supply towards the end of the year that many orders could not be met. Besides, our printer lost the majority of his employees to conscription, with the result that, regrettably, production possibilities were also restricted. Nevertheless, we were successful in doubling the 1914 sales figures, and achieving profits which can be termed satisfactory.'[3]

However, these statements are seen in another light – indeed, they take on a hint almost of wishful thinking – when one reads, in the same report, about the general state of affairs in the Wiener Werkstätte: 'As regards the desire to buy and the demand for our products, we have to consider two distinct periods in 1915, which are in quite sharp contrast with each other. The first four months were overshadowed by a deep economic depression and consequently demand was greatly reduced. This situation was altered by a noticeable improvement shortly before the memorable breakthrough at Gorlice,[4] i.e. towards the end of April; shortly afterwards, however, during the initial embroilment with Italy, this trend was suddenly reversed and only showed a gradual improvement after mid-August. However, almost simultaneously with the improvement of sales opportunities, production difficulties became much more acute, so that demand could no longer be met to a satisfactory degree.'[5]

Shortage of materials, lack of skilled labour and the reduced call for luxury products must have affected all departments. Not the least of the reasons for the particular difficulty in correctly evaluating the fortunes of the Wiener Werkstätte is that the reports made during the war seem not to have been very objective. Even so, the textile department was very likely the most successful financially.

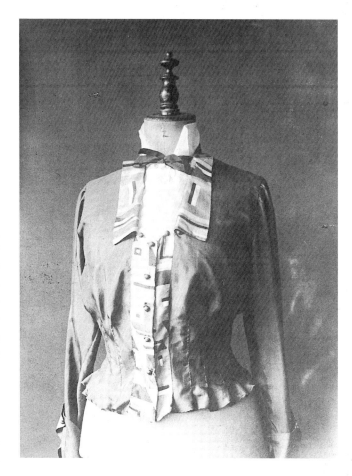

Dagobert Peche worked with great commitment for the entire Wiener Werkstätte, probably making occasional contributions from 1911 on, and then from 1915 onwards as a permanent member. From 1917 he was head of the Wiener Werkstätte branch in Zurich, returning to Vienna in 1919. During the war the Wiener Werkstätte, or at least its fashion and textile departments, had established elaborately fitted out showrooms in the best locations in Vienna, not exactly a sign of inactivity, rather a demonstration of its single-minded business policy, also a reason for its having to rely on the support of patrons. Projects initiated by Wiener Werkstätte artists between 1914 and 1918 involving the collaboration of the textile department were not limited to the few exhibitions taking place at that time. Hoffmann continued to work on interior design, for example for the Knips apartment,[6] and, apart from fitting out the showrooms already mentioned, he designed a new Wiener Werkstätte showroom in Marienbad.[7] Moreover, printed silks were used for accessories and gowns in the fashion department,[8] where, in November 1914, a section

173 Knips apartment, Vienna, designed by Josef Hoffmann, 1915/16. Living room with upholstery and lampshades featuring PELARGONIE (1913/16) by Felice Rix. DA in DBK 1916/18

for blouses was set up, an especially suitable outlet, it seemed, for the colourful fabrics.[9]

Before the outbreak of the war in 1914, namely from May onwards, a large and lengthily prepared Werkbund Exhibition took place in Cologne, where the Wiener Werkstätte was represented as an independent institution in the Austrian pavilion. Its room was designed by Wimmer-Wisgrill and incorporated many of his own works, including a wall devoted to his fashion drawings (fig. 59). His well-known textile pattern 'Ameise' was woven as a fitted carpet and adapted as an upholstery fabric for voluminous armchairs. Arthur

174 Knips apartment, Vienna, designed by Josef Hoffmann, 1915/16. Library with upholstery covered in ARBE (1910/11) by Ugo Zovetti. DA in DBK 1916/18

Berger's 'Mekka' provided the background for a long wall showcase.

The architect of the Austrian pavilion in Cologne was Josef Hoffmann, and he too remained loyal to Wiener Werkstätte fabrics in the room he designed for the furniture manufacturers Jacob and Josef Kohn. His almost compulsive tendency to invent patterns, already observed in his earlier work, led him to decorate the upholstery and carpet of a single room with four very different printed fabrics, all with bold colours and expressive motifs. Wimmer-Wisgrill's 'Ameise' was again used here in the fitted carpet. For the suite of furniture he chose 'Rosengarten' by Peche (figs. 79, 159), Kalhammer's 'Kaisergarten' and 'Schönau' (fig. 130), as well as Frömel-Fochler's 'Krammetsvogel' (figs. 42, 164),[10] while in the entrance hall of the pavilion, also furnished by Hoffmann, the new pattern 'Basel' by Maria Likarz matched the Hoffmann style of furniture, being used for both upholstery and curtains.[11] That Hoffmann was not alone in his penchant for combining different bold patterns is demonstrated by Karl Witzmann's room for the display of handicrafts; its walls and showcases, decorated with Peche's Wiener Werkstätte wallpaper 'Wundervogel', contrasted boldly not only with the exhibits but also with the large repeat of the carpet design.[12]

Dagobert Peche was also active during the pre-war years as an exhibition designer: for the International Exhibition of Art held in Rome in 1914 he refurbished the Austrian pavilion built by Hoffmann for the exhibition of 1911;[13] he designed a lady's boudoir for the Werkbund Exhibition,[14] and in 1915/16 was the architect responsible for a large fashion exhibition held at the Österreichisches Museum für Kunst und Industrie (fig. 175).[15] In each of these projects Peche used his own pattern 'Rom', obviously designed for the first of them: in Rome as curtains in the main hall and in a semi-circular room dedicated to Klimt, also as wallpaper in other rooms; in Cologne as an upholstery fabric for a chaise-longue; in Vienna as a wallpaper and upholstery design. Apart from this, the fashion department used 'Rom' for an extravagant coat made in 1913 (fig. 176). The pattern's large, oval bouquets, here in white on a black ground, were evidently one of Peche's favourite motifs, which he used in sculptural form as gilded ornament on black furniture – a small table and a cupboard –

175 Fashion exhibition at the Österreichisches Museum für Kunst und Industrie, designed by Dagobert Peche, 1916. Wallpaper: ROM (1911/13) by Dagobert Peche. DK 1916

wallpaper; 'Rosenkavalier' (Peche) for curtains; and, for the floor-covering, a velour carpet produced by Backhausen using Hoffmann's 'Sanduhr'. The second showroom for the textile department – likewise designed by Hoffmann – opened in mid-1918; this was located at 32 Kärntnerstraße, on the corner across the street from no. 41; here, however, Wiener Werkstätte fabrics and wallpaper were not part of the fixed furnishings (figs. 285, 287, 290). In the Zurich branch and in the showroom in Marienbad, Peche and Hoffmann used Berger's 'Mekka' once again as wallpaper (figs. 165, 166), in exactly the same way as they had sought to achieve stylistic homogeneity in the branches described above (figs. 167–169).[18]

The leading role played by Wiener Werkstätte textiles in interior design up till the outbreak of war and beyond stands in stark contrast with their decline after 1918. Even so, such materials continued to be produced for use as curtain fabrics, tablecloths or lampshades. The textiles' erstwhile function of determining the character of a room had, however, been lost.[19]

again in 1914.[16] No documentary material relating to this pattern, apart from the secondary sources already mentioned, has survived in any Wiener Werkstätte archival records.

On 1 April 1916 the Wiener Werkstätte opened its fashion department showroom at 41 Kärntnerstraße in Vienna (fig. 169).[17] The rooms were designed by Josef Hoffmann in collaboration with Wimmer-Wisgrill. Wiener Werkstätte patterns were used for all furnishings: 'Mekka' (Berger), 'Daphne' (Peche) and 'Semiramis' (Peche) for the

176 Coat designed by Eduard J. Wimmer-Wisgrill, 1913, featuring ROM (1911/13) by Dagobert Peche

[1] Minutes of the board meeting of 9 June 1914.
[2] Minutes of the board of directors' sixth session, held on 9 October 1915. An example of the advertising campaign takes the form of a sheet of paper with a small fabric sample attached to it; the text promotes silks available for sale, and the reverse bears a list of selling agents in Germany (see fig. 300).
[3] Minutes of the board meeting of 19 June 1916, p. 6.
[4] In Galicia early in May 1915, Austrian and German forces broke through the Russian front line at Gorlice; the Wiener Werkstätte pattern name 'Gorlicze' by Angela Pietrovska (fig. 124) thus probably refers to this event, a topic of considerable public interest at the time.
[5] Minutes of 19 June 1916, p. 2 (cf. note 3 above).
[6] Supplement to DA XXI (1916/18): 'Die bildenden Künste', pls. 14f.
[7] Sekler 1985, cat. no. 198, p. 377.
[8] Die Damenwelt, March-July 1917. Völker 1984, p. 79, fig. 101; p. 84, fig. 109; p. 90, fig. 119; p. 99, fig. 134; p. 103, fig. 139; p. 104, fig. 141.
[9] Minutes of the board of directors' third session, held on 15 April 1915; cf. also Völker 1984, pp. 83ff.
[10] Sekler 1985, cat. no. 183, p. 365.
[11] Koch 1916, pp. 30f.
[12] DA XX (1914/15), pls. 62, 63; DK XVII (1914), pp. 470ff.
[13] Eisler 1916, p. 38; Eisler 1925, p. 8.
[14] Eisler 1925, p. 9.
[15] Wien 1915/16 (exhib. cat.), pp. 9, 14; DK XXIV (1916), pp. 229ff.; DKD XXXVIII (1916), pp. 79ff.
[16] DKD XXXIV (1914); the cupboard is owned by the Österreichisches Museum für angewandte Kunst, inv. no. H.2184.
[17] Report on trading in the financial year 1916, p. 1; Völker 1984, pp. 250ff., figs. 348ff.
[18] Koch 1923, n.p.
[19] Angela Völker, 'Textilien zur Wiener Innenraumgestaltung 1918–1938' in Wien 1980 NW (exhib. cat.), pp. 59ff.

178 *Hilda Jesser. BAUERNGARTEN (1912/19).*
Fabric sample

Opposite
177 *Reni Schaschl. LUFTSCHLOSS (1916/18).*
Fabric sample

179 *Felice Rix. TANAGRA (1916).*
Fabric sample

After the war the Wiener Werkstätte fashion and textile departments continued in business as usual without any interruption.[1] Business reports are again the main sources illustrating the day-to-day background to the artistic side of the enterprise. The report of 9 December 1920 describes the general situation of the Wiener Werkstätte in the financial year 1919: 'Business progress last year was satisfactory, although it was handicapped by the difficulties of importing and exporting, the uncertain foreign exchange rates, the spread of socialism, and various measures undertaken by the state. The greater part of Altösterreich [the former Austro-Hungarian Empire] was lost as a market; this was offset by sales opportunities in the entente countries [Czechoslovakia, Rumania and Yugoslavia], which were exploited only with a degree of restraint so as to allow customers to familiarize themselves with our taste gradually, to bring our products onto the market in the right way ... Our main market has remained Germany, a country in which artistic trends approximate most closely to our own.'[2] The textile department had sold merchandise to a total value of 10.5 million crowns, even though it 'had been subject to shortages of charcoal and dyes at the printing works.' The tone remained optimistic: 'We are hoping for good sales figures in the entente countries, since marketing our printed fabrics calls for fewer introductory procedures than do fashion and handicrafts.'

The Wiener Werkstätte now began to take part in various trade fairs, especially in Germany. Photographs taken at the Leipzig Trade Fair, where it exhibited from 1918,[3] reveal the organization's current style of self-presentation: The 'fabric and handicraft room' on the premises of the Dresdner Bank was decorated with a Wiener Werkstätte wallpaper (fig. 181). Items from the various departments were displayed on shelves and on tables. Wiener Werkstätte fabrics were used as upholstery and for lampshades. Besides familiar fabrics from older collections, like Zovetti's 'Stichblatt' (fig. 261), more recent new designs were on show: 'Bauerngarten' (Jesser, fig. 178), 'Luftschloss' and 'Columbia' (Schaschl, figs. 177, 186, 187), 'Tanagra' (Rix, fig. 179) and 'Vogelweide' (Löw, fig. 285). From 1920 to 1922 the Wiener Werkstätte took part in the Frankfurt Trade Fair. In 1920 and

181 Wiener Werkstätte fabric and handicraft display at the Leipzig Trade Fair, 1920. Photograph album 137

Left
180 Wiener Werkstätte fashion room at the Frankfurt Trade Fair pavilion, 1920, with wallpaper featuring DAPHNE (1918) by Dagobert Peche. Photograph album 137. (Insets) DAPHNE. Fabric samples

1921 it put up its own pavilions there, luxuriously fitted out with its own furniture, fabrics and wallpapers.[4] Fashion shows were already taking place by 1920, to much publicity and acclaim: 'The absolute highlight is provided by the Wiener Werkstätten, appearing at the Frankfurt Trade Fair for the very first time. An association of artists with Prof. Hoffmann, Vienna, as director, is displaying here artistic innovations of its own design in the form of silk gowns, blouses, summer dresses and hand-printed fabrics.'[5]

At exhibitions and trade fairs the Wiener Werkstätte was always represented by its textiles as well:

182 Third Vienna Trade Fair, autumn 1922. Wallpaper: DIE ROSE (1922) by Dagobert Peche. Photograph album 137

Right
184 Sigmund Berl
House, Freudenthal,
designed by Josef
Hoffmann 1919/22 with
upholstery featuring
TROPENBLUME
(1916/18) by Reni
Schaschl. MBF 1925

185 Reni Schaschl.
TROPENBLUME
(1916/18). Fabric sample

Opposite
183 Wiener Werkstätte
branch in New York,
1922: Josef Urban's office
with wall-covering
featuring PAPPEL-
ROSE (1911/16) by
Dagobert Peche.
Photograph album 137

186 Reni Schaschl. COLUMBIA (1912/17). Colour proof on paper

plant motifs on a dark ground is well suited to the simple forms and provides visual accents in a room that is otherwise kept plain. In 1924/5, the armchairs in the dining room and hall of the villa which Hoffmann built for Sonja Knips in Vienna were upholstered with Peche's 'Viola' (fig. 188).[17] The velour carpet, with a pattern of rhombuses made up of leaf-shaped forms 'in shades of purple and dark green',[18] was designed by Julius Zimpel and manufactured by Backhausen. Here again we encounter Hoffmann's preference for highly expressive and brightly coloured textile patterns which aim to create variety and a lively effect.

As already noted, textiles played a less prominent role in interior decoration during the 1920s than in the years after 1910. The visual effect is now considerably more subdued and the use of plain textiles,

187 Lampshade designed by Josef Hoffmann and featuring COLUMBIA (1912/17) by Reni Schaschl. Photograph album 118

in 1920 at the Landesgewerbemuseum in Stuttgart,[6] in 1922 at the Deutsche Gewerbeschau in Munich,[7] and at the opening of the Wiener Werkstätte's New York branch (fig. 183)[8] as well as the third Wiener Messe (fig. 182);[9] in 1923 at the Ausstellung von Arbeiten des modernen österreichischen Kunsthandwerks, which was dedicated to the memory of Dagobert Peche,[10] and likewise in 1924,[11] and of course in 1925 at the Exposition Internationale des Arts Décoratifs et Industriels Modernes in Paris[12] (figs. 202, 204); this was followed in 1927 by the exhibition 'Europäisches Kunstgewerbe' held at the Grassi Museum in Leipzig.[13] Finally, two exhibitions presented in Vienna at the Österreichisches Museum für Kunst und Industrie deserve mention:'Wiener Raumkünstler'(1929/30)[14] and the Ausstellung des Österreichischen Werkbunds (1930).[15]

After the war Josef Hoffmann collaborated a great deal with the Wiener Werkstätte on his commissions for house and interior design schemes. A good example of Hoffmann's exploitation of textiles at that time was the Sigmund Berl house in Freudenthal (*c.* 1922), where he used the Wiener Werkstätte fabric pattern 'Tropenblume' (figs. 184, 185) by Reni Schaschl for upholstering a suite of furniture.[16] The bold pattern of colourful stylized often handwoven in a single colour, or of leather, now predominates. In Oskar Strnad's view, 'Fabrics are the garb of a room, its decoration ... the fabric lives within the room as a free being. Therefore, no suites of furniture, but individual elements; that means the use of a variety of fabrics. Pure colours ... ; no repeating patterns ... Best of all, only those created purely by weaving techniques. No industrial products, they are too empty, only what is handwoven and enriched by the weaving process.'[19] This opinion was to a great extent a direct contradiction of Hoffmann's ideas. In sympathy with Hoffmann, on the other hand, were Josef Frank's arguments: 'For example, fewer patterned fabrics of a hardwearing and durable quality are being manufactured, but they are being replaced by printed cretonne, which we are using not only because it is cheaper but also because we find it more pleasing.'[20]

The few boldly patterned fabrics, mostly prints, provided focal accents and underlined the curving forms of furniture with their playfully decorative designs or formed an attractive contrast to severe shapes. Hoffmann's interior design schemes were in accordance with these principles, as when he aimed to produce a pleasing effect with his patterned upholstery materials in the Berl house. In Sonja Knips's villa his ideas were based on his personal predilection for using as many different patterns as possible; on the other hand, he was then greatly influenced by Dagobert Peche, whose seemingly limitless powers of formal invention were much appreciated by Hoffmann.

Peche himself, with his commitment to the use of eccentric forms of ornament and varied materials, as well as to the resolving of problems created by the latter, was in sympathy with the trends of international Art Déco. These were in stark and often clearly defined contrast with modern realism (*Sachlichkeit*), which strove for the reduction of ornament and for design to be appropriate to the material used. It was especially in surface patterns for fabrics and wallpaper that Peche's exuberant powers of formal invention knew no limits. The influence of his inventions went far beyond the Wiener Werkstätte. 'The whole of Germany has been ushered into a new epoch by Peche's patterns. And take a look at France, England and at the large showrooms of industry; these carpets, cretonne goods, wallpapers, everything about them is orna-

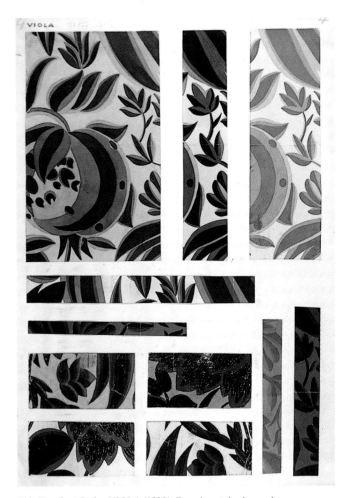

188 Dagobert Peche. VIOLA (1923). Experimental colour-schemes; gouache on paper

ment from Peche's bounty, colour from Peche's palette', was Hoffmann's assessment of his younger colleague, whose influence caused Hoffmann himself to develop a new repertoire of forms.[21]

The extent of the reverberations of Peche's influence and its effect on the Wiener Werkstätte's style and public image is best measured by reference to post-war articles and illustrations devoted to him and his works, especially textile designs. Museum acquisitions and the use of his fabrics in fashion and interior design schemes also demonstrate the popularity of his patterns. Three new fabrics, 'Hymen' (figs. 277, 278), 'Vergissmeinnicht' (fig. 313) and 'Endigung' (fig. 347), were illustrated in *Die bildenden Künste* in 1920. Peche's 'Irrgarten' (figs. 189, 199) was used by Carl Witzmann for armchair upholstery in the exhibition entitled 'Einfacher Hausrat' (simple household effects) held at the Österreichisches Museum für Kunst und Industrie in the same year.[22] Peche's 'Diomedes'

(fig. 191) was well received abroad in 1921: Fritz August Breuhaus from Cologne used the pattern for a four-poster bed canopy in a lady's bedroom,[23] and Paul Poiret designed a coat in which it was used for the lining.[24] Also in 1921, *Wasmuths Monatshefte für Baukunst* included an illustration of Peche's 'Pan' (fig. 194) and 'Hesperidenfrucht'. The latter was manufactured as fabric and wallpaper, and was also used in the fashion department for one of their extremely popular pyjama designs (fig. 197). 'Pan' (figs. 193, 194) is an example of the *ombré* effect, much favoured and frequently used by Peche; this was a characteristic feature of the time, achieved by gradually blending coloured stripes into each other. Other designs by Peche illustrating this technique are 'Kardinal' (fig. 192), 'Gletscherblume' (fig. 301) and 'Krone' (fig. 314).

Peche's influence can be detected not only in the works of Hoffmann, but also in those of Mathilde Flögl, Felice Rix and Maria Likarz. However, more important than the occasionally rather overt borrowing of his patterns, seems to be the fact that

Opposite and below
189, 190 Dagobert Peche. IRRGARTEN (1913). Length of fabric and window of the Wiener Werkstätte branch in Zurich, designed by Dagobert Peche, 1917, with fabric on display. Photograph album 137

191 Dagobert Peche. DIOMEDES (1919). Colour proof on paper

Peche fundamentally changed the general trend within the Wiener Werkstätte. This led to the adoption of principles of form and technique which, having eventually taken a negative course years after Peche's death, made many works by Wiener Werkstätte artists appear so trivial and out-of-date. Hans Tietze, art historian, civil servant and prescient observer of the Viennese art scene in the years between the wars, had described this tendency as early as 1919 on the occasion of the Ausstellung österreichischer Kunstgewerbe held at the Museum für Kunst und Industrie.[25] Peche was an avowed opponent of industrial production and after the First World War his arguments were still in line with the declared aims of the Wiener Werkstätte as set out in the work programme of 1905.[26] Actively supported by Hoffmann, he persisted in pursuing a course which aimed at luxurious decoration perfectly and individually crafted by hand. However, in the early years of the Wiener Werkstätte, in projects such as the Palais Stoclet, this principle had resulted in ambivalent effects

193, 194 *Dagobert Peche. PAN (1919).*
Pyjamas. Photo by d'Ora, 1920.
(Above) Fabric sample

Opposite
192 *Dagobert Peche. KARDINAL (1911/13).*
Length of fabric

195 *Anny Schröder. ARABESKE (1920/21).*
Colour proof on paper

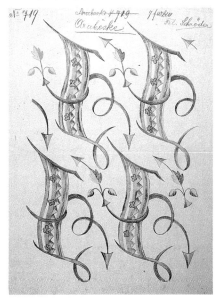

196 Anny Schröder. *ARABESKE (1920/21). Fabric sample and (inset) pyjamas photographed by d'Ora, 1920*

197 Dagobert Peche. HESPERIDENFRUCHT (1919). Fabric sample and (inset) pyjamas photographed by d'Ora, 1920

derived from exuberance that was not always decorous. Most likely this was attributable to a surfeit of technical and material possibilities. Peche's influential aesthetic ideas eventually paved the way for the demise of the Wiener Werkstätte, whose products lapsed into slickness and what can be negatively termed 'arts and crafts'.

The pre-emption of art by decoration, felt to be 'typically Viennese',[27] was in marked contrast to the reduced formal vocabulary of artists such as Adolf Loos, Oskar Strnad, Ernst Plischke or the architect Friedrich Kiesler. They tended to favour strict *Sachlichkeit* and functionalism, internationally represented by the likes of Le Corbusier or Mies van der Rohe. Japan played an influential role again. In 1925 Le Corbusier wrote a pamphlet attacking the exhibition in Paris, and especially the emphasis given to decoration, rejecting it as inadequate for modern times.[28]

That Vienna also experienced comparable trends and produced works to vie with the international avant-garde can be demonstrated through personalities such as Franz Cizek, initiator of a course on ornamental forms, his pupil Erika Giovanna Klien, with her kinetic paintings, and Friedrich Kiesler, probably the most impressive of all, with the international exhibition he organized at the Konzerthaus in 1924 devoted to new theatrical techniques,[29] but it may be less well known that these trends also found an echo within the Wiener Werkstätte, and above all in the textile department. Thus, Maria Likarz, Mathilde Flögl, Felice Rix and Max Snischek, although influenced by Peche, were all able to give new impetus to their work through the abstract trends which were so relevant at that time. Maria Likarz had already made a start around 1912 with her versatile pattern 'Irland', still being put to practical use in 1929 (figs. 99–102, 172, 251).

Adolf Loos was not alone in frowning upon the Wiener Werkstätte and its artists as the embodiment of the reprehensible ornamental trends. It was a subject of ridicule that here an unusual proportion of the artists were women who dominated the artistic climate within the organization; this was combined with the prejudiced view that *Sachlichkeit*, abstraction and a repertoire of geometric forms did not exist in the Wiener Werkstätte between the wars.[30] A look into the textile department proves the opposite. However, one should not expect to seek the new image in official disputes.

*198 Reni Schaschl.
BOSTON (1912/17).
Length of fabric*

It was especially after the war that women had a virtual monopoly in determining how the Wiener Werkstätte and its products would be viewed, leaving aside the leading (male) members – Hoffmann, Wimmer-Wisgrill, Max Snischek, Peche, and his successor Julius Zimpel. As in the founding years of the textile department, the new arrivals were again mainly students from Hoffmann's class at the Kunstgewerbeschule, among whom Reni Schaschl, Hilda Jesser and Fritzi Löw deserve special mention; the first two artists designed about twenty-five patterns each, the last about forty-five for the Wiener Werkstätte. 'Boston' (fig. 198) is typical of Schaschl's style, while 'Bauerngarten'

*199 Fritzi Löw.
OSIRIS (1910/17).
Fabric sample*

(fig. 178) and 'Osiris' (fig. 199) are characteristic patterns for Jesser and Löw respectively. Hoffmann's pupils all belonged to the same generation, and at the time were between twenty-five and twenty-nine years old, while Camilla Birke and Gertrud Höchsmann were a little younger. Also active in other areas, they designed all manner of objects besides fabric patterns in various departments of the Wiener Werkstätte. The art critic Max Eisler, in contrast to Hans Tietze, was encouraging and yet critical. In 1920 he wrote: 'In addition, the Wiener Werkstätte … is making provision for development in its own way through its young, indeed youngest possible, workforce. Even if this is happening at the moment only in cheap fabrics, rather as window-dressing and moulding, and solely with the obvious intention of keeping the hand supple and inventive ideas in good humour, it is imperative, especially in this waiting period, not to underestimate it. It [the Wiener Werkstätte] could, of course make things easier for itself and forgo experimentation, which after all, is expensive, as well as such liberal employment of the next generation of artists. Within a large-scale enterprise such as this one has become, economic expansion cannot be hindered in the long run.'[31]

In the context of handicrafts the most important exhibition held in the 1920s was without doubt the Exposition Internationale des Arts Décoratifs et Industriels Modernes, staged in Paris in 1925, from the title of which the entire epoch acquired the name Art Déco. It goes without saying that the Wiener Werkstätte was well represented. Josef Hoffmann, the Austrian exhibition commissioner, chose to present its products crammed into large, lavishly decorated showcases, the framework of which had been covered on the outside with a stylized floral pattern (fig. 202). An additional and colourful feature was the use of lengths of fabric as supplementary decoration. As far as one can judge from the black-and-white photographs of the time, Hoffmann's apparent aim in presenting such a profusion of wares was to demonstrate in no uncertain terms the artists' powers of invention and the general versatility of the Wiener Werkstätte; he wanted to present an international audience with as many of the Wiener Werkstätte treasures as possible.

A brief look at the other Viennese artists and institutions participating in the Paris exhibition shows that the Wiener Werkstätte and its associated artists

200 Camilla Birke. TAHITI (1924). Fabric sample

were not alone in setting stylistic trends in the city between the wars. The exhibition of works by Austrian architects organized by Hoffmann's pupil and assistant Oswald Haerdtl, Friedrich Kiesler's theatre section and his *Raumstadt*, as well as the display presented by the Kunstgewerbeschule, all bear witness to a general involvement in the international movement towards abstraction.[32]

The multiplicity of styles and attitudes in art was entirely in keeping with Hoffmann's intentions. As exhibition commissioner, he had personally chosen the various artists for their current contributions. Apart from which, his obvious and pronounced penchant for variety and contrast and his almost

201 Camilla Birke. TIBET (1925). Colour proof on paper

202 Wiener Werkstätte showcases at the international exhibition, Paris, 1925. Photograph by Henri Manuel, Paris. Photograph album 137

203 Josef Hoffmann. SALAMBO (1910/15). Fabric sample

204 Room at the international exhibition in Paris, 1925, with Austrian exhibits from Prof. Cizek's youth art course. Curtain featuring SALAMBO (1910/15) by Josef Hoffmann

uncanny adaptability were demonstrated – perhaps without his active participation – in the use of his fabric pattern 'Salambo' (figs. 203, 204) for curtains and coverings in the Kunstgewerbeschule display and the architecture section in Paris. This abstract pattern in two colours was entirely in sympathy with the functional style of the exhibits. In the furniture section – his own design – he demonstrated yet again his fondness for decorative patterns by using Camilla Birke's wallpaper 'Tahiti' (fig. 200), a design which was also on show as a fabric, and another wallpaper with a lively marbled pattern.[33]

In trying to assess the Wiener Werkstätte fabrics in the context of the Paris exhibition as a whole, it should be borne in mind that the display also included examples of Sonia Delaunay's textiles, both fabrics and garments,[34] and that artists of the Russian avant-garde were exhibiting a variety of characteristic handicrafts, including fabrics,[35] and, moreover, that objects by the Italian Futurists were on show.[36] These in fact represented the very trends that were received with the most spontaneous interest and artistic enthusiasm and achieved the greatest success. The artistic climate was also influenced by the avant-garde style of pavilions, such as those by Melnikov, Le Corbusier and Mallet-Stevens, while the Austrian pavilion, designed by Hoffmann and with a Café by the German architect Peter Behrens, then a professor at the Akademie der Künste in Vienna, was an example of international co-operation.[37]

Adolf Loos was not alone in his fierce and sometimes polemical criticism of the Wiener Werkstätte, his diatribes becoming more vehement after 1925. The architect Armand Weiser, Hoffmann's later biographer, was equally harsh in his judgment of the Paris exhibits. In his words, 'What we now see in the showcases is just the same as what we have been getting in the displays of the Wiener Werkstätte, the Werkbund and the Kunstgewerbemuseum exhibitions for more than a decade. It is all so similar that it makes one think that taste is subject to automation ... Unfortunately, nearly everything on show has as its objective the creation of luxury, a luxury that has become prohibitive and has long been superfluous both for us and for those nations which understand our individuality'.[38] The German author Benno Reifenberg was aware of the tensions just described, as is evident from what he

205 Maria Likarz. MAHARADSCHA (1925). Length of woven fabric

wrote about the showcases in Hoffmann's pavilion: '... the Wiener Werkstätte has poured its trifling life into these showcases, the bric-à-brac of the boudoir, fashion and toys; a motley pile out of Santa Claus's sack. It is difficult to grasp what this new Austria is up to ... They are just playing around. For instance, the windows are fitted in slightly below the base to avoid structural integrity at all costs ... Meanwhile, in the architecture exhibition at the Grand Palais, Vienna is showing an example of modern building more or less as we could have presented it; the power of the Weimar Bauhaus can be felt, Peter Behrens is also a determining element.'[39]

The Wiener Werkstätte presentation in 1925 must have served as an exposure of the one-sided conservative tendencies that existed within the artists' association. As far as the textile department was concerned, the reproach seems paradoxical in a certain sense, since Wiener Werkstätte fabrics were after all the very products which had already shown early evidence of modern trends early on – trends

which also continued to develop after 1925. Nor were abstract patterns absent from the Wiener Werkstätte presentation in Paris, which included, for instance, 'Natter' (Flögl), 'Mandarin' (Rix) and Likarz's 'Maharadscha' (fig. 205), the last originally a wallpaper pattern,[40] and one of the few weaves still being produced by Backhausen for the Wiener Werkstätte. However, the profusion of objects and patterns on view in endless showcases ruined any chance that such forward-looking tendencies might have had to make any real impression; the abstract patterns could not assert themselves in the context of a massed display.

In 1926 the Wiener Werkstätte was yet again in a grave crisis. Its conversion from a limited company to a public one was meant to help, but this never came about: it was the cause of a fundamental review, which can be seen from a report of 18 July 1927 in the archive.[41] Today the document's function appears to be that of an inventory giving precise details of numbers of employees and existing merchandise in stock. The Wiener Werkstätte, it is recorded, had a total of '63 employees and 93 workers, furthermore an average of about 40 outworkers'.[42] A detailed breakdown relating to the staffing levels of the individual departments is not included. The textile department's wares were classified logically into 'raw materials, fabrics of one colour, and patterned merchandise (printed, coloured, woven, etc.)'. The report also describes the high value of artists' design drawings and of the printing blocks.

In the years after 1927 the Wiener Werkstätte placed its fabrics almost exclusively at the disposal of the fashion department. The surviving stock registers make it clear that linen and cotton fabrics were nevertheless still being printed for interior design. Accessories, *Galanteriewaren* (fancy goods) and cushions in bizarre shapes (figs. 273, 274), mostly making use of printed silk, also formed part of its own production. Thus, the designing and manufacture of fabrics continued at the usual level. Given the high esteem in which the fabrics were held, one can imagine that the retail trade began to play an even more important role. The impression that this was the case is conveyed by a stock register with the title *Textil detail* started on 1 January 1920; unfortunately the situation is somewhat con-

206 *Maria Likarz. EBRO (1926). Fabric sample*

fused, since it only contains seemingly endless lists of the fabrics manufactured and supplied by various firms, without allowing sufficient insight into sales success.

There was more or less an equal ratio of decorative and abstract tendencies shaping the last ten years of the Wiener Werkstätte. The distinctive 'handwritings' identifying the various artists – a programmatic requirement for inclusion as a member in the Wiener Werkstätte – did now seem to some extent to lose their individuality, but there was never a homogeneous style. Maria Likarz and Max Snischek, both holding leading positions in the fashion department as well, drew strictly geometric patterns in exciting colour-schemes, as well as patterns with stylized plants or other motifs – e.g. figures or skyscrapers (figs. 244, 377) – corresponding to the current vogue. Felice Rix and Mathilde Flögl were effective and artistically prolific members of the association, whose repertoire of forms had a similarly wide range. Josef Hoffmann also continued to work in the textile department to the very end, designing patterns which provided clear evidence of his exploration of modern – even abstract – trends, but which never ceased to bear the stamp of his very personal inventive skills (fig. 383). However, with such a profusion of patterns a tendency towards a dissipation of ideas becomes evident, a factor which in the end must have been disconcerting to the consumer, no longer able to discern a clear line in the surfeit of choice. Despite this, however, with the late patterns one can generally be certain of correctly distinguishing Wiener Werkstätte creations from those from other sources, errors occurring only rarely.

Probably the most striking feature of the Wiener Werkstätte fabrics is its use of colour-schemes that were often unusual yet always featured tasteful combinations. They were evidently impossible to imitate or surpass and even in the case of very simple, almost banal patterns had an effect that was both strongly expressive and stylistically influential. Some patterns are known to exist in more than twenty different colour-schemes. The colour sense of the Wiener Werkstätte artists will have reached such a consummate level thanks to their experience of working in different departments and of handling a variety of materials.

207 Maria Likarz. Dress design featuring EBRO (1926); pencil and watercolour on paper

208 Felice Rix. WELLEN (1927). Woven fabric sample

The need for a commercialization of the Wiener Werkstätte continued to grow, but this stood little chance of being realized, since the organization's practically unaltered programme and work structure were based on premises that were much too idealistic and had meanwhile become outdated; accordingly, the textile department tried various experiments in fabric production. Zimpel, Flögl and Hoffmann thus created small-patterned silks suitable for neckties.[43] Maria Likarz (fig. 205), Mathilde Flögl (fig. 209), Felice Rix (fig. 208) and occasionally other artists produced designs for woven

209 Mathilde Flögl. DORNEGG (1927). Woven fabric sample

fabrics, which were manufactured by various firms, including Backhausen.[44] Simple striped cottons, known as *Heliosripse* (literally 'sun reps'), as well as light, chequered *Voiles Fantasie*. The experimental stage is recognizable not least because of the small number of fabrics and the short space of time during which they were produced. Nevertheless, in their formal features they are entirely in keeping with the development of printed fabrics, even if their tones were more muted, in response to the demand for a degree of reticence in fabrics intended for interior decorative schemes.

Finally, one other typical product of the late 1920s remains to be mentioned, the so-called *Spritzdrucke* (sprayed prints), which Hoffmann, Likarz, Flögl and Snischek designed. Clara Posnanski, who produced the sprayed prints on silk and cotton for the Wiener Werkstätte, was herself an artist, and designed a whole series of mainly abstract patterns using this technique for the textile department (figs. 210, 348–351). All that is known about Clara Posnanski today is that she ran a textile-finishing business *(Werkstätte für Textilveredelung nach eigenen künstl. Entwürfen)* at 57 Pernerstorferstraße in Vienna's tenth district.

The patterns, applied with stencils and fine spray jets, were probably inspired by the so-called *ombré* stripes like 'Kardinal' (fig. 192), so often used by Peche; they in turn were derived from abstract painting. Sharp outlines of the elements within a pattern alternate with the fuzzy effect of sprayed outlines, and overlap each other. Clara Posnanski's patterns conform to the general design trends of the Wiener Werkstätte: there were bold and colourfully contrasted designs such as 'Paul' (fig. 351) and 'Paliuri' (fig. 350), but also unpretentious and small-patterned designs such as 'Brioni' (fig. 210) and 'Höflein' (fig. 349), as well as a whole series of striped patterns which were particularly striking in their use of colour. Clara Posnanski also used this technique to design shawls, which were sold in the fashion and textile departments. The Wiener Werkstätte sprayed prints were given a separate numbering system, beginning with 5001, designating 'Sakatali' by Josef Hoffmann.

An effect similar to that produced by spraying can be achieved by hand-painting, a significantly more complicated technique for colouring fabrics, which was practised in the Wiener Werkstätte in the early years until about 1920. Nearly all the

210 Clara Posnanski. BRIONI (1926). Fabric sample

known examples were executed by Gabriele Möschl, who had her own workshop for silk printing in Auhofstraße in Vienna XIII, and finished articles were made up to order in the fashion and textile departments. Unfortunately, the tiny sample strips still surviving in the stock books and in the so-called small card index can now convey only a very vague impression of her designs. They were obviously not intended as pattern samples, but related to whichever type of article was involved – fashion, accessories or fancy goods.

1 Völker 1984, p. 138.
2 The passage quoted appears on pp. 4f. of the official report.
3 *Annalen* 83, 237.
4 For the 1920 pavilion see Schweiger 1984, p. 112; for the 1921 pavilion see WW photo album 137, p. 60; Völker 1984, p. 191 (figs.).
5 *Frankfurter Mittagsblatt*, 3 May 1920; see *Annalen* 83, 365, 366ff. and 464ff.
6 *Annalen* 83, 434f.
7 Ibid., 558 ff.; WW photo album 137, p. 75; Munich 1922 (exhib. cat.); Koch 1923, n.p.
8 *Annalen* 83, 575ff.; WW photo album 137, p. 78.
9 WW photo album 137, p. 76.
10 Wien 1923 (exhib. cat.), p. 9; WW photo album 137, p. 78.
11 Wien 1924 (exhib. cat.), pp. 21ff.
12 *Annalen* 84, 797ff.
13 Leipzig 1927 (exhib. cat.), p. 56; Wien 1989/90 (exhib. cat.), pp. 262, 562 (no. V/4/51).
14 Wien 1929/30, p. 14.
15 Wien 1930 (exhib. cat.), pp. 16, 27.
16 *MBF* XXIV (1925), p. 294; Sekler 1985, cat. no. 226.
17 *MBF* XXV (1926), pp. 356ff.; Sekler 1985, cat. no. 265.
18 Sekler 1985, p. 402.
19 Oskar Strnad, 'Neue Wege der Wohnraumeinrichtung' in *ID* XXXIII (1922), p. 324.
20 Josef Frank 'Zum Formproblem' in Wien 1931/32 (exhib. cat.), p. 12.
21 Berta Zuckerkandl, 'Erinnerungen an Dagobert Peche' in *Wiener Journal*, 19 April 1923 (*Annalen* 83, 589).
22 *DBK* III (1920), p. 32; *DA* XXIII (1920), p. 85.
23 *ID* XXXII (1921), p. 202.
24 Berlin 1977 (exhib. cat.), no. 43.
25 Hans Tietze, 'Ausstellung österreichischer Kunstgewerbe' in *Der neue Tag*, 16 December 1919 (*Annalen* 83, 335), and a reply to a reader's letter – 'Die Frage des österreichischen Kunstgewerbes' – which appeared in the issue of 1 February 1920 (*Annalen* 83, 336).
26 Wien 1967 (exhib. cat.), p. 21; Schweiger 1984, pp. 41ff.
27 Cf. for example E. J. Wimmer-Wisgrill's foreword in the exhibition catalogue *Raum und Mode*, Vienna 1931–2, n. p. He wrote: '… and we believe, that once this wholesome bath of purification has been completed, we may dare to think more about the decoration of our rooms.'
28 Le Corbusier (1925) 1987.
29 Marietta Mautner-Markhof, 'Franz Cizek und die "moderne Kunst". Ornamentale Formenlehre an der Kunstgewerbeschule in Wien' in Wien 1985, Cizek (exhib. cat.), pp. 15 ff.; Wien 1988 (exhib. cat.); Lesak 1988, pp. 99ff.
30 Schweiger 1984, p. 120 (and notes); Bouillon 1989, pp. 107ff.
31 Max Eisler in *Der Morgen*, 19 January 1920 (*Annalen* 83, 333).
32 Wien 1978 (exhib. cat.), p. 23; Wien 1988 (exhib. cat.), pp. 21ff.; Österreichisches Museum für angewandte Kunst, K.I. 8961, division 361.
33 Paris 1925 (exhib. cat.); *Amour de l'Art*, vol. 8, August 1925 (special number); Edgar Brandt, *L'Exposition Internationale des Arts Décoratifs et Industriels Modernes, Paris 1925*, p. 319.
34 Guy Weelen, 'Robes Simultanées' in *L'Oeil*, vol. 60, December 1959, pp. 82 ff.
35 Paris 1925 (exhib. cat.) – U.S.S.R.; cf. also Alexander Lavrentiev, *Varvara Stepanova. The Complete Work*, Cambridge, Mass. 1988, p. 79.
36 Venice 1986 (exhib. cat.), p. 425 (Balla).
37 *Amour de l'Art* (op. cit.), see note 33 above.
38 *Neues Wiener Tagblatt* (*Annalen* 84, 913).
39 Benno Reifenberg, 'West-Kunst-Gewerbe. Zur internationalen Ausstellung in Paris' in *Frankfurter Zeitung*, 5 August 1925 (*Annalen* 83, 744).
40 Völker/Pichler 1989, vol. II, figs. 13ff.
41 The full title of the report was 'Revisions-Bericht betreffend die Umwandlung der Wiener Werkstätte Ges.m.b.H., Wien, in eine Aktiengesellschaft'.
42 In 1920/21 there were 120 employees and 250 workers in Vienna, as well as three employees in the Berlin branch, three in Marienbad and two in Karlsbad.
43 Examples in the large card index are: 'Assyrien' and 'Belsazar' by Julius Zimpel, 'Cilli' by Mathilde Flögl, and 'Everest', 'Kauri' and 'Luzern' by Josef Hoffmann.
44 Examples in the large card index are: 'Maharadscha' by Maria Likarz, 'Almata' by Felice Rix and 'Arizona' by Julius Zimpel.

211 Franz von Zülow. PASSION (1924).
Fabric sample

212 Franz von Zülow. BERGWALD (1924).
Fabric sample

213 Johanna Wintersteiner. MEXIKO (1923).
Fabric sample

Opposite
214 Franz von Zülow. ALGIER (1925).
Fabric sample (actual size)

124

215 Vally Wieselthier. QUADERN
(1916/19). Fabric sample

216 Lilly Jacobsen. FESTSCHMUCK
(1918). Fabric sample

217 Reni Schaschl. GITTERBLUME
(1912/17). Fabric sample

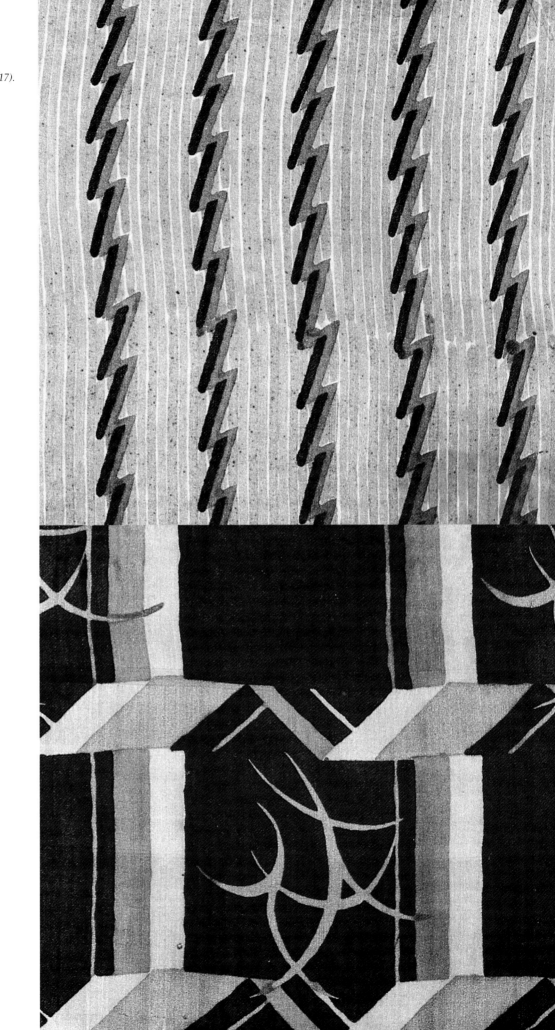

218 *Fritzi Löw. BADEN (1910/17).*
Fabric sample

219 *Maria Jungwirth. KREUZ-*
BAND (1919). Fabric sample

220 Heddi Hirsch.
LAVA (1916/18).
Fabric sample

221 Julius Zimpel.
VALENCIA (1925).
Fabric sample

128

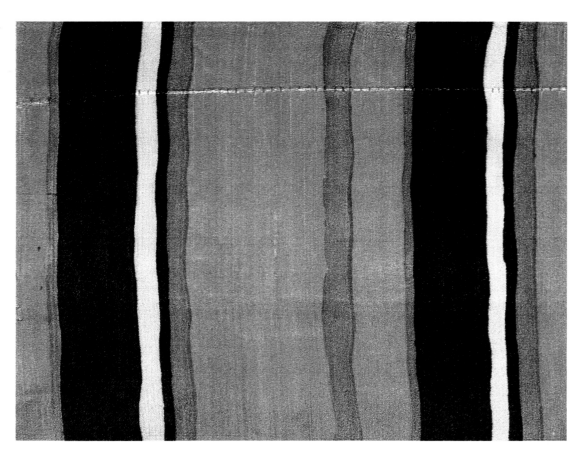

222 *Vally Wieselthier.*
ANDROMACHE
(1919). Fabric sample

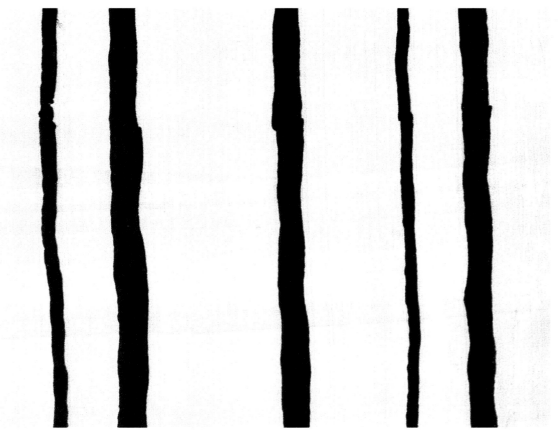

223 *Vally Wieselthier.*
ANDROMACHE
(1919). Fabric sample

129

224 *Erna Kopriva. PHILIPP (1927). Fabric sample*

225 *Thea Angerer. MENGO (1927). Fabric sample*

226 Gertrud Höchsmann. YAP (1925). Colour proof on paper

Opposite (from top left to bottom right)
227–232 *Fabric samples:*

227 *Hilde Blumberger. QUARTETT (1928).*
228 *Susi Singer. STANIOL (1923)*
229 *Hilda Jesser. FLOCKENTANZ (1912/22)*
230 *Ernst Lichtblau. GROSSVESIR (1916/18)*
231 *Camilla Birke. CIRCUS (1925).*
232 *Reni Schaschl. TROJA (1912/17).*

234 *Julius Zimpel. BIMINI (1927). Fabric sample*

235 *Julius Zimpel. ZWERGPALME (1928). Fabric sample*

236 *Julius Zimpel. GUINEA (1928). Fabric sample*

Opposite
237 *Julius Zimpel. BATAVIA (1925). Fabric sample*

134

FORMS AND LOCATIONS OF PRODUCTION

239 *Maria Likarz. PORTEPEE (1923).*
Printing block in the fashion collection of the
Historisches Museum der Stadt Wien

Opposite
238 Maria Likarz. PORTEPEE (1923).
Colour-schemes, gouache on paper

240 Maria Likarz. PORTEPEE (1923). Colour-
schemes, gouache on paper

Fabrics bearing the Wiener Werkstätte label were predominantly prints, namely linens, cottons and silks. The process used – block-printing – fulfilled the requirements of the Wiener Werkstätte for producing work of hand-crafted and artistic perfection resulting from the partnership between artist and craftsman. The printing of textiles with blocks is one of the earliest forms of producing decorative fabrics, and is a technique which offers opportunities that are appreciably less complicated than weaving patterns. Although far more variety can be achieved than is possible with woven patterns, creative and precise skills are required of all those involved in the printing process. As long as block-cutters and printers are qualified and experienced craftsmen, the artist can put his design ideas on paper in the knowledge that scarcely any limits will be imposed by technical considerations. However, the optimum result is achieved when all parties work together with a clear understanding of each other's limitations. Artistic freedom, working within the scope of the qualified craftsman's skills, always had priority in the Wiener

Werkstätte. Although it was a prerequisite for exceptional products, it also often became a bone of contention where financial success and profits were concerned. It thus came about that items – or, in this case, lengths of fabric – were manufactured at a cost which often bore no relation to their sales potential.

Technical difficulties can arise in block-printing if the fabric pattern has a complex differentiated colour-scheme. The number of blocks needed to print a single pattern is at least one for each colour employed, and the print quality also depends on whether all the blocks are perfectly matched with each other. In this respect, too, the Wiener Werkstätte fabrics measure up to the highest technical standards, with some patterns requiring up to twenty-four blocks.

The wooden blocks (fig. 239) are prepared by block-cutters, who trace the outlines of the final pre-print drawings on to each one. The wooden block is made of layers of softwood and pearwood glued together. The lines forming the pattern can be carved out of the wood, leaving raised areas to be printed; or, as was the more common practice with the Wiener Werkstätte blocks, the

137

241 Camilla Birke. MOORLAND (1924). Drawing in pencil, ink and watercolour, bought by the Wiener Werkstätte for 50,000 crowns on 17 January 1924

pattern is 'etched' with insets of copper and brass, thus forming the outlines of the pattern. For patterns needing large sets of blocks a combination of both types is often used. Each block has a set of projecting pins, one at each corner, as a guide for the printer, so ensuring the accuracy of their positioning one to another; the pins themselves have to be adjusted with a special device in order to guarantee precision. The individual blocks are numbered in accordance with the appropriate stage of the operation. The larger elements of a pattern have to be divided up and distributed over several blocks, since individual blocks need to be heavy but still capable of being moved by the printer using one hand to hold the fitted handle.

The printing process begins with the stretching of the fabric along the length of a long printing table. The first block, or – in the case of a large repeat – several blocks, for each pattern element is then used to print the whole length of the fabric. Each of the colours is allowed to dry before the next group of

blocks is applied to the fabric. The block is pressed onto a pre-soaked dye-pad and thus the raised areas receive the dye. After the printer, with a single carefully aimed movement, has placed the block in its exact position on the fabric, he strikes it several times with the handle of a weighted mallet (maul), leaving an evenly distributed impression. As a rule, one printer works on the full length of the fabric, rarely more. An assistant checks that the dye supply is always evenly distributed over the dye-pad before the block is recharged.

It can be safely assumed that the textile department never undertook the most complicated and elaborate operations in its own workshops; however, the preparatory procedures before the printing of the fabrics were probably carried out on the Wiener Werkstätte's premises. Thus it most likely arranged for the artists to design the majority of the numerous patterns on the spot. It is known that Hoffmann, as well as Peche after him, worked in their own offices within the Wiener Werkstätte workshops situated in the Neustiftgasse.[1] From 1916 on, Wimmer-Wisgrill and his successors had workrooms in the same building as the department's showroom.[2] The students of the Kunstgewerbeschule, whom Hoffmann had introduced in such numbers, worked on their designs mainly in the so-called 'artists' workshop' (*Künstlerwerkstätte*). It is still not known exactly when this came into existence – perhaps in 1913 – or where it was located.[3] The students and artists closely or only loosely associated with the Wiener Werkstätte could work here without having to pay for the use of the premises or for raw materials. The Wiener Werk-

242 Plan for the new Wiener Werkstätte workshops at 32-34 Neustiftgasse, dated 28 September 1917; pencil and crayon on tracing paper

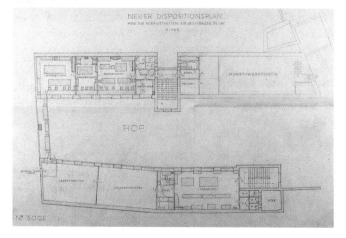

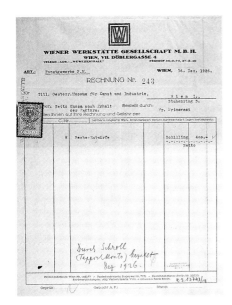

243 Invoice to the Österreichisches Museum für Kunst und Industrie, dated 16 December 1926, for the purchase of 8 designs by Dagobert Peche

*Below right
244 Colour-schemes for: Max Snischek, SPORT (1928); Dagobert Peche, ARIADNE (1919) and BLATTWINDE (1911/13); Josef Hoffmann, HOPFEN (1910/17). Gouache on paper*

stätte would buy from them those patterns which suited the organization's programme (fig. 241).

Once accepted, a pattern was copied by a specially engaged draughtsman working in co-operation with the artist, and the final pre-print drawing eventually served as a guide for the block-cutter.[4] Apart from this, the various colour-schemes had to be established. A great many of the dyeing patterns and final drawings are still extant and so make a significant contribution in completing the overall picture of the fabric patterns' range and variety in terms of their colour-schemes (figs. 11, 238, 240, 244, 245, 250). A number of the final pre-print drawings were preserved with the artists' original designs; the latter were regarded by the Wiener Werkstätte as being valuable financial assets. In 1927 it was recorded that 'the Wiener Werkstätte possesses over 13,000 drawings by artists, some of whom are world-famous. These designs have a very considerable, almost inestimable, value, and are occasionally offered for sale.'[5] At first the colour-schemes were kept in envelopes, but later they were pasted onto large sheets of paper which were systematically organized to allow a comprehensive view of the production. Today they are evidence of the efforts made by the Wiener Werkstätte to record its own history and promote its image.

The procedures described here – designing, completion of pre-print drawings, fixing of colour-schemes – all preceded the making of the blocks. This operation apparently took place in part on the Wiener Werkstätte premises, but was also, perhaps

more frequently, a function of outside firms. A block-cutter is registered in a list of employees dating from 1916,[6] and there is even a mention of a block-cutting workshop *(Modelstecherei)*, indicating the presence of specialized facilities which may have been understaffed during the war years. Moreover, the names of block-cutters are recorded in the two surviving production files of the textile department, although the names entered there are usually those of independent block-printing workshops.[7] All blocks cut in the Wiener Werkstätte itself are marked either *'Haus'* or *'Wiener Werkstätte'* in the files.[8] Finally, fabric-printing factories are also named as block-cutters: this may reflect incorrect information concerning production, or it could mean that certain blocks were indeed prepared on the spot at the printers' premises.[9] The fact that the block-cutting workshop was located together with the other Wiener Werkstätte

SPORT

ARIADNE

HOPFEN

BLATTWINDE

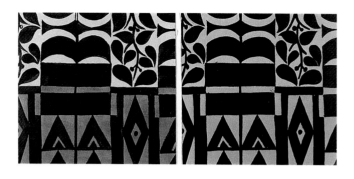

workshops, for a certain time at least, is an indication of the well-known assiduity with which the organization's members sought to approach the supervision of each phase of the merchandise's production. However, the complexity of the individual stages involved in fabric printing seems to have made it impossible to accommodate the entire production process within the Wiener Werkstätte's own group of workshops. Indeed, it led in the end to a lessening of the importance attached to this kind of supervision. The value of the printing blocks, however, was estimated to be fairly high; they are referred to in the *Revisions-Bericht* of 1927, where it is stated that 'We have in stock around 3,000 sets of these manufacturing aids, so vital for an enterprise such as the Wiener Werkstätte. Their value is based not only on how long the firm itself has a use for them, but they also have their own intrinsic value, in that those blocks which are no longer needed are usually sold off to hand-printers in the provinces.'[10]

The supervision of the printing blocks, such as was practised at least at the beginning by the Wiener Werkstätte itself, naturally made storage an im-

portant factor. Since the blocks were part of the Wiener Werkstätte's assets, it is evident from the production files that they were either kept on the premises of the Wiener Werkstätte[11] or, if the pattern was involved in current production, handed directly to the printers.[12] As a result, only a comparatively small proportion of the blocks were still held in stock at the time of the Wiener Werkstätte's liquidation.[13] As mentioned previously, the majority – some 2,000 sets still in the possession of the Basle manufacturer, were sold by Alfred Hofmann in the late 1930s to another Swiss printing firm, which tried unsuccessfully to reactivate the Wiener Werkstätte patterns.[14]

Apart from this, a large collection of colour prints on paper has survived in the archive (e.g. figs. 15, 54, 110, 186, 226, 344); these trial prints were used by printers, artists and clients as a first check. It is conceivable that this proofing stage was carried out in the Wiener Werkstätte itself before the blocks and colour-schemes were distributed to outside firms. There is, however, another possible explanation, one that is more probable especially in relation to the later period, namely, that the printers would

246 *Josef Hoffmann. DORFSCHWALBE (1910/12). Small card index, verso with pattern sample*

247 *Josef Hoffmann. RAGUSA (1910/12). Small card index, verso with pattern sample*

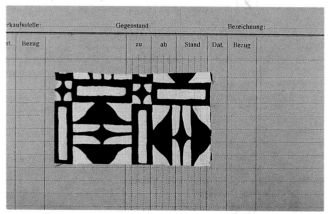
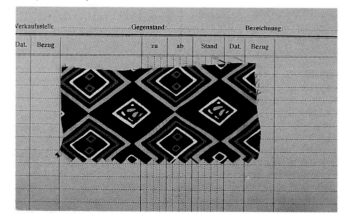

248 Maria Likarz. LHASA
(1925). Fabric samples in various
colour-schemes. Large card index

Opposite
245 Josef Hoffmann.
MONTEZUMA (1910/12).
Colour-schemes, gouache on paper

249 Max Snischek. LENGLEN
(1927). Fabric samples in various
colour-schemes. Large card index

141

prepare the proofs for submission to the Wiener Werkstätte for a final check before the order was confirmed.

On a very much smaller scale, the Wiener Werkstätte also commissioned the production of stencil prints,[15] mainly in the later years. This process, which is similar to modern screen-printing, was also carried out manually, but the production method was markedly less complex than block-printing. The stencils have a much shorter life-span than blocks and unfortunately none of these is known to have survived.

The production files, the two stock registers and, of course, invoices and correspondence provide information today on the fabric printers working for the Wiener Werkstätte, firms which in every respect produced work of a high level of craftsmanship: in Austria firms such as Gustav Ziegler,[16] Teltscher, the Neunkirchen printing works, Ströbel & Co.,[17] M. B. Neumann's Söhne[18] or the firm of Franz Bujatti;[19] in Switzerland work was commissioned from the Färberei & Appretur-Gesellschaft[20] in Basle and from the Alpenländische Druckfabrik; however, firms in Germany[21] and France[22] were also employed. The raw materials used by the Wiener Werkstätte were likewise drawn from various sources. The complicated and elaborate production method of block-printing did not permit the printing of extensive lengths of fabric.[23] An exact account of sales was kept in the so-called large card index (figs. 248, 249, 250, 252). The quantity

251 Felice Rix. MOOSBLUMEN (1924). Colour-schemes, gouache on paper

250 Maria Likarz. IRLAND (1910/13). Fabric samples in various colour-schemes. Large card index

252 Josef Hoffmann. CSIKOS (1930). Fabric samples in various colour-schemes. Large card index

142

in metres and date of sale, or the details of retail trading were noted, and such records often provide the only firm dating for a pattern. From this same evidence it is also possible to see that certain patterns were sold over a very long period – for example Josef Hoffmann's 'Kiebitz' (fig. 141) was available from 1910/12 until 1928 – and that other less successful patterns, such as 'Csikos' in 1930 (fig. 252), also by Hoffmann, lasted for only one season.

253 Looms in the Wiener Werkstätte weaving department. Photograph

purchased eight designs by Peche for 400 Schillings, a transaction organized through Frau Primavesi, who must have had responsibility for such matters. See fig. 243.

6. Minutes of board meeting of 15 April 1915, p. 7.

7. Examples of such names are: Formenstecherei Franz Süss, Meidlinger Hauptstraße 67, Vienna XII; Leopold Weiß (or Weihs); Kunz (Guntramsdorf); Wolff Müllers Erben (Frankenberg); Genossenschaft (or Produktionsgenossenschaft) der Formenstecher Wiens.

8. These designations appear in the large and small card indexes, respectively.

9. For example, at the printing works of the Färberei & Appretur Gesellschaft, Clavel & Lindenmeyer, in Basle, or of Gillet & Fils in Lyons.

10. Cf. note 5 above; passage quoted from p. 18 of this report.

11. Cf. Schweiger 1984, pp. 98f., citing *Moderne Welt* 12 (1920/21), pp. 26f.

12. Thus in 1913 blocks held in store by the firm of Ziegler – the Wiener Werkstätte's principal collaborator during these years and later – were used as collateral in connection with payments due to the printing company. See first general meeting, 2 May 1914 (report and elections), p. 3. In the balance sheet for 1914 (minutes of 15 April 1915 – see note 6 above) these blocks ('Modelle bei Ziegler') are likewise entered as assets.

13. Cf. above, p. 20, note 9.

14. Langenthal 1986 (exhib. cat.), p. 167, note 171.

15. The firms concerned included Vetter of Dornbirn and Schenk of Vienna.

16. Cf. note 12 above.

17. This company was based in Hütteldorf, near Penzing.

18. At no. 14 Börsegasse, Vienna I.

19. At no. 8 Zieglergasse, Vienna VII.

20. Cf. note 9 above.

21. Pausa, Mechanische Weberei, Stuttgart.

22. G. A. Bossert & Cie, Lyons.

23. Orders were placed for lengths varying from about 25 m to over 70 m. Cf. the listings of fabrics in the 'Textilwarenbuch I' (covering the period 1 January 1920 to 21 December 1923) and 'Textilwarenbuch III' (February 1924 to 18 April 1932). Retail sales of individual patterns are noted in the volume entitled 'Textil detail' (with effect from January 1920), though no information is given concerning the customers.

1. See *Der Flächeninhalt der Arbeitsräume und Magazine der Wr. Werkstätte*, VII, n.d.

2. Völker 1984, p. 257.

3. Schweiger 1984, p. 97. Here it is suggested that this workshop was probably established in 1913, its address being the Wiener Werkstätte's rented premises at 4 Döblingergasse. In the archival documents a *Künstler-Werkstätte* is mentioned for the first time in the report on business activity in 1916 ('Geschäftsbericht über das Geschäftsjahr 1916', p. 1), and a floor-plan of the premises in the Neustiftsgasse from 28 September 1917 indicates one large room with this description. These documentary references cannot, however, be taken as conclusive proof that the workshop was first set up in 1916, and it is also possible that its location was changed in 1917.

4. Cf. Schweiger 1984, p. 99. Among the surviving drawings from the Wiener Werkstätte archive there are a few rather roughly sketched items on sheets of tracing paper, some of which are inscribed 'Original Rapportpause' ('original tracing of pattern'), so indicating that they were used in the trial stages of relating a pattern to the fabric to be printed.

5. Report *(Revisions-Bericht)* concerning the conversion of the artists' association into a limited company, 18 July 1927, p. 19. An invoice dated 16 December 1926 (K.I. 13.743/13) provides evidence that the Österreichisches Museum für Kunst und Industrie ordered and

255 Ladies' shoes covered in POSEIDON (1912/17) by Josef Hoffmann

Opposite
254 Josef Hoffmann. CYPERN (1910/15. Fabric sample. The pinafore dress (inset) features CYPERN and the umbrella is covered in AMANDA (1910/17) by Fritzi Löw. Photo by d'Ora, 1917

256 Corsages featuring KARDINAL (1911/13) and REGENBOGEN (1919) by Dagobert Peche

As numerous examples make clear, Wiener Werkstätte fabrics appear in the source literature mostly in the form of finished products, and as a result we can claim to have a fairly good knowledge of their versatile applications. Furthermore, the Wiener Werkstätte archive includes not only photograph albums (e.g. figs. 167–169, 180–183) but other extant photographs showing various items either made from fabrics or decorated with them (e.g. figs. 196, 197). Fashion drawings (e.g. figs. 55, 56) provide further information. Since any customer could buy lengths of fabric by the metre, architects or dressmakers not associated with the Wiener Werkstätte also made use of them. Among the former, Viennese architects were of course the principal clients, including Wilhelm Margold, Otto Prutscher and Karl Bräuer;[1] there is in addition evidence illustrating their use by non-Viennese artists.[2]

When Wiener Werkstätte fabrics were used in the context of fashion, we are nowadays confronted with the problem of distinguishing a garment which can be considered a Wiener Werkstätte product, i.e. whether it really was designed and made up in the fashion department, from one in which only the fabric employed was a Wiener Werkstätte original. A genuine Wiener Werkstätte model can still be identified today through the fabric name-tag sewn to it. Because of the 'mobility' of these forms of identification, corroboration by reference to surviving drawings or photographs may provide incontrovertible proof of genuineness. In reality, many museums, including the Österreichisches Museum für angewandte Kunst, own more fashion items made of Wiener Werkstätte fabrics than they do examples known to have been created by the fashion department.

Interested members of the Viennese *haute bourgeoisie* – whose ranks are known to have been the source of most of the Wiener Werkstätte's regular clients – such as Sonja Knips, Friederike Beer-Monti and Mäda Primavesi, evidently surrounded themselves with Wiener Werkstätte objects suitable for all aspects of everyday life. Besides their houses or apartments, usually designed by Hoffmann, in which Wiener Werkstätte textiles were utilized for carpets, curtains or upholstery, the organization's wealthy clients also possessed items produced by various other departments. A revealing example can be seen in the National Gallery of Victoria in Melbourne; in addition to the Gallia family's furnishings designed by Hoffmann in 1913, other objects on view range from porcelain figures to silver vessels to a sample book from the textile department.[3] Moriz Gallia was well-known as a Wiener Werkstätte shareholder and leading patron.

A photograph of Sonja Knips shows her wearing an early dress from the fashion department featuring Wimmer-Wisgrill's 'Ameise' (fig. 257), this dress can be seen in a photograph in the Wiener Werkstätte fashion album.[4] Friederike Beer-Monti owned most of the articles of clothing which can be identified today as genuine Wiener Werkstätte products, either original models, or at least garments made from its materials. Their intriguing elegance is conveyed by two photographs showing her wearing Wiener Werkstätte houserobes (figs. 258, 262);[5] two others show her in a dress or blouse using Czeschka's 'Bavaria'[6] and in an afternoon dress for which Hoffmann's 'Ragusa' was used (fig. 260).[7] In the portrait of her painted by Gustav Klimt (fig. 92) she is depicted wearing a

257 Sonja Knips wearing a dress, c. 1911, featuring AMEISE (1910/11) by Eduard J. Wimmer-Wisgrill

258 Friederike Beer-Monti wearing a houserobe, c. 1913, featuring AMEISE (1910/11) by Eduard J. Wimmer-Wisgrill

Wiener Werkstätte creation featuring Peche's 'Marina';[8] this dress still exists. Over it she wears a coat inside-out to give a full view of the colourful lining; this is also reputedly a Wiener Werkstätte garment.[9] Finally, the dress she wears in the portrait painted by Egon Schiele is also supposed to have come from the same source.[10] Mäda Primavesi, wife of the Wiener Werkstätte's second business manager and for many years a dominant force in the association of artists, certainly possessed a fair number of creations produced by the fashion department, although, as far as we know, there is no contemporary record of them in photographs or paintings. Her dress depicted in the portrait of her painted by 1913/14 could well have been an original from the Wiener Werkstätte fashion department, but unfortunately it is not possible to identify it.[11] And as a last example there is the robe featuring Martha Alber's fabric design 'Blätter' which envelops Johanna Staude right up to the neck in the unfinished portrait by Klimt of 1917/18 (fig. 263).[12] One can imagine that many an old Viennese family album includes ladies in dresses purchased from the Wiener Werkstätte or made of Wiener Werkstätte materials.[13]

The portraits and photographs mentioned here derive mainly from the years after 1913, a time when Wiener Werkstätte fabrics were being increasingly put to use in the fashion department. In the years after 1910 they were comparatively rarely made up into dresses, blouses and cloaks, and were more often used for accessories or as linings to enliven costumes, jackets or coats in plain colours.[14] It was only after the mid-1920s that their own materials also played a major role in the activities of the fashion department. This is made evident, for instance, by the fact that each model was named after the fabric employed (figs. 207, 269, 303, 342).[15] In its latter years the fashion department eventually commissioned the production of hand-woven woollen fabrics; in the early 1920s Wiener Werkstätte artists had already been designing knitting patterns, which had been realized and presented

260 Friederike Beer-Monti wearing a dress, c. 1913, featuring RAGUSA (1910/12) by Josef Hoffmann

259 Josef Hoffmann. RAGUSA (1910/12). Fabric sample

with great success.[16] These were experiments in which the textile department apparently took only little interest; at all events, the surviving documents refer solely to the fashion department. Hand-woven examples have not been preserved in the Wiener Werkstätte archive; they are documented only as finished products in photographs and in the sole account book kept by the fashion department.[17] Coats made of hand-woven or knitted materials are to be found in the fashion collection of the Hochschule für angewandte Kunst, Vienna, and in private possession.[18]

In the beginning Wiener Werkstätte fabrics were employed far more frequently in the furnishing of houses or apartments than in the fashion department. Immediately after the founding of the textile department, the artists of the Wiener Werkstätte – especially, of course, Joseph Hoffmann – began to make exclusive use of the organization's own materials for interior decoration, in accordance with

261, 262 Ugo Zovetti. STICHBLATT (1910/11). Fabric sample (opposite) and Friederike Beer-Monti wearing a houserobe, c. 1913, featuring this pattern

263 Gustav Klimt, Portrait of Johanna Staude, 1917/18, oil on canvas (Österreichische Galerie, Vienna); the sitter is shown wearing a dress featuring BLÄTTER (1910/11) by Martha Alber

264 Martha Alber. BLÄTTER (1910/11). Jewish New Year greetings card; see also figs. 279-81

the Wiener Werkstätte concept of designing complete ensembles. The most important examples of the early years have already been illustrated (see pp. 33 ff.). The Palais Stoclet must be cited as an exception, for although it was finished by 1911, no Wiener Werkstätte materials were used in the furnishings. This seemingly odd situation is explained by the fact that the building and its furnishings planned years before the Wiener Werkstätte considered undertaking fabric production in its own name. However, it is also possible that the fabrics available were not to the client's taste.

As the war progressed, there was apparently a change of emphasis in production in favour of printed silks.[19] That meant a concentration on fashions, accessories, *Galanteriewaren* (fancy goods), as well as lampshades and retail sales, as is confirmed by the establishment of showrooms for fabrics from 1916 onwards. Although the separation of Hoffmann's architectural practice from the Wiener Werkstätte and the diminishing number of his commissions he received after the war contributed to a reduction in the use of Wiener Werkstätte fabrics in interior decorating, there were also stylistic reasons to be considered: the growing preference for 'discreet' materials and colours was at least as influential a factor.

Nevertheless, two marginal areas of interior design continued to be dominated by silk prints up till the disbandment of the Wiener Werkstätte: lampshades (e.g. figs. 267, 275) and cushion-covers. Both were available in the textile department's showroom. Whilst Wiener Werkstätte fabrics had been used for lampshades since the earliest days of their production, cushions notable for their inventive, even fantastical, forms were confined mainly to the later years. Earlier cushions, in contrast, had simple forms and relied on the fabric patterns to provide a striking effect (fig. 274). The cushions of the 1920s were made in the most bizarre shapes, sometimes using only one fabric, sometimes featuring a combination of very diverse patterns (fig. 273). Unfortunately, no examples of these cushions has survived, hence the not very vivid impression given by contemporary black-and-white photographs must suffice to suggest their appearance; their effect in the original colours can be gauged only from surviving samples of fabrics. In the Wiener Werkstätte archive there are several paper patterns still extant, and these help us to

265, 266 *Maria Jungwirth.*
GABRIEL (1914/17). Fabric
sample and (right) dress, c. 1922

267, 268 *Felice Rix. Lampshade*
covered in GESPINST (1924) and
(below) fabric sample

270 Wiener Werkstätte business postcard incorporating ST. ANDRA (1911/14) by Leopold Blonder

Left
269, 271 Max Snischek. Design for house jacket using PAPAGENA (1928) by Mathilde Flögl, and (below) fabric sample

Below
272 Felice Rix. TOKIO (1924). Corsage

gain an impression of the cushions' forms and dimensions.

It was especially in the period immediately after 1910, rarely later, that Wiener Werkstätte fabrics appear to have been used in making umbrellas (figs. 61, 254) and fancy goods (e.g. fig. 71).[20] Various so-called account or model books provide information about these applications. They list prices and the wage costs of the outworkers who made the objects, and usually give the exact date of production as well. From this information it can be deduced that the items recorded were produced in small series of up to a few dozen and seldom repeated in more than one year. St Nicholas figures and their bogie-like counterparts (Krampusse) were even produced singly. Small sketches and the few surviving objects in this general category (figs. 276–278) give us an idea of how far the Wiener Werkstätte seems to have fallen in the estimation of many critics, being accorded the status of a workshop for the production of trivial bric-à-brac.

Umbrellas and boxes, books, albums or Easter eggs covered with Wiener Werkstätte fabrics can be found today in public and private collections (figs. 60, 63); other applications include corsages (figs. 256, 272), hats, bonnets, as well as fashion accessories such as lined vanity bags, fans (fig. 93), shoes (fig. 255) or handbags. Finally, a series of fabric-covered animal figures was designed, mostly by Peche and not necessarily as toys, in which Wiener Werkstätte silks were used (figs. 276–278).[21] Shawls and stoles, tablecloths and napkins were also

made from Wiener Werkstätte fabrics. The original products all bore the trade mark, the monogram 'WW' or the full name; items made of Wiener Werkstätte fabrics but produced by other firms are mostly unmarked.

An unusual, indeed unique, secondary use of early fabric patterns is found in a series of postcards. These were not published by the Wiener Werkstätte itself, but – as is indicated on the reverse of one of the postcards – by the Lehrlingsheim Zukunft in Vienna; they had them printed by the largest postcard publishers in the monarchy, Brüder Kohn, who probably sold the cards to the general public in large numbers. In each case the fabric pattern forms the background for an oval, round or rectangular inset in which appears a greeting in Hebrew and German for the Jewish New Year (figs. 264, 279–281). There are seventeen such cards in the collection of the Österreichisches Museum für angewandte Kunst, though they do not derive from

Above
273 Cushions covered in ROSENHAIN (1927) by Felice Rix, BOZEN (1928) by Maria Likarz and MANISSA (1925/26) by Max Snischek

274 Cushion covered in SCHATTEN (1916) by Dagobert Peche

153

275 Lampshades covered in KRONE (1919) by Dagobert Peche and
KIRSCHGARTEN (1922) by Felice Rix

276 Toy elephant covered in PARASIT (1919) by Dagobert Peche.
Photograph album 106

the Wiener Werkstätte archive.[22] The familiar patterns – among them 'Blätter' (fig. 264), 'Wienerwald' (fig. 281), 'Kropftaube' (fig. 280) and 'Anninger' (fig. 279) – are designs by Alber, Jonasch,
Czeschka, Häusler and other artists of the early period. Could it be that the Wiener Werkstätte had
placed the patterns at the institution's disposal as
a charitable gesture? The reverse side, also typographically designed, cites the name of the fabric
designer, notes that it is a fabric reproduction and

also names the Wiener Werkstätte. The postcards
have very little similarity to the series published by
the Wiener Werkstätte itself (figs. 5, 51, 72).[23] Some
examples have small pictures with altogether trivial motifs instead of printed words. The best one
can say about these is that they are indicators of the
patterns' general popularity.

To sum up the practical uses of Wiener Werkstätte
fabrics, it still remains to be noted that all departments within the organization made almost exclu-

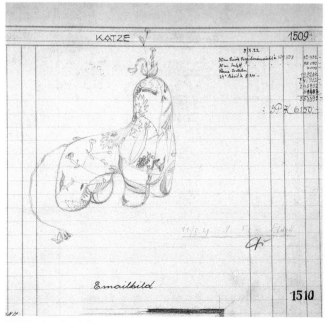

277 Design sketch for toy cat, 1922, covered in HYMEN (1919) by
Dagobert Peche. book 'Diverses' 74

278 Design for toy cat, 1922, covered in HYMEN (1919) by
Dagobert Peche. Photograph album 106

279–281 Jewish New Year greetings cards featuring Wiener Werkstätte patterns
279 Philipp Häusler. ANNINGER (1910/11)
280 Carl Otto Czeschka. KROPFTAUBE (1910/11)
281 Wilhelm Jonasch. WIENERWALD (1910/11).

sive use of the materials produced on its behalf and that, initially, their production was subject to the strictest supervision. The association often exploited their individuality and characteristic patterns as a kind of trade mark. This becomes very obvious

from references to the fabrics appearing in fashion-show reports. One such report in 1928 notes: 'Every dress is recognizable from miles away as Wiener Werkstätte from its material, along with praise and criticism.'[24] The Wiener Werkstätte's own advertising and business graphics also made use of fabric patterns as background or eye-catching features (fig. 270), and its showrooms and branches were furnished with its own fabrics, not least among its intentions being the desire to give its products greater exposure and to emphasize their exclusive character (figs. 167–169). This was a conscious gesture in keeping with the idea of 'corporate identity', though admittedly not as firmly based on theory as the concept is today. Almost contemporaneous with the early Wiener Werkstätte was Peter Behrens' more wide-ranging development of a company image on behalf of AEG in Berlin.[25]

[1] *DKD* XXXIII (1913/14), p. 456; *DI* XIV (1913), pls. 152ff.
[2] *ÖBWK* IV (1927/28), p. 65 (Alexander Popp); *DKD* XLVII (1920/21), p. 317 (Karl Bertsch, Deutsche Werkstätten); *ID* XXXII (1921), p. 202 (August Breuhaus, Cologne).
[3] Melbourne 1984 (exhib. cat.).
[4] Völker 1984, p. 13, fig. 6; Nebehay 1979, fig. 149.
[5] Fischer 1987, pp. 84f., figs. 92, 94.
[6] New York 1986 (exhib. cat.), p. 33, fig. 33.
[7] Fischer 1987, p. 85, fig. 95.
[8] Cf. p. 64, note 13. Another blouse owned by Friederike Beer-Monti and made from a Wiener Werkstätte fabric is illustrated in Fischer 1987, p. 47, fig. 39.
[9] Nebehay 1976, p. 268.
[10] Fischer 1987, p. 72, fig. 74.
[11] New York 1986 (exhib. cat.), p. 45, fig. 6.
[12] Völker 1984, fig. XXXII.
[13] The Österreichisches Museum für angewandte Kunst recently received a bequest from a Viennese lady who in the 1920s had purchased a length of Felice Rix's 'Kiuschiu' direct from the Wiener Werkstätte. From it she made a wide-skirted dress which she took with her when she was forced to emigrate after 1938; the dress was subsequently altered to a slimmer style, and when the owner finally returned to Vienna after the Second World War she used the remaining fabric to make a small bolero to be worn over a black dress. This she left to the museum, together with photographs showing her wearing the garments described at each stage of the fabric's history.
[14] Völker 1984, p. 79, fig. 101.
[15] Völker 1984, pp. 215ff.
[16] Op. cit., p. 190, figs. 268, 269.
[17] Op. cit., p. 213 and note 185 (inv. no. WWMO 182), pp. 242f., fig. 336.
[18] Tokyo 1989 (exhib. cat.), pp. 354 f., no. 478; Wien 1967 (exhib. cat.), p. 80, nos. 384, 387 (fig. 52).
[19] Minutes of committee meeting held on 19 June 1916.
[20] Cf. Wiener Werkstätte pattern book 54.
[21] Eisler 1925, p. 76.
[22] Wiener Werkstätte postcards 881/1, 916/1–4, 917/1–3, 918/1–2, 919/1–3, 920/1–4.
[23] Hansen 1982.
[24] *Die Freiheit*, Vienna, 1 June 1928 (*Annalen* 85, 1613).
[25] Buddensieg / Rogge 1979.

282 Design for an advertisement announcing Wiener Werkstätte fabrics; pencil and ink on paper

Opposite
283 Mathilde Flögl. Design for a poster, c. 1925; pencil and gouache on paper

The fact that the Wiener Werkstätte seemingly had no plans to set up its own fabric showroom in the early years of its textile department's existence is understandable, since the fabrics were used mainly for its own interior design schemes and in the field of Wiener Werkstätte fashions. The raw materials and finished products were stored in the workshop building in the Neustiftgasse (fig. 242), where there was an office for the textile department as well as a fabric storeroom.[1] We can surmise that after the founding of the new department a gradual start was made in building up retail sales, though documentary evidence for this is lacking. Such transactions took place in the small showroom established by the Wiener Werkstätte in the Graben; however, by the spring of 1914 this arrangement was no longer considered satisfactory by the business manager, Adelbert Kurz: 'Our present office facilities and workshops in the Neustiftgasse together with those in the Doeblergasse are as unsuitable as they could possibly be, and we must, if we wish to work successfully in a properly organized way, consider renting other premises, or, better still, erect a building of our own. Just

as unsatisfactory is the present showroom in the Graben; it is impossible to display our products effectively here, especially those of the fashion department.'[2] The situation for the textile department improved two years later. On 19 June 1915 a business report noted, with regard to the textile department, that '... for Austria more favourable conditions will be created for retail sales through the establishment of our own premises in the Maysedergasse [a side-street off Kärntnerstraße]'.[3]

The establishment of individual showrooms for different products reflects the importance which the Wiener Werkstätte attached to the relevant departments and, more generally, gaining wider public acceptance. As far as the organization's 'market strategy' was concerned, it was now possible to cater for those customers who wished to purchase fabrics, ribbons or lace by the metre. Larger orders were hardly to be expected on account of the 'general economic depression'[4] and the outbreak of war in September 1914. Since the appeal of Wiener Werkstätte luxury products was restricted to a public with a certain spending power and a receptiveness to the Wiener Werkstätte philosophy,

157

Left
284 Reni Schaschl. Design for an advertisement announcing the Wiener Werkstätte showroom at 32 Kärntnerstraße, c. 1917; pencil and ink on paper

Right
285 Reception room and stairway leading to the first floor of the textile department at 32 Kärntnerstraße, 1918. Upholstery and screen featuring VOGELWEIDE (1910/17) by Fritzi Löw, Photo by Atelier Reiffenstein in photograph album 137

Left
286 Vally Wieselthier. Design for an advertisement announcing the showroom at 4 Maysedergasse, 1916; pencil and ink on paper

Right
287 The staircase leading to the textile sales department, 1918. Photo by Atelier Reiffenstein in photograph album 137

the only retail locations considered suitable were in the centre of the city, e.g. in the Graben, Kärntnerstraße and their immediate surroundings.

The first fabric showroom at 4 Maysedergasse opened for business on 15 August 1916.[5] There are no photographs of the premises, only plans for an apartment unit at mezzanine level, identified as office space (*Büroräume*) in a handwritten annotation. Newspaper advertisements, posters (figs. 282, 286, 288) and letter headings confirm that business was being conducted at this address – a trial operation, so to speak, for the better documented second showroom of the textile department. At the end of June 1918, the third Wiener Werkstätte showroom in Vienna, namely, the new premises of the textile department situated at the junction of Kärntnerstraße and Führichgasse, was ready for opening.[6] The design concept was Hoffmann's; assisting him in the furnishing and interior decoration were Felice Rix, who created the ornamental motifs on the walls and furniture, and Hilda Jesser, who executed two mural paintings on the Kärntnerstraße stairwell (fig. 287). Both the reception room and the narrow staircase are recorded in photographs (figs. 285, 290) which show two chairs and a screen upholstered with 'Vogelweide' by Fritzi Löw and a free arrangement of fabrics displayed in the narrow shop window – featuring 'Persien' (Anny Wirth, fig. 291) and 'Indigo' (Maria Vera Brunner, fig. 292) – as well as a glass showcase containing small textile items. The actual salerooms were situated on the first floor (figs. 293, 294).

Besides rooms for the use of customers on the upper floor, the blueprint plan (fig. 289) also shows areas reserved for the staff. Contemporary photographs and other illustrations also show the salerooms, which were furnished with built-in cupboards and large tables.[7] They are described as the *Spitzenraum* (lace room), *Stoffraum* (fabric room) and a *Verkaufsraum für Beleuchtungskörper* (saleroom for light fixtures; fig. 295). According to the floor-plan, the cash-desk was situated on the upper staircase landing. Other facilities indicated in the plan refer to *Manipulation, Sanitärräume* (toilets and washroom) and a *Kleiderablage* (cloakroom), all with access from a horseshoe-shaped corridor. A spacious office for the director and a further large room, divided into anteroom, telephone area and *Wasch- und Kleiderraum* (washroom and cloakroom) would not have been accessible to visitors.

288 Dagobert Peche. Poster for the textile department, 1917

As to who used this director's office, or, more concretely, who the director actually was, emerges neither from this nor from any other document. In her capacity as artistic director of the textile department and on account of the quality and quantity of her fabric designs, Maria Likarz seems the most likely candidate. The suggestion that it could have been Max Snischek, simultaneously director of the fashion and textile departments, is also tenable on

289 The Wiener Werkstätte showroom, Kärntnerstraße and Führichgasse. Blueprint of ground plan

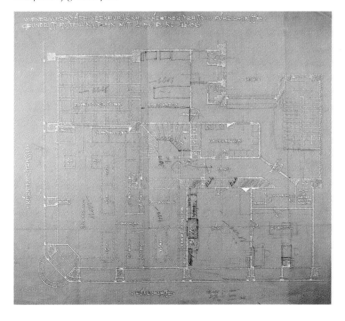

291 Anny Wirth. PERSIEN (1910/11). Colour proof on paper

292 Maria Vera Brunner. INDIGO (1910/17). Fabric sample

Opposite
290 Entrance to the reception area of the textile showroom at 32 Kärntnerstraße, 1918; lengths of Maria Vera Brunner's INDIGO (1910/17) and Anny Wirth's PERSIEN (1910/11) are on display. Photo by Atelier Reiffenstein from photograph album 137

293 Fabric saleroom of the textile department,1918. Photo by Atelier Reiffenstein in photograph album 137

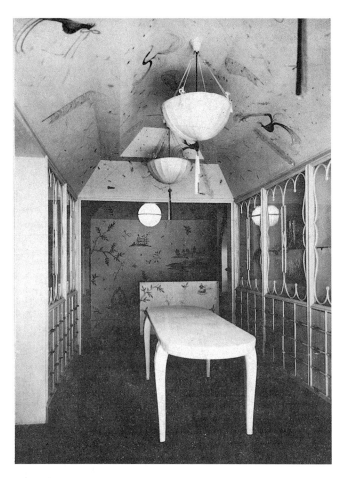

294 Ribbon and lace room of the textile department, looking towards the stairs, 1918. Photo by Atelier Reiffenstein in photograph album 137

295 Lighting appliances saleroom in the textile department, 1919. Photo by Atelier Reiffenstein in photograph album 137

similar grounds, but only from 1922, or even 1924, the year of his first post-war fabric designs.[8]

Quite intentionally, Hoffmann dispensed with colours and any wallpaper with a repeating pattern in his design concept for the brightly lit salerooms (fig. 293). The materials were kept in closed cupboards, so the effect of showing the fabrics one at a time must then have been all the more impressive. The *Spitzenraum* (fig. 294), in contrast, was furnished with glass showcases, in which lace, ribbons or other merchandise such as flowers or shawls were on display. The liveliest impression was made by the saleroom for light fixtures (fig. 295), with its open display of colourful lampshades and the diversity of shapes. The whole interior furnishing scheme imparted a feeling of tasteful reticence and at the same time, with its buoyant and playful wall paintings and the curved details on the enamelled furniture, bore the stamp of Hoffmann's well-known love of decorative detail. In the fabric saleroom, where comfortable chairs – not upholstered with Wiener Werkstätte fabrics – were placed in front of the tables, each customer received punctiliously individual attention. First of all, the visitor had to gain access to these upper rooms via the narrow staircase (fig. 287) and overcome any 'threshold *angst*' when confronted by such select surroundings. In keeping with the spirit of the Wiener Werkstätte and its lofty aims, the sales methods employed had no hint of vulgarity, but were discreet and low-key. The tasteful elegance of the surroundings was supposed to match the standard of the products, useful articles being given the aura of works of art through the skill of the presentation.

The purchasers of Wiener Werkstätte fabrics will have differed little from the customers of the other departments. Well-to-do artists and intellectuals, the educated upper middle classes or no doubt simply 'people with money' shopped here, members of the circle of those who were familiar with and supported the aims of the Wiener Werkstätte. Some clients were identical with the association's members, notably Waerndorfer, Gustav Klimt, the Primavesis, Moriz Gallia and Kuno Grohmann.

After the fashion showroom at 41 Kärntnerstraße and the small shop on the Graben had to close in 1931 on account of the Wiener Werkstätte's catastrophic financial situation, the branch dealing in textiles and light fixtures at 32 Kärntnerstraße became the sole retail outlet in Vienna for the entire range of Wiener Werkstätte products.[9] No visual record of the changes arising from this move is known to have survived.

How sales of Wiener Werkstätte fabrics were organized before the establishment of its own retail premises can only be surmised today. Given the lack of space in the cramped premises on the Graben, were customers simply shown the fabric sample books? Supporting this supposition is the fact that many sample books dating from the early years of the textile department (figs. 296, 297) still exist. Evidently some of them were in the possession of private individuals, as we know from Moriz Gallia.[10] Not only could each customer obtain an overall view of the available fabrics in this way, but representatives were also supplied with sample books in order to be able to give wholesalers, other branches or any commissioning body a comprehensive idea of the fabric production.

It is standard practice to display in sample books a specific collection, or the entire range of available merchandise. The Wiener Werkstätte apparently adopted this practice, for there exist today various sample books, each containing a different number of fabric samples. In the Österreichisches Museum für angewandte Kunst there are three types of sample books containing between 37 and 180 items. Arranged according to fabric type, they displayed the available range of printed linens and silks. Two linen sample books illustrate how the current collection and the general range of merchandise might have been presented to clients (figs. 17, 49, 120, 129, 141, 297); they correspond to what was probably the most frequently used Wiener Werkstätte sample book, examples of which are found in other collections. The fabric samples, each measuring about 15 x 20 cm (6 x 8 in.), are bound together along one of the shorter sides, and the outer cover bears the Wiener Werkstätte monogram. On the reverse of each sample is attached a label (figs. 17, 49, 297, 302), with details specifying the pattern, the designer and the price. The books are marked I and II respectively and were apparently intended to complement each other.[11] Sample book I includes 37 patterns from the new collection in their various colour-schemes; in its counterpart, book II, the remaining selection of 65 further patterns was displayed, but without the range of available colour-schemes. As possible proof that

296 Josef Hoffmann. SANTA SOPHIA (1910/12) and HIRSCHENZUNGE (1910/12). Silk sample book, c. 1912

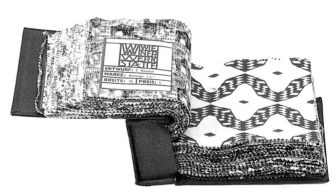

297 Kolo Moser. BAUMMARDER (1910/11). Linen sample book I, before 1914

298 Gertrud Höchsmann. BASRA (1925). Sample card, c. 1928

299 Title page of the magazine 'Die Damenwelt'. Design by Otto Lendecke, 1917, showing skirt featuring GLETSCHERBLUME (1911/13) by Dagobert Peche

the reverse is not the case, a comparison can be made with the contemporary Wiener Werkstätte wallpaper collection, a group of about thirty patterns, which can be more accurately identified as a range of entirely new designs.[12] Moreover, it is probable that the sample book with the choice of colour-schemes presented the full range of new patterns rather than those already in stock. The style of the linen patterns suggests an early date of production, and the post-1914 market strategy quoted above, namely, that of drastically reducing linen prints in favour of silks, supports the likelihood that their date of origin was before 1914.

Another sample book in the Österreichisches Museum für angewandte Kunst is typographically more elaborate and larger (fig. 296).[13] The printed silks, of different sizes, and with some patterns presented in various colour combinations, are pasted onto thin sheets of cardboard on which the name 'WIENER WERKSTÄTTE' is printed in large type at the top and bottom. Small panels adjacent to the pattern samples include printed details of the name, colour, material, designer and price. The loose-leaf binding arrangement made it possible for individual leaves to be replaced easily. This book appears to be the only one of its kind to have survived; it was acquired by the museum from the descendants of Franz von Zülow in 1968. Blank pages, missing patterns – surely never even included – make it likely, when taken in conjunction with its provenance, that the book served an internal purpose within the Wiener Werkstätte itself. The 180 patterns it contains are again of fabric designs originally created before the First World War. Lavishly designed, and especially oriented to project

Above right
300 Wiener Werkstätte advertising leaflet issued during the First World War, incorporating fabric sample of Lotte Frömel-Fochler's MIGNON (1910/17)

301 Dagobert Peche. GLETSCHERBLUME (1911/13). Fabric sample

the 'image' of the Wiener Werkstätte, this kind of book may well have served as a demonstration sampler for representatives to show their opposite numbers in negotiations.

Finally, the Vienna museum possesses a third type of sample 'book' (fig. 298), in reality a collection of pattern cards, which entered the collection as part of the Wiener Werkstätte archive.[14] The collection of loose, thin cards, each measuring about 25 x 30 cm (10 x 12 in.) and folded once, is held between two covers lined with blue Wiener Werkstätte pasting paper, tied with Wiener Werkstätte silk ribbons. In this case the individual cards are also graphic designs in themselves: identified by the Wiener Werkstätte monogram, each is annotated with the pattern name and the colour number. The designer's name and the pattern number were added in pencil; the pattern name was also hand-written, and as such is part of the original presentation. A relatively large sample of printed silk is pasted on to the front; small fabric specimens are attached on the inside, illustrating the available colour-schemes, but no indication of price is given. This collection – 177 patterns – was probably a reflection of the production current at the time. The stylistic features and a comparison with firmly dated patterns in the so-called large card index suggest a dating of *c.* 1928. Since the pattern card collection was still part of the Wiener Werkstätte archive, it could have belonged to the late experimental stage, perhaps representing an attempt to give the sample books of the early period a new form.

The fabric pattern collection from the Wiener Werkstätte archive kept today in the Österreichisches Museum für angewandte Kunst was probably intended above all to be a documentation of its own production. Apart from unmarked pieces, it contains fabric samples supplied with various Wiener Werkstätte tags – either pasted or pinned on – naming the patterns and often the designers (see, for example, fig. 102). They could likewise have been the ones shown to the customer as examples, or even fabric samples which the customer could take home.

Clearly the business policy of the Wiener Werkstätte also included publicity, evidence of which is found in, for instance, the collection of press cuttings. The minutes of meetings also contain reports: thus, in 1915 it was noted that 'Despite the initial undertaking of a comprehensive and expensive publicity campaign for the textile department, which must be regarded mainly as a preparatory operation for peacetime, … the financial balance for this department is … a very good one and we can count on a continued, thriving development.'[15] In 1916: '… in the last six months [i.e. the second half of 1915] comprehensive advertising and extensive publicity campaigns, succeeded in achieving a remarkable reactivation of trade in our textile products.'[16] The entire range of advertising material for the Wiener Werkstätte was designed by its own artists. Posters, newspaper and magazine advertisements (figs. 282–284, 286, 287, 300), business cards and other advertising material such as was distributed to customers, give us an idea of the scope of this campaign.[17] Otto Lendecke (fig. 299) and Peche (fig. 288) created effective posters

and advertisements. The textile department was also represented, together with the other departments, in the lavish book published by the Wiener Werkstätte on the occasion of its 25th anniversary in 1928, and two years later illustrations and an article on the textile department appeared in an issue of *Wiener Mode* devoted to the Wiener Werkstätte.[18] An art magazine on the Wiener Werkstätte published in Japan in 1928 is the most notable documentary evidence of the extent of its international renown;[19] its cover was decorated with Peche's pattern 'Schwalbenschwanz' (fig. 153).

1 Minutes of the board meeting held on 15 April 1915. In the minutes of the committee meeting held on 19 June 1916, reference is made to 'Central warehouse depot: silk, linen, ribbons, brocade, woven upholstery fabrics, printed silk gauze, woven braid trimmings, crêpe de chine and cretonne, woollen crepe and muslin, various fabrics, tablecloths and table-napkin remnants.' Examples of this wide variety and of the enthusiasm shown for experimentation are preserved in both the stock registers and the large card index.
2 Minutes of general meeting held on 2 May 1914, report and elections. Cf. also minutes of first board meeting, 9 June 1914.
3 Minutes of committee meeting, 19 June 1916.
4 Minutes of general meeting (see note 2 above), p. 7.
5 Report on business activity for 1916, p. 2.
6 *Ostdeutsche Rundschau*, 27 July 1918 (*Annalen* 83, 241). This report states that 'The Wiener Werkstätte has put up new business premises in addition to the existing branches, namely the textile and lace department (Kärnterstraße 32), which was opened at the end of June.' Sekler 1982, cat. no. 208, p. 380.
7 *DKD* XLIII (1918/19), pp. 373 ff. (WW photo album 137).
8 The sources provide no other information and there is no further mention of the 'textile industry expert' (*Fachmann für die Textilindustrie*) engaged in June 1914; equally elusive is the Geo. Michaelis (see above, p. 95), who was supposed to establish an English-American department for the Wiener Werkstätte. See minutes of meeting, 9 June 1914.
9 Völker 1984, p. 259.
10 Cf. Melbourne 1984 (exhib. cat.), no. 72, p. 79.
11 T 11.379a and 379b.
12 Völker / Pichler 1989. If we compare the previously mentioned annual output of new patterns (cf. p. 64, note 6), i. e. a total of about 70, the discrepancy could be explained if there were two collections presented each year.
13 T 10.621, measuring approximately 35 x 20 cm (14 x 8 in.).
14 T 11.502, accessioned later.
15 Minutes of the board meeting held on 9 October 1915.
16 Minutes of committee meeting held on 19 June 1916, p. 7.
17 For example, a sheet with attached fabric pattern and bearing a strongly nationalistic text; this was apparently aimed at the German market, since the reverse carries a list of 54 agents from whom Wiener Werkstätte fabrics could be obtained in Germany, including the Hohenzollern Kunstgewerbehaus in Berlin and Karstadt in Brunswick, Hanover and Kiel.
18 'Die Wiener Werkstätte 1903–1928. Modernes Kunstgewerbe und sein Weg. Wien 1929'; Rolf Haybach, 'Stoffe und Kissen, Spitzen und Schals', in *Wiener Mode*, vol. 2 (1930), n.p.
19 Schweiger 1984, p. 124.

ENTWURF: W. Jonas

MARKE: Vorgarten I L/I

BREITE: 70 **PREIS:** 3.50

ENTWURF: D. Peche

MARKE: Gartenwinde I S/I

BREITE: 90 **PREIS** 10.25

WIENER WERKSTÄTTE

Marke: *Vase 2 S 6*

Meter:

Breite:

Preis:

WIENER WERKSTÄTTE

Dessin *Nihon*

Mtr. 0'50 *Col.* 8

Qualität Pongis 8 m/m

Nr 19608 b *Breite* 82

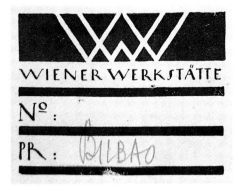

WIENER WERKSTÄTTE

N°:

PR: BILBAO

302 *Labels for Wiener Werkstätte fabrics*

304 Max Snischek. MANISSA (1925/26). Fabric sample

Opposite
303 *Max Snischek. Design sketch using his own pattern MANISSA (1925/26), pencil and gouache on paper*

305 *Max Snischek.*
Wiener Werkstätte fashion postcard, c. 1929

The role played by individual artists in the Wiener Werkstätte's development of fabric pattern design, especially in the early years, has already been described and analyzed above (see pp. 49ff.). To recapitulate: Carl Otto Czeschka's ideas on ornamentation were already influencing the decorative surface patterns produced by Wiener Werkstätte artists even before the textile department was founded, and their effect before *c.* 1914 should not be underestimated. In contrast, Kolo Moser produced only a few patterns, small in scale and predominantly geometric in form, most of which he had already invented around 1900 and which were evidently of minor significance for the Wiener Werkstätte. Eduard Josef Wimmer-Wisgrill, a pupil of Hoffmann much influenced by his mentor in creating fabric patterns, produced very successful designs such as 'Ameise' (figs. 55–59, 257, 258), which was used both in the fashion department and in interior design schemes and was even woven as a carpet (fig. 59). He designed fabric patterns only in the initial years, even though he was director of the fashion department until 1922. Besides the various well-known artist personalities already men-

tioned, numerous young pupils of Hoffmann were helping to establish the image of the textile department. There was no question of a uniform approach, for Hoffmann evidently encouraged individual expression in order to attain the greatest possible variety. Mitzi Friedmann, for instance, with 'Feldpost' (fig. 115) or 'Karst' (fig. 118), designed highly expressive patterns utilizing strong colours and unconventional forms. Lotte Frömel-Fochler's contribution is characteristic for its variety and range. She invented such diverse patterns as the unpretentiously pretty 'Krebs' (fig. 106) and the colourful abstract 'Sada Jacco' (fig. 20). The popularity and importance of the 'Expressionists' amongst the Wiener Werkstätte designers – Franz von Zülow, Ugo Zovetti and Ludwig H. Jungnickel – have already been described above.

Josef Hoffmann's fabric patterns formed a stylistic continuum conveyed through his personal presence from the founding years to the closure of the textile department. His creative potential, his ability to adopt ideas and his single-minded preoccupation with the invention of ornament and patterns inevitably led him not only to absorb new im-

306 *Josef Hoffmann. SCHWARZBLATT (1910/12). Fabric sample*

Opposite
308 *Josef Hoffmann. OZON (1923). Fabric sample*

307 *Eduard J. Wimmer-Wisgrill. SEEROSE (1910/12). Fabric sample*

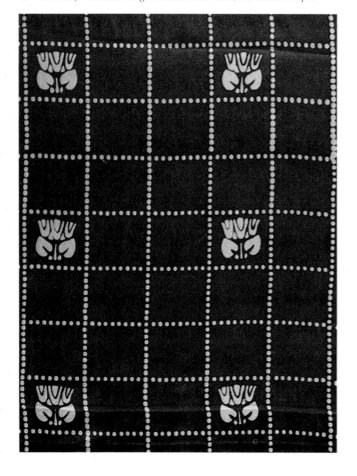

pulses, but to instigate them as well.[2] As an example, one can contrast his 'Schwarzblatt' (fig. 306) with Wimmer-Wisgrill's 'Seerose' (fig. 307). Both patterns have the same basic squares filled in with floral motifs – and it is hard to say who influenced whom. Hoffmann was able to take any innovative current trend as a model and adapt the stimuli to his own ideas: his adoption of motifs from Czeschka's *Nibelungen* illustrations (fig. 67) for his 'Montezuma' (figs. 22, 68, 245) has already been mentioned. Further examples of Hoffmann's fabrics which were influenced by Czeschka's repertoire are 'Apollo' (figs. 3–5, 71) and 'Kohleule' (fig. 309). Inspired by Dagobert Peche, Hoffmann changed his mode of expression once again, as in 'Hopfen' (figs. 143, 244), a design which transposes Peche's style of draughtsmanship into a repeating pattern made up of small elements. Furthermore, we encounter fabrics in Hoffmann's textile oeuvre where the same compositional elements were combined anew to make different patterns, for example 'Alpenfalter' (fig. 98) and 'Dorfschwalbe' (fig. 246), where he used the same curved motif in different combinations, or in 'Guido' (fig. 385) and 'Carus' (fig. 381), where he combined linear patterns within a square grid. He often revived his own earlier inventions, reworking them without being at all repetitive, as in 1923 with 'Ozon' (fig. 308), in which he used a pattern principle which originated before 1917, namely that of 'Cypern' (fig. 254).

Hoffmann's receptivity to creative ideas seems to have known no limits, otherwise he could never have combined such diverse influences in his own works, nor, for instance, could he have juxtaposed Neue Sachlichkeit and Art Déco as he did in Paris in 1925. Evidently a man quite without envy, Hoffmann also frequently chose to use fabrics designed by other Wiener Werkstätte artists because of their effectiveness in his own interior designs. Hoffmann's keen interest in innovations of form and new talent shaped the style and work of the Wiener Werkstätte; however, his clinging to out-of-date programmes and forms of production would finally lead to its demise.

For Hoffmann, fabric designing was admittedly always only a sideline – although a welcome one – which fitted into the overall framework of his many other activities. He developed a total of about 75 patterns for the textile department, and these

309 Josef Hoffmann.
KOHLEULE (1910/15).
Silk sample book, c. 1912

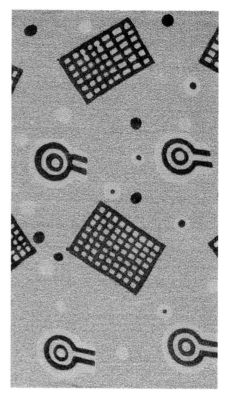

310 Josef Hoffmann.
CSIKOS (1930).
Fabric sample

provide a reflection of developments over twenty fairly eventful years. However, the quantitative and also most probably the qualitative emphasis belongs to the early years of the department, e.g. in patterns such as 'Santa Sophia' (figs. 70, 296), 'Miramar' (fig. 150), 'Hirschenzunge' (figs. 151, 296) or 'Adler' (figs. 98, 147), which, in their strict adherence to two colours and geometric patterning present ideas that are characteristic of Hoffmann's most productive phase. As a comparison of an early and a late design, 'Kohleule' (fig. 309) can be contrasted with 'Csikos' (fig. 310). The first, an assertive, expressive pattern dating from a period that was fascinated by ornament, has little chance of being subordinate to the object it was used for. On the other hand, 'Csikos', with its small motifs and simple geometric forms, blends into the background when put to practical use; it is a pattern which consciously exploits banal forms.

Like Hoffmann, Dagobert Peche was an extremely prolific designer in all categories of handicraft. He worked in fashion as well as in furniture design, lace and graphics. In the relatively short period of his association with the Wiener Werkstätte, Peche designed 113 fabric patterns. It is probably correct to assume that he started working for the textile department soon after he met Hoffmann in 1911.

Examples of his ideas can be found in the early sample books and in the dated stock register. At all events, some of the early wallpaper designs from the 1913 collection are derived from his fabric patterns, besides which there are examples of dresses utilizing fabrics with patterns based on designs datable to 1912.[3]

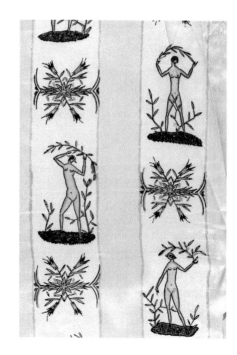

311 Dagobert Peche.
FREUDE (1911/19).
Fabric sample

Peche's designs for the textile department are distinctive for their stylistic homogeneity. His preference for naturalistic motifs or stylized versions of them is their most outstanding feature. Delicate plant forms ('Daphne', fig. 180), the amalgamation of animal and plant motifs ('Semiramis', fig. 312), figures ('Schatten', fig. 274; and 'Freude', fig. 311) or sprays of blossom ('Rom', figs. 175, 176), as well as oddly shaped architectural components as in 'Endigung' (fig. 347), are among Peche's favourite motifs. Many patterns have relatively large repeats, as for instance in 'Säule' (fig. 344) and 'Falte' (figs. 342, 343). Peche loved patterns in which their graphic origin is still apparent, such as 'Chytera' (fig. 345) and 'Vergissmeinnicht' (fig. 313). Forms owing their effectiveness to the flat surface or to painting – 'Marina' (figs. 22, 88–92, 169) or 'Doris' (fig. 316) – occur less often, but are nonetheless as pleasing. Occasionally, despite his capacity for invention, even Peche would repeat himself, as when he used the same tendril of stylized blossom, once in a zig-zag form and another time as a rhomboid frame, in 'Gartenwinde' and 'Venusgärtchen'. Abstract patterns are comparatively infrequent in Peche's repertoire, examples such as 'Rax' (figs. 10, 163), 'Spinne' (figs. 160, 162) or 'Ariel' (fig. 315) are especially effective. Also simple designs of small hand-drawn elements, such as 'Osten' (fig. 157) or 'Flut' (fig. 158), show Peche's interest in graphic effects. His artistic development expressed itself in an increasing freedom of draughtsmanship; furthermore, in his later years, he tended to use larger repeats. Early patterns by Peche consist of compact, individual motifs, often in series, as in 'Pierrot' (fig. 96) or 'Gletscherblume' (fig. 301). Lavishness of line is already becoming noticeable in simple plant compositions such as 'Daphne' (fig. 180) and finally in patterns such as 'Vergissmeinnicht' (fig. 313) or 'Säule' (fig. 344). Many of Peche's fabric designs can be called refined in the best sense, especially the *ombré* patterns, with their cunningly arranged colour-schemes, where he was not always satisfied simply with using simple stripes, as in 'Kardinal'

312–314 *Samples of fabric designs by Dagobert Peche:*

312 SEMIRAMIS (1911/14)
313 VERGISSMEINNICHT (1911/17)
314 KRONE (1919)

316 Dagobert Peche. DORIS (1923). Fabric sample

Opposite
315 Dagobert Peche. ARIEL (1911/13). Fabric sample

and which – as evidence of how little known the young artist was – is attributed there to one 'Olga Sikarz'.[4] In later records the mistake is corrected. In 1916, Maria Likarz went to Germany,[5] and it was only in 1920 that she returned to Vienna and the Wiener Werkstätte, where she stayed until the association was disbanded, working mostly in the fashion and textile departments.[6]

Maria Likarz did not only design a large number of fabric patterns, but like other influential artists of the Wiener Werkstätte she too showed an astonishing stylistic range in her work. In her repertoire stylized floral and geometric motifs are found in equal numbers; in the former she appears to have been mainly influenced at first by Peche. Her pattern 'Tamara' (fig. 318), for instance, gives the impression of being a variation on Peche's 'Vase'. Designs such as 'Borneo' (fig. 319) and 'Fidelio' (fig. 360), in contrast, are derived from Peche's style in a more general way. 'Nachthimmel' (fig. 362) is related to Peche's graphic designs. In inventions such as 'Brindisi' (fig. 320), 'Bozen' (figs. 273, 361), 'Liliom' (fig. 358) or 'Winkel' (fig. 352), however, Likarz's own originality is very pronounced, a

317 Maria Likarz. KAYALA (1930). Fabric sample

(fig. 192), but added delicate blossoms as extra embellishment, as seen in 'Pan' (figs. 193, 194) and 'Krone' (fig. 314).

Peche's lasting influence on the members of the Wiener Werkstätte and their concern with international trends towards abstraction is clearly exemplified in the fabric patterns of Maria Likarz. With about 200 designs to her credit, she was the most prolific artist in the Wiener Werkstätte textile department. While still a pupil of Hoffmann at the Kunstgewerbeschule, Maria Likarz was already working for the association of artists. Hoffmann used her pattern 'Basel' in Cologne at the German Werkbund exhibition held in 1914. She had already invented the fabric design which she called 'Irland' (figs. 99–102, 172, 250), but which is erroneously listed as 'Schottland' (Scotland) in the early large-format sample book already mentioned,

quality with which she in turn impressed her colleagues Felice Rix, Mathilde Flögl and Max Snischek.

The most outstanding results were achieved by Maria Likarz in her abstract patterns. 'Irland' (figs. 99–102, 172, 250) had already shown that she did not rely solely on her immediate surroundings for sources of inspiration. This striking pattern, with its subtlety in all kinds of colour-schemes and its impressive effect, has no parallel in designs by other contemporary Wiener Werkstätte artists. Not only this example, but also later developments in Likarz's designs, clearly demonstrate that she must have become actively interested in international trends towards abstraction.

In terms of geometric and abstract fabric designs, Maria Likarz's only equal was Sonia Delaunay, who had been active in textile design since 1911, but whose fabrics were actually produced in Lyons only in 1925, when they were shown in Paris with great success (fig. 325).[7] It will be difficult to ascertain whether or not Maria Likarz was familiar with Sonia Delaunay's designs, but she could have been introduced to them in connection with the Exposition Internationale des Arts Décoratifs in 1925. At all events, Hoffmann, who as an exhibition commissioner in Paris will not have been unaware of them, seems to have been influenced by Delaunay's work, especially in his late pattern 'Reifen' (fig. 383), one of the most accomplished fabric designs the architect ever created.[8] Like the Wiener Werkstätte artists, Delaunay used fine silk, often pongee, for many of her creations. Her mainly abstract patterns display a distinctive feeling for colour, in primary shades as well as in subtle nuances, and one could suppose that in some of Maria Likarz's patterns – for example, 'Martin' (fig. 357), 'Marelli' (fig. 355), both datable to 1927, or 'Ali' (fig. 324) dated 1929 – there could have been some direct contact with the Franco-Russian artist. An embroidered coat designed by Delaunay, now in private ownership in Vienna, perhaps provides an indication of possible connections which have yet to be researched.

318–320 Samples of fabric design by Maria Likarz:
318 TAMARA (1920/21)
319 BORNEO (1920/21)
320 BRINDISI (1925)

In designing her fabrics Sonia Delaunay was led by the desire and the concept of being able to express her creative ideas concerning the simultaneity of colours not only in paintings but even more immediately in textiles. Freed from working in two dimensions on canvas, she was able to adopt a sculptural and three-dimensional approach to fabrics and clothing as they related to the human body or to interior spaces. Although she created industrial products and fashion articles, her printed materials and embroidered or knitted models do not in any way give the impression of being 'fashionable' or 'dated' in the ephemeral sense. Sonia Delaunay attained in her fabrics and garments that synthesis of art and handicraft which is so often sought after yet so seldom achieved. The homogeneous effect is based on the transference of her painterly ideas to a medium that was totally suited to her talents.

In contrast to Delaunay, Maria Likarz's creative momentum and starting point did not derive from an integrated artistic theory; she invented fabric patterns with consciously planned, infinite repeats, corresponding to their own complexity and their own rules. In addition, there was the range and variety of the design elements, which extended from abstract geometric to stylized naturalistic forms. Because of this, both colour and form in Likarz's inventions showed greater variation, and were also less homogeneous. Patterns such as 'Skorpion' (fig. 321), 'Kayala' (fig. 317), 'Mombasa' (fig. 354) or 'Bridge' (fig. 359) are reminiscent of the consistency of a Delaunay. By contrast, 'Romulus' (fig. 364) and 'Whisky' (fig. 356), with their large repeats and bold motifs, are without parallel in contemporary designs. Amongst the abstract designs by Likarz there are also unpretentious patterns composed of small elements, such as 'Adonis' (fig. 323) or 'Onix' (fig. 363). 'Radio' (fig. 8) and 'Bermuda' (fig. 322) belong, however, among her most original creations.

Maria Likarz's fabric patterns, except for the early designs, were all created within a period of about ten years. Any attempt at dating the individual pat-

321–323 Samples of fabric design by Maria Likarz:

321 *SKORPION (1919)*
322 *BERMUDA (1928)*
323 *ADONIS (1929)*

terns precisely is difficult, however: just as 'Irland' was far ahead of its time, Maria Likarz's patterns in general have a timeless quality while also being clearly products of their time. In many of the designs the 'fashionable' aspect is absent – another reason why her fabrics are most appropriately compared to those of Sonia Delaunay.

Mathilde Flögl and Felice Rix, pupils of Hoffmann who worked in the textile department in the early pre-war phase as well as after 1918, were remarkably prolific designers. In all, 113 patterns can be attributed to Felice Rix, and 128 to Mathilde Flögl. Both artists made important contributions to the style of fabric patterns between the wars by responding to Peche's and Likarz's work and by realizing their own ideas. The artistic demands still being upheld by Peche and Likarz in keeping with the Wiener Werkstätte programme were modified here in favour of a more practical approach. It was no longer exclusively or unconditionally the individual personality and style of either artist that was to find expression; trends that were typical, popular, even fashionable at the time were taken into consideration, and this resulted in a shift to a more generally decorative concept, as in 'Quaste' (Flögl, fig. 328) or 'Japanland' (Rix, fig. 329). The

patterns are variously composed of: stylized plant forms such as 'Curzola' (Flögl, fig. 370) and 'Camille' (Rix, fig. 327); geometric elements as in 'Amanullah' (Flögl, fig. 372) and 'Archibald' (Rix, fig, 366). Repeats range between very large, eye-catching examples – 'Cannes' (Flögl, fig. 332) and 'Krasnojarsk' (Rix, fig. 333) – and small-scale patterning – 'Chypre' (Flögl, fig. 330) and 'Sylvester' (Rix, fig. 335). Here the use of colour is the most striking feature. In contrast to the contemporary purist and future-oriented fashion for using hand-woven fabrics in subdued colours for interiors, the artists of the Wiener Werkstätte adhered to decorative patterns and colour-schemes that were full of variety.

The same is also true of Max Snischek, from 1922 head of the fashion department, who also engaged in fabric design in the Wiener Werkstätte from 1924. Between 1912 and 1914, Snischek had only produced one pattern, 'Märchen', which he apparently developed for the Wiener Werkstätte in his student days, and which relied on the kind of folk-art ornament that was so popular at that time.[9]

Snischek's geometric abstract patterns, such as 'Phantom' (fig. 376), 'Zyprian' (fig. 379) or 'Manissa' (figs. 273, 303, 304), are qualitatively on a par

326 Mathilde Flögl.
HORTENSIE (1928).
Fabric sample

327 Felice Rix.
CAMILLE (1929).
Fabric sample

Below
328 Mathilde Flögl.
QUASTE (1930).
Fabric sample

Below
329 Felice Rix.
JAPANLAND (1923).
Fabric sample

with those of Likarz. 'Berggeist' (fig. 373) and 'Lenglen' (figs. 249, 336), as well as 'Samoa' (fig. 338), are decorative-abstract patterns that are more closely linked to their time. Finally, with 'Moldau' (fig. 341) and 'Vorau' (fig. 375) Snischek

invented patterns whose repertoire of forms – figures and plants in abstract lines and surface formations – could only date from the late 1920s. Even more typical of their time are floral designs like 'Missouri' (fig. 339), 'Elbasan' (fig. 337) and

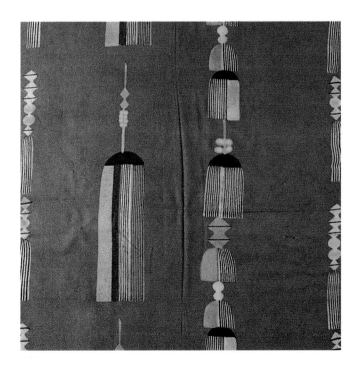

331 Felice Rix. GERANIE (1929).
Fabric sample

Left
330 Mathilde Flögl. CHYPRE (1928).
Fabric sample

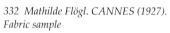

332 Mathilde Flögl. CANNES (1927).
Fabric sample

333–335 Samples of fabric designs
by Felice Rix:

333 KRASNOJARSK (1929)
334 DONNERWETTER (1919)
335 SYLVESTER (1924)

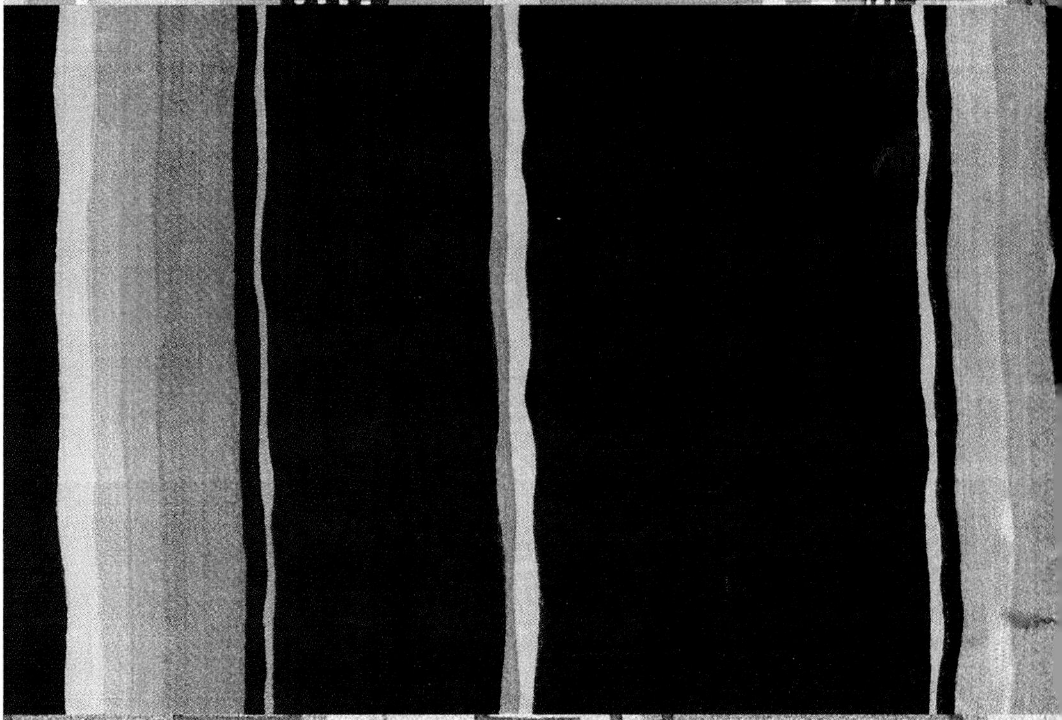

'Celebes' (fig. 340). Snischek's stylized plants, figures, animals and scenes, and even more so his use of colour – often pastel shades, as in 'Biel' (fig. 374) – nevertheless make him one of the most forward looking designers in the Wiener Werkstätte textile department. In the late 1920s he gave expression to principles of form and colour which would be revived in the fabric designs of the 1950s.

1 Angela Völker, 'Josef Hoffmanns Gesamtkunstwerk. Ornament und Muster', in Wien 1986/87 (exhib. cat and stock register), p. 14.
2 Völker / Pichler 1989, nos. 19–21.
3 For example, a dress based on Poiret's neo-Empire style features the pattern 'Einsame Blume'; WW photograph album 169 / 101.
4 Cf. Österreichisches Museum für angewandte Kunst, inv. no. T 10.261, p. 141.
5 Katja Schneider, *Burg Giebichenstein*, Weinheim 1992, p. 157.
6 The patterns by Maria Likarz which must have originated before 1914/16, or which were sent by her to the Wiener Werkstätte form Germany, are: 'Rosanna', 'Balkan', 'Spalato' and 'Venusschuh'.
7 Zurich 1987 (exhib. cat.).
8 Malochet 1984, p. 56.
9 In 1932 Snischek went to Munich to become a teacher at the school of fashion. Cf. *Mode für Deutschland* (exhib. cat.), Munich 1981; Völker, 1984, p. 250.

336-338 Samples of fabric designs by Max Snischek:

336 LENGLEN (1927)

337 ELBASAN (1928)

338 SAMOA (1928)

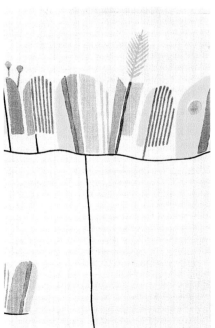

Above
339 Max Snischek.
MISSOURI (1925).
Fabric sample

Left
340 Max Snischek.
CELEBES (1929).
Fabric sample

341 Max Snischek.
MOLDAU (1928).
Fabric sample

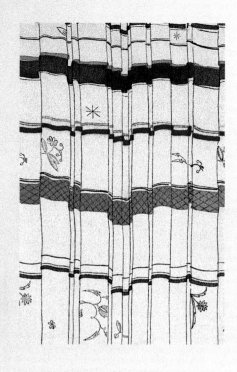

Talte

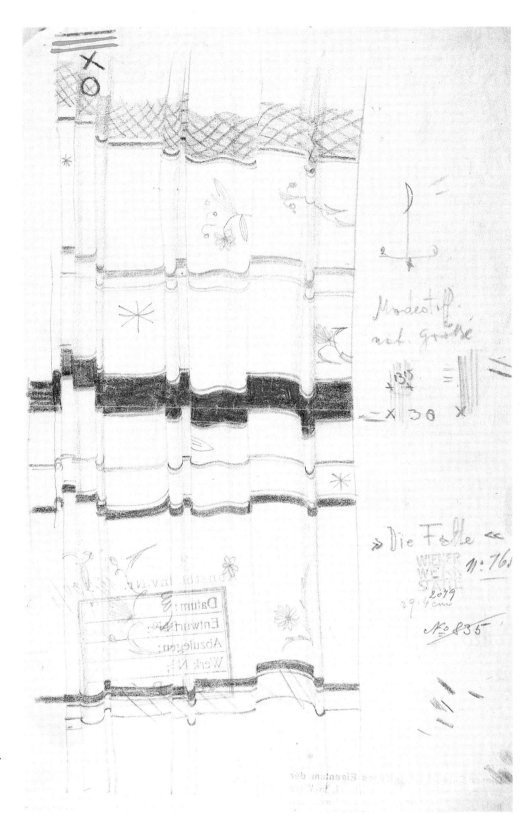

344 Dagobert Peche. SÄULE (1919). Colour proof on paper

345-347 *Samples of fabric designs*
by Dagobert Peche:

345 CHYTERA *(1911/19)*
346 EDISON *(1911/17)*
347 ENDIGUNG *(1911/19)*

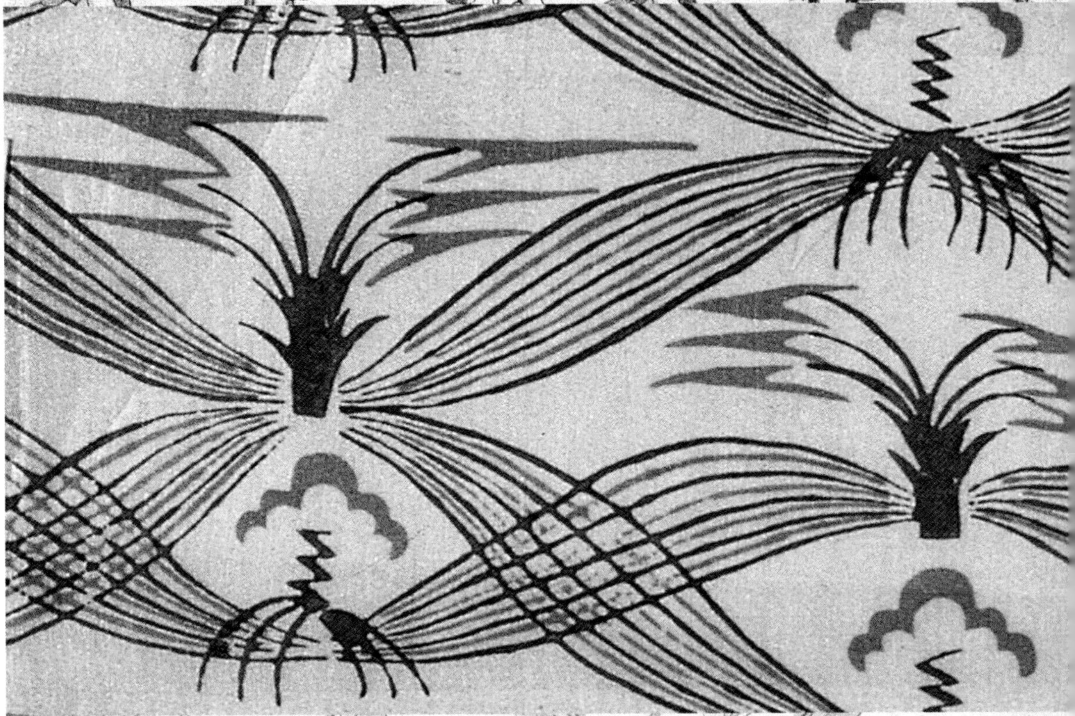

348–350 *Samples of fabric designs
by Clara Posnanski:*

348 *EPIRUS (1928)*
349 *HÖFLEIN (1926)*
350 *PALIURI (1928)*

351 *Clara Posnanski. PAUL (1927). Fabric sample*

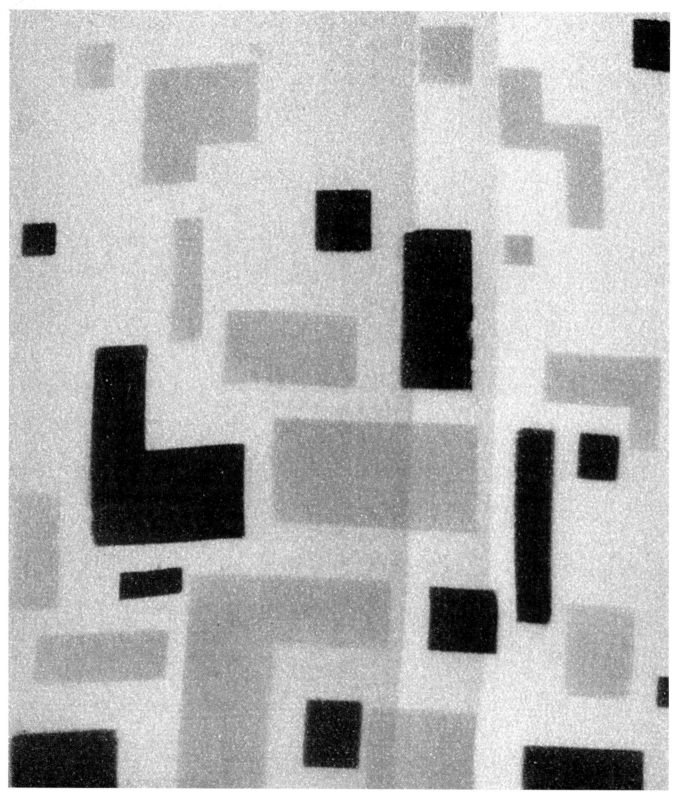

352 Maria Likarz. WINKEL (1927). Fabric sample

Opposite
353–358 Samples of fabric designs by Maria Likarz.
From top left to bottom right: 353 LUTHER (1927); 354 MOMBASA (1928); 355 MARELLI (1927); 356 WHISKY (1929);
357 MARTIN (1927); 358 LILIOM (1927)

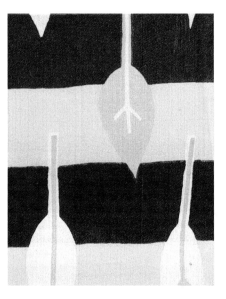

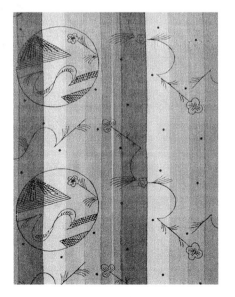

359-363 Samples of fabric designs by Maria Likarz.

From top left to bottom right:
359 BRIDGE (1928)
360 FIDELIO (1924)
361 BOZEN (1928)
362 NACHTHIMMEL (1921/22)
363 ONIX (1930)

Opposite
364 Maria Likarz. ROMULUS (1928).
Fabric sample (actual size)

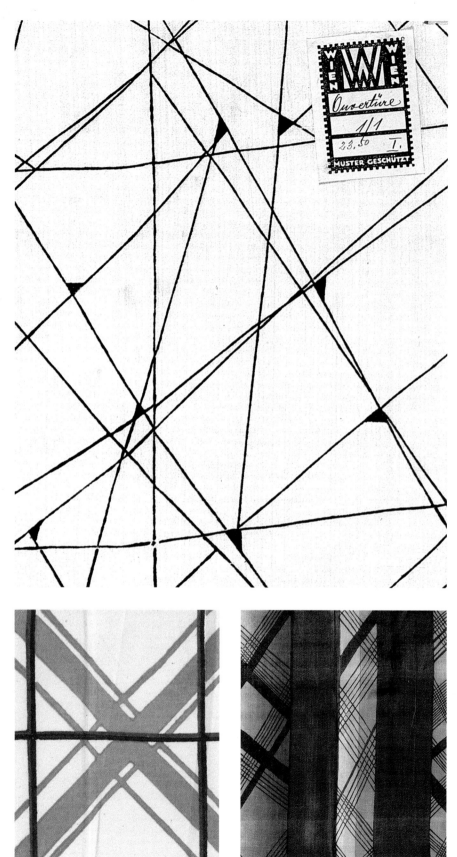

Opposite
368 Felice Rix. SARGANS (1926). Fabric sample

Right
370–372 Samples of fabric designs by Mathilde Flögl:

370 *CURZOLA (1925)*
371 *BLUES (1928)*
372 *AMANULLAH (1928)*

WIENER WERKSTÄTT

Opposite
369 Mathilde Flögl. BAMBI (1925).
Fabric sample (actual size)

373–378   Samples of fabric designs by Max Snischek: (upper register from left to right) BERGGEIST (1924), BIEL (1928) and VORAU (1928); (lower register) PHANTOM (1924), NEW YORK (1928) and ENOS (1926)

Opposite
379 Max Snischek. ZYPRIAN (1924). Fabric sample (actual size)

198

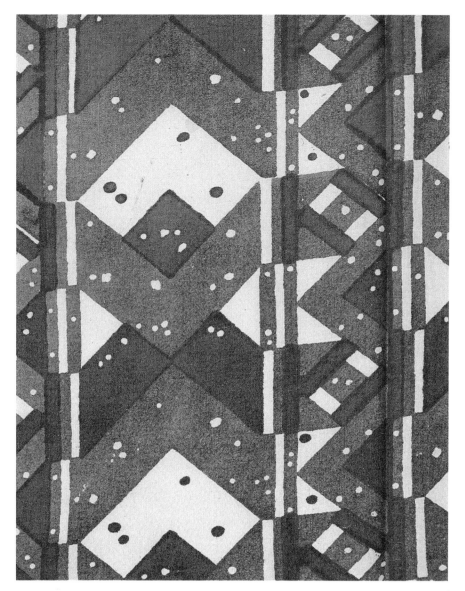

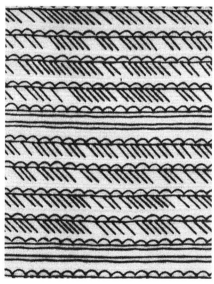

*380–384 Samples of fabric designs
by Josef Hoffmann: (top left) MIRA
(1926), (top right) CARUS (1929),
(above) ODER (1928), (far left) REIFEN
(1929), and (left) TENOR (1928)*

*Opposite
385 Josef Hoffmann. GUIDO (1929).
Fabric sample*

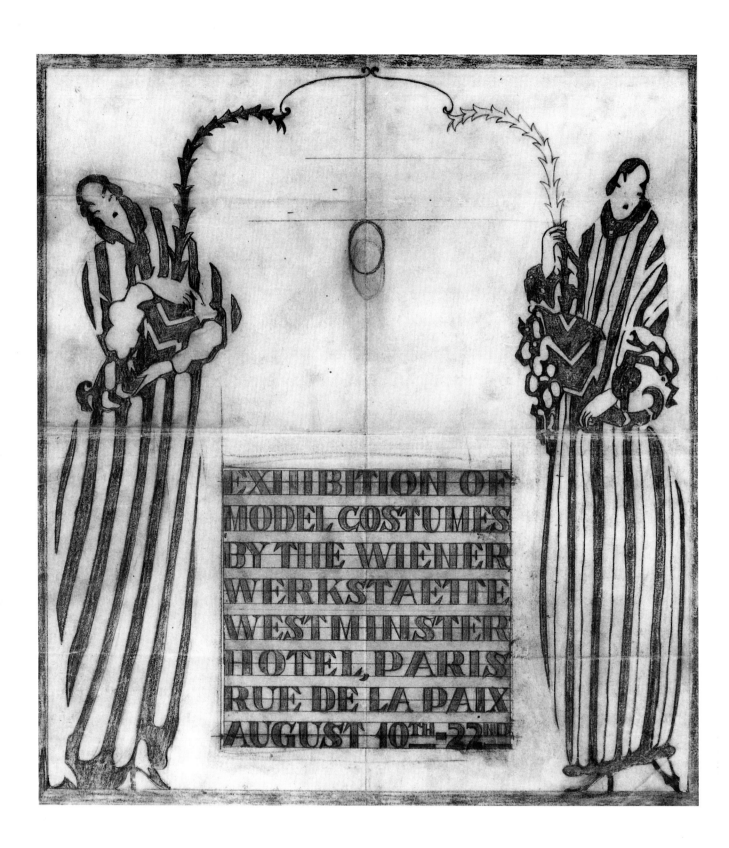

EXHIBITION OF
MODEL COSTUMES
BY THE WIENER
WERKSTAETTE
WESTMINSTER
HOTEL, PARIS
RUE DE LA PAIX
AUGUST 10TH – 22ND

WIENER WERKSTÄTTE FABRICS:
INTERNATIONAL RESONANCES

387 *Label for the*
'Wiener Werkstätte of America', New York

Opposite
386 *Arnold Nechansky. Drawing for a poster*
announcing a Wiener Werkstätte fashion show
in Paris, c. 1925, pencil on tracing paper

388 *Studio Martine, Paris. Printed fabric (1924).*
Courtesy, the Art Institute of Chicago
(gift of Robert Allerton)

Links and parallels with international trends in contemporary fabric design demonstrate the considerable extent and importance of Viennese artists' involvement with surface patterns after 1900.

At about the same time in Paris the leading fashion designer Paul Poiret was working on new fabric pattern concepts which were attuned to his own designs and ideas in the field of fashion. With Poiret a realistic reform of fashion had been initiated, which, in contrast to the artistic reforms of the years around 1900, was very successful and also influenced the Wiener Werkstätte. Following the Austrian and German example, Poiret founded in Paris a craft school, whose young students were to give an important new impetus to textile design. At the same time he inspired the painter Raoul Dufy to take an interest in the creation of fabric designs.[1] Thus, in 1911 the Ecole d'art décoratif Martine was established, and later the Studio Martine, where textiles and other handicrafts were designed and produced.[2] Poiret was acquainted with the Wiener Werkstätte, and had much admired Hoffmann's pavilion in Rome in the summer of 1911; in November that year he visited the Austro-Hungarian capital in order to purchase large quantities of new Wiener Werkstätte fabrics.[3]

Poiret's predilection for Oriental style, for the radiant colours of the costumes and stage designs of Diaghilev's Ballets Russes and for East European folk art found its parallel in Vienna: in 1912 and 1913 audiences had the opportunity to marvel at the brilliance of the Ballets Russes when the company toured Austria. The aesthetic revaluation of folk art in Vienna precipitated a great number of publications on the subject, as well as a flurry of activity in collecting.[4] The influence of folk art on the Wiener Werkstätte textile department was restricted to its early years and has been reviewed above.

Whilst Poiret had a direct influence on Wimmer-Wisgrill in the realm of fashion, the fabric patterns reflect a movement in the opposite direction: designs by Dufy and the Studio Martine are variations on original Wiener Werkstätte patterns and were often executed using the same technique, the printing-block method.[5] Interest in Wiener Werkstätte fabrics in France was probably limited to the pre-war years and appears to have been associated above all with Poiret.

However, the quite early acquisitions made by the museum in Mulhouse can hardly be connected with Poiret. The fact that an internationally famous Paris dealer was selling Wiener Werkstätte fabrics provides clear evidence that the fabrics were being well received elsewhere, and not just by the museum, Poiret or Dufy. Inevitably, the war and the new directions in art will have brought about a break in such sympathies – a rift which not even the success of the Wiener Werkstätte at the Paris exhibition in 1925 was able to bridge.

Evidence of specific points of contact such as those that existed between Vienna and Paris in the field of textiles and fashion cannot be found in other cities and countries. Parallels, certainly not unfamiliar to the Wiener Werkstätte artists – indeed, as their works demonstrate, they must in fact have seemed important to them – were not far away. In 1912 Josef Gocar founded in Prague the handicraft workshop 'Artel', which was based on the Wiener Werkstätte model. In that artists' association, firmly bound stylistically to Czech Cubism, textile design was not practised at all; however, the parallels could have been of a formal and theoretical nature.[6]

In Italy the Futurist painters, once again with the concept of the *Gesamtkunstwerk* in mind, showed an interest in handicrafts, and specifically in surface patterns. From 1912 Giacomo Balla designed abstract compositions of a pattern-like character for the interior decor of the Löwenstein house in Düsseldorf, and began inventing fabric designs in the following year.[7] Until *c.* 1930 Futurist artists were designing not only fabrics but also women's and men's clothing.[8]

In July 1913 Roger Fry founded the Omega Workshops in London – also following the Wiener Werkstätte model – which practised all categories of handicrafts. Their fabrics were for the most part intended for use in interior design.[9]

Those materials made in Paris, London and Italy after 1910 which aspired to artistic recognition were almost exclusively printed fabrics, apparently an international trend which also influenced the Wiener Werkstätte. In their patterns the Futurists and, later, the Russian Constructivists employed the abstract vocabulary familiar in contemporary painting or the graphic arts, whilst Dufy and with him Studio Martine preferred flowers, animals or patterns with small scenes. Dufy's designs were also woven into rich brocades. The Wiener Werkstätte chose a middle way: its designers experimented with abstract geometric forms as well as with floral motifs and naturalistic forms, all in great variety.

After the First World War a reform movement in handicrafts was started anew, its declared aim, in keeping with the times, being to work with in-

389 Paul Poiret(?): fashion model. Photograph from the Wiener Werkstätte fashion department's collection

390 Paul Poiret(?): fashion model. Photograph from the Wiener Werkstätte fashion department's collection

dustrial products. In Russia, where in the meantime Communism had taken hold, it was incumbent on artists to adapt new ideas and the creative achievements of Constructivism to handicrafts and above all to industrial production. Correspondingly, in the early 1920s, artists such as the painter Liubov Popova (1889–1924) and the graphic artist Varvara Stepanova (1894–1958) began designing fabrics with completely abstract, decorative patterns in brilliant colours. Other Soviet designers drew fabric patterns with very direct naturalistic or stylizing motifs alluding to the new age. It is not known whether these fabrics found their way out of the Soviet Union, but in any event they were never acquired for museum collections abroad, either in Europe or in America.[10]

In Germany too, the founding of the Bauhaus in 1919 brought the start of a new era in handicraft production. The hand-made object was to be designed in such a way that it could serve as a prototype for industrial production. It was not only on account of its fundamentally different aims – as is well known, the Wiener Werkstätte, with varying degrees of strictness, rejected to the bitter end the very idea of a collaboration with industry – that the Bauhaus stood apart from the Wiener Werkstätte; above all, there was a structural disparity. As a place of training, where pupils studied with artists in order to work later as designers in industry, it had aims that were primarily ideological, and in no way commercial. The Wiener Werkstätte also frequently drew on students from the city's school of arts and crafts, the Kunstgewerbeschule, as collaborators, but never with the slightest intention of training them specifically within its own workshop organization. The artists' workshop offered artists and students an opportunity of working – perhaps even of learning – but certainly not one of being given training in any formal sense. Notwithstanding the high level of handicraft and artistry, the Wiener Werkstätte produced objects and fabrics first and foremost with the aim of selling them.

It is only an apparent paradox that the Wiener Werkstätte, rather than undertake fabric production itself, employed certain outside firms to do it for them, while the Bauhaus manufactured hand-woven patterned materials in its own workshops. The method of block-printing practised in printing works on behalf of the Wiener Werkstätte is a technique of pure handicraft. Block-prints were not in-

391 Paul Poiret: fashion model. Photograph from the Wiener Werkstätte fashion department's collection

tended to serve as models for industrial printing processes. The Bauhaus weavers, by contrast, made prototypes for fabrics which were to be produced industrially and woven by machine, for instance those intended for use in tubular steel furniture. On the other hand, wall-hangings were woven at the Bauhaus as single items, and these – strictly geared to the technical demands of weaving – display abstract compositions in delicate colour combinations.[11] There is no known evidence of such works having been produced in the Wiener Werkstätte.

In the Wiener Werkstätte archive hardly any specific records can be found of a confrontation with the general tendencies described above, or any proof of individual artists showing an interest in international trends.[12] Written statements, letters or reports, also illustrative material such as drawings, photographs or magazines, for example from Paris, are absent. On the other hand, we can surmise that newspapers, books, catalogues and exhibitions had probably been helping to make the new repertoire of forms known, hence they would have been assimilated by Vienna as well. As an example, the major exhibition held in Paris in 1925 presented an opportunity of experiencing international standards at first hand. Here Hoffmann will certainly have taken an interest in much more than the latest designs by Sonia Delaunay, who was apparently a special source of inspiration for Wiener Werkstätte artists. The works of these artists, above all their fabric designs, demonstrate a profound and intense involvement with a wide-ranging variety of contemporary artistic ideas.

The fact that information on international trends that were in no sense indigenous to Vienna was absorbed and developed there can be seen in the case of individuals including Adolf Loos, Franz Cisek, Friedrich Kiesler and, last but by no means least, Josef Hoffmann, who were internationally renowned and acclaimed. Their travels and activities suggest that they cultivated private contacts for themselves which have not been documented. Furthermore, it is known that in the Vienna of the 1920s there were many occasions which offered anybody who was interested opportunities to become acquainted with the avant-garde and with international art events.[13]

But what impact did the Wiener Werkstätte and its fabrics have during the 1920s in the countries which offered them such diverse sources of inspiration? The Wiener Werkstätte was fully aware that Germany provided the most important outlet for its products. Exhibitions and fashion shows, as well as representation in the Deutsche Werkstätten from 1908 onwards, evidently caused the Wiener Werkstätte to become an important partner of and influence on its neighbour. Newspaper cuttings collected in the *Annalen* illustrate vividly the positive reception given to the Wiener Werkstätte fabrics in particular. The Bauhaus innovations were not always seen in a favourable light by German artists and craftsmen, but it would be unfair to assign those who purchased Wiener Werkstätte fabrics exclusively to the conservative camp.

During the war years the Wiener Werkstätte maintained contracts with fifty-three German firms for the sale of silk fabrics.[14] Museums abroad also showed an interest in the Wiener Werkstätte, purchasing – probably from as early as 1913 onwards

392 *Studio Martine, Paris. Printed fabric (1920). Courtesy, the Art Institute of Chicago (gift of Robert Allerton)*

(see p. 20) – fabrics and other products from the textile department. Three examples may be mentioned here. In 1921, the Landesgewerbemuseum in Stuttgart acquired two fabrics: Peche's 'Freude' (fig. 311) and Flögl's 'Mittagstee'.[15] It is also known that in 1926 the Neue Sammlung in Munich purchased a series of Wiener Werkstätte fabric samples and corsages.[16] Finally, the Grassi Museum in Leipzig, on the occasion of the exhibition of arts and crafts entitled 'Europäisches Kunstgewerbe' held in 1927, bought fourteen lengths, some extensive, of Wiener Werkstätte fabrics, or accepted them in settlement of the rent owed for the use of the trade fair stand.[17]

The establishment by the Wiener Werkstätte of a branch in New York in 1922 signalled the confirmation of an awakening of interest in its fabrics in America.[18] In 1923, this time in Vienna, a curator of the Brooklyn Museum purchased a collection of sixteen fabrics by different designers, mostly dating from the early years.[19] The Metropolitan Museum of Art in New York owns examples of fabrics, as well as small sample books, but it is not known if the museum acquired them by direct purchase from the Wiener Werkstätte. The Art Institute of Chicago received a gift of several silk fabrics in

393 Lotte Frömel-Fochler. GRÜNFINK (1910/11). Fabric sample

1924: these included Wiener Werkstätte patterns, fabrics from the Studio Martine, as well as materials based on designs by Leon Bakst, the stage and costume designer of the Ballets Russes, thus demonstrating that the very high standards achieved in the Wiener Werkstätte fabrics had been widely noted.[20]

The fabrics produced by the Wiener Werkstätte clearly prove that this association of artists was more than just a part of the cultural phenomenon of 'Vienna around 1900', nowadays often endowed with an aura of mystery. It is undeniable that many designs dating from the early Wiener Werkstätte period were constituents of the systematically proclaimed aesthetic utopia, in which art and life merge, ornaments of that 'ideal community of all creators and appreciators', which was the vision entertained by Gustav Klimt in 1908. It is, however, also undeniable that in many Wiener Werkstätte fabric designs produced after 1918, especially those of Maria Likarz, Mathilde Flögl or Max Snischek, elements of the European avant-garde were assimilated and developed in such an original and superlative way that today it is difficult to comprehend why they have so far received virtually no recognition in the context of art history.

[1] Dufy worked from 1911 until 1928 with the Lyons textile factory Bianchini-Férier: cf. Bouillon 1989, p. 65.
[2] Bowman 1985, pp. 26ff.; Bouillon 1989, p. 54.
[3] *Annalen* 83, 606; 87, 102.
[4] Völker 1984, pp. 51ff.; Hohe Warte I, 1904/05, with several articles on folk art; Wien 1985 WW (exhib. cat.); Fischer 1987 (Emilie Flöge). Only recently staff of the Österreichisches Museum für angewandte Kunst discovered Josef Hoffmann's collection of folk-art textiles in his home village Brtnice, Moravia, now in the Czech Republic, cf. Wien/Brtnice 1992 (exhib. cat.).
[5] Bowman 1985, p. 49, shows a Dufy fabric which clearly derives from Peche patterns such as 'Semiramis'. In the textile collection of the Art Institute of Chicago there is also a fabric from the Studio Martine (inv. no. 1924.205), which derives from Frömel-Fochler's 'Grünfink'.
[6] Bouillon 1989, p. 70. For Czech Cubism see Düsseldorf 1992 (exhib. cat.) in which there are textile designs by Czech artists associated with Artel.
[7] Venezia 1986 (exhib. cat.), p. 86; Crispolti 1986, pp. 156ff.
[8] Crispolti 1986.
[9] Bouillon 1989, pp. 70f.
[10] Yasinskaya/Bowlt 1983; Pesaro 1987 (exhib. cat.); Zurich/Salzburg 1989 (exhib. cat.).
[11] Pesaro 1985 (exhib. cat.); Berlin 1987 (exhib. cat.).
[12] There are small photographs of designs by Poiret in the Wiener Werkstätte archives, but one may search in vain for evidence of direct involvement with him or with textile artists in Europe.
[13] Matthias Boeckl; 'Kiesler und die Wiener Architekten' in Wien 1988 (exhib. cat.), pp. 305ff.; Lesak 1988, pp. 33ff. and 99ff.; Wien 1924 (exhib. cat.).
[14] Textile department, advertising brochure KI 13.742/25. Amongst them were the Hohenzollern Kunstgewerbehaus in Berlin, and Karstadt in Brunswick, Hanover and Kiel.
[15] Inv. nos. 21.93 and 21.91. For this information I would like to thank the curator of the textile collection of the Württembergisches Landesmuseum in Stuttgart.
[16] Cf. Wichmann 1990 (stock cat.), pp. 94, 95, 112, 114, 115, 122, 124, 125, 146–49.
[17] Cf. p. 108, above. For this information I would like to thank Frau Angela Grzesiak. Her list contains (including some losses which occurred during the war, here marked with an asterisk) the following patterns which at that time were quite up-to-the-minute and in current production: inv. no. 27.69 'Traum' (Posnanski), 27.70 'Phantom' (Snischek), 27.71 'Palamos' (Rix), 27.72 'Double Fox' (Flögl), 27.73 'Falter' (Flögl), *27.75 'Helene' (Likarz), *27.76 'Missouri' (Snischek), 27.77 'Sommerfalter' (Rix), 27.78 'Rebhuhn' (Likarz), *27.79 'Kobra' (Rix), 27.80 'Tahiti' (Birke), *27.81 'Prater' (Likarz) and *27.82 'Sünde' (Flögl). Cf. also Wichmann 1990 (exhib. cat.), pp. 265ff.
[18] *Annalen* 83, 575ff.; interior of the Wiener Werkstätte showroom in New York in photo album 137, pp. 84ff.
[19] According to information provided by Elizabeth Coleman, former Curator of Dress and Costume in the Brooklyn Museum, to whom I wish to express my thanks, the following fabrics are in the museum's collection and in the Fashion Institute of Technology in New York, which today holds part of the textile collection of the Brooklyn Museum: 'Vorgarten' and 'Hameau' (Jonasch), 'Ruth' (Zimpel), 'Waldidyll' (Czeschka), 'Biene' and 'Kiebitz' (Hoffmann), 'München' and 'Flora' (Blonder), 'Pelargonie' (Rix), 'Schatten' (Peche), 'Waldwiese' (Heigl), 'Luxemburg' (Frömel-Fochler), 'Märchen' and 'Schwan' (Snischek), 'Bauerngarten' (Jesser), 'Rübezahl' (Friedmann), 'Mekka' (Berger), 'Medea' (Friedmann), 'Felsenhuhn' (Martens) and 'Artischoke' (Paradeiser).
[20] The Wiener Werkstätte fabrics are: 'Osterglocken' (Zülow), inv. no. 1924.214, and 'Waldfee' (Rix), inv. no. 1924.215.

CATALOGUE

The catalogue which follows includes only those patterns that can be documented by direct reference either to fabric samples or to the detailed records in the Wiener Werkstätte archival material now in the collection of the Österreichisches Museum für angewandte Kunst. Some designs which were never executed, and those patterns for which no visual identification is possible from the available records (even though documentary references may exist in the archives), have been disregarded and thus do not feature in the present listing.

The patterns listed are grouped under the names of individual artists arranged alphabetically. The sequence of the entries follows, in ascending order, the system of numbering adopted in the Wiener Werkstätte records and, although that system was not strictly chronological, the presentation gives an approximate idea of the historical development of each artist's contribution.

Within each catalogue entry the available information about the pattern is presented in the following order:

Number in the present catalogue (1–1335)

Name of pattern (with alternative German name in parentheses where appropriate) and translation or alternative spelling, e.g. of place names

Date of introduction / names of firms involved in production (sequence based on entries recorded in Wiener Werkstätte card indexes)

Wiener Werkstätte number

Method of production / pattern repeat intervals (height and width) if known / number of colour combinations recorded

Bibliographical references in chronological order (for full details of abbreviated titles of publications see the separate list of Bibliographical Sources)

Illustration number in this book

Martha ALBER (1893–)

1
Blätter (Leaves)
1910/11
262
Block printed / repeat height
not ascertainable:15 cm / 1
ID XXV, 1914, p. 77 (blouse),
p. 203 (cushion)
263, 264

2
Helenental
1910/11 / Bujatti, Klinger,
Ziegler
334
Block printed / 30:30 cm / 1
TKI VII, 1914, p. 54 (length of
fabric)

3
Kahlenberg
1910/11
363
Block printed / 25:25 cm / 1
DKD XXXI, 1912/13, p. 102
(corsage)
Kessler-Aurisch 1983, pp. 225,
344; fig. 424
69

Thea (Mea) ANGERER
(1877–1955)

4
Rialto
1927 (July) / Müller's Erben,
Teltscher
1086
Block printed / 15:31 cm / 9
MBF XXX, 1931, p. 509 (curtain)

5
Fregoli
1927 (July) / Müller's Erben,
Teltscher, Hermann
1089
Block printed /16:16 cm / 9

6
Lese (Vintage)
1928 (13 Oct. 1928) / Vetter
5128
Spray printed / 116:117 cm,
napkins 35:34 cm / 7

7
Theba
1926 (19 Oct. 1926) / Vetter
5143
Spray printed / repeats not
ascertainable / 4

8
Delia
1927 (August) / Müller's Erben,
WW ('Haus')
5206
Spray printed / repeats not
ascertainable / 7

9
Kalkutta (Calcutta)
1927 (August) / Müller's Erben

5207
Spray printed / repeats not
ascertainable / 7

10
Mengo
1927 (July) / Müller's Erben,
Ama, Teltscher, Ziegler
5209
Spray printed / 30.5:31 cm / 7
225

11
Sonja
1927 (July) / Müller's Erben,
WW ('Haus')
5211
Spray printed / 15.5:15.5 cm / 7

Gudrun BAUDISCH-
WITTKE (1907–1982)

12
Haag
1928 (21 Apr. 1928)
13817 (archive no.)
Plush / repeats not ascertainable / 5

Arthur BERGER
(1892–1981)

13
Wolkenstern (Star of the Clouds)
1911/13 / Ziegler
236
Block printed / repeats not
ascertainable / 1

14
Mekka (Mecca)
1911/13 / Ziegler, Teltscher
405
Block printed / repeat height
not ascertainable:45 cm / 7
DK XVII, 1914, p. 476 (facing of a
showcase)
DKD XXXIV, 1914, p. 369 (facing
of a showcase)
DK XXIII, 1915, p. 236 (lamp-
shade, curtain, upholstery)
JDW 1915, p. 7 (facing of a show-
case)
DK XXIV, 1916, p. 124 (jacket)
DKD XXXVIII, 1916, p. 213
(lampshade, upholstery, bed-
spread)
ID XXVII, 1916, pp. 152 (lamp-
shade)
Eisler 1916, p. 188 (jacket)
ID XXVIII, 1917, p. 376 (wall-
paper)
DKD XLV, 1919/20, fig. between
p. 78 and p. 80 (wallpaper)
WMB VI, 1921/22, p. 173
(lampshade, upholstery, bed-
spread)
Koch 1923, p. 64 (wallpaper)
Fabelli 1976, III, fig. 588
Baroni/D'Auria 1981, p. 132,
fig. 323; p. 136, fig. 331, 332
Schweiger 1984, p. 95, fig.;
p. 107, fig.; p. 128
Venice 1984 (exhib. cat.), p. 249,

fig. 1
Völker 1984, p. 77, fig. 98; p. 84,
fig. 109; p. 250, fig. 348; p. 251,
fig. 349; p. 282
Gmeiner/Pirhofer 1985, p. 34,
fig. 18
Tokyo 1989 (exhib. cat.), pp. 337,
351; p. 366, cat. no. 527
22, 75, 165, 166, 167, 168, 170, 171

15
Mela
1911/13 / Bujatti, Ziegler
425
Block printed / 14.7:12.7 cm / 2

16
Flitter (Spangles)
1916/18 / Ziegler
609
Block printed / repeat height
not ascertainable:7.5 cm / 4

17
Riva-See
1916/18 / Blumenegg
636, 636a
Block printed / 45.5:43 cm / 17

Fritzi BERGER

18
Kultur (Culture)
1920/21 / Ziegler
716
Block printed / repeats not
ascertainable / 2

19
Jansa
1920/21 / Ziegler
732
Block printed / 5:5.8 cm / 12

Camilla BIRKE-EBER
(1905–1990)

20
Tahiti
1924 (blocks produced 14 Jan.
1925) / Ziegler
889
Block printed / 44:30 cm / 7
MBF XXIV, 1925, p. 287 (length
of fabric)
Paris 1925 (exhib. cat.), length of
fabric
Amour de l'Art 1925, no. 9, p. 335
(length of fabric)
200

21
Tibet
1925 / Ziegler
895
Block printed / 44:30 cm
201

22
Cirkus (Circus)
1925 (blocks produced 25 Mar.
1925)
897
Block printed / 38:30.5 cm / 11
231

Leopold BLONDER
(1893–)

23
Aussee
1911/14 / Ziegler
17
Block printed / 17.5:30 cm /14
Wichmann 1990 (stock cat.),
p. 122

24
Ägypten (Egypt)
1911/14
31
Block printed / 23:39 cm / 9
270

25
Georgine
1911/14 / Ziegler
76, 76a
Block printed / 11.5:16 cm / 5

26
Kamilla
1911/14
80
Block printed / 11.2:8.1 cm / 2

27
Smyrna
1911/14 / Bujatti, Ziegler
81
Block printed / 10.1:10 cm / 5

28
Monastir
1911/14 / Ziegler
92
Block printed / 10:10 cm / 5

29
Ilonka
1911/14
168
Block printed / 15.6:7.4 cm / 3

30
Orlow
1911/14 / Ziegler
190
Block printed / 35:29.3 cm / 1

31
Nero
1911/14 / Ziegler
251
Block printed / 10:16.5 cm / 9

32
Diskus (Discus)
1911/14 / Ziegler
253
Block printed / 10:8.8 cm / 9

33
Kongo (Congo)
1911/14 / Ziegler
273
Block printed / 32.2:32.2 cm / 8

34
Federgans (Feather Goose)
1911/14 / Bujatti, Ziegler
301, 301a
Block printed / 9:10 cm / 1

35
Flagge (Flag)
1911/14 / Ziegler
306
Block printed / 12:29.5 cm / 3

36
Flora
1911/14 / Ziegler, Teltscher
308
Block printed / 30.5:repeat
width not ascertainable / 22
Eisler 1916, p. 216 (length of
fabric)
DKD XLI, 1918, p. 121 (length of
fabric)
DBK in DA XXI, 1916/18, pl. 14
(upholstery, lampshade)
Neuwirth 1984, pp. 162 f.
Wien 1985 WW (exhib. cat.),
no. 87
Bouillon 1989, p. 87
123, 295

37
Grado
1911/14 / Ziegler
327
Block printed / 31: 30 cm / 13
DKD LII, 1923, p. 97 (lamp-
shade)
AeD XLVI, 1924, p. 61 (up-
holstery)
Kleiner 1927, p. 26 (upholstery)
Neuwirth 1984, p. 146
Wien 1985 WW (exhib. cat.),
no. 74

38
Goldfisch (Goldfish)
1911/14
331
Block printed / 11.4:14.9 cm / 1

39
Java
1911/14 / Bujatti
358
Block printed / 18.3:10 cm / 1

40
Lawine (Avalanche)
1911/14 / Ziegler
397
Block printed / 45:49 cm / 1

41
München (Munich)
1911/14 / Ziegler
409
Block printed / 32.2:21.8 cm / 5
22

42
Macedonien (Macedonia)
1911/14 / Klinger, Bujatti,
Ziegler
410
Block printed / 45:30 cm / 4

43
Parsifal
1911/14 / Teltscher, Ziegler
456
Block printed / 30:30 cm / 9

44
Sternwarte (Observatory)
1911/14 / Ziegler, Teltscher, Sax
500
Block printed / 24.3:28.5 cm / 10

45
St. Andrä
1911/14 / Bremges & G.,
Albouts, Finkh & Co, Ziegler
501, 501a
Block printed / 19.5:6 cm / 10
DK XXIV, January 1916, p. 128
(length of fabric)

46
Teheran
1911/14 / Bremges & G.,
Albouts, Finkh & Co, Ziegler
506
Block printed / 12.5:14.6 cm / 11
Eisler 1916, p. 216 (length of
fabric)

47
Vogelkönig (King of the Birds)
1911/14 / Ziegler
524
Block printed / 18.6:21.9 cm / 6

48
Wiedehopf (Hoopoe)
1911/14 / Bremges & G.,
Albouts, Finkh & Co, Ziegler
537, 537a
Block printed / 5.6:14.8 cm / 9

49
Zugspitze (Head of Parade)
1911/14 / Bremges & G.,
Albouts, Finkh & Co, Ziegler
541
Block printed / 37.5:30.3 cm / 1

50
Unterwelt (Underworld)
1916/18 / Ziegler
561
Block printed / 8:5.9 cm / 1

51
Hermada
1916/18
621
Block printed / 10:9.7 cm / 8

52
Isphahan (Isfahan)
1912/17
791
Block printed / 17.2:10.5 cm / 3
15

53
Mauerwerk (Brickwork)
1921/22
795
Block printed / 16:12.7 cm / 9
117

54
Intarso (Marquetry)
1921/22
801
Block printed / 22.7:27 cm / 6

55
Sternhimmel (Starry Sky)
1928 (blocks produced 11 May
1928) / Ziegler
1014
Block printed / repeats not
ascertainable

56
Simplicius
1911/22
Silk brocade / repeats not
ascertainable / 9

Hilde BLUMBERGER (1903–)

57
Krassin
1928 (25 Oct. 1928) / Ziegler,
Teltscher
1072
Block printed / 13.8:15.2 cm / 19
DKD LXVI, 1930, p. 128 (length
of fabric)

58
Quartett (Quartet)
1928 (November) / Ziegler
1082
Block printed / 41.5:30.5 cm / 14
227

59
Sinaia
1928 (November) / Ziegler
1083
Block printed / 32:32 cm / 9
DKD LXVI, 1930, p. 127 (length
of fabric)

Maria Vera BRUNNER-FRIEBERGER (1885–1965)

60
Malacca
1910/17 / Ziegler, Alpen-
ländische Druckfabrik
117
Block printed / 8:5.9 cm / 4

61
Indigo
1910/17
184
Block printed / 52:30 cm / 2
Brussels 1987 (exhib. cat.), p. 176
Tokyo 1989 (exhib. cat.), p. 351
292, 300

62
Steinbrecher (Stone Breaker)
1910/18 / Ziegler
185
Block printed / 29.5:29.5 cm / 9

63
Tulipan
1910/18 / Ziegler, Alpen-
ländische Druckfabrik
186
Block printed / 44:44 cm / 9

64
Leonardo
1910/18 / Ziegler
187
Block printed / 12.5:15 cm / 3

65
Tanz (Dance)
1916/18 / Ziegler
630
Block printed / 5:5 cm / 9

Charlotte Alice (Lotte) CALM-WIERINK (1897–)

66
Akustik (Acoustics)
1923 / Ziegler, Teltscher
845
Block printed / 5.2:1.5 cm / 12

67
Kristiania
1925 (15 Nov. 1925) / Ziegler,
Teltscher
930
Block printed / 23:10 cm / 7

68
Kandidus
1927 (August) / Schenk
5158
Spray printed / 28 cm:repeat
width not ascertainable / 7

69
Tanne (Fir Tree)
1926 (before 2 June 1926) / Vogel
9688
Woven fabric / repeat height not
ascertainable:15.5 cm / 25

Carl Otto CZESCHKA (1878–1960)

70
Bavaria
1910/11
13
Block printed / 75.2:102 cm,
pattern staggered / 8
DI XIII, 1912, pl. 57 (border)
DI XIV, 1913, pl. 70 (lampshade),
pl. 137 (lampshade, bedspread,
upholstery of a chair), pl. 150
(lampshade), pl. 156 (lampshade, bedspread, upholstery of
a chair, curtain)
DKD XXXIII, 1913/14, p. 459
(lampshade), p. 461 (lampshade), p. 464 (upholstery of a
stool), p. 465 (upholstery)
ID XXV, 1914, p. 105 (wallpaper)
DKD XXXV, 1914/15, p. 294
(wallpaper)
ID XXVI, 1915, p. 184 (bedspread), p. 186 (lampshade,
curtain, upholstery, wall-
covering), p. 188 (lampshade,
curtain, upholstery, wall-
covering, curtain holder),
p. 189 (wall-covering, lampshade, upholstery, curtain
holder), p. 213 (lampshade)

DK XXIII, 1915, p. 237 (lamp-shade, upholstery of a chair, curtain)
DKD XXXVIII, 1916, p. 214 (lampshade, upholstery of a chair, curtain)
Eisler 1916, pp. 188, 189 (curtain)
DBK 1916/17, in: DA XXI, 1916/18, p. 21 (curtain, wall-covering)
DW, March 1917, p. 21 (cushion)
DA XXIV, 1921/22, p. 94 (up-holstery)
Wien 1934 (exhib. cat.), p. 11 (wallpaper), p. 79 (curtain, wall-paper), p. 83 (lampshade, curtain, upholstery, curtain holder)
Völker 1984, p. 53, fig. 58; p. 272
Schweiger 1984, p. 133, fig. below right
Tokyo 1989 (exhib. cat.), p. 366, no. 524
77, 138, 139

71
Apfel (Apple)
1910/11 / Ziegler
36
Block printed / 8.5:8.3 cm / 7
DK XXIV, 1916, p. 128 (length of fabric)
134

72
Feldlerche (Skylark)
1910/11 / Bremges & G., Ziegler
299
Block printed / 3.5:2 cm / 2
98

73
Fischreiher (Heron)
1910/11 / WW
303
Block printed / 2.8: 3.6 cm / 4
ID XXIV, 1913, p. 110 (lampshade)
Fanelli 1976, fig. 609
132

74
Hase (Hare)
1910/11
336
Block printed / repeat height not ascertainable:4.2 cm / 3
Fanelli 1976, fig. 608

75
Haushund (House Dog)
1910/11 / Ziegler
337
Block printed / 1.5:4.2 cm / 2
96

76
Hecht (Pike)
1910/11
338
Block printed / 1.6:3.2 cm / 4

77
Herbst (Autumn)
1910/11
345
Block printed / 12.4:6 cm / 11

78
Kropftaube
1910/11 / Ziegler
368
Block printed / 32:28.5 cm / 4
DI XIV, 1913, pl. 70 (lampshade), pl. 142 (curtain, bedspread, upholstery, lampshade), pl. 143 (lampshade, curtain, upholstery of a chair)
Fanelli 1976, fig. 610
92, 280

79
Kaninchen (Rabbit)
1910/11 / WW
384
Block printed / repeats not ascertainable / 1

80
Löwe (Lion)
1910/11 / Ziegler
394
Block printed / repeats not ascertainable / 2
TKI VIII, 1915, p. 201 (length of fabric)
96

81
Po-Ho
1910/11 / Ziegler, Alpen-ländische Druckfabrik
445
Block printed / 25.5:33.6 cm / 1
Brussels 1927 (stock cat.), p. 384, no. 450 (length of fabric)
135

82
Waldidyll (Forest Idyll)
1910/11 / WW, Ziegler
531
Block printed / 36:37.5 cm / 3
TKI VIII, 1915, p. 202 (length of fabric)
Brussels 1927 (stock cat.), p. 385, no. 451 (length of fabric)
DKD XXXVIII, 1916, p. 209 (lampshade)
DKD XLI, 1917/18, p. 212 (length of fabric)
Schweiger 1984, p. 222, fig. below right (attributed to Zülow)
Sekler 1985, p. 130, fig. 162
Paris 1986 (exhib. cat.), p. 187
81, 82, 83, 84, 133

83
Wasserorgel (Hydraulic Organ)
1910/12 / Ziegler
534
Block printed / 43.2:22 cm / 5
TKI VII, 1914, p. 56 (length of fabric)
136, 137

Ignaz DOSTAL

84
Patria
1910/19 / Ziegler, Alpen-ländische Druckfabrik
118
Block printed / 32:22 cm / 5

85
Wildling (Imp, Tomboy)
1910/19 / Ziegler
119
Block printed / 15.4:14.4 cm / 6
Brussels 1987 (exhib. cat.), p. 180, no. 9.12

86
Kokos (Coconut)
1923 / WW, Rodauner Druck-fabrik, Ziegler
840
Block printed / 5.8:5.8 cm / 7

Christine EHRLICH
(1903–)

87
Malmö
1926
954
Block printed / 35:32 cm / 1

88
Morelia
1928 / WW ('Haus')
1077
Block printed / 32:32 cm / 1

Hugo FALKENSTEIN
(1891–)

89
Eisbär (Polar Bear)
1910/11 / Ziegler
295
Block printed / 6.2 cm:repeat width not ascertainable / 6

Mathilde FLÖGL
(1891–1950)

90
Allegro
1910/17 / Ziegler, Ama
77
Block printed / 19:15 cm / 23
Brussels 1987 (exhib. cat.), p. 181, no. 9.13
Wichmann 1990 (stock cat.), p. 125

91
Ballade
1910/17
78
Block printed / repeat height not ascertainable:14.5 cm / 4

92
Sevilla (Seville)
1910/16 / Ziegler
86
Block printed / 26:15 cm / 9
SSR XVIII, 1917/18, p. 183 (bag)
DW, March 1917, p. 21 (house dress)

93
Erzerum
1910/17 / Ziegler
198
Block printed / 11:7.5 cm / 10

94
Einfalt (Simplicity)
1910/18 / Ziegler
210
Block printed / 29:15 cm / 5
Völker 1984, p. 114, fig. 155; p. 275

95
Chin-Chang
1910/18 / Ziegler, Blumenegg
212, 212a
Block printed / 33:30 cm / 9

96
Distel (Thistle)
1910/17 / Bujatti, Ziegler, Neu-mann
283
Block printed / 37.5:30 cm / 15

97
Tennis
1910/17
513
Block printed / 23:29.3 cm / 10

98
Veilchen (Violet)
1910/19 / Ziegler
559
Block printed / 16:15 cm / 9

99
Granit (Granite)
1910/19
572
Block printed / repeats not ascertainable / 1

100
Mittagstee (Midday Tea)
1910/19
615, 615a
Block printed / 40:29.2 cm / 9

101
Blumenzaun (Flower Hedge)
1910/19 / Ziegler, Teltscher
626
Block printed / 39:29 cm / 15

102
Riesenblatt (Giant Leaf)
1910/19 / Ziegler
631
Block printed / 79:88 cm / 6

103
Schiras
1910/19 /Ziegler, Sax
632
Block printed / repeats not ascertainable / 5

104
Der Garten Erde (Gartenerde) (Garden Mould)
1910/19 / Teltscher, Ziegler
637
Block printed / repeats not ascertainable / 6

105
Buchenwald (Beech Forest)
1919 / Teltscher, Ziegler
666
Block printed / 58:44.5 cm / 17

106
Granatblüte (Garnet Flower)
1919 / Albouts, Finkh & Co
667
Block printed / repeats not
ascertainable / 9

107
Sondervogel
1910/21 / Ziegler
738
Block printed / 90:43.5 cm / 5

108
Baumblüten (Blossom of a Tree)
1910/21 / Ziegler
751
Block printed / repeats not
ascertainable / 2

109
Oliven (Olives)
1910/21 / Teltscher, Ziegler
762
Block printed / 34.5:21.5 cm / 1

110
Gratianus
1910/21
763
Block printed / 22.8:22 cm / 6

111
Burgenland
1910/22 / Ziegler
816
Block printed / 30.5:43 cm / 6

112
Florentina
1924 (blocks produced 5 Nov.
1924) / Teltscher, Lörrach, Ama,
Ziegler
878
Block printed / 48.5:30 cm / 14
MBF XXIV, 1925, p. 287 (length
of fabric)
DK XXXIV, 1925/26, p. 227
(length of fabric)

113
Sünde (Sin)
1924/25 (blocks produced 14
Jan. 1925) / Ziegler
885
Block printed / 35:34.7 cm / 9

114
Falter (Butterfly, Moth)
1924 (blocks produced 3 Dec.
1924) / Teltscher, Ziegler
886
Block printed / 32:30 cm / 26
DKD LVII, 1925/26, p. 86
(length of fabric)
Wien 1929 (exhib. cat.), p. 23
(length of fabric)
Weiser 1930, p. 23 (length of
fabric)
MW 43, 1930, no. 2

115
Natter (Adder, Viper)
1924 (blocks produced 14 Jan.
1925) / Ziegler
887
Block printed / 20:30 cm / 10
Kleiner 1927, p. 65 (length of
fabric)

116
Curzola
1925 / Gillet & Fils, Ziegler
890
Block printed / 32:29 cm / 14
370

117
Petrograd
1925 (blocks produced 18 Mar.
1925) / Teltscher, Ziegler
893
Block printed / 48.5:40 cm / 15

118
Krokus (Crocus)
1925 / Ziegler
922
Block printed / 10.5:50 cm

119
Andante
1925 (15 Nov. 1925) / Ziegler
926
Block printed / 45.5:20.5 cm / 8

120
Bambi
1925 (15 Nov. 1925) / Ziegler,
Teltscher
932
Block printed / 29:29.5 cm / 9
369

121
Monaco
1925/26 / Ziegler
933
Block printed / 45:18 cm / 6

122
Mosel
1926 (July) / Ziegler, Teltscher,
M. B. Neumann's Söhne, Sax
941
Block printed / 10.8:10.2 cm / 30

123
Ob
1926 (July) / Ziegler, Teltscher
942
Block printed / 16.2:10.2 cm / 21
SSR XXX, 1929/30, p. 164
(corsage, cushion)
DKD LXVIII, 1931, p. 56
(cushion)

124
Mur
1926 (July) / Teltscher, Ziegler
943
Block printed / 15:7.7 cm / 15

125
Inn
1926 (July) / Ziegler, Teltscher
948
Block printed / 8:6.1 cm / 16

126
Perlis
1926 (31 Dec. 1926) / Ziegler,
Teltscher
958
Block printed / 12:15.2 cm / 10

127
Panama
1927 (March) / Ziegler
969
Block printed / 18:15.3 cm / 9
Wien 1929 (exhib. cat.), p. 60
(length of fabric)
Neuwirth 1981, p. 262, fig. 171
Tokyo 1989 (exhib. cat.), p. 318,
no. 376

128
Cannes
1927 (October) / Ziegler, Teltscher
978
Block printed / 38:30.5 cm / 8
332

129
Pacific
1927 (October) / Ziegler, Teltscher
981
Block printed / 37:30.3 cm / 11
Wien 1928 (sales cat.), p. 1101
(dress)
Wien 1929 (exhib. cat.), pp. 32,
75 (dress)
Völker in WKK 1984, no. 1, p. 47,
fig. 13
Völker 1984, p. 225, fig. 316;
p. 281
Wien 1985 (exhib. cat.), p. 398,
no. 13/11/50
Munich 1986/87 (exhib. cat.),
p. 608

130
Krim (Crimea)
1927 (October) / Teltscher,
Ziegler
984
Block printed / 40:30.5 cm / 5

131
Sudan
1927 (December) / Teltscher
994
Block printed / 31.7:42.7 cm / 9

132
Peking
1928 (February) / Ziegler, Teltscher
997
Block printed / repeats not
ascertainable / 12
Tokyo 1989 (exhib. cat.), p. 317,
no. 375

133
Amanullah
1928 (March)
1000
Block printed / 15.2:15.2 cm / 10
372

134
Iltis (Polecat)
1928 (1 Apr. 1928) / Ziegler
1006
Block printed / 30:30.5 cm / 9

135
Clan
1928 (April) / Teltscher, Ziegler,
Ama
1007
Block printed / 10:1 cm / 16

136
Mitsu
1928 (31 Mar. 1928) / Ziegler
1008
Block printed / 20:31 cm / 13

137
Kentucky
1928 (March) / Ziegler
1009
Block printed / 6:2.5 cm / 8

138
Hortensie (Hydrangea)
1928 (April) / Ziegler, Teltscher
1011
Block printed / 30:30.5 cm / 11
326

139
Chypre (Cypress)
1928 (April) / Ziegler
1012
Block printed / 15:6.2 cm / 13
330

140
Sambesi (Zambesi)
1928 (July) / Teltscher
1031
Block printed / 32:29.5 cm / 11

141
Papagena
1928 (July) / Ziegler
1040
Block printed / 30.3:30.5 cm / 12
MW, March 1929, vol. 12, no. 1,
p. 19 (cocktail dress)
Völker 1984, p. 230, fig. 321;
p. 231, fig. 322; p. 281
Wien 1985 (exhib. cat.), p. 398,
nos. 13/11/51, 13/11/52
269, 271

142
Perlen (Pearls)
1928 (20 June 1928) / Ziegler,
Teltscher
1043
Block printed / repeats not
ascertainable / 9

143
Hobby
1928 (21 Aug. 1928) / Ziegler,
FAG
1048
Block printed / 45:30 cm,
pattern staggered / 7

144
Marchesa
1928 (blocks produced 28 Aug.
1928) / Ziegler
1049
Block printed / 43.5:31 cm / 10

145
Byzanz (Byzantium)
1928 (24 Sep. 1928) / Ziegler
1054
Block printed / 17:10.2 cm / 8

146
Tientsin
1928 (24 Sep. 1928) / Ziegler
1058
Block printed / 11.5:10.3 cm / 10

147
Priel
1928 (22 Oct. 1928) / Ziegler
1070
Block printed / 15:30.5 cm / 13

148
Pergola
1928 (24 Nov. 1928) / Ziegler,
Teltscher
1081
Block printed / 7.5:7.5 cm / 22

149
Kab
1928 / Ziegler
1084
Block printed / 8:47 cm

150
Wiese (Meadow)
1929 (25 Apr. 1929) / Ziegler
1106
Block printed / 30.5:30.5 cm / 8
Pichler 1992 (stock cat.), p. 51,
fig. 9

151
Amazonas
1929 (30 Apr. 1929) / Ziegler,
Ama
1108
Block printed / 33.5:32.5 cm / 15

152
Domingo
1929 (7 May 1929) / Ziegler
1112
Block printed / 6.6:11.5 cm / 12
Völker 1984, p. 227, fig. 318;
p. 281

153
Triglav
1929 (21 May 1929) / Ziegler
1122
Block printed / 15.9:16 cm / 13

154
Leila
1929 (blocks produced 11 Dec.
1929) / Ziegler
1163
Block printed / 39:34.5 cm / 14

155
Quaste (Tassel)
1930 (January) / Ziegler, Ama,
Teltscher
1172
Block printed / 32:30 cm / 10
Tokyo 1989 (exhib. cat.), p. 317,
no. 374
328

156
Caliopsis
1930 (October) / FAG
1182
Block printed / repeats not
ascertainable / 7

157
Zinnia (Zimnia)
1930 (November) / Clavel &
Lindenmeyer
1189
Block printed / 24.5:64.5 cm / 9
Fanelli 1976, fig. 731

158
Sumba
1930 (December) / FAG
1193
Block printed / 15.5:16.3 cm / 9
Fanelli 1976, fig. 731

159
Kresse (Cress, Peppergrass)
1930 (November) / FAG, Ziegler
1194
Block printed / 33:33 cm / 12

160
Violantha
1930 (December) / FAG
1201
Cylinder printed / repeats not
ascertainable / 11

161
Sitter
1928 (February) / Posnanski,
Großmann, WW ('Haus')
5071
Spray printed / repeat height
not ascertainable:47 cm / 9

162
Thur
1928 (February) / Posnanski
5078
Spray printed / repeats not
ascertainable / 3

163
Blues
1928 (21 Apr. 1928) / Vetter
5118
Spray printed / 31:39.2 cm / 13
371

164
Don
1927 (February) / Schenk
5149
Spray printed / repeats not
ascertainable / 4

165
Felix
1927 (March) / Schenk
5151
Spray printed / 22:15 cm / 7

166
Forsitie (Forsythia)
1927 (April) / Denk
5153
Spray printed / repeats not
ascertainable / 6

167
Fox
1927 (23 Mar. 1927) / Schenk
5154
Spray printed / repeats not
ascertainable / 13

168
Kosmos (Cosmos)
1926 (1 Mar. 1926) / Schenk
5159
Spray printed / 16:15 cm / 11

169
Monos (Monkeys)
1927 (February) / Schenk
5166
Spray printed / repeats not
ascertainable / 4

170
Regia
1927 (16 Mar. 1927) / Schenk,
Guttmann
5175
Spray printed / repeats not
ascertainable / 5

171
Odessa
1928 (25 Sep. 1928) / Neumann,
Mülrath
5191
Spray printed / 24.3 cm:repeat
width not ascertainable / 10

172
Neapel (Naples)
1928 (25 Sep. 1928) / Neumann,
Hämmerle & Rhoner
5193
Spray printed / 26.5:repeat
width not ascertainable / 11
Völker 1984, p. 221, fig. XXI; p. 270
Wien 1985 (exhib. cat.), p. 398,
no. 13/11/48

173
Alexander
1929 (26 Feb. 1929) / Presser
5229
Block printed / repeats not
ascertainable / 6

174
Karmena (Karmenia)
1929 (December) / Wasservogel,
Ziegler, Posnanski, WW ('Haus')
5252
Spray printed / 33.5 cm:repeat
width not ascertainable / 6

175
Cadillac
1930 / Wasservogel, Schenk,
Ziegler, Posnanski, Hämmerle &
Rhoner, Mülrath, WW ('Haus')
5253
Spray printed / repeat width 34
cm / 8

176
Abbadie
1929
5257
Spray printed / repeats not
ascertainable

177
Kioto (Kyoto)
1929 (January) / Wasservogel,
WW ('Haus')
5258
Spray printed / repeats not
ascertainable / 6

178
Uranus
1927 (July) / Vogel
0129
Woven fabric / repeat width
31 cm / 8

179
Helis
1927 (October) / Vogel
0135
Woven fabric / repeat height not
ascertainable:31.5 cm / 8

180
Azur
1927 / Vogel(?)
0136
Woven fabric / repeats not
ascertainable

181
Epinglé
1927 / Vogel
0461
Woven fabric / repeats not
ascertainable / 2

182
Bedonia
1928 / Vogel
01016
Woven fabric /30 cm:repeat
width not ascertainable / 11

183
Rogate
1927 / Vogel
01019
Woven fabric / 32:30.5 cm / 7

184
Dornegg
1927 / Vogel
01022
Woven fabric / repeat height not
ascertainable:28.5 cm / 10
209

185
Azania
1927 / Vogel
01023
Woven fabric / 28.3 cm:repeat
width not ascertainable / 3

186
Firming
1927 / Vogel
01035
Woven fabric / repeats not
ascertainable / 3

187
Orina
1925/27 / Vogel
01072
Woven fabric / 29:29.7 cm / 7

188
Baja (Descent)
1926
12230 (archive no.)
Woven fabric / repeats not
ascertainable

189
Ätna (Etna)
1927 (4 Jan. 1927) / Giger
12231 (archive no.)
Woven fabric / repeats not
ascertainable / 3

190
Korfu (Corfu)
1927 (July) / Vogel
12789 (archive no.)
Woven fabric / repeat width
31.2 cm / 4

191
Kansas
1927 (July) / presumably Vogel
0206
Woven fabric / 27.5:28.5 cm / 2

192
Miami
1927 (July) / Vogel
0207
Woven fabric / repeats not
ascertainable / 2

193
Fels (Rock)
1927 (1 Feb. 1927)
Roller printed / repeats not
ascertainable / 9

Wilhelm FOLTIN (1890–   )

194
Blattpflanze (Foliage Plant)
1916/18 / Blumenegg, Ziegler
581
Block printed / 48:22 cm / 9

195
Lemberg
1916/18 / Ziegler, Alpen-
ländische Druckfabrik
620
Block printed / 17.6:14.5 cm / 9

196
Karo (Diamond)
1919 / Ziegler, Teltscher
646
Block printed / 10:9.7 cm / 8

197
Schraube (Screw)
1919 / Ziegler
649
Block printed / 10:10 cm / 5

198
Gewitter (Thunderstorm)
1919 / Teltscher, Ziegler
657
Block printed / 18:10 cm / 5

199
Schlinge (Loop)
1919 / Ziegler
658
Block printed / 10:5.2 cm / 1

200
Eisfigur (Ice Figure)
1919 / Ziegler
661
Block printed / 30:30 cm / 9

201
Kokoro
1919 / Ziegler
693
Block printed / 11.6:11.2 cm / 9

Josef FRANK (1885–1967)

202
Schöpfung (Creation)
1916/18 / Ziegler
634
Block printed / repeats not
ascertainable / 2

FREUND

203
Globus (Globe)
1916/18
558
Block printed / 8.7:14.8 / 4

FRIEDL

204
Thun (Tuna)
1927 (October) / Vogel
0163
Woven fabric / repeat height not
ascertainable:15.6 cm / 24

205
Tatra (Tatra Mountains)
1928 (21 Apr. 1928) / Teltscher
1052
Block printed / repeat height
not ascertainable:32.7 cm / 8

Marie Rosalie (Mitzi) FRIEDMANN-OTTEN (1884–1955)

206
Habsburg (Hapsburg)
1910/14 / Bujatti
42
Block printed / 26.8:10.1 cm / 7

207
Asta
1910/14
174
Block printed / 29:29.5 cm / 9
Fanelli 1976, pl. 137
112

208
Gartenstadt (Garden City)
1910/14 / Ziegler
175
Block printed / 17.5:22 cm / 1

209
Medea
1910/14 / Teltscher, Ziegler
176
Block printed / 26.5:15 cm / 12
Koch 1926, p. 25 (cushion)

210
Juno
1910/14
177
Block printed / 13.7:15 cm / 1
113

211
Schilfblüte (Reed Blossom)
1910/14 / Bujatti, Ziegler
178
Block printed / 19:30 cm / 4

212
Aschermittwoch (earlier
'*Carneval*') (Ash Wednesday)
1910/14
179
Block printed / 46:36 cm / 2
Brussels 1987 (exhib. cat.), p. 181,
no. 9.14
114

213
Feldpost (Army Postal Service)
1910/14 / Ziegler
180
Block printed / 23:38 cm / 1
115

214
Karst
1910/14 / Ziegler, Teltscher
181
Block printed / 30.2:30.2 cm / 2
117

215
Croatien (Croatia)
1910/14 / Ziegler
270
Block printed / 10.5:36.5 cm / 2
TKI VII, 1914, p. 101 (length of
fabric)

216
Dammhirsch (Fallow Deer)
1910/14 / Ziegler
277
Block printed / 29:9.5 cm / 1
TKI VII, 1914, p. 101 (length of
fabric)

217
Rübezahl (Sprite of the
Mountains)
1910/14 / Bremges & G.,
Albouts, Finkh & Co, Ziegler
469
Block printed / 44:41 cm / 4

218
Strohblume(n) (Strawflowers)
1910/14 / Ziegler
498
Block printed / 16:8 cm / 1
TKI VII, 1914, p. 101 (length of
fabric)
Fanelli 1976, fig. 628

219
Halbmond (Half-moon)
1916/18
550
Block printed / 42.2:29.5 cm / 4

220
Seestern (Starfish)
1920/21 / Ziegler
717
Block printed / 19.5:33.5 cm,
pattern staggered / 5

221
Seekoralle (Sea Coral)
1920/21 / Ziegler
750
Block printed / 14.5:11 cm / 9

222
Blumenblitz (Flower Lightning)
1920/21 / Ziegler
752
Block printed / 15:21.8 cm / 6

223
Romeo
1922 / Ziegler
813
Block printed / 24.5:11.5 cm / 7

224
Neptun (Neptune)
1922 / Ziegler
818
Block printed / 12.5:11.5 cm / 6
MBF XXIX, 1930, p. 82 (length of
fabric)

225
Coriandoli
1922 / Ziegler, Teltscher
826
Block printed / 30:35.5 cm / 3
Kleiner 1927, p. 65 (length of
fabric)

226
Gitterstern (Lattice Star)
1922 / Ziegler
827
Block printed / 7:6 cm / 8

227
Bethlehem
1922
832
Block printed / 19:11.5 cm / 16
233

Lotte FRÖMEL-FOCHLER (1884–   )

228
Bergfink (Brambling)
1910/11
9
Block printed / 7.8:4 cm / 1

229
Akropolis (Acropolis)
1910/11 / Teltscher
18
Block printed / 10:7.5 cm / 9

230
Eismeer (Polar Sea)
1910/17 / Ziegler
167
Block printed / repeats not
ascertainable / 1

231
Buenos-Aires
1910/17 / Bremges & G.,
Albouts, Finkh & Co
258
Block printed / repeats not
ascertainable / 1

232
Citronenfalter (Brimstone Butterfly)
1910/17 / Bremges & G.,
Albouts, Finkh & Co, Ziegler
269
Block printed / 12:8 cm / 2

233
Eiderente (Eider Duck)
1910/11
288
Block printed / 8:6.2 cm / 1
Wien 1912 (exhib. cat.), p. 28,
no. 86 (length of fabric)
Fanelli 1976, fig. 616

234
Eisfuchs (Arctic Fox)
1910/11
289
Block printed / 15:8 cm / 6
Wien 1912 (exhib. cat.), p. 28,
no. 83 (length of fabric)
Wien 1967 (exhib. cat.), p. 77,
no. 356
Florence 1978 (exhib. cat.),
p. 147, fig. 127; pp. 162f.

235
Fledermaus (Bat)
1910/17 / Bremges & G.,
Albouts, Finkh & Co
296
Block printed / repeats not
ascertainable / 6
Paris 1986 (exhib. cat.), p. 187

236
Flamingo
1910/11 / Bremges & G.,
Albouts, Finkh & Co, Ziegler
298
Block printed / 4.5:4 cm / 3
Wien 1912 (exhib. cat.), p. 28,
no. 85 (length of fabric)
TKI VII, 1914, p. 51 (length of
fabric)
Neuwirth 1985, p. 239, fig. 286

237
Forelle (Trout)
1910/11
300
Block printed / 7.5:10.2 cm / 1
Wien 1912 (exhib. cat.), p. 28,
no. 88 (length of fabric)

238
Fuchs (Fox)
1910/11 / Bremges & G.,
Albouts, Finkh & Co, Ziegler
307
Block printed / 8.4:8 cm / 1

239
Fasching (Carnival)
1910/13 / Ziegler
311
Block printed / 20.5:45 cm / 1
TKI VII, 1914, p. 60 (length of
fabric)
Brussels 1987 (exhib. cat.),
pp. 174f.
105

240
Gemse (Chamois)
1910/11 / Bujatti, Ziegler
316, 316a
Block printed / 2:4 cm / 5
Wien 1912 (exhib. cat.), p. 28,
no. 94
Fanelli 1976, fig. 614

241
Gazelle
1910/11 / Bujatti, Ziegler
317, 317a
Block printed / 22:16 cm / 1
Wien 1912 (exhib. cat.), p. 28,
no. 92 (length of fabric)
TKI VII, 1914, p. 52 (length of
fabric)
DK XXIV, January 1916, p. 129
(length of fabric)
Fanelli 1976, fig. 136
Neuwirth 1984, pp. 126, 128

242
Grasmücke (Warbler)
1910/11
319
Block printed / 2:4 cm / 4
Wien 1912 (exhib. cat.), p. 28,
no. 91 (length of fabric)
Wien 1967 (exhib. cat.), p. 77,
no. 358

243
Grünfink (Greenfinch)
1910/11
321
Block printed / 25:8.4 cm / 1
KKHW XIV, 1911, p. 683 (length
of fabric)
Völker 1984, pp. 26, 28, fig. 30;
p. 271
2, 393

244
Geier (Vulture)
1910/11 / Teltscher
322
Block printed / 14.6:8.2 cm / 3
KKHW XIV, 1911, p. 682 (length
of fabric)
TKI VII, 1914, p. 51 (length of
fabric)

245
Gorilla
1910/13
326
Block printed / 4:8 cm / 1
TKI VII, 1914, p. 51 (length of
fabric)
DA XXI, 1916/18, p. 94 (lampshade, wall-covering, furniture
covering)

246
Goldfasan (Golden Pheasant)
1910/11 / Klinger, Bujatti
328
Block printed / 7.5:8.5 cm / 1
Wien 1912 (exhib. cat.), p. 28, no.
95 (length of fabric)

247
Hermelin (Ermine)
1910/11
333
Block printed / 8:4 cm / 1
Wien 1912 (exhib. cat.), p. 28,
no. 84 (length of fabric)

248
Herzegowina (Hercegovina)
1910/17
335
Block printed / repeats not
ascertainable / 7

249
Kohlmeise (Great Titmouse)
1910/11 / Bremges & G.,
Albouts, Finkh & Co, Ziegler
364
Block printed / 8:8 cm / 2
Wien 1912 (exhib. cat.), p. 28,
no. 89 (length of fabric)

250
Kolibri (Humming-Bird)
1910/11 / Bremges & G.,
Albouts, Finkh & Co
367
Block printed / 2:4 cm / 1
Wien 1912 (exhib. cat.), p. 28,
no. 87 (length of fabric)

251
Kram(m)et(s)vogel (Fieldfare)
1910/11 / Ziegler
369
Block printed / 11:16 cm / 2
Wien 1912 (exhib. cat.), p. 28,
no. 90 (length of fabric)
KKHW XV, 1912, p. 344 (length
of fabric)
MBF XII, 1913, pp. 11, 13, 17
(cushion)
Wien 1964 (exhib. cat.), p. 102,
no. 799
Wien 1967 (exhib. cat.), p. 77,
no. 357
Hansen 1984, p. 142
Schweiger 1984, p. 221, fig. centre
right
Bouillon 1989, p. 38
42, 164

252
Krebs (Cancer, Crab)
1910/11 / Ziegler
377
Block printed / 8:8.3 cm / 1

253
Luxemburg
1910/17 / Bremges & G.,
Albouts, Finkh & Co, Ziegler
398, 398a
Block printed / 8:4.4 cm / 6
Fanelli 1976, fig. 612

254
Mauerblümchen (Wallflower)
1910/13 / Klinger, Bujatti
411
Block printed / 10 cm:repeat
width not ascertainable / 3
Eisler 1916, p. 15 (lampshade,
upholstery, tablecloth)
ID XXVII, 1916, p. 130 (upholstery), p. 131 (upholstery of a
chair, curtain), p. 133 (upholstery)
DKD XXXVIII, 1916, p. 219
(lampshade, curtain, wallpaper)
DBK in DA XXI, 1916/18, p. 20
(lampshade, upholstery, tablecloth), pl. 14 (curtain)
DKD XLIV, 1919, p. 130 (suit)
ID XXVIII, 1917, p. 394 (curtain),
p. 428 (curtain)
ÖBWK II, 1925/26, p. 52 (upholstery, curtain)
Kleiner 1927, p. 13 (upholstery),

p. 20 (lampshade, curtain, wall-
covering)
Fanelli 1976, fig. 615
64, 65

255
Mignon
1910/17 / WW
426
Block printed / 8.2:4.3 cm / 8
Neuwirth 1985, p. 238, fig. 285
300

256
Nizza (Nice)
1910/13 / Bremges & G.,
Albouts, Finkh & Co
431
Block printed / 8.2:4.3 cm / 5
TKI VII, 1914, p. 52 (length of
fabric)

257
Nordkap (North Cape)
1910/13 / Bremges & G.,
Albouts, Finkh & Co
432
Block printed / repeats not
ascertainable / 9

258
Peking
1910/17 / Bremges & G.,
Albouts, Finkh & Co, Ziegler
447
Block printed / 35:32.2 cm / 2

259
Samtente (Velvet Scoter)
1910/11 / Ziegler, Klinger,
Bujatti
474
Block printed / 29.5:28.2 cm / 1
Wien 1912 (exhib. cat.), p. 28,
no. 93 (length of fabric)
KKHW XV, 1912, p. 345 (length
of fabric)
DI XIV, 1913, pl. 1 (upholstery)
TKI VIII, 1915, p. 197 (length of
fabric)
Eisler 1916, p. 215 (length of
fabric)
DKD XL, 1917 II, p. 174 (length
of fabric)
DKD XLI, 1917/18, pp. 58f.
(cushion)
Fanelli 1976, fig. 613
Brussels 1987 (exhib. cat.), p. 182,
no. 9.16
Wichmann 1990 (stock cat.),
p. 114
53, 54

260
Sumatra
1910/17 / Ziegler
477
Block printed / 10.5:10 cm / 1
107

261
Sada Jacco
1910/13
479
Block printed / repeats not
ascertainable / 1

262
Trocadero
1910/17 / Bremges & G.,
Albouts, Finkh & Co
505
Block printed / 36.5:7.5 cm / 4

263
Waldkapelle (Forest Chapel)
1910/13 / Ziegler
536
Block printed / repeat height
not ascertainable:16.8 cm / 1
DKD XXXVIII, 1916, p. 221
(lampshade, curtain, bedspread)
85

264
Tunis
1910/13 / Ziegler
568
Block printed / 20:10 cm / 1

265
Feuerwerk (Fireworks)
1910/19 / Ziegler
647
Block printed / 20:19.5 cm / 3

266
Indien (India)
1910/19 / Ziegler
660
Block printed / repeats not
ascertainable

G. HACKL

267
Ellen
1925/26
Hand painted / repeats not
ascertainable / 2

268
Flamme (Flame)
1925
Hand painted / repeats not
ascertainable / 1

269
Irrlicht (Will o' the Wisp)
1925 (23 July 1925)
Hand painted / repeats not
ascertainable / 1

270
März (March)
1925
Hand painted / repeats not
ascertainable / 1

271
Violetta
1925
Hand painted / repeats not
ascertainable / 1

Philipp HÄUSLER
(1887–1966)

272
Anninger
1910/11 / Ziegler

24
Block printed / 7:4.7 cm / 4
TKI VI, 1913, p. 242 (length of
fabric)
279

273
Laubfrosch (Tree Frog)
1910/11 / Bremges & G.,
Albouts, Finkh & Co, Ziegler
390
Block printed / 7:5.5 cm / 2

274
Spätsommer (Late Summer)
1910/11 / Bremges & G.,
Albouts, Finkh & Co
475
Block printed / 39 cm:repeat
width not ascertainable / 1
DI XIV, 1913, pl. 153 (curtain),
pl. 154 (curtain, lampshade,
upholstery)

Lotte HAHN
(1906–)

275
Morena
1928 (June) / Neumann, Schenk
5167
Spray printed / 28:27 cm / 5

Guido HEIGL
(1890–)

276
Waldwiese (Forest Glade)
1912/16 / Ziegler
538
Block printed / 30:60 cm / 7
Venice 1984 (exhib. cat.), p. 502,
fig. 1
Schweiger 1984, p. 235

Heddi HIRSCH-
LANDESMANN (1895–)

277
Stachelrose (Thorny Rose)
1912/17 / Ziegler
107
Block printed / 22:30 cm / 2

278
Münchhausen
1912/17 / Ziegler
108
Block printed / 21.5:15 cm / 4

279
Bergkristall (Rock Crystal)
1915/18
109
Block printed / 8.5:15 cm / 2

280
Tanzpaar (Dancing Couple)
1915 / Ziegler
551
Block printed / 7:7.5 cm / 6

281
Lava
1916/18 / Ziegler
612
Block printed / 12:21.8 cm / 9
220

282
Nedschibe
1916/18 / Ziegler, Neumann,
Teltscher
624
Block printed / 10:17.3 cm / 6

283
Lymphe (Lymph)
1923 (11 June 1923) / Ziegler,
Teltscher, Neumann
844
Block printed / 26:29.5 cm / 17

Gertrud HÖCHSMANN
(1902–1990)

284
Loanda
1925 (22 Oct. 1925)
166
Block printed / repeats not
ascertainable

285
Basra
1925 (15 Nov. 1925) / Teltscher,
Ziegler
934
Block printed / 32.5:30 cm / 9
298

286
Elbe
1926 (July) / Ziegler
947
Block printed / 30.5:30.5 cm / 19

287
Risa
1925 (15 Nov. 1925) / Ziegler,
Teltscher
935
Block printed / 30:30 cm / 11

288
Wolga (Volga)
1925 (15 Nov. 1925) / Ziegler,
Teltscher
928
Block printed / 16:15 cm / 10

289
Yap (Jap)
1925 (15 Nov. 1925) / Ziegler,
Teltscher
937
Block printed / 26.5:30 cm / 10
226

Josef HOFFMANN
(1870–1956)

290
Biene (Bee)
1910/11
4
Block printed / 11.5:5 cm / 11
Wien 1986/87 (exhib. and stock
cat.), p. 325, nos. T 11, T 14
St Petersburg 1991 (exhib. cat.),
p. 54, no. 92; p. 56, no. 118
New York 1992/93, p. 222,
fig. 377; p. 322
13, 14

291
Alpenfalter (Alpine Butterfly)
1910/11 / Ziegler, Bremges & G.,
Albouts, Finkh & Co
28
Block printed / 5:4.9 cm / 4
Wien 1986/87 (exhib. and stock
cat.), p. 325, nos. T 10, T 11
98

292
Adler (Eagle)
1910/12 / Teltscher, Ama,
Ziegler
29
Block printed / 5:2.5 cm / 9
TKI VI, 1913 , p. 242 (length of
fabric)
Wien 1986/87 (exhib. and stock
cat.), pp. 186f.; p. 325, no. T 15
New York 1992/93, p. 216,
fig. 352; p. 321
98, 147

293
Apollo
1910/11 / Bremges & G.,
Albouts, Finkh & Co
30
Block printed / 26:8 cm / 8
DKD XXXI, 1912/13, p. 105 (box)
MBF XII, 1913, p. 17 (curtain)
DK XXXIV, 1916, p. 129 (length
of fabric)
DBK in DA XXI, 1916/18, pl. 14
(curtain, lampshade)
DKD XLI, 1917/18, p. 59 (pillow-
case)
ÖBWK II, 1925/26, p. 53
(curtain, lampshade)
Brussels 1927 (stock cat.), p. 382,
no. 446 (length of fabric)
Florence 1978 (exhib. cat.), vol. 1,
p. 135, fig. 32; p. 159
Völker 1984, p. 24, fig. 22, 23;
p. 25, fig. 24; p. 271
Hansen 1984, p. 71
Wien 1986/87 (exhib. and stock
cat.), p. 325, no. T 11
Bouillon 1989, p. 88
3, 4, 5, 71

294
Theben (Thebes)
1910/15 / Ziegler
49
Block printed / 11.2:8.5 cm / 1
Wien 1986/87 (exhib. and stock
cat.), pp. 186, no. T 16; p. 325
149

295
Salambo
1910/15 / Neumann, Teltscher
224
Block printed / repeats not
ascertainable / 8
MBF XXIV, 1925, p. 270 (tablecloth)
Wien 1986/87 (exhib. and stock
cat.), pp. 186f., 325, no. T 17
203, 204

296
Cypern (Cyprus)
1910/15 / Ziegler, Teltscher

274
Block printed / 11.3:12.1 cm / 17
DW, July 1917, p. 8 (skirt with
shoulder straps)
Völker in WKK 1983, no. 2,
p. 135, fig. 16
Völker 1984, p. 104, fig. 141;
p. 275
Wien 1985 (exhib. cat.), p. 397,
no. 13/11/24
Wien 1986/87 (exhib. and stock
cat.), pp. 186f., no. 22; p. 325,
no. T 18
Varnedoe 1986, p. 103
St Petersburg 1991 (exhib. cat.),
p. 55, no. 101
New York 1992/93, p. 217,
fig. 356; p. 321
254

297
Dorfschwalbe (Common Swallow)
1910/12 / Albouts, Finkh & Co,
Bremges & G., Ziegler
275
Block printed / 8:8 cm / 2
DKD XXXIII, 1913/14, p. 82
(upholstery of a chair)
Fanelli 1976, fig. 601
Völker amk, p. 5
Kessler-Aurisch 1983, pp. 225,
344, fig. 422
Hansen 1984, p. 142
Schweiger 1984, p. 221, fig. centre
left
Wien 1986/87 (exhib. and stock
cat.), p. 325, nos. T 10, T 11
246

298
Erlenzeisig (Siskin)
1910/11 / Ziegler
290
Block printed / 6:4.5 cm (repeats
of the flower) / 2
DI XIV, 1912, pl. 6 (curtain)
MBF XII, 1913, p. 146 (curtain)
ID XXIX, 1918, p. 146 (wallpaper), p. 147 (curtain)
ID XXXI, 1920, p. 313 (lampshade)
ID XXXII, 1921, p. 295 (curtain,
bedspread, covering of a side
table)
Fanelli 1976, fig. 600
Neuwirth 1984, p. 136
Wien 1986/87 (exhib. and stock
cat.), pp. 186f., fig. 29; p. 325,
nos. T 10, T 19
St Petersburg 1991 (exhib. cat.),
p. 54, no. 91
New York 1992/93, p. 218, fig.
362; p. 321
18

299
Feiertag (Holiday)
1910/12 / Albouts, Finkh & Co,
Bremges & G., Ziegler
304
Block printed / 13.8:12 cm / 5
Fanelli 1976, fig. 605
Wien 1986/87 (exhib. and stock
cat.), p. 325, no. T 10
95

300
Grünspecht (Green Woodpecker)
1910/15
320
Block printed / 3.5:3.5 cm / 1
Wien 1986/87 (exhib. and stock
cat.), p. 325, nos. T 10, T 11

301
Herzblatt (Leaf Bud)
1910/15
335
Block printed / 8:4.7 cm / 5
Wien 1986/87 (exhib. and stock
cat.), p. 325, nos. T 11, T 20
New York 1992/93, p. 216,
fig. 353; p. 321

302
Hirschenzunge (Hart's Tongue)
1910/12
342
Block printed / 12:8 cm / 3
Wien 1986/87 (exhib. and stock
cat.), p. 325, no. T 21
St Petersburg 1991 (exhib. cat.),
p. 56, no. 114, fig. 114
New York 1992/93, p. 222,
fig. 379; p. 322
151, 296

303
Hopfen (Hops)
1910/17 / Bujatti
350
Block printed / 7.8:10 cm / 5
Eisler 1925, p. 25 (lampshade)
Wien 1986/87 (exhib. and stock
cat.), p. 325, no. T 23
St Petersburg 1991 (exhib. cat.),
p. 55, no. 102
143, 244

304
Isonzo
1910/15
356
Block printed / 7.6:4.1 cm / 4
DK XXIV, 1916, p. 129 (length of
fabric)

305
Jagdfalke (White Gyrfalcon)
1910/11
357
Block printed / 38:54 cm / 5
DI XIII, 1911, p. 96 (upholstery
of a sofa)
KKHW XIV, 1911, p. 619 (upholstery of a sofa)
TKI V, 1912, p. 50 (wall-covering)
MBF XII, 1913, p. 20 (wallpaper)
DI XIV, 1913, pl. 90 (wallpaper),
pl. 91 (wallpaper), pl. 141
(curtain, bedspread, upholstery)
DKD XXXIII, 1913/14, p. 82
(curtain)
ID XXV, 1914, p. 111 (curtain,
wall-covering)
ID XXVI, 1915, p. 174 (curtain,
wall-covering, upholstery),
p. 176 (curtain, upholstery, wall-
covering), p. 177 (upholstery,
wall-covering)
TKI VIII, 1915, p. 204 (length of
fabric)
SSR XV, 1915, p. 134 (length of
fabric)

ID XXVII, 1916, p. 224 (wallpaper)
Eisler 1916, p. 131 (wallpaper)
DKD XXXIX, 1916/17, p. 178
(dress), p. 209, 210 and 211
(wallpaper)
Brussels 1927 (stock cat.), p. 383,
no. 447 (length of fabric)
Kleiner 1927, p. 21 (wallpaper)
Wien 1934 (exhib. cat.), p. 82
(wall-covering, curtain, upholstery)
Wien 1967 (exhib. cat.), p. 87,
no. 444, fig. 47
Florence 1978 (exhib. cat.),
p. 135, fig. 33; p. 159
Völker 1984, p. 9, fig. 1; pp. 24,
25, figs. 22, 24; p. 35, fig. 38;
pp. 217f.
Schweiger 1984, p. 220, fig. centre
right
Wien 1985 (exhib. cat.), p. 396,
no. 13/11/9
Wien 1986/87 (exhib. and stock
cat.), p. 325, nos. T 9a, T 9b, T 12
Varnedoe 1986, p. 102
Brussels 1987 (exhib. cat.), p. 185,
fig. 24, no. 9.24
60, 61, 62, 63

306
Kiebitz (Peewit)
1910/15
365
Block printed / 12.7:5.7 cm / 10
DKD XLI, 1917/18, p. 107 (dress
in window display)
Wien 1986/87 (exhib. and stock
cat.), p. 186, no. T 24; pp. 187,
325, nos. T 12, T 24; p. 342
New York 1992/93, p. 199, fig.
324; p. 218, fig. 363; pp. 319, 321

307
Kohleule
1910/15 / WW, Teltscher
366
Block printed / 16:10 cm / 1
Völker amk, pp. 10ff.
Wien 1986/87 (exhib. and stock
cat.), p. 325, nos. T 10, T 12,
T 25; p. 342
St Petersburg 1991 (exhib. cat.),
p. 56, no. 115
New York 1992/93, p. 222, fig.
376; p. 322
309

308
Kernbeisser (Hawfinch)
1910/12 / Ziegler, Teltscher
371
Block printed / repeats not
ascertainable / 1
ID XXIV, 1913, p. 354 (curtain,
lampshade)
ID XXV, 1914, p. 102 (wallpaper,
lampshade, curtain)
TKI VII, 1914, p. 58 (length of
fabric)
ID XXVI, 1915, p. 180 (wallpaper)
DK XXIV, 1916, p. 330 (length of
fabric)
DKD XXXVIII, 1916, p. 220 (curtain, lampshade, bedspread,
upholstery of a chair)

ID XXXII, 1921, p. 303 (cushion)
Fanelli 1976, fig. 604
Kessler-Aurisch 1983, pp. 225,
230, 344, fig. 424
Wien 1986/87 (exhib. and stock
cat.), p. 325, nos. T 10, T 12
17

309
Luchs (Lynx)
1910/12 / Ziegler, Bremges & G.,
Albouts, Finkh & Co
389
Block printed / 8.5:16 cm / 3
Völker 1984, pp. 31f., fig. 36;
p. 272
Wien 1986/87 (exhib. and stock
cat.), p. 325, nos. T 12, T 26
New York 1992/93, p. 217,
fig. 357; p. 321
144

310
Lerche (Lark)
1910/11 / Bremges & G.,
Albouts, Finkh & Co, Bujatti
392, 392a
Block printed / 2.1:1.5 cm / 3
Fanelli 1976, fig. 594
Wien 1986/87 (exhib. and stock
cat.), p. 325, nos. T 10, T 12
St Petersburg 1991 (exhib. cat.),
p. 55, no. 104
New York 1992/93, p. 219, fig.
364; p. 321
142

311
Lyon (Lyons)
1910/15
401
Block printed / 5.5:4.3 cm / 4
Fanelli 1976, fig. 597
Wien 1986/87 (exhib. and stock
cat.), p. 325, nos. T 10, T 12
Tokyo 1989 (exhib. cat.), p. 318,
no. 377

312
Montezuma (Monte Zuma)
1910/12 / Teltscher, Ziegler
417
Block printed / 23:10.3 cm / 14
DKD XXXIII, 1913/14, p. 456
(lampshade, upholstery)
ÖBWK IV, 1927/28, p. 65 (cur-
tain, bedspread, wall-covering)
Florence 1978 (exhib. cat.),
p. 135, fig. 34; p. 159
Sekler 1985, p. 130, fig. 162
Völker in WKK 1983, no. 2,
p. 125, fig. 4a
Völker 1984, p. 42, fig. 46, p. 272
Neuwirth 1984, pp. 122f.
Neuwirth 1985 (exhib. cat.),
no. 67
Paris 1986 (exhib. cat.), p. 187
Wien 1986/87 (exhib. and stock
cat.), p. 325, nos. T 12, T 27
Wichmann 1990 (stock cat.),
pp. 94f.
St Petersburg 1991 (exhib. cat.),
p. 54, no. 89; p. 55, fig. 110; p. 56,
no. 110
New York 1992/93, p. 220,
fig. 368; p. 321
22, 68, 245

313
Martha
1910/15 / Bremges & G.,
Albouts, Finkh & Co, Ziegler
419, 419a
Block printed / 4:2 cm / 7
DK XXIV, 1916, p. 128 (length of
fabric)
Wien 1986/87 (exhib. and stock
cat.), p. 186, no. T 28; pp. 187,
325
St Petersburg 1991 (exhib. cat.),
p. 54, no. 95
New York 1992/93, p. 218,
fig. 360; p. 321

314
Miramar
1910/15 / Teltscher, Ziegler
420
Block printed / 6.4:4.5 cm / 6
DK XXIV, 1916, p. 129 (length of
fabric)
Wien 1986/87 (exhib. and stock
cat.), pp. 186, 325, no. T 29
St Petersburg 1991 (exhib. cat.),
p. 54, no. 93, fig. 95
New York 1992/93, p. 217,
fig. 359; p. 321
150

315
Nil (Nile)
1910/17 / Bujatti, Teltscher
435
Block printed / 23.5:10 cm / 4
Wien 1986/87 (exhib. and stock
cat.), p. 325, no. T 30; p. 342
St Petersburg 1991 (exhib. cat.),
p. 55, fig. 197; p. 56, no. 109
New York 1992/93, p. 222, fig.
378; p. 322
152

316
Riva
1910/13 / Ziegler
461
Block printed / 5:4 cm / 7
TKI VII, 1914, p. 55 (length of
fabric)
Wiener Mode XXVIII, no. 5,
1915, p. 491 (book cover)
Fanelli 1976, fig. 602
Wien 1986/87 (exhib. and stock
cat.), p. 325, no. T 10
10, 140, 141

317
Rollschnecke
1910/12 / Bremges & G.,
Albouts, Finkh & Co
462
Block printed / 11:8.8 cm / 1
DKD XXXI, 1912/13, p. 105 (box)
Wien 1986/87 (exhib. and stock
cat.), p. 325, no. T 10
9, 71

318
Rhombus (Rhomb)
1910/12 / Bremges & G.,
Albouts, Finkh & Co, Teltscher
463
Block printed / repeat height
not ascertainable:12.4 cm / 14

ID XXVI, 1915, p. 464 (tea cosy)
DKD XXXIII, 1913/14, p. 110
(skirt suit)
Sekler 1985, p. 130, fig. 162
Paris 1986 (exhib. cat.), p. 187
Wien 1986/87 (exhib. and stock
cat.), p. 325, nos. T 10, T 12, T 31
7

319
Ragusa
1910/12 / WW, Ziegler,
Neunkirchner Druckfabrik
464
Block printed / 4.5:4 cm / 2
Fanelli 1976, fig. 598
Wien 1986/87 (exhib. and stock
cat.), p. 186, no. T 32; p. 187;
p. 325, nos. T 10, T 32
New York 1992/93, p. 223,
fig. 385; p. 322
247, 259, 260

320
Santa Sophia (Santa Sofia)
1910/12
473
Block printed / 29 cm:repeat
width not ascertainable / 3
DI XIV, 1913, pl. 155 (curtain)
TKI VI, 1913, p. 445 (length of
fabric)
DKD XXXIV, 1914, p. 140 (wallpaper)
DK XXXVII, 1929, p. 254
(curtain, cushion)
Wien 1986/87 (exhib. and stock
cat.), p. 325, no. T 10; p. 342
Bouillon 1989, p. 42
70, 296

321
Serpentin (Serpentine)
1910/15 / Ziegler
485
Block printed / 4.2:4.2 cm / 10
Wien 1986/87 (exhib. and stock
cat.), p. 158, no. Z 68; p. 325,
no. T 33; p. 329, nos. Z 68, Z 69;
p. 342
St Petersburg 1991 (exhib. cat.),
p. 55, no. 99
New York 1992/93, p. 192,
fig. 314; p. 194, fig. 315; p. 319
145

322
Schwarzblatt (Black Leaf)
1910/12 / Ziegler
487
Block printed / 10.5:11.5 cm / 5
Fanelli 1976, fig. 606
Wien 1986/87 (exhib. and stock
cat.), p. 325, no. T 10; no. T 34
St Petersburg 1991 (exhib. cat.),
p. 54, no. 90; p. 55, no. 100
New York 1992/93, p. 221, fig.
375; p. 322
306

323
Tulpe (Tulip)
1910/15 / Albouts, Finkh & Co,
Bremges & G., Teltscher
504
Block printed / 3:2 cm / 6

Wien 1986/87 (exhib. and stock
cat.), p. 325, no. T 35
New York 1992/93, p. 220,
fig. 370; p. 321

324
Triangel (Triangle)
1910/13 / Klinger, Ziegler,
Bujatti
507
Block printed / 8:9.5 cm / 5
Fanelli 1976, fig. 603
Hansen 1984, p. 142
Schweiger 1984, p. 221, fig. centre
right
Wien 1986/87 (exhib. and
stock cat.), p. 325, nos. T 10, T 12,
T 36
St Petersburg 1991 (exhib. cat.),
p. 56, no. 108
New York 1992/93, p. 221,
fig. 373; p. 321
146

325
Wasserfall (Waterfall)
1910/12 / Ziegler, Teltscher
530
Block printed / 10:6 cm / 7
DK XVII, 1914, p. 472 (lamp-
shade)
DKD XXXIV, 1914, p. 375
(lampshade)
DK XXIV, 1916, p. 127 (dress)
ID XXVII, 1916, p. 202 (lamp-
shade)
Eisler 1916, p. 189 (dress)
Koch 1916, pp. 34, 45 (lamp-
shade)
Fanelli 1976, fig. 599
Wien 1986/87 (exhib. and stock
cat.), pp. 186, 325, nos. T 10, T 37;
p. 342
St Petersburg 1991 (exhib. cat.),
p. 56, no. 116
New York 1992/93, p. 217,
fig. 358; p. 321
148

326
Zebra
1910/15
545
Block printed / repeat height
not ascertainable:9.4 cm / 3
Wien 1986/87 (exhib. and stock
cat.), p. 325, no. T 12; p. 342

327
Waldrand (Edge of the Woods)
1912/21 / Ziegler
774
Cylinder printed / repeats not
ascertainable / 1

328
Ozon (Ozone)
1923 (27 Mar. 1923) / Ziegler
833
Block printed / 9:7 cm / 7
Wien 1986/87 (exhib. and stock
cat.), p. 325, no. T 38
New York 1992/93, p. 216,
fig. 355; p. 321
308

329
Gotemba
1925 (15 Nov. 1925) / Ziegler
939
Block printed / 16.5:6 cm / 6
Wien 1986/87 (exhib. and stock
cat.), p. 325, no. 39
St Petersburg 1991 (exhib. cat.),
p. 56, no. 111
New York 1992/93, p. 221,
fig. 372; p. 321

330
Tenor
1928 (21 July 1928) / Ziegler,
Clavel & Lindenmeyer
1034
Cylinder printed / 15.5:13.2 cm /
12
Wien 1986/87 (exhib. and stock
cat.), pp. 186f., no. T 40; p. 325
St Petersburg 1991 (exhib. cat.),
p. 55, no. 106
New York 1992/93, p. 223,
fig. 387; p. 322
384

331
Bremen
1928 (July) / Ziegler, Alpenländische Druckfabrik
1036
Block printed / 16:30.5 cm / 10
Wien 1986/87 (exhib. and stock
cat.), p. 325, no. T 41; p. 342
St Petersburg 1991 (exhib. cat.),
p. 56, no. 107
New York 1992/93, p. 223,
fig. 386; p. 322

332
Athos
1928 (July) / Ziegler
1039
Block printed / 12.4:6.2 cm / 13
Wien 1986/87 (exhib. and stock
cat.), p. 341
St Petersburg 1991 (exhib. cat.),
p. 55, no. 97
New York 1992/93, p. 202, fig.
327; p. 320

333
Jordan
1928 (July) / Teltscher, Ziegler
1044
Block printed / 33.5:22 cm / 7
Wien 1967 (exhib. cat.), no. 371
Wien 1980 NW (exhib. cat.),
p. 86, no. 103
Wien 1986/87 (exhib. and stock
cat.), p. 174, no. Z 76; p. 186,
cat. nos. T 13, T 42; pp. 325, 329
Tokyo 1989 (exhib. cat.), p. 348,
no. 465
New York 1992/93, p. 200, fig.
325; p. 218, fig. 361; pp. 319, 321

334
Hedin
1928 (July) / Ziegler, Alpenländische Druckfabrik
1045
Block printed / 19.6:1 cm / 14
Wien 1986/87 (exhib. and stock
cat.), p. 342

335
Save
1928 (July) / Ziegler
1046
Block printed / repeats not
ascertainable / 9
Wien 1986/87 (exhib. and stock
cat.), p. 342

336
Oder
1928 (July) / Ziegler
1051
Block printed / 30.5:10.2 cm / 13
Wien 1986/87 (exhib. and stock
cat.), p. 325, no. T 43; p. 342
St Petersburg 1991 (exhib. cat.),
p. 56, no. 112
New York 1992/93, p. 219, fig.
365; p. 321
382

337
Ibera
1928 (2 Oct. 1928) / Ziegler,
Teltscher
1065
Block printed / 10.2:10.2 cm / 10
ID XLII, 1931, pp. 122 (design for
a living room and a bedroom)
MBF XXX, 1931, p. 71 (design for
a living room and a bedroom)
Wien 1986/87 (exhib. and stock
cat.), p. 325, no. T 44; p. 342
St Petersburg 1991 (exhib. cat.),
p. 55, no. 98
New York 1992/93, p. 219,
fig. 366; p. 321

338
Mira
1926 (November) / Haendel,
WW ('Haus')
1075
Block printed / 17.5:16 cm / 4
Wien 1986/87 (exhib. and stock
cat.), p. 325, no. T 45
New York 1992/93, p. 220,
fig. 371; p. 321
380

339
Reifen (Hoop)
1929 (23 Oct. 1929) / Teltscher,
Ziegler
1103
Block printed / 38.5:32 cm / 11
Wien 1986/87 (exhib. and stock
cat.), p. 325, no. T 48; p. 342
St Petersburg 1991 (exhib. cat.),
p. 54, no. 88; p. 56, no. 117; p. 56,
fig. 117
New York 1992/93, p. 201,
fig. 326; p. 320
382

340
Carus
1929 (25 Apr. 1929) / Ziegler
1104
Block printed / 15:15.5 cm / 13
Wien 1986/87 (exhib. and stock
cat.), p. 325, no. T 47
St Petersburg 1991 (exhib. cat.),
p. 55, no. 103
New York 1992/93, p. 196, fig.
318; p. 197, fig. 321; p. 319
381

341
Guido
1929 (25 Apr. 1929) / Ziegler
1105
Block printed / 30.5:30.5 cm / 17
DKD LXV, 1930, p. 331 (length
of fabric)
Wien 1986/87 (exhib. and stock
cat.), p. 325, nos. T 46a, T 46b;
p. 342
St Petersburg 1991 (exhib. cat.),
p. 56, no. 113
New York 1992/93, p. 222, fig.
380; p. 322
385

342
Refrain
1929 (26 July 1929) / Sax
1142
Block printed / 10.5:11 cm / 13
Die Form, V, 1930, no. 10, p. 265
(length of fabric)
Wien 1986/87 (exhib. and stock
cat.), p. 326, no. T 49; p. 342
St Petersburg 1991 (exhib. cat.),
p. 54, no. 94
New York 1992/93, p. 220,
fig. 369; p. 321
6

343
Bacchus
1929 (26 Aug. 1929) / Sax
1143
Block printed / 32:27 cm / 14
Die Form, V, 1930, no. 10, p. 265
(length of fabric)
Völker 1984, p. 234, fig. 328;
p. 281
Wien 1986/87 (exhib. and stock
cat.), p. 326, no. T 50b; p. 341
St Petersburg 1991 (exhib. cat.),
p. 55, no. 105

344
Csikos
1920 (November) / Ziegler
1190
Block printed / 12:17.8 cm / 9
Wien 1986/87 (exhib. and stock
cat.), p. 168, nos. Z 82, Z 83;
p. 326, no. T 52; pp. 329, 342
St Petersburg 1991 (exhib. cat.),
p. 54, no. 87, fig. 87
New York 1992/93, p. 198,
figs. 322, 323; p. 319
252, 310

345
Sakatali
1929 (3 Jan. 1929) / Schenk
5001
Spray printed / repeats not
ascertainable / 1

346
Styx
1927 (January) / Posnanski
5077
Spray printed / 9:8 cm / 16

347
Bantu
1926 (19 Oct. 1926) / Vetter
5085
Spray printed / repeats not
ascertainable / 5

348
Speda
1928 (15 Dec. 1928) / Posnanski
5213
Spray printed / repeats not
ascertainable / 5
Wien 1986/87 (exhib. and stock
cat.), p. 342

349
Pompadour
1929/30
5270
Spray printed / repeats not
ascertainable / 1
Wien 1986/87 (exhib. and stock
cat.), p. 342

350
Dornier
1929 (19 Aug. 1929) / WW
('Haus'), Großmann
5284
Spray printed / repeats not
ascertainable / 5

351
Stanley
1929 (19 Aug. 1929) / Großmann
5286
Spray printed / repeats not
ascertainable / 8
Wien 1986/87 (exhib. and stock
cat.), p. 342

352
Zell
1928 (July)
14020 (archive no.)
Wien 1986/87 (exhib. and stock
cat.), p. 342

353
Lady
1928 (20 June 1928)
14465 (archive no.)
Spray printed / repeats not
ascertainable / 7
Wien 1986/87 (exhib. and stock
cat.), p. 342

354
Balaton
1928 (20 June 1928)
14467 (archive no.)
Spray printed / repeats not
ascertainable / 8
Wien 1986/87 (exhib. and stock
cat.), p. 342

355
Erlau
1929
15384 (archive no.)
Wien 1986/87 (exhib. and stock
cat.), p. 342

356
Gracilis
1931
Wien 1986/87 (exhib. and stock
cat.), p. 343

357
Isis
1912/17
Brocade/ repeats not ascertainable / 5

358
Poseidon
1912/17
Brocade/ 2:1.5 cm / 4
Trad. u. Exper. 1988, fig. 90,
p. 307
255

359
Rosita
1931
Wien 1986/87 (exhib. and stock
cat.), p. 343

360
Rubin (Ruby)
1931
Wien 1986/87 (exhib. and stock
cat.), p. 343

**Franz HUDEC
(1897–)**

361
Lenz (Spring)
1914/17 / Klinger, Ziegler,
Bujatti
400
Block printed / 7:3.8 cm / 6

**Karolina Lilly JACOBSEN
(1895–)**

362
Blütenstaub (Pollen)
1916/18 / Ziegler
589
Block printed / 9.7:9.9 cm / 11

363
Nebelstreifen (Streak of Mist)
1918 / Teltscher, Ziegler
590
Block printed / 9:9.8 cm / 3

364
Jugend (Youth)
1916/17 / Ziegler, Alpen-
ländische Druckfabrik
591
Block printed / 6.6:4.2 cm / 11

365
Zephir (Zephyr)
1916/17 / Ziegler
592
Block printed / 5.5:7.4 cm / 8

366
Milchstraße (Milky Way)
1916/17 / Blumenegg, Ziegler,
Teltscher, Neumann, Haendel
593
Block printed / 7.3:7.4 cm / 12
DW, April 1919, p. 19 (length of
fabric)

367
Frohsinn (Cheerfulness)
1916/18 / Ziegler
607, 607a
Block printed / 10:5.9 cm / 9

368
Festschmuck (Festive Decoration)
1918 / Neumann, Teltscher,
Ziegler
608
Block printed / 7.3:7.3 cm / 23
216

369
Sachsen (Saxony)
1918 / Ziegler, FAG
611
Block printed / 6:11.6 cm / 13

370
Seraphin (Seraph)
1918 / Ziegler
625
Block printed / 8.5:7.2 cm / 6

371
Roland
1918 / Ziegler, Alpenländische
Druckfabrik
627
Block printed / 10:7.2 cm / 3

372
Frühlingshimmel (Spring Sky)
1919 / Ziegler
682, 682a
Block printed / 13.5:14.9 cm / 8

373
Liebesgarten (Garden of Love)
1920/21 / Ziegler
721
Block printed / 71:90 cm

Hilda JESSER-SCHMID
(1894–   )

374
Titania
1912/17 / Ziegler
39
Block printed / 17:10 cm / 11
Völker 1984, p. 245, fig. 339;
p. 281
Trad. u. Exper. 1988, p. 74

375
Hallensee
1912/17 / Ziegler, Teltscher
67
Block printed / 17:22.6 cm / 9

376
Tylli
1912/17 / Ziegler
90
Block printed / 16.6:15 cm / 9

377
Gavotte
1912/19 / Ziegler
91
Block printed / 0.5:10 cm / 6

378
Schattenriß (Silhouette)
1912/19 / Ziegler, Teltscher
129
Block printed / 10:10 cm / 14

379
Eilido
1912/19 / Ziegler
183
Block printed / repeat height
not ascertainable:30 cm / 3

380
Bauerngarten (Country Garden)
1912/19 / Ziegler, Teltscher
218
Block printed / 30:30 cm / 8
DK XXIX, 1921, p. 240 (lampshade)
Wien 1923 (sales cat.), p. 9
(lampshade)
Tokyo 1989 (exhib. cat.), p. 351
178

381
Nelke (Pink, Carnation)
1912/19 / Ziegler
219
Block printed / 33.5:11 cm / 3

382
Lorbeer (Laurel)
1912/21 / Ziegler, Klinger,
Bujatti
220
Block printed / 7.5:7.5 cm / 3

383
Traumblume (Dream Flower)
1912/17
221
Block printed / 10:5 cm / 18

384
Zickzack (Zigzag)
1912/21 / Ziegler
552
Block printed / 10.7:5 cm / 9

385
Blumenspitze (Tip of a Flower)
1912/21 / Ziegler
614
Block printed / 20:14.5 cm / 8

386
Wiesenglocke (Meadow Bell)
1912/21 / Ziegler
618
Block printed / 29.5:14.5 cm / 9

387
Riedgras (Sedge)
1912/21 / Teltscher, Ziegler,
Neumann
623
Block printed / 38:14.2 cm / 7

388
Opium
1912/21 / Ziegler
681
Block printed / 20:22 cm / 9

389
Abruzzen (Abruzzi)
1919 / Neumann, Teltscher,
Ziegler
697
Block printed / 35:28.5 cm / 9

390
Sommerlust (Summer Joy)
1912/21 / Ziegler
715
Block printed / repeats not
ascertainable / 2

391
Abendröte (Sunset Glow)
1912/21 / Ziegler
737
Block printed / 18.7:7.5 cm / 2

392
Blumensockel (Floral Base)
1912/21 / Ziegler
747
Block printed / repeats not
ascertainable

393
Primula
1912/22 / Ziegler, Alpen-
ländische Druckfabrik
785
Block printed / 18.5:14.5 cm / 4

394
Segelstangen (Sail Yards)
1912/22 / Ziegler, Teltscher
786
Block printed / 45:30 cm / 4

395
Flockentanz (Dance of the Snow
Flakes)
1912/22 / Ziegler
787
Block printed / 10.1:10.2 cm / 15
229

Wilhelm JONASCH
(1892–   )

396
Cobenzl
1910/11 / WW, Ströbel
268
Block printed / repeat height
not ascertainable:11 cm / 4
TKI VI, 1913, pp. 242, 250 (length
of fabric)
ID XXVI, 1915, p. 181 (lampshade, curtain)
Eisler 1916, p. 108 (curtain, tablecloth)
Buxbaum 1986, p. 343

397
Hameau
1910/11
339
Block printed / 6.5:7 cm / 5
TKI VI, 1913, p. 242 (length of
fabric)
Fanelli 1976, fig. 618
129

398
Krieau (Kriau)
1910/11 / Ziegler
379
Block printed / repeat height
not ascertainable:46 cm / 1

DKD XXXI, 1912/13, p. 102 (corsage), p. 182 (curtain, upholstery
of a chair), p. 183 (curtain),
p. 185 (upholstery of a chair)
DI XIV, 1913, pl. 36 (upholstery)
ID XXVII,1916, p. 368 (lampshade, wallpaper, upholstery)
Eisler 1916, p. 97 (lampshade,
wallpaper, upholstery)
Kleiner 1927, p. 14 (upholstery)
Wien 1980 Kaffeehaus (exhib.
cat.), p. 106, nos. 227/1, 228;
p. 107, no. 227/2
Trad. u. Exper. 1988, p. 64
72, 73, 74

399
Vorgarten (Front Garden)
1910/11 / Ziegler
521
Block printed / 20.5:18.5 cm / 10
KKHW XV, 1912, p. 331 (upholstery of a chair), p. 332
(upholstery, curtain), p. 333
(upholstery of a chair, curtain),
p. 334 (curtain)
ID XXIII, 1912, p. 463 (curtain)
DK XX, 1912, p. 480 (curtain)
DI XIII, 1912, p. 58 (upholstery
of a chair), p. 64 (curtain), pl. 57
(upholstery of a chair, curtain)
DKD XXXI, 1912/13, p. 182
(upholstery of a chair, curtain),
p. 183 (curtain), p. 185 (upholstery of a chair)
Baroni/D'Auria 1981, p. 12
Neuwirth 1984, p. 137
95

400
Wienerwald (Vienna Woods)
1910/11 / Alpenländische
Druckfabrik, Albouts, Finkh &
Co, Ziegler
529
Block printed / 14.5:12.5 cm / 9
DKD XXXII, 1913, p. 366 (cushion)
TKI VII, 1914, p. 61 (length of
fabric)
281

Ludwig Heinrich JUNG-
NICKEL (1881–1965)

401
Hochwald (High Forest)
1910/11
341
Block printed / repeats not
ascertainable / 4
DKD XXXIV, 1914, p. 142 (wallpaper), p. 385 (lampshade)
DK XXIII, 1915, p. 239 (curtain,
lampshade)
Koch 1916, p. 55 (lampshade)
DKD XXXVIII, 1916, p. 217
(curtain, lampshade)
ID XXVIII, 1917, p. 242 (covering
of a cabinet)
Brussels 1927 (stock cat.), p. 383,
no. 448 (length of fabric)
Wichmann 1990 (stock cat.),
p. 112
24, 80

402
Nachtfalter (Night Moth)
1910/11 / Bremges & G.,
Albouts, Finkh & Co, Ziegler
430
Block printed / 34:29.5 cm / 9

403
Papageienwald (Parrot's Forest)
1910/11 / Ziegler, Teltscher,
Neumann
454
Block printed / 23.7 cm:repeat
width not ascertainable / 1
ID XXIV, 1913, p. 353 (wallpaper)
DKD XXXIV, 1914, p. 384
(upholstery of an armchair)
Koch 1916, p. 54 (cocktail dress)
DKD XXXVIII, 1916, p. 212
(upholstery, curtain)
DKD XLVI, 1921, p. 211 (upholstery of an armchair)
76

404
Urwald (Primeval Forest)
1910/11 / Ziegler
519
Block printed / repeats not
ascertainable / 1
DKD XXXII, 1913, p. 360 (length
of fabric)
ID XXVI, 1915, p. 465 (cushion)

Maria JUNGWIRTH
(1894–1968)

405
Komet (Comet)
1914/17 / Ziegler
45
Block printed / 10.5:10 cm / 4

406
Pilot
1914/17 / Ziegler, Blumenegg
112
Block printed / 13:14.7 cm / 9

407
Susanna
1914/17 / Ziegler
225
Block printed / 11.5:9.8 cm / 10
ID XXX, 1919, p. 96 (length of
fabric)

408
Gabriel
1914/17 / Ziegler
226
Block printed / 8:7.5 cm /6
265, 266

409
Nihilit
1914/17 / Ziegler, Ama
240
Block printed / 44:38 cm /10
DKD LXV, 1929/30, p. 420
(cushion)
Leipzig 1930 (exhib. cat.), p. 195
(cushion)

410
Schwertlilie (Iris)
1916/18 / Teltscher, Ziegler
554
Block printed / 8:10 cm / 4

411
Kreuzband (Cross-beam)
1919 / Ziegler
680
Block printed / 22.4:19 cm / 2
MBF XXVII, 1929, p. 415
(cushion)
219

KAESTNER

412
Kubin
1926 / Vogel
9695
Woven fabric / 11.3:15.5 cm / 2

413
Opal
1925 / Vogel
9698
Woven fabric / 27:15.6 cm / 5
Tokyo 1989 (exhib. cat.),
pp. 350f., no. 472

Gustav KALHAMMER
(1886–1919?)

414
Adria (Adriatic Sea)
1910/11 / Bremges & G.,
Albouts, Finkh & Co, Ziegler
23
Block printed / 5.5:5.5 cm / 1

415
Bukarest (Bucharest)
1910/11 / Alpenländische
Druckfabrik, Ziegler
261
Block printed / 7:7.5 cm / 1

416
Dornröschen (The Sleeping
Beauty)
1910/11 / Ziegler
281
Block printed / 8:8 cm / 1

417
Gloggnitz
1910/12 / Ziegler, Teltscher
324
Block printed / repeats not
ascertainable / 4

418
Kaisergarten (Imperial Garden)
1910/12
376
Block printed / 29.5:15.8 cm / 1
JDW 1915, p. 62 (lampshade,
upholstery)
Eisler 1916, p. 30 (lampshade,
upholstery)

419
Pepita
1910/12 / Albouts, Finkh & Co,
Ziegler
449, 449a
Block printed / 8:8 cm / 2

420
Schönau
1910/12 / Bremges & G.,
Albouts, Finkh & Co
486
Block printed / 7.5:7.8 cm / 2
DK XXIV, 1916, p. 330 (length of
fabric)
DBK in DA XXI, 1916/18, pl. 15
(upholstery)
130

421
Venedig (Venice)
1910/12 / Ziegler
526
Block printed / 12:8 cm / 1

422
Wachau
1910/12 / Ziegler
535
Block printed / 8:3.8 cm / 10

Melanie Leopoldina
KÖHLER-BROMAN
(1885–1960)

423
Geisha
1910/12 / Bremges & G.,
Albouts, Finkh & Co, Ziegler
314
Block printed / 60:24.5 cm / 1
ID XXV, 1914, p. 480 (lamp-
shade)
DKD XXXV, 1914/15, p. 88
(lampshade)
TKI VIII, 1915, p. 201 (length of
fabric)
Koch 1916, p. 149 (lampshade)
110

Erna KOPRIVA
(1894–   )

424
Herzblüten (Bleeding Heart)
1916/18
587
Block printed / 10:9.9 cm / 3

425
Ginefra
1928 (12 Apr. 1928) / Ziegler,
Teltscher
1024
Block printed / 46.5:30.5 cm / 7

426
Ernestine
1927 (August) / Kurz-Fisch
5194
Spray printed / repeat height
not ascertainable:41.5 cm / 9

427
Hiaz
1927 (August) / Kurz-Fisch,
Schenk
5195
Spray printed / repeats not
ascertainable / 7

428
Philipp
1927 (August) / Kurz-Fisch
5198
Spray printed / repeats not
ascertainable / 7
224

Valentine KOVACIC
(1895–   )

429
Schottland (Scotland)
1913/18 / Ziegler, Teltscher
139
Block printed / 24:22.8 cm / 13
Wichmann 1990 (stock cat.),
p. 122

430
Narew
1913/18 / Ziegler
232
Block printed / 18:21.5 cm / 11

431
Jamaika (Jamaica)
1913/18
243
Block printed / 18:11 cm / 1

432
Herbstwind (Autumn Wind)
1916/18
556
Block printed / 20.3:15 cm / 4

433
Anilin (Aniline)
1916/18 / Ziegler
570
Block printed / 18:29.5 cm / 5

434
Fischotter (Otter)
1916/18 / Ziegler, Teltscher
616
Block printed / 35:39 cm / 3

435
Harlem
1916/18 / Ziegler, Teltscher,
Haendel
619
Block printed / 31:15 cm / 16

436
Maskenzauber
1920/21 / Ziegler
740
Block printed / 64:87 cm / 1

Carl KRENEK
(1880–1948)

437
Blitz (Lightning)
1910/11 / Klinger, Bujatti
7
Block printed / 7.8 cm:repeat
width not ascertainable / 2
Neuwirth 1984, p. 139, cat.
no. 102
Wien 1985 WW (exhib. cat.),
no. 73
122

438
Diabolo
1910/11 / Ziegler
276
Block printed / 12:12 cm / 1

439
Granate (Grenade)
1910/11
323
Block printed / 8:16 cm / 4
Fanelli 1976, fig. 595
Neuwirth 1984, p. 138, cat. nos.
100, 101
Brussels 1987 (exhib. cat.), p. 54,
no. 9.18
121

440
Mosaik (Mosaic)
1910/12 / WW
414
Block printed / 9:5 cm / 1
120

441
Monte Carlo
1910/12 / Bremges & G.,
Albouts, Finkh & Co, Ziegler
422
Block printed / 30:25 cm / 1
Fanelli 1976, fig. 626
16

442
Raket(t)en (Rocket)
1910/12 / Ziegler
466
Block printed / repeats not
ascertainable / 1
10

443
Ischl
1912/17
Silk brocade/ 16:10.7 cm / 7

Rose KRENN
(1894–)

444
Backfisch (Teenage Girl)
1910/11
10
Block printed / repeat height
not ascertainable:49 cm / 9
Brussels 1927 (stock cat.),
pp. 386f., no. 455 (length of
fabric)

445
Liverpool
1910/12 / Ziegler
395
Block printed / 23:18.5 cm / 2

446
Ninon
1910/12 / Bremges & G.,
Albouts, Finkh & Co, Ziegler
434
Block printed / 45:22 cm / 1

447
Wasservogel (Water Bird)
1910/12 / Ziegler
533
Block printed / 22.5:43.5 cm / 10
TKI VII, 1914, p. 59 (length of
fabric)
Wien 1967 (exhib. cat.), p. 77,
no. 360
Florence 1978 (exhib. cat.),
p. 146, fig. 122; p. 162

448
Dronte
1912/17
Silk brocade / repeats not
ascertainable / 10

449
Freude (Joy)
1912/17
Silk brocade / repeats not
ascertainable / 8

450
Frühlingslied (Spring Song)
1912/17
Silk brocade / repeats not
ascertainable / 4

451
Oase (Oasis)
1912/17
Silk brocade / repeats not
ascertainable / 7

Ernst LICHTBLAU
(1883–1963)

452
Großvesir (Grand Vizier)
1916/18
635
Block printed / repeats not
ascertainable / 4
230

LIEPMANN

453
Bonn
1927 (July) / Müller's Erben,
Ama, Ziegler
5205
Spray printed / 36.5:32.7 cm / 7

Maria LIKARZ-STRAUSS
(1893–1971)

454
Basel (Basle)
1910/13

1
Block printed / repeats not
ascertainable / 1
ID XXV, 1914, p. 446 (upholstery
of a sofa)
DK XVII, 1914, pp. 470f. (upholstery)
DKD XXXIV, 1914, pp. 360f.
(upholstery of a sofa)
JDW 1915, p. 5 (upholstery of a
chair, curtain)
Eisler 1916, p. 57 (upholstery of a
chair, curtain)
Koch 1916, p. 30 (upholstery),
p. 31 (upholstery, curtain)
AeD XLVI, 1924, p. 55 (upholstery of a sofa)
Kleiner 1927, p. 31 (upholstery,
curtain)
Weiser 1930, p. 19 (upholstery of
a chair), p. 21 (upholstery of a
sofa)

455
Rosanna
1910/17 / Ziegler
169, 169a
Block printed / 15:31 cm / 11
Wien 1967 (exhib. cat.), p. 78,
no. 369
Florence 1978 (exhib. cat.),
p. 147, fig. 125; p. 162

456
Balkan (Balkans)
1910/13 / Ziegler, Bremges & G.,
Albouts, Finkh & Co
265
Block printed / 48:44 cm / 1

457
Spalato (Split)
1910/17 / Ziegler, Bremges & G.,
Albouts, Finkh & Co
480
Block printed / 50.5:48 cm / 1

458
Irland (*Irrland, Schottland*)
(Ireland)
1910/13 / Ziegler, Teltscher
491
Block printed / 48.5:30 cm / 13
Brussels 1927 (stock cat.), p. 386,
no. 454 (length of fabric)
Wien 1929 (exhib. cat.), p. 106
(length of fabric)
Wien 1967 (exhib. cat.), p. 77,
no. 361, fig. 51
Graz 1972 (exhib. cat.), p. 28,
no. 58, fig. 20
Lucerne 1974 (exhib. cat.),
no. 340
Florence 1978 (exhib. cat.),
p. 162, no. 123
Völker amk, p. 9
Völker in WKK 1983, no. 2,
p. 132, fig. 12
Kessler-Aurisch 1983, pp. 225,
230, 344, fig. 423
Völker 1984, p. 90, fig. 119;
p. 247
Venice 1984 (exhib. cat.), p. 294,
fig. 3
99, 100, 101, 102, 172, 251

459
Venusschuh (Venus's Shoe)
1910/17 / Ziegler
522
Block printed / 45.5:43.5 cm / 4

460
Laura
1919 / Ziegler
665
Block printed / repeat height
not ascertainable:6.3 cm / 10

461
Skorpion (Scorpion)
1919 / Teltscher, Ziegler
673
Block printed / 11:10 cm / 19
321

462
Sparta
1919 / Ziegler
674
Block printed / repeats not
ascertainable / 7

463
Nayade
1919 / Ziegler
675
Block printed / 22:22 cm / 6

464
Gardasee (Lake Garda)
1918 / Ziegler, Alpenländische
Druckfabrik
676
Block printed / 7.2:3.7 cm / 8

465
Narwal (Narwhal)
1919 / Ziegler
677
Block printed / 10:16 cm / 1

466
Mai (May)
1919 / Albouts, Finkh & Co
678
Block printed / 14.9:22 cm / 9

467
Lillith
1919 / Ziegler
679
Block printed / 22:22 cm / 9

468
Pfau (Peacock)
1920/21
726
Block printed / repeats not
ascertainable

469
Dubary
1920/22 / Ziegler
739
Block printed / repeats not
ascertainable / 7

470
Weltkugel (Globe)
1920/21 / Ziegler, K. G.
746
Block printed / repeats not
ascertainable

471
Streifen (Stripes)
1920/21 / Ziegler
748
Block printed / 21:17 cm,
pattern staggered / 8

472
Knabenkraut (Orchis)
1920/23 / Ziegler
749
Block printed / 18:22 cm,
pattern staggered / 8

473
Tamara
1920/21 / Ziegler
782
Block printed / 15.1:11.1 cm / 12
318

474
Treppe (Staircase)
1921 / Ziegler, Teltscher
784
Block printed / 1:10 cm / 9

475
Florestan
1921/22 / Ziegler
799
Block printed / 15:14 cm / 9

476
Nachthimmel (Night Sky)
1921/22 / Ziegler
804
Block printed / 10.5:30.5 cm / 7
362

477
Borneo
1920/21 / Ziegler
805
Block printed / 13:23.5 cm / 11
319

478
Robinson
1921/22 / Ziegler
806
Block printed / 15.9:23 cm / 10

479
Gräser (Grasses)
1922 / Neumann, Teltscher
809
Block printed / 12:12 cm / 9

480
Titus
1922 / Ziegler
810
Block printed / 26:23 cm / 12

481
Luzia
1922 (blocks produced 7 Oct.
1922) / Ziegler, Neumann
815
Block printed / 43.5:31.5 / 18

482
Morrer
1922 (blocks produced 25 Oct.
1922) / Ziegler, Neumann
817
Block printed / 43:46.5 cm / 5

483
Umbra (Umber)
1922 (blocks produced 29 Dec.
1922) / Ziegler
819
Block printed / repeats not
ascertainable / 15

484
Prolog (Prologue)
1922 / Ziegler
828
Block printed / 41:25.5 cm / 22

485
Fixstern (Fixed Star)
1923 (27 Mar. 1923) / Ziegler,
Teltscher, Neumann
829
Block printed / 15.3:16 cm / 13

486
Portepee (Sword Knot)
1923 (25 June 1923) / Ziegler,
Teltscher
837
Block printed / 12.8:15.8 cm / 11
238, 239, 240

487
Terzett (Trio)
1923 (25 Apr. 1923) / Ziegler,
Haendel, Teltscher
842
Block printed / 11.3:6.3 cm / 14
Wien 1967 (exhib. cat.), p. 83,
no. 421
Tokyo 1989 (exhib. cat.), p. 358,
no. 494

488
Ethik (Ethics)
1923 (5 May 1923) / Ziegler,
Teltscher, Clavel & Lindenmeyer
843
Block printed / 13:10.4 cm / 21
DKD LXI, 1928, I, p. 72 (length of
fabric)

489
Novelle (Short Novel)
1923 (blocks produced 11 June
1923) / Ziegler, Teltscher,
Neumann
847
Block printed / 2:3.7 cm /19

490
Kommers (Drinking Bout)
1923 (blocks produced 3 July
1923) / Ziegler
849
Block printed / 23.7:23.2 cm / 7

491
Gallus
1924 (blocks produced 16 Jan.
1925 and 2 May 1927) / Ziegler,
Haendel, Clavel & Lindenmeyer,
Rodauner Druckfabrik
856, 856a
Block printed / 18.9:23 cm / 15

492
Revue
1924 (blocks produced 9 Apr.

1924) / Ziegler
861
Block printed / 10.5:15 cm / 8

493
Phantast (Dreamer)
1924 / Ziegler
862
Block printed / 30:26 cm / 8

494
Vorwitz (Forwardness)
1924 / Haendel, Ziegler
863
Block printed / 9.5:15.2 cm / 9

495
Orakel (Oracle)
1924 / Ziegler
865
Block printed / 23.4:15.1 cm / 1

496
Stockrose (Rose Mallow)
1924 / Neumann, Ziegler,
Teltscher
870
Block printed / repeat height
not ascertainable:23.5 cm

497
Fidelio
1924 (blocks produced 1 July
1924) / Ziegler, Teltscher
871
Block printed / 28.5:31 cm / 13
ID XLV, 1934, p. 144 (curtain)
Wichmann 1990 (stock cat.),
p. 149 and jacket
360

498
Rebhuhn (Partridge)
1924 (blocks produced 30 Aug.
1924) / Ziegler, Teltscher
872
Block printed / 17:15 cm / 12

499
Verona
1924 (blocks produced 8 Oct.
1924) / Ziegler, Teltscher
874
Block printed / 42:45 cm / 12

500
Roma (Rome)
1924 (blocks produced 5 Nov.
1924) / Ziegler, Teltscher
881
Block printed / 6:10.1 cm / 17

501
Schönbrunn
1924
882
Block printed / 67:64.3 cm

502
Helena
1924/25 (blocks produced 18
Mar. 1925) / Ziegler
888
Block printed / 45:70 cm / 9

503
Brindisi
1925 (blocks produced 10 June
1925) / Ziegler
909
Block printed / repeat height
not ascertainable: 23 cm / 9
320

504
Ajax
1925
911
Block printed / repeat height
not ascertainable:15.5 cm

505
Uruguay
1925 / Ziegler
916
Block printed / 25.9:15 cm
11

506
Lhasa
1925 (blocks produced 28 July
1925) / Clavel & Lindenmeyer,
Ziegler, Teltscher
918
Block printed / 12.4:20 cm / 10
11, 248

507
Prater
1925 (blocks produced 30 June
1925) / Clavel & Lindenmeyer,
Ziegler
923
Block printed / 15:15.3 cm / 13
11

508
Morphium (Morphine)
1925 (blocks produced 11 Feb.
1926) / Ziegler, Teltscher
931
Block printed / 3:15 cm / 10

509
San Sebastian
1925 / Ziegler
936
Block printed / 40:23 cm

510
Andorra
1926 (July) / Ziegler, Teltscher
945
Block printed / 38:30.8 cm / 14

511
Ebro
1926 (July) /Ziegler, Teltscher
946
Block printed / 7.5:15.4 cm / 15
206, 207

512
Aare
1926 (August) / Ziegler,
Teltscher
951
Block printed / repeat height
not ascertainable:61 cm / 15

513
Ticino (Picino)
1926 (August) / Ziegler
955
Block printed / 7:6.1 cm / 10

514
Lugo (Lucca)
1927 (March) / Ziegler, Teltscher
961
Block printed / 15.7:19 cm / 11

515
Liliom
1927 / Ziegler
963
Block printed / 25:15.5 cm
358

516
Leda
1927 (March) / Ama, Ziegler
970
Block printed / 19:24 cm / 7

517
Amaro
1927 (August) / Ziegler
972
Block printed / 25.5:30.5 cm / 7

518
Florenz (Florence)
1927 (August) / Teltscher,
Ziegler
973
Block printed / 3.3:1 cm / 9

519
Fano
1927 (August) / Teltscher,
Ziegler
974
Block printed / 1:7.2 cm / 7

520
Mantua
1927 (August) / Teltscher,
Ziegler
975
Block printed / 1:1 cm / 10
Munich 1986/87 (exhib. cat.),
p. 608

521
Margerith
1927 (October) / Ziegler
977
Block printed / 32:30.5 cm / 11

522
Lindbergh
1927 (October) / Ziegler,
Neumann
986
Block printed / 30.5:30.5 cm / 14
Wien 1928 (sales cat.), p. 303
(cushion)

523
Marmon
1927 (October) / Ziegler
987
Block printed / 15:10.5 cm / 19

524
Muratti
1927 (November) / Ziegler,
Teltscher
988
Block printed / repeat height
not ascertainable:42 cm / 8

525
Martin
1927 (November) / Ziegler
992
Block printed / repeats not
ascertainable / 8
357

526
Montblanc
1928 (January) / Teltscher,
Ziegler
995
Block printed / 16.8:7.7 cm / 14

527
Menorea
1928 (January) / Teltscher, FAG
998
Block printed / 31:31 cm / 14

528
Baker
1928 (4 Apr. 1928) / Ziegler
999
Block printed / 32.5:25.5 cm / 15

529
Bridge
1928 (16 Mar. 1928) / Ziegler
1001
Block printed / 26.5:30 cm / 23
359

530
Marizza (without grid)
1927 (December) / Teltscher,
Ziegler
1005
Block printed / 30:32.5 cm / 14

531
Bozen
1928 (April) / Ziegler, Teltscher
1016
Block printed / 34.5:31.5 cm / 13
DKD LXVI, 1930, p. 308 (length
of fabric)
DKD LXVIII, 1931, p. 56
(cushion)
Leipzig 1930 (exhib. cat.), p. 155
(cushion)
273, 361

532
Stabilo
1928 (5 June 1928)
1021 (1022)
Spray printed / 30.5:31 cm,
pattern staggered / 13

533
Nelson
1928 (April) / Ziegler, Teltscher
1026
Block printed / 34:15.3 cm / 14

534
Evian
1928 (July) / Ziegler
1030
Block printed / 9:8 cm / 5

535
Romulus
1928 (July) / Ziegler, Teltscher
1037
Block printed / repeat height
not ascertainable:29.5 cm / 13
SSR XXIX, 1928/29, pp. 12f.
(cushion)
Leipzig 1930 (exhib. cat.), p. 155
(cushion), p. 263 (length of
fabric)
DKD LXVI, 1930 II, p. 301
(length of fabric)
MBF XXIX, 1930, pp. 79, 95
(upholstery and mattress cover)
DKD LXVIII, 1931, p. 56 (neck
cushion)
MBF XXX, 1931, p. 44 (cushion)
Neuwirth 1981, p. 328, fig. 248
Völker 1984, p. 220, fig. XXVIII;
p. 245, fig. 339; pp. 269, 281
Wien 1985 (exhib. cat.), p. 398,
no. 13/11/46
Trad. u. Exper. 1988, p. 74
New York 1992/93, p. 19
364

536
Gallia
1928 (July) / Ziegler
1041
Block printed / 30.5:35 cm / 8
DKD LXVI, 1930, p. 308 (length
of fabric)

537
Mauritius
1928 (24 Sep. 1928) / Ziegler,
FAG
1056
Block printed / 41.5:32 cm / 16

538
Mombasa
1928 (25 Sep. 1928) / Ziegler,
Teltscher
1059
Block printed / 34:30.5 cm / 8
354

539
Bermuda
1928 (19 Oct. 1928) / Ziegler,
Teltscher
1069
Block printed / 12:15.5 cm / 12
322

540
Azoren (Azores)
1928 (19 Oct. 1928) / Ziegler, Sax
1071
Block printed / 12.8:15.5 cm / 14

541
Carlton
1928 (29 Oct. 1928) / Ziegler
1074
Block printed / repeat width 10
cm / 11

SSR XXXI, 1930/31, p. 129
(cushion)
DKD LXVII, 1930/31, p. 207
(cushion)
ID XLII, 1931, pp. 33f. (cushion)

542
Meleda
1928
1076
Spray printed / repeat height
not ascertainable:11 cm / 5

543
Royal
1928 (6 Nov. 1928) / Ziegler
1079
Block printed / 30.3:10 cm / 15
DKD LXVII, 1930/31, p. 207
(cushion)
SSR XXXI, 1930/31, p. 129
(cushion)
ID XLII, 1931, p. 33 (cushion)

544
Fritz
1928 (8 Nov. 1928) / Ziegler
1080
Block printed / repeat width 30
cm / 11

545
Marelli
1929 (July) / Müller's Erben,
Teltscher, Neumann, Sax
1090
Block printed / 41.5:31 cm / 7
355

546
Whisky
1929 (9 Jan. 1929) / Teltscher
1091
Block printed / 63:79 cm / 16
MBF XXIX, 1930, pp. 93f. (upholstery of a chair, covering of a
music case)
Leipzig 1930 (exhib. cat.),
pp. 261f. (upholstery of a chair,
covering of a music case and of a
music cabinet)
Weiser 1930, p. 55 (upholstery of
a chair, covering of a music
cabinet), p. 58 (upholstery of a
chair, covering of a music case
and of a music cabinet)
356

547
Sining
1929 (22 Jan. 1929) / Ziegler
1092
Block printed / 9:18.2 cm / 10

548
Yokohama
1929 (28 Jan. 1929) / Ziegler
1094
Block printed / 15.5:15.5 cm / 16

549
Alzette
1929 (15 Mar. 1929) / Teltscher,
Ziegler
1099
Block printed / 32:30.5 cm / 16

550
Korinth (Corinth)
1929 (20 Mar. 1929) / Ziegler
1100
Block printed / 39.5:30.5 cm / 14

551
Apistin(o)
1929 (23 Apr. 1929) / Ziegler,
Teltscher
1102
Block printed / 30.5:30.5 cm / 16

552
Isabella
1929 (6 May 1929) / Teltscher,
Ziegler
1110
Block printed / 43:31.5 cm / 9

553
Kassandra (Cassandra)
1929 (6 May 1929) / Teltscher,
Ziegler
1113
Block printed / 40:31.5 cm / 12
MBF XXX, 1931, p. 494 (up-
holstery)

554
Nephrit (Nephrite)
1929 (July) / Ziegler
1115
Block printed / 35:32.2 cm / 12

555
Asunta
1929 (May) / Ziegler, Teltscher
1116
Block printed / 45:37.5 cm / 14

556
Portici
1929 (May) / Teltscher,
Dresdner Druckfabrik, Ama
1117
Block printed / 40.5:31.5 cm / 10

557
Weekend
1929 (13 May 1929) / Teltscher
1119
Block printed / 30:28.5 cm / 9

558
Nyitra
1929 (15 May 1929) / Teltscher
1121
Block printed / 41.5:31.5 cm / 9

559
Hockey
1929 (19 June 1929) / Ziegler
1124
Block printed / 46:50 cm / 7

560
Indus
1929 (25 June 1929) / Teltscher,
Ziegler
1125
Block printed / repeats not
ascertainable / 7

561
Ramona
1929 (25 June 1929) / Ziegler

1126
Block printed / 45:45 cm / 7
Völker 1984, p. 232, fig. 326;
p. 278

562
Girl
1929 (26 July 1929) / Ziegler
1140
Block printed / 40:32 cm / 7

563
Bora
1929 (26 Oct. 1929) / Sax, Ama
1150
Block printed / 39:39 cm / 11
MBF XXX, 1931, p. 511 (upholstery)

564
Samun
1929 (26 Oct. 1929) / Ama,
Ziegler, FAG
1151
Block printed / 38:33.4 cm / 12

565
Panath
1929 (28 Oct. 1929) / Ama,
Teltscher
1156
Block printed / 38.3:64.7 cm / 11

566
Ali
1929 (5 Nov. 1929) / Ama, FAG
1158
Block printed / 46.5:32 cm / 17
324

567
Ottilie
1929 (7 Nov. 1929) / Ama,
Teltscher
1159
Block printed / 31:30 cm / 13

568
Adonis
1929 (6 Nov. 1929) / Sax
1160
Block printed / 34:32 cm / 19
323

569
Timur (Tamerlane)
1929 (7 Nov. 1929) / Ziegler
1161
Block printed / 32:32 cm / 19

570
Paleika
1929 (2 Nov. 1929) / Ama, FAG,
Bruggmann
1162
Block printed / 38:31 cm / 13
DSH XXXV, no. 6, 1931/32,
pp. 192f. (curtain)
ID XLV, 1934, p. 103 (curtain,
bedspread)

571
Vanity
1929 (December) / Ama, Teltscher
1164
Block printed / 32:32 cm / 15

572
Fatima
1929 (December) / Sax
1165
Block printed / 16:16 cm / 10

573
Radio
1930 (January) / Ziegler
1166
Block printed / 32:32 cm / 14
8

574
Fiori
1930 (January) / Ama, Teltscher,
Ziegler
1169
Block printed / 42:32 cm / 11

575
Apollonia
1930 (January) / Ama, Ziegler
1170
Block printed / 32:30.5 cm / 9

576
Onix (Onyx)
1930 (February) / Ama, Ziegler
1173
Block printed / 9.6:10.6 cm / 12
363

577
Magig
1930 (January) / Ziegler
1174
Block printed / 38:32 cm / 10

578
Melodram (Melodrama)
1930 (February) / Ama, Teltscher, Ziegler
1176
Block printed / 32:34 cm / 7

579
Tamaris
1930 (October) / FAG
1178
Block printed / 38.5:30.7 cm / 15

580
Delos
1930 (October) / Ama, Clavel &
Lindenmeyer
1179
Block printed / 45:32.5 cm / 11

581
Kayala
1930 (October) / Ama, Teltscher,
Ziegler
1180
Block printed / 31:38 cm / 10
317

582
Sandy
1930 (October) / Clavel &
Lindenmeyer
1181
Block printed / 18:14 cm / 10

583
Florio
1930 (November) / FAG
1183
Block printed / 38:37 cm / 9

584
Cyma
1930 (November) / FAG
1184
Block printed / 33 cm:repeat
width not ascertainable / 13

585
Aras
1930 (November) / Köchlin &
Baumgartner, Lörrach, WW
('Haus')
1186
Block printed / 32:32 cm / 6

586
Fayal
1930 (November) / FAG
1188
Block printed / 12.4:6.4 cm / 14

587
Aulus
1930 (December) / Clavel &
Lindenmeyer
1191
Block printed / 30 cm:repeat
width not ascertainable / 9

588
Sibu
1930 (November) / FAG
1196
Block printed / 30:30.5 cm / 10

589
Panay
1930 (November) / Ziegler,
Clavel & Lindenmeyer
1197
Block printed / 33.5:37 cm / 10

590
Waikiki
1930 (December) / FAG
1198
Block printed / 32:32 cm / 14

591
Akita
1930 (November) / Clavel &
Lindenmeyer
1199
Block printed / 31:40.5 cm / 11

592
Mungo
1930 (December) / Clavel &
Lindenmeyer
1200
Block printed / 16:16 cm / 11
Völker in WKK, 1984, no. 1,
p. 50, fig. 16

593
Rana
1930 (December) / Lörrach
1204
Block printed / 40:40 cm / 8

594
Nepal
1931 (January) / Lörrach, FAG
1205
Block printed / 30:63 cm / 12

595
Ambrass
1930 (December) / Lörrach, WW
('Haus')
1206
Block printed / 40.5 cm:repeat
width not ascertainable / 8

596
Page
1928 / Haus, Fritsch & Sohn
5001
Spray printed / repeats not
ascertainable / 9

597
Minsk
1928 / Posnanski
5006
Spray printed / repeats not
ascertainable / 1

598
Hall
1928 / Posnanski
5007
Spray printed / repeats not
ascertainable / 1

599
Lakme
1927 (2 May 1927) / Posnanski
5037
Spray printed / 12:25 cm / 11

600
Lissy
1927 (January) / Posnanski,
Großmann, Wasservogel
5041
Spray printed / 11:12.8 cm / 19

601
Luther
1927 (November) / Posnanski
5044
Spray printed / repeat height
not ascertainable:24 cm / 5
353

602
Mozart
1928 (21 July 1928) / Posnanski
5047
Spray printed / repeats not
ascertainable / 7

603
Nussdorf
1928 (16 Aug. 1928) / Posnanski
5049
Spray printed / 38.5:10.5 cm / 9

604
Maorie
1928 (March) / Vetter
5129
Spray printed / repeats not
ascertainable

605
Meledek
1927 (2 Feb. 1927)
5130
Spray printed / 20 cm:repeat
width not ascertainable / 3

606
Oran
1927 (July) / Vetter
265, 5135
Block printed and spray
printed / 89:64 cm / 6

607
Rummy
1928 (March) / Vetter
5139
Spray printed / 23:24 cm /6

608
Sommer (Summer)
1928 (February) / Vetter
5141
Spray printed / repeats not
ascertainable / 9

609
Ziermücke
1928 (February) / Vetter
5146
Spray printed / 40:34.2 cm / 7

610
Levante (Levant)
1927 (16 Mar. 1927) / Schenk
5160
Spray printed / repeat height
not ascertainable:22.8 cm / 6

611
Rengo
1927 (September) / Vetter,
Schenk, Hämmerle & Rhoner
5176
Spray printed / 36:44 cm / 7

612
Vielblatt (Multifoil)
1928 (22 Mar. 1928) / Schenk
5189
Spray printed / 10:10 cm / 10

613
Wolkenkratzer (Skyscraper)
1927 (March) / Schenk
5190
Spray printed / repeats not
ascertainable / 10

614
Lima
1926 (November) / Kurz-Fisch
5196
Spray printed / 31:27.4 cm / 4

615
Passo
1927 (September) / Denk
5202
Spray printed / repeats not
ascertainable / 12

616
Santos
1927 (September) / Denk

5203
Spray printed / repeats not
ascertainable / 3

617
Winkel (Angle)
1927 (9 Apr. 1927) / Denk,
Fritsch, Friedjung & Schmedh
5102
Spray printed / repeats not
ascertainable / 10
352

618
Maskat
1927 (July) / WW ('Haus')
Müller's Erben
5208
Spray printed / repeats not
ascertainable

619
Morris
1927 (October) / WW ('Haus'),
Müller's Erben
5210
Spray printed / 16:16 cm / 10

620
Ginzano (*Cinzano*)
1928 (14 Nov. 1928) / Vetter
5214
Spray printed / repeats not
ascertainable / 7

621
Frascati
1928 (17 Nov. 1928) / Vetter
5216
Spray printed / repeats not
ascertainable / 9

622
Ostende
1929 / Karstadt
5219
Spray printed / repeats not
ascertainable

623
Ava
1929 (28 Mar. 1928) / Posnanski
5233
Spray printed / repeats not
ascertainable / 6

624
Tua
1929 (28 Mar. 1928) / Posnanski
5234
Spray printed / repeats not
ascertainable / 7

625
Cinta
1929 (26 Mar. 1929) / Posnanski
5235
Spray printed / repeats not
ascertainable / 6

626
Oporto
1929 (26 Mar. 1929) / Posnanski
5236
Spray printed / repeats not
ascertainable / 6

627
Sirene (Siren)
1929 (31 May 1929) / Schenk
5243
Spray printed / repeats not
ascertainable / 7

628
Bluefox
1929 (24 June 1929) / Schenk
5245
Spray printed / repeats not
ascertainable / 9

629
Arlberg
1927 / Vogel
9685
Woven fabric / repeat height not
ascertainable:31 cm / 8

630
Maloja
1927 / Vogel
0128
Woven fabric / repeats not
ascertainable / 4

631
Loja
1927 (October) / Vogel
0140
Woven fabric / repeat height not
ascertainable:22 cm / 3

632
Ariano
1930 (January) / Vogel
0418
Woven fabric / 23:30 cm / 3

633
Arbino
1933 (January) / Vogel
0439
Woven fabric / repeat height not
ascertainable:29.5 cm / 3

634
Sabino
1927 / Vogel
0476
Woven fabric / repeats not
ascertainable / 1

635
Escali
1927 / Vogel
0666
Woven fabric / 31.5 cm:repeat
width not ascertainable / 3

636
Maharadscha (Maharaja)
1925 / Backhausen
10040 (archive no.)
Woven fabric / repeat height
80 cm, width of weave 135 cm / 1
Wien 1967 (exhib. cat.), p. 78,
no. 367, fig. 50
Wien 1980 NW (exhib. cat.),
p. 84, no. 92, fig. 92
Hansen 1984, p. 149
Schweiger 1984, p. 222, fig. top
right
204

637
Ragaz
1926 (August)
10577 (archive no.)
Block printed / repeats not
ascertainable / 7

638
Marius
1925
11248 (archive no.)

639
Mercedes
1925
11248 (archive no.)

640
Berna
1925
11249 (archive no.)
Woven fabric / repeats not
ascertainable

641
Tami
1927 (4 Jan. 1927) / Giger
12230 (archive no.)
Woven fabric / 11:17.5 cm / 3

642
Habana (Havana)
1927 (4 Jan. 1927) / Giger
12292 (archive no.)
Woven fabric / 10:17 cm / 3

643
Leopold
1927 (July) / Vogel
12764 (archive no.)
Woven fabric / repeat width
25 cm / 3

644
Castello (Castle)
1927 (September) / Giger
12867 (archive no.)
Woven fabric / repeats not
ascertainable / 1

645
Halifax
1927 (September) / Giger
12868 (archive no.)
Woven fabric / repeat width
21.6 cm (stripes) and 18.9:23 cm
(diamond) / 4

646
Flandern (Flanders)
1927 (September) / Giger
12869 (archive no.)
Woven fabric / repeat width
19 cm (stripes) and 17.5:17.5 cm
(square) / 4

647
Molia
1927
13265 (archive no.)

648
Fabeltier (Fabulous Creature)
1929
14921/19 (archive no.)
Block printed / repeats not
ascertainable / 7

649
Südfrucht (Tropical Fruit)
7479/90119 (archive no.)

650
Grönland (Greenland)
1928/30
7701 (archive no.)

651
Lipiti
1927/29
Colour proof only

652
Magnus
1912/13
Block printed / repeats not
ascertainable / 7

653
Raps
1927/29
Colour proof only

654
Romana
1912/23
Block printed / repeats not
ascertainable / 5

655
Tamia
1927 (January) / Thanel, Stern-
berg
Woven fabric / repeat width
20 cm / 4

Friederike (Fritzi) LÖW-LAZAR (1891–1975)

656
Alland (Baden, Vöslau)
1910/17 / Bremges & G.,
Albouts, Finkh & Co, Teltscher
14
Block printed / 1.5:2.8 cm / 7
218

657
Vogelweide (Aviary)
1910/17 / Teltscher, Ziegler
48
Block printed / 36:43 cm / 11
Tokyo 1989 (exhib. cat.), p. 351
285

658
Vorgarten (Front Garden)
1910/17
48
Block printed / repeats not
ascertainable

659
Klein Zaches (*Klein Zack*)
1910/17
50
Block printed / 13:10.3 cm / 5
21

660
Himmelschlüssel (Primrose)
1910/17
51
Block printed / repeat height
not ascertainable:7.6 cm / 2

661
Amanda
1910/17 / Bujatti, WW, Ziegler
52
Block printed / 10:7.7 cm / 2
Völker in WKK 1983, p. 135,
fig. 16
Völker 1984, p. 104, fig. 141;
p. 162, fig. 228; pp. 276, 278
Varnedoe 1986, p. 103

662
Glacis
1910/17
53
Block printed / 10.5:10.5 cm / 3

663
Osiris
1910/17 / Bujatti, Ziegler
58
Block printed / 10:10 cm / 9
199

664
Weingartl (Vineyard)
1910/17 / Klinger, Bujatti,
Blumenegg
60, 60a
Block printed / 10:4.7 cm / 4

665
Ähre (Ear of Corn)
1910/17 / Ziegler
61
Block printed / 15:23 cm / 9

666
Sommerblume (Summer Flower)
1910/16 / Ziegler
63
Block printed / 60:92.5 cm / 9
DW, 1917, no. 12, p. 19 (house
dress)

667
Zarte Bänder
1910/17 / Ziegler
73
Block printed / 2.5:5 cm / 7

668
Ehrenpreis (Speedwell)
1910/17 / Bujatti
74, 74a
Block printed / 2.7:2.7 cm / 6

669
Vorfrühling (Early Spring)
1910/17 / Ziegler
75
Block printed / 7.5:5 cm / 7

670
Abisag
1910/17 / Ziegler
89
Block printed / 27:30.5 cm / 9

671
Neckar
1910/17 / Ziegler, Teltscher
103
Block printed / 8:7.5 cm / 7

672
Zuidersee
1910/17 / Ziegler
165
Block printed / 43.2:30 cm / 1

673
Rappelkopf (Hothead)
1910/17 / Bujatti
194
Block printed / 7.5:5 cm / 4

674
Pamina
1910/17 / Bujatti, Ziegler
195
Block printed / 6:10 cm / 7

675
Treuherz (True Heart)
1910/18 / Ziegler
201
Block printed / 10:10 cm / 2

676
Zerbinetta
1910/18 / Ziegler
206
Block printed / 10.6:9.9 cm / 5

677
Adventstern (Advent Star)
1910/18 / Ziegler
207
Block printed / 6:5.5 cm / 4

678
Freimaurer (Freemason)
1910/18 / Ziegler
208
Block printed / 5:4.2 cm / 5

679
Libelle (Dragonfly)
1910/18 / Bujatti
209
Block printed / 6.5:5 cm / 5

680
Kongreß (Congress)
1910/1918 / Ziegler
235
Block printed / 5:7.5 cm / 2

681
Sonnenglanz (Splendour)
1910/18 / Ziegler
238
Block printed / 9:4 cm / 5

682
Portorose
1910/18 / Ziegler
241
Block printed / 4.5:7.5 cm / 2

683
Birma
1910/19 / Ziegler, FAG
244
Block printed / 8.5:6 cm / 7

684
Kassiopäa (Cassiopeia)
1910/19 / Ziegler
362
Block printed / 10:10 cm / 17
DKD XLVI, 1921, p. 151 (lampshade)

685
Kaktus (Cactus)
1910/18
383
Block printed / 21.5:19.8 cm / 14

686
Kornblume (Cornflower)
1910/19 / Klinger, Ziegler,
Bujatti
385
Block printed / 3.7:1.8 cm / 6

687
Limanova
1910/15 / Teltscher, Haendel,
Ziegler
388
Block printed / 11:12.8 cm / 6
Sekler 1985, p. 130, fig. 162
Paris 1986 (exhib. cat.), p. 187

688
Lohengrin
1910/16 / Ziegler
399
Block printed / 8.5:10.5 cm / 1

689
Millesfleurs (Millfleur)
1910/17
418
Block printed / 3.5:2.2 cm / 5
DK XXIV, January 1926, p. 128
(length of fabric)

690
Quodlibet
1910/17 / Bujatti, Teltscher
460
Block printed / 30 cm:repeat
width not ascertainable / 4

691
Torpedo
1910/15 / Neumann, Albouts,
Finkh & Co, Ziegler, Teltscher
503, 503a
Block printed / 37.5:30 cm / 19

692
Windling
1910/18 / Teltscher, Ziegler,
Neumann
577
Block printed / 4.2:4.2 cm / 9

693
Blütenflocken
1910/18 / Ziegler
586
Block printed / 5:5 cm / 11

694
Wadin
1910/19 / Ziegler, Neumann
664
Block printed / 2.5:2.2 cm / 9

695
Winde (Bindweed)
1910/17
Block printed / repeats not
ascertainable / 1

**Grete LUZATTO
(1898–   )**

696
Rosmarin (Rosemary)
1916/17 / Ziegler, Blumenegg
603, 603a
Block printed / 13:9.8 cm / 10

697
Tunnel
1916/17 / Neunkirchner Druckfabrik, Ziegler
606, 606a, 606b
Block printed / 9:9.7 cm / 14

**Josef MANFREDA
(1890–1967)**

698
Königskerze (Mullein)
1910/12 / WW, Teltscher
386
Block printed / repeats not
ascertainable / 1
TKI VIII, 1915, p. 198 (length of
fabric)

Wilhelm MARTENS

699
Felsenhuhn (Stone Grouse)
1910/12 / WW, Ziegler, Neunkirchner Druckfabrik
312
Block printed / repeat height
not ascertainable:25 cm / 3

700
Holztaube (Wood Pigeon)
1910/12 / WW, Teltscher
347
Block printed / repeats not
ascertainable / 2

701
Kranich (Crane)
1910/12 / Bremges & G.,
Albouts, Finkh & Co
373
Block printed / 5.5:10.5 cm / 3
TKI VII, 1914, p. 55 (length of
fabric)

702
Kranichgeier (Secretary Bird)
1910/12 / Bremges & G.,
Albouts, Finkh & Co, Ziegler
374
Block printed / 8.6:7.1 cm / 3
127

703
Lama
1910/12 / WW, Teltscher
402
Block printed / 15:9.5 cm / 1
TKI VII, 1914, p. 55 (length of
fabric)

**Gabriele Maria MÖSCHL-
LAGUS (1887–   )**

704
Steppe
1916/18
574
Hand painted / repeats not
ascertainable / 1

705
Schiene(n) (Rail)
1916/18
575
Hand painted / repeats not
ascertainable / 1

706
Küste (Coast)
1920/21
775
Hand painted / repeats not
ascertainable / 9

707
Theiss
1920/21
776
Hand painted / repeats not
ascertainable / 7

708
Walpurga
1920/21
777
Hand painted / repeats not
ascertainable / 9

709
Saturn
1920/21
778
Hand painted / repeats not
ascertainable / 6

710
Markus
1920/21
779
Hand painted / repeats not
ascertainable / 5

711
Bonifaz
1920/21
788
Hand painted / repeats not
ascertainable / 1

712
Julia
1921/22
789
Hand painted / repeats not
ascertainable / 2

713
Angela
1920/21
790/3
Hand painted / repeats not
ascertainable / 1

714
Martina
1920/21
791
Hand painted / repeats not
ascertainable / 1

715
Alarich
1920/21
791/5
Hand painted / repeats not
ascertainable / 1

716
Valentin
1920/21
793
Hand painted / repeats not
ascertainable / 1

717
Florian
1921/22
794/7
Hand painted / repeats not
ascertainable / 1

**Koloman (Kolo) MOSER
(1868–1918)**

718
Bergfalter (Mountain Butterfly)
1910/11
5
Block printed / 10:7.3 cm / 5
Quelle 1901, p. 10 (fabric design)
Fanelli 1976, fig. 214
Völker 1984, p. 23, fig. 20; p. 271
50, 51

719
Baummarder (Pine Marten)
1910/11
6
Block printed / 10:8.3 cm / 7
Fanelli 1976, fig. 215
297

720
Bachstelze (Wagtail)
1910/11
11
Block printed / repeat height
not ascertainable:4 cm / 2
Quelle 1901, p. 8 (fabric design)
Fanelli 1976, fig. 216

721
Baumfalke (Hobby [bird])
1910/11
12
Block printed / 2:3 cm / 3
Quelle 1901, p. 5 (fabric design)
Fanelli 1976, fig. 607
103

722
Amsel (Blackbird)
1910/1911 / WW
32
Block printed / 8.6:9 cm / 4
48, 49

MÜLLNER

723
Starling (Troupial)
1910/18 / Teltscher
173
Block printed / 11:10 cm / 9

724
Kitty
1910/18 / Ziegler
200, 200a
Block printed / 20:7.4 cm / 2

725
Ellen Petz
1910/18 / Ziegler, Neumann,
Teltscher
214
Block printed / 4.5:2.5 cm / 8

726
Ebenholz (Ebony)
1910/18 / Ziegler
215
Block printed / 12:14.7 cm / 5

Arnold NECHANSKY
(1888–1938)

727
Blumenkorb (Flower Basket)
1910/11
260
Block printed / repeats not
ascertainable / 1

728
Pompeji (Pompeii)
1910/11 / WW, Ziegler
453
Block printed / 40:38 cm / 3
TKI VII, 1914, p. 53 (length of
fabric)
Brussels 1927 (stock cat.), p. 384,
no. 449 (length of fabric)
MBF XXVI, 1927, p. 119
(curtain)
26

729
Toska (Tosca)
1910/11 / Ziegler, Bujatti
514
Block printed / 45:43 cm / 1

730
Kairo (Cairo)
1912/17
Silk brocade / repeats not
ascertainable / 1

B. OBERMANN

731
Ceylon
1910/12 / WW, Ziegler,
Neunkirchner Druckfabrik
271
Block printed / repeats not
ascertainable / 1

Erna PAMBERGER

732
Kursk
1927 (August) / Kurz-Fisch
5197
Spray printed / repeats not
ascertainable / 4

733
Zaglul
1927 (August) / Kur-Fisch
5199
Spray printed / repeats not
ascertainable / 14

Leopold PARADEISER
(1890–   )

734
Jupiter
1911/13
359
Block printed / 14.4:7.4cm / 1

735
Zeus
1911/13 / Ziegler
544
Block printed / 15.4:7.8 cm / 1

736
Adelgunde
1920/21 / Ziegler
743
Block printed / repeats not
ascertainable / 9

Dagobert PECHE
(1887–1923)

737
Blumenstrauß (Bunch of Flowers)
1911/12 / Ziegler, Teltscher
2
Block printed / repeats not
ascertainable / 2

738
Blumenhorn
1911/12 / Ziegler
8
Block printed / 18.3:15.5 cm / 11
DI XIV, 1913, pl. 70 (lampshade),
pl. 119 (wallpaper)
DKD XXXII, 1913, p. 373 (wall-
paper), p. 374 (length of fabric)
TKI VI, 1913, p. 464 (wallpaper)
TKI VII, 1914, p. 44 (cushion)
DA XXI, 1916/18, p. 143 (cushion)
ID XXIX, 1918, p. 29 (cushion)
DA XXIV, 1921/22, p. 95 (wall-
paper)
Fanelli 1976, fig. 633

739
Blattwinde
1911/13 / Ziegler
15
Block printed / 15:15 cm / 10
244

740
Blütenzweig (Flower Spray)
1911/13 / Bremges & G.,
Albouts, Finkh & Co, Ziegler
16, 16a
Block printed / 15:15 cm / 12

741
Amur (Amor)
1911/13 / Ziegler, Teltscher
34
Block printed / 22.3:20.3 cm / 8
Pichler 1992 (stock cat.), p. 106,
no. 15

742
Velden
1911/13 / Ziegler
35
Block printed / 3:3 cm / 1

743
Vase
1911/13 / Ziegler
37
Block printed / 15:7.5 cm / 3

744
Dilon (Dillon, Frass, Trass)
1911/13 / Ziegler, Klinger,
Alpenländische Druckfabrik,
Teltscher
38
Block printed / 1.7:4.8 cm / 3

745
Möven (Sea Gulls)
1911/13 / Ziegler, Teltscher,
Ama
40
Block printed / 13:22 cm / 14
22

746
Palme (Palm)
1911/13 / Ziegler
41
Block printed / 15:15 cm / 15

747
Rosengarten (Rose Garden)
1911/13 / Ziegler,
Alpenländische Druckfabrik
43
Block printed / 68:31.5 cm / 6
DKD XXXIV, 1914, p. 218 (length
of fabric)
DK XXIII, 1915, p. 232 (curtain,
upholstery of a chair), p. 235
(curtain, upholstery of a chair,
lampshade)
JDW 1915, p. 62 (upholstery)
DK XXIV, 1916, p. 406 (curtain)
DKD XXXVIII, 1916, p. 205
(curtain, upholstery of a chair,
lampshade)
ID XXVII, 1916, p. 179 (curtain,
upholstery of a chair, lampshade)
ID XXVIII, 1917, p. 164 (curtain,
upholstery of a chair)
AeD XLV, 1924, p. 63 (curtain,
upholstery of a chair, lampshade)
Kleiner 1927, p. 19 (curtain,
upholstery of a chair, lampshade)
79, 159

748
Semiramis
1911/13 / Ziegler
44
Block printed / 29.5:15 cm / 10
312

749
Gletscherblume (Glacier Flower)
1911/13 / Ziegler

47
Block printed / 15:30 cm / 28
DW, May 1917, no. 3, p. 5
(umbrella)
DW, July 1917, no. 4, p. 8 (dress)
Koch 1926, p. 25 (cushion)
Wien 1967 (exhib. cat.), p. 78,
no. 364
Florence 1978 (exhib. cat.),
p. 147, fig. 129; p. 162
Kessler-Aurisch 1983, pp. 254,
257, 346, 347; fig. 479, 492
Völker 1984, p. 99, fig. 134;
p. 114, fig. 155; p. 275
Tokyo 1989 (exhib. cat.), p. 349,
no. 469; p. 367, no. 528
299, 301

750
Kardinal (Cardinal)
1911/13 / Ziegler, Posnanski,
Haendel
47
Block printed / repeat height 8.3
cm / 30
Koch 1926, p. 25 (lampshade)
Wien 1929 (exhib. cat.), p. 28
(animal)
Wien 1967 (exhib. cat.), p. 83,
no. 421
Neuwirth 1981, p. 262, fig. 171
Neuwirth 1984, p. 198
Brussels 1987 (exhib. cat.), p. 196,
no. 10.5
Tokyo 1989 (exhib. cat.), p. 358,
no. 490
192, 256

751
Jaguar
1911/13 / Ziegler, Bujatti
54
Block printed / 10:6 cm / 1

752
Ariel
1911/13
55
Block printed / 15:15 cm / 3
315

753
Liszt
1911/13 / Bujatti, Ziegler
59
Block printed / 2.7:5 cm / 3

754
Lurko
1911/13 / Klinger, Bujatti,
Ziegler
62
Block printed / 30.2:30.2 cm / 1

755
Capri
1911/13 / Ziegler
101
Block printed / repeats not
ascertainable / 4

756
Epos (Epic Poem)
1911/13 / Teltscher, Ziegler
106
Block printed / 2:6 cm / 9

757
Orpheus
1911/13 / Ziegler
131
Block printed / 5:2.5 cm / 11
Völker 1984, p. 125, fig. 166;
p. 276

758
Körmend
1911/13
132
Block printed / 7.5:10 cm / 10

759
Edison
1911/17 / Bujatti, WW,
Teltscher
133
Block printed / 7.5:15 cm / 1
346

760
Juvelle
1911/17
158
Block printed / 3:5 cm / 2

761
Diana
1911/17 / Ziegler
216, 216a
Block printed / repeat height
not ascertainable:22.5 cm / 8
ÖBWK, IV, 1927/28, p. 140 (bedspread)

762
Diomedes
1919 (Block printed 1919, spray
printed 10 Feb. 1928) / Ziegler,
Vetter
217, 5122
Block printed, spray printed /
34.5:22 cm / 23
ID XXXII, 1921, p. 202 (canopy)
191

763
Merkur (Mercury)
1911/13 / Rodauner Druck-
fabrik, Ziegler, WW
222
Block printed / 20.5:15 cm / 9

764
Bouquet
1911/17
223
Block printed / repeats not
ascertainable / 9

765
Fantasie (Fantasy)
1911/17 / Ziegler
223a
Block printed / 33.3:23 cm / 4

766
Sieg (Victory)
1911/17 / Ziegler
227
Block printed / 16.5:14 cm / 2

767
Daphne
1918 / Ziegler, Neumann, Ama,
Teltscher

228
Block printed / 24.5:18 cm / 34
DKD XLVII, 1920/21, p. 317
(wallpaper)
DKD LXV, 1929/30, p. 420
(curtain)
Leipzig 1930 (exhib. cat.), p. 193
(curtain)
MBF XXXI, 1932, p. 96 (curtain),
p. 98 (curtain)
Völker 1984, p. 191, figs. 270,
271; p. 279
Wien 1987 Peche (exhib. cat.),
p. 21, fig. 12
Tokyo 1989 (exhib. cat.), pp. 348,
no. 467

768
Dezember (December)
1911/17
229
Block printed / 24:10 cm / 10

769
Vergissmeinnicht (Forget-Me-
Not)
1911/17 / Clavel & Lindenmeyer, Teltscher, Ziegler
231
Block printed / 30:46 cm / 7
DBK III, 1920, p. 32 (length of
fabric)
313

770
Blumenregen (Flower Rain)
1911/17 / Teltscher, Ziegler
264
Block printed / 14.5:15 cm / 22

771
Delphinen (Dolphin)
1911/17 / Ziegler, N(eumann?)
279
Block printed / 21.6:22 cm / 8
DKD XLI, 1917/18, p. 169
(length of fabric)

772
Danaeblume
1911/17 / Bujatti
282, 282a
Block printed / 20:30 cm / 8

773
Draperie (Drapery)
1911/17 / WW
285
Block printed / repeats not
ascertainable / 7

774
Einsame Blume(n) (Lonely
Flowers)
1911/12 / Ziegler, Teltscher
287
Block printed / 33.5:37 cm / 8
DKD XXXII, 1913, p. 374 (length
of fabric)
TKI VII, 1914, p. 69 (length of
fabric)
ID XXV, 1914, p. 480 (lamp-
shade)
DKD XXXV, 1914/15, p. 88
(lampshade)
Koch 1916, p. 149 (lampshade)

ID XXVIII, 1917, p. 219 (lampshade), p. 224 (curtain), p. 393
(lampshade)
Venice 1984 (exhib. cat.), p. 248,
fig. 2

775
Freudenau
1911/13 / Ziegler
297
Block printed / 14.2:7.4 cm / 9

776
Frühling (Spring)
1911/13 / Ziegler, N(eumann?)
309
Block printed / 50:93.5 cm / 10

777
Flut (Flood Tide)
1911/16 / Ziegler, Teltscher
310, 310a
Block printed / 22.2:15.8 cm / 6
158

778
Gartenwinde (Sweet Pea)
1911/13 / Bremges & G.,
Albouts, Finkh & Co, Ziegler
315
Block printed / 27:25 cm / 5
DKD XXXII, 1913, pp. 372
(curtain, upholstery)
TKI VII, 1914, p. 44 (length of
fabric)

779
Ganges
1911/17 / Bujatti, Bremges & G.,
Albouts, Finkh & Co, Ziegler,
WW
329, 329a
Block printed / 15:15 cm / 6

780
Harlekin (Harlequin)
1911/13
344
Block printed / repeats not
ascertainable / 9
DKD XXXII, 1913, p. 374 (length
of fabric)

781
Irrgarten (Maze)
1913 / Neumann, Teltscher,
Haendel, Ziegler
360
Block printed / 42.3:44.6 cm / 24
DKD XLV, 1920, p. 76 (length of
fabric)
KKHW XXIII, 1920, p. 256
(upholstery)
Wien 1967 (exhib. cat.), p. 78,
fig. 48, no. 363
Lucerne 1974 (exhib. cat.),
no. 337
Schweiger 1984, p. 221, fig. top
left
Hansen 1984, p. 146
Neuwirth 1984, p. 155
Langenthal 1986 (exhib. cat.),
p. 129
Tokyo 1989 (exhib. cat.), pp. 348,
no. 468
Wichmann 1990 (stock cat.),
p. 114
189, 191

782
Labyrinth
1911/17 / Ziegler
403
Block printed / 15:15 cm / 3
Völker 1984, p. 103, fig. 139;
p. 275
161

783
Mäander (Meander)
1911/17 / Ziegler
403
Block printed / 15:15 cm / 1

784
Spinne (Spider)
1911/17 / Ziegler
403
Block printed / 15:15 cm / 5
Neuwirth 1984, pp. 147, 149
Brussels 1987 (exhib. cat.), p. 55,
no. 9.19
160, 162

785
Marina
1911/12 / Haendel, Teltscher,
Ziegler
407
Block printed / 46.1:28 cm / 12
ID XXV, 1914, p. 104 (curtain,
upholstery of a chair, small
cloth)
DK XXIV, 1916, p. 123 (umbrella),
pp. 407 f. (curtain, upholstery of
a chair, small cover)
Eisler 1916, p. 100 (upholstery of
a chair), p. 101 (curtain, upholstery of a chair, small cover),
p. 192 (doll's dress)
Eisler 1925, fig. 3 (upholstery of
a chair), fig. 6 (upholstery), fig. 7
(curtain, upholstery, small
cover)
Fanelli 1976, fig. 633
Völker amk, p.16
Kessler-Aurisch 1983, pp. 254,
313; fig. 479
Völker 1984, endpaper
Neuwirth 1985, p. 93, fig. 7
22, 88, 89, 90, 91, 92

786
Marmor (Marble)
1911/17 / Bremges & G.,
Albouts, Finkh & Co, Ziegler
424
Block printed / 33:7.4 cm / 1

787
Medina
1911/17 / Ziegler
427
Block printed / 25:14 cm / 5

788
Olympia
1911/17 / Ziegler
427
Block printed / 13.5:16.5 cm / 5

789
Narcyssus
1911/17 / Ziegler, Albouts,
Finkh & Co
436
Block printed / 13:14.7 cm / 25

790
Norden (North)
1911/17 / Bujatti, WW
438
Block printed / 15:10 cm / 8

791
Osten (East)
1911/17 / Bujatti, Teltscher,
Ziegler
438
Block printed / 15:10 cm / 10
157

792
Othello
1911/13 / Ziegler
439
Block printed / repeat height
not ascertainable:30 cm / 1
DKD XXXIV, 1914, p. 216 (length
of fabric)

793
Pierrot
1911/12 / Klinger, Bujatti
448
Block printed / repeats not
ascertainable / 1
96

794
Paradiesvogel (Bird of Paradise)
1911/13 / Clavel & Lindenmeyer, Teltscher, Ziegler
451
Block printed / 46:21 cm / 24
DK XXIII, 1915, p. 238 (curtain,
lampshade)
DKD XXXVIII, 1916, pp. 202
(curtain, lampshade)
Florence 1978 (exhib. cat.),
p. 147, fig. 128; p. 162
Wichmann 1990 (stock cat.),
p. 148
78

795
Pappelrose
1911/16 / Ziegler
452
Block printed / 59:99.5 cm / 14
Schweiger 1984, p. 115, fig.
183

796
Rosenkavalier
1911/12 / Ziegler
465
Block printed / 23.8:40 cm / 19
10

797
Riviera
1911/13 / Ziegler, Teltscher,
Neumann
468
Block printed / repeats not
ascertainable / 2
10

798
Rax
1911/17 / Ziegler, Teltscher
471
Block printed / repeats not
ascertainable / 1
10, 163

799
Sizilien (Sicily)
1911/14 / WW, Teltscher
484
Block printed / repeats not
ascertainable / 1

800
Schwalbenschwanz (Swallowtail)
1911/13 / Ziegler, F. K. Gröbel
& Co, Neunkirchner Druck-
fabrik, Teltscher
488
Block printed / 58:69.5 cm / 3
DKD XXXIV, 1914, p. 216 (length
of fabric)
TKI VIII, 1915, p. 199 (length of
fabric)
ID XXVII, 1916, pp. 131ff.
(upholstery); pp. 223f. (up-
holstery)
Eisler 1916, p. 131 (upholstery)
DKD XXXVIII, 1916, II, pp. 199ff.
(upholstery, curtain)
DKD XXXIX, 1916/17, p. 209
(upholstery)
Kleiner 1927, p. 21 (upholstery of
a chair)
Völker amk, p. 15
Völker in WKK 1983, no. 2,
p. 127, fig. 6
Völker 1984, p. 57, fig. 63; p. 272
Varnedoe 1986, p. 103
Brussels 1987 (exhib. cat.), p. 57,
no. 9.32
Tokyo 1989 (exhib. cat.), p. 348,
no. 466
New York 1992/93, p. 299
153, 154, 155

801
Schuppen (Scales)
1911/17 / Bujatti
489
Block printed / 7.5:5 cm / 3

802
Stakete (Stakette)
1911/17 / Ziegler, FAG
495
Block printed / 27.5:30 cm / 18
Eisler 1925, p. 25 (lampshade)
Neuwirth 1984, p. 152
Wien 1985 WW (exhib. cat.),
no. 83
Bouillon 1989, p. 110

803
Storchenschnabel (Storchschnabel)
(Stork's or Crane's Bill)
1911/17 / Ziegler, Teltscher
496
Block printed / 17.5:22.7 cm / 14
DA XXIV, 1921/22, p. 40 (lamp-
shade)
DK XXIX, 1921, pp. 212, 216
(lampshade)
ID XXXII, 1921, p. 157 (lamp-
shade)

804
Thymian (Thyme)
1911/17 / Ziegler
516
Block printed / 26:23.1 cm / 3

805
Venusgärtchen (Venus's Garden)
1911/17 / Ziegler, Teltscher
525
Block printed / 25.6:10.1 cm / 3
Fanelli 1976, fig. 632

806
Wunderbaum (Castor Oil Plant)
1911/16 / Ziegler
539
Block printed / 28.6:30.8 cm / 12

807
Wörthersee
1911/17 / Ziegler, Teltscher
540
Block printed / 5:5 cm / 3

808
Schatten (Shadow)
1916 / Ziegler, W.(Wasservogel?), Teltscher
546
Block printed / 14:15.6 cm / 9
274

809
Glückspilz (Lucky Fellow)
1911/18
548
Block printed / 11:9.8 cm / 8

810
Cloe (Chloe)
1919 (January) / WW
553
Block printed / repeats not
ascertainable / 1
DKD XLV, 1919/20, p. 98
(length of fabric)

811
Wundervogel (Miraculous Bird)
1911/19 / Ziegler, Blumenegg
564, 564a
Block printed / 22:14.8 cm / 10

812
Chytera
1911/19 / (Zurich)
573
Block printed / 21.5:9 cm / 1
345

813
Tropen (Tropics)
1911/19 / Ziegler
583
Block printed / 22.5:22 cm / 7

814
Freude (Joy)
1911/19 / Zurich
638
Block printed / 35:19 cm / 1
DKD XLVII, 1920/21, p. 342
(length of fabric)
311

815
Kristall (Crystal)
1911/19 / Zurich
639
Block printed / repeats not
ascertainable

816
Pandora
1911/19 / Zurich
640
Block printed / repeat height
not ascertainable:18.5 cm / 1

817
Wein (Wine)
1911/19
642
Block printed / 55.5:30.5 cm / 5

818
Krone (Crown)
1919 / Clavel & Lindenmeyer
643
Block printed / 33:47.7 cm / 6
DKD XLV, 1919/20, p. 98
(length of fabric)
DKD LII, 1923, pp. 87, 91
(lampshade)
Wien 1923 (sales cat.), p. 9
(lampshade)
Koch 1923, fig. between pp. 179,
180 (length of fabric)
Eisler 1925, p. 22 (lampshade),
p. 76 (stuffed animal)
Wien 1929 (exhib. cat.), p. 56
(stuffed animal)
Wiener Mode XLIII, 1930, issue 2
(cushion)
SSR XXXII, 1931/32, p. 149
(cushion)
New York 1986 (exhib. cat.),
p. 32, fig. 30
Brussels 1987 (exhib. cat.), p. 56,
no. 931; p. 187
Tokyo 1989 (exhib. cat.), p. 350,
no. 470

819
Ariadne
1919 / Neumann, Ama, Alpenländische Druckfabrik, Ströbel,
Ziegler, Teltscher, Zurich
644, 644a
Block printed / 58.8:91 cm / 17
244

820
Wicken (Vetches)
1919 / Clavel & Lindenmeyer,
Ziegler, Teltscher
651
Block printed / 49.5:46.5 cm / 10
Wien 1967 (exhib. cat.), p. 79,
no. 375
New York 1980 (exhib. cat.),
p. 155
Tokyo 1989 (exhib. cat.),
pp. 354f., no. 480
156

821
Die Endigung (Endigung) (The
End)
1911/19 / WW, Zurich, Basle
652
Block printed / repeats not
ascertainable / 1
DBK III, 1920, p. 32 (length of
fabric)
347

822
Regenbogen (Rainbow)
1919 / Clavel & Lindenmeyer,
Wasservogel
653
Block printed / variable repeat
widths / 45
Wien 1929 (exhib. cat.), p. 98
(cushion)
SSR XXXII, 1929/30, p. 28
(cushion)
ID XLII, 1931, p. 34 (cushion)
ÖK III, 1932, no. 10, p. 8
(cushion)
Wien 1967 (exhib. cat.), p. 83,
no. 42
Brussels 1987 (exhib. cat.), p. 196,
no. 10.5
Tokyo 1989 (exhib. cat.), p. 358,
no. 491
256

823
Hymen
1919 / Clavel & Lindenmeyer
654
Block printed / 55:45 cm / 8
DKD XLV, 1919/20, p. 98
(length of fabric)
DBK III, 1920, p. 32 (length of
fabric)
ID XXXIV, 1923, p. 32 (lampshade)
Wien 1923 Peche, fig. 14 (length
of fabric)
Koch 1923, fig. between pp. 26,
27 (length of fabric)
DKD LIV, 1924, p. 55 (length of
fabric)
ÖBWK II, 1925/26, p. 365
(lampshade)
Wiener Mode XLIII, 1930, no. 2
(cushion)
MBF XXX, 1931, pp. 509f.
(curtain, length of fabric)
277, 278

824
Säule (Column)
1919 / Clavel & Lindenmeyer,
Ziegler, Neumann, Teltscher
662
Block printed / repeat height
not ascertainable:22.5 cm / 7
KKHW XXIII, 1920, p. 178
(length of fabric)
Eisler 1925, fig. 75 (length of
fabric)
344

825
Parasit (Parasite)
1919 / Clavel & Lindenmeyer,
FAG, Teltscher
708
Block printed / repeats not
ascertainable / 4
DKD LII, 1923, p. 9 (lampshade)
Wien 1929 (exhib. cat.), p. 117
(lampshade)
Wien 1967 (exhib. cat.), p. 83,
no. 421
Brussels 1987 (exhib. cat.), p. 196,
no. 10.5
Tokyo 1989 (exhib. cat.), p. 358,
no. 498
276

826
Pan
1919 / Clavel & Lindenmeyer
709
Block printed / 44:47.7 cm / 5
DKD XLVII, 1921, p. 343 (length
of fabric)
WMB VI, 1921/22, p. 180 (length
of fabric)
Eisler 1925, p. 75 (length of
fabric)
Kleiner 1927, p. 65 (length of
fabric)
SSR XXIX, 1928/29, p. 8
(cushion)
Wien 1928 (sales cat.), p. 304
(cushion)
Wien 1929 (exhib. cat.), pp. 45,
100 (cushion), p. 117 (lampshade)
Berlin 1977 (exhib. cat.), pp. 33,
144
Völker 1984, p. 176, fig. 246;
p. 278
Schweiger 1984, p. 234
Wien 1985 (exhib. cat.), p. 397,
no. 13/11/37
New York 1986 (exhib. cat.),
p. 92, fig. 117
Trad. u. Exper. 1988, p. 70
Bouillon 1989, p. 111
193, 194

827
Hesperidenfrucht (Fruit of the
Hesperides)
1919
710
Block printed / 48:44 cm / 2
KKHW XXIII, 1920 I, p. 178
(length of fabric)
DKD XLVII, 1920/21, p. 342
(length of fabric)
WMB VI, 1921/22, p. 180 (length
of fabric)
Völker in WKK 1984, no. 1, p. 40,
fig. 4
197

828
Falte (Fold)
1923 (blocks produced 25 Apr.
1924)
835
Block printed / 29.5:15.8 cm / 18
Eisler 1925, fig. 75 (length of
fabric)
MBF XXXI, 1932, p. 85 (bedspread)
Wichmann 1990 (stock cat.),
p. 115
342, 343

829
Große Blätter (Large Leaves)
1923 (blocks produced 22 Oct.
1923) / Neumann, Haendel
850
Block printed / 41.5:52.5 cm / 4

830
Tausendblumen (Thousand
Flowers)
1923 (blocks produced 4 Dec.
1923 and 9 Apr. 1924) / Ziegler,
Neumann
851, 851a
Block printed / 41.8:33 cm / 7

831
Die Ranke (The Tendril)
1923 (blocks produced 4 Dec.
923) / Neumann, Haendel
853
Block printed / repeat height
not ascertainable:110.5 cm / 5

832
Viola
1923 / Teltscher, Ziegler
855
Block printed / 39.5:76.5 cm
(and 40.5:84 cm) / 12
ID XXXVI, 1925, p. 81 (wall-
hanging)
MBF XXV, 1926, pp. 356, 359,
360 (upholstery of an armchair)
MBF XXVI, 1927, p. 21 (upholstery)
Kleiner 1927, pp. 54 (upholstery
of an armchair)
MBF XXXVII, 1928, pp. 145, 147
(wall-covering, curtain)
DKD LXI, 1927/28, p. 452
(curtain)
The Studio, no. 97, 1929, pp. 385,
387 (upholstery of a chair)
Wien 1967 (exhib. cat.), p. 78,
no. 368
Wien 1980 NW (exhib. cat.),
p. 84, fig. 104 ; p. 86, no. 104

833
Doris
1923 (blocks produced 3 Mar.
1930) / Ama, Teltscher, Ziegler
1177
Block printed / 50:33 cm / 12
316

834
Rhomben (Rhombus)
1922 / Vogel
9190
Woven fabric / 34:10.5 cm / 9

835
Die Tulpen (The Tulips)
1922 / Vogel
9627
Woven fabric / repeat height not
ascertainable:62 cm / 9

836
Wien (Vienna)
1922 / Vogel
9680
Woven fabric / repeats not
ascertainable / 11

837
Dolomiten (Dolomites)
1923 / Vogel
9707
Woven fabric / repeats not
ascertainable / 6
DKD XXXVII, 1929, p. 41 (upholstery of a chair)

838
Claudia
1923 / Vogel
9708
Woven fabric / repeats not
ascertainable / 8

839
März (March)
1923 / Vogel
9717
Woven fabric / different
repeats / 19

840
Faser (Fibre)
1922
10352/St.7 (archive no.)
Roller printed / repeats not
ascertainable / 53

841
Alaun (Alum)
1922
Roller printed / 8.5:7.5 cm / 55

842
Cyan
1922
Roller printed / repeats not
ascertainable / 15

843
Federwisch (Feather Duster)
1922 (August)
Roller printed / 16.8:12.1 cm / 5

844
Irrweg (Wrong Way)
1922
Roller printed / repeats not
ascertainable / 27

845
Nuance
1922
Roller printed / repeats not
ascertainable / 42

846
Orleans
1922 (August)
Roller printed / repeats not
ascertainable / 10

847
Palatin
1922 (August)
Roller printed / repeats not
ascertainable / 32

848
Prisma (Prism)
1922 (August)
Roller printed / repeats not
ascertainable / 37

849
Rom (Rome)
1911/13
Repeats not ascertainable
DA XX, 1914/15, pl. 63
(curtain)
ID XXVII, 1916, p. 23 (up-
holstery)
Eisler 1916, p. 39 (curtain), p. 125
(upholstery)
DK XXIV, 1916, p. 405 (curtain)
Eisler 1925, p. 9 (upholstery)
175, 176

Marianne PERLMUTTER (1891–)

850
Bergen
1910/17
94
Block printed / 18.4:22 cm / 1

851
Zakopane
1910/17 / Bujatti
95
Block printed / 33.5:29 cm / 1
108

852
Säge (Saw)
1910/17 / Ziegler, Klinger, Bujatti
96
Block printed / 2:6 cm / 9

853
Windblume
1910/17 / Ziegler
126
Block printed / repeats not ascertainable

854
Hellbrunn
1910/17
254
Block printed / 60:29.5 cm / 10

855
Donauwellen (Waves of the Danube)
1910/17 / Bujatti, Ziegler
284
Block printed / 36:30 cm / 4

856
Donau (Danube)
1916/18 / Ziegler
622
Block printed / 7.5:4.8 cm / 4

Camilla PEYRER (1894–)

857
Wintergarten (Winter Garden)
1912/17 / WW
528
Block printed / repeats not ascertainable / 1

Angela PIOTROVSKA-WITTMANN (1898–)

858
Gorlicze
1914/15
237
Block printed / 47:43.3 cm / 10
124

859
Anastasius
1914/15 / Ziegler, Alpenländische Druckfabrik
246
Block printed / 46:43.8 cm / 9
110

Clara POSNANSKI

860
Akka
1928 (23 Nov. 1928) / Posnanski
5005
Spray printed / repeats not ascertainable / 15

861
Amely
1927 (January) / Posnanski
5006
Spray printed / 3.3:6.6 cm / 8

862
Andros
1928 (stencil produced 31 Oct. 1928) / Posnanski
5007
Spray printed / 14:23 cm / 9

863
Brioni
1926 (December) / Posnanski
5008
Spray printed / 5:5 cm / 5
210

864
Chios
1928 (stencil produced 31 Aug. 1928) / Posnanski
5010
Spray printed / repeat height not ascertainable:20 cm / 7

865
Dachstein
1926 (August) /Posnanski
5013
Spray printed / 21.5 cm:repeat width not ascertainable / 2

866
Dornbach
1928 (4 Jan. 1928) / Posnanski
5015
Spray printed / 8.8:12 cm / 8

867
Edfu
1928 (4 Jan. 1928) / Posnanski
5016
Spray printed / repeat width 16.4 cm / 13
SSR XXXI, 1930/31, p. 129 (cushion)
DKD LXVII, 1930/31, p. 207 (cushion)
ID XLII, 1931, p. 33 (cushion)

868
Edlach
1928 / Posnanski
5017
Spray printed / repeats not ascertainable / 12

869
Epirus
1928 (24 Nov. 1928) / Posnanski
5019
Spray printed / repeats not ascertainable / 11
348

870
Finis
1928 (October) / Posnanski
5021
Spray printed / 7.5:11.8 cm / 8

871
Fluchthorn
1928 (4 Jan. 1928) / Posnanski
5021
Spray printed / 14.3:20 cm / 10

872
Grinzing
1926 (July) / Posnanski
5023
Spray printed / 4:2.2 cm, *ombré* / 2

873
Hallstadt
1926 (July) / Posnanski
5024
Spray printed / repeat height not ascertainable:25 cm / 6

874
Hatasu
1928 (4 Jan. 1928) / Posnanski
5025
Spray printed / repeat width 17 cm / 9

875
Hekla
1928 (23 Nov. 1928) / Posnanski
5026
Spray printed / 15:41 cm / 15

876
Höflein
1926 (August) / Posnanski
5029
Spray printed / 17.5:16 cm / 7
349

877
Jena
1928 (24 Nov. 1928) / Posnanski
5031
Spray printed / 73.5:45 cm / 14

878
Josta
1928 (October) / Posnanski
5032
Spray printed / 11.7:2 cm / 8

879
Ischl
1926 (July) / Posnanski
5033
Spray printed / repeats not ascertainable / 1

880
Kanton
1928 (February) / Posnanski
5033
Spray printed / 14:8 cm / 9

881
Kieneck
1926 (August) / Posnanski
5034
Spray printed / repeats not ascertainable / 1

882
Linz
1928 / Posnanski
5040
Spray printed / repeat height not ascertainable:20.5 cm / 13

883
Milos
1927/28 / Posnanski
5046
Spray printed / repeats not ascertainable / 11

884
Muttler
1928 (4 Jan. 1928) / Posnanski
5048
Spray printed / repeats not ascertainable / 8

885
Paul
1927 (October) / Posnanski
5051
Spray printed / 18:13 cm / 4
351

886
Paulus
1927 (16 May 1927) / Posnanski
5052
Spray printed / repeats not ascertainable / 4

887
P
1927 / Posnanski
5053
Spray printed / repeats not ascertainable / 1

888
Pegasus (Thalia)
1927 (16 May 1927) / Posnanski
5054
Spray printed / 2:2 cm / 7

889
Pelusium
1928 / Posnanski
5055
Spray printed / 8.7:7.5 cm / 7

890
Pest
1927 (October) / Posnanski
5056
Spray printed / 20:20 cm / 6

891
Pierre
1927 (16 May 1927) / Posnanski
5057
Spray printed / repeats not ascertainable / 5

892
Pintus
1927 (October) / Posnanski
5058
Spray printed / 5.6:13 cm / 9

893
Plato
1927 (October) / Posnanski
5059
Spray printed / 12.8:13.2 cm / 7

894
Pola
1927 (October) / Posnanski
5060
Spray printed / 18:15 cm / 8

895
Pram
1928 (23 Nov. 1928) / Posnanski
5061
Spray printed / repeats not
ascertainable / 8

896
Preblau
1928 (23 Nov.1928) / Posnanski
5062
Spray printed / repeat height
not ascertainable:18 cm / 14

897
Prix
1928 (October) / Posnanski
5063
Spray printed / repeats not
ascertainable / 6

898
Prosa (Prose)
1927 (October) / Posnanski
5064
Spray printed / 9: 11.6 cm / 6

899
Rütli
1928 (February) / Posnanski
5065
Spray printed / repeats not
ascertainable / 2

900
Salzburg
1926 (July) / Posnanski
5066
Spray printed / repeats not
ascertainable / 1

901
Samnaun
1928 (4 Jan. 1928) / Posnanski
5067
Spray printed / 9:20 cm / 15

902
Schöpfl
1926 (August) / Posnanski
5068
Spray printed / repeats not
ascertainable / 1

903
Sievering
1926 (July) / Posnanski
5069
Spray printed / 14.5:15 cm / 4

904
Silvretta
1928 (4 Jan. 1928) / Posnanski
5070
Spray printed / repeat width
13 cm / 10

905
Soslon
1928 (4 Jan. 1928) / Posnanski
5073
Spray printed / repeats not
ascertainable / 6

906
Spree
1928 (23 Nov. 1928) / Posnanski
5074
Spray printed / 17:12 cm / 16

907
Stettin
1928 (23 Nov. 1928) / Posnanski
5075
Spray printed / 22:21.5 cm / 14

908
Strauss
1928 (October) / Posnanski
5076
Spray printed / 10:4 cm / 8

909
Tinos
1928 / Posnanski
5079
Spray printed / 14:14 cm / 7

910
Tulln
1928 (31 Aug. 1928) / Schenk
5081
Spray printed / repeats height
not ascertainable:49 cm / 10

911
Tyrol
1928 (October) / Posnanski
5082
Spray printed / 10:5 cm / 7

912
Ulm
1928 (24 Nov. 1928) / Posnanski
5083
Spray printed / repeat height
not ascertainable:43.5 cm / 12

913
Zara
1926 (August) / Posnanski
5084
Spray printed / 19.5:18 cm / 1

914
2002
1928 (4 Jan. 1928) / Posnanski
5116
Spray printed / repeats not
ascertainable / 3

915
2005
1928 (4 Jan. 1928) / Posnanski
5117
Spray printed / repeats not
ascertainable / 4

916
Traun
1926 (July) / Posnanski
5145
Spray printed / repeat width
10.8 cm / 32
SSR XXIX, 1928/29, pp. 8, 75
(cushion)
ID XLII, 1931, p. 34 (cushion)

917
Jonny
1929 (14 Jan. 1929) / Posnanski
5228
Spray printed / repeats not
ascertainable / 6

918
Antonio
1931 (June) / Posnanski
5272
Spray printed / repeats not
ascertainable / 5

919
Ferro
1931 (June) / Posnanski
5273
Spray printed / repeat height
not ascertainable:33 cm / 7

920
Kama
1931 (June) / Posnanski
5274
Spray printed / repeats not
ascertainable / 5

921
Loanda
1931 (June) / Posnanski
5276
Spray printed / repeats not
ascertainable / 5

922
Lucano
1931 (June) / Posnanski
5277
Spray printed / repeats not
ascertainable / 5

923
Magnus
1931 (June) / Posnanski
5278
Spray printed / repeats not
ascertainable / 5

924
Niger
1931 (June) / Posnanski
5279
Spray printed / repeats not
ascertainable / 4

925
Planei
1929 (14 Jan. 1929) / Posnanski
5280
Spray printed / repeat width
12.3 cm / 7

926
Saffi
1931 (June) / Posnanski
5281
Spray printed / repeat height
not ascertainable:23.3 cm / 4

927
Tigris
1931 (June) / Posnanski
5282
Spray printed / 9 cm:repeat
width not ascertainable / 5

928
Tizi
1931 (June) / Posnanski
5283
Spray printed / repeats not
ascertainable / 5

August POSPISCHIL

929
April
1910/12 / Bremges & G.;
Albouts, Finkh & Co
22
Block printed / 11:7 cm / 2
ID XXIV, 1913, p. 110 (lamp-
shade)
DKD XXXIII, 1913/14, p. 82
(lampshade)

930
Alpenweide (Alpine Pasture)
1910/12 / Bujatti, Ziegler
27
Block printed / 7.5:11.2 cm / 10

931
Schönbrunn
1910/12 / Ziegler
493
Block printed / repeats not
ascertainable / 1
Fanelli 1976, fig. 617
98

Maria PRANKE (1891–   )

932
Dschungel (Jungle)
1910/17 / Ziegler
120
Block printed / 16:15 cm / 8

Otto PRUTSCHER
(1880–1949)

933
Saragossa
1910/12 / Ziegler
110
Block printed / repeat width
22.2 cm / 1

934
Glockenblume (Bellflower)
1910/12
330
Block printed / repeats not
ascertainable / 1
DI XIII, 1912, pl. 58 (wallpaper,
curtain)
DKD XXXI, 1912/13, p. 186
(wallpaper), p. 187 (wallpaper,
curtain)

Margarethe REINOLD
(1901–   )

935
Savonarola
1925 (blocks produced 11 Jan.
1925) / Ziegler, Teltscher
929
Block printed / 5:10 cm / 8

Karl RIEDEL
(1890–)

936
Klatschrose (Poppy)
1910/11 / Ziegler
372
Block printed / repeats not
ascertainable /1
DKD XXXI, 1912/13, p. 102
(dress)
TKI VI, 1913, p. 445 (folding
screen)
69, 70

Felice RIX-UENO
(1893–1967)

937
Gotland
1913/17 / Ziegler
93
Block printed / 30:27.1 cm / 13

938
Archibald
1913/17 / WW ('Haus'),
Haendel, Teltscher, Ziegler
193
Block printed / 29:30 cm / 19
Koch 1926, p. 25 (cushion),
p. 121 (curtain, bedspread)
Ritter 1933, p. 118 (curtain)
Wien 1967 (exhib. cat.), p. 78,
no. 379
Florence 1978 (exhib. cat.),
p. 146, fig. 124; p. 162
Völker 1984, pp. 114f., 124f., 276
Wichmann 1990 (stock cat.),
p. 122
366

939
Traviata
1913/17 / Ziegler
205
Block printed / 68.5:92 cm / 4

940
Mondscheinblume (Moonlight
Flower)
1913/17/ Ziegler, Neumann
211
Block printed / 31:29.5 cm / 11

941
Waldfee (Fairy of the Woods)
1913/17 / Ziegler
230
Block printed / 45:30 cm / 11
Koch 1923, p. 151 (covering of a
showcase)

942
Davos
1913/17 / Ziegler, Neumann,
Teltscher
233
Block printed / repeat width
43.5 cm / 12
Völker 1984, p. 216, fig. 309;
p. 245, fig. 339; pp. 280f.
Trad. u. Exper. 1988, p. 74

943
Pelargonie (Pelargonium)
1913/16 / Teltscher, Ziegler
266
Block printed / repeats not
ascertainable / 14
MBF XXVI, 1927, p. 399 (upholstery)
MW XI, issue 13, 1930, p. 13
(upholstery of a chair)
DKD LXV, 1929/30, p. 276
(upholstery of a chair)
Wiener Mode XLIII, 1930, WW
special number (upholstery of a
chair)
MBF XXX, 1931, p. 509 (upholstery of a stool)
Wien 1980 NW (exhib. cat.),
pp. 46f., fig. 44
172

944
Junker (Junka)
1913/17
361
Block printed / repeats not
ascertainable / 1

945
Rispen (Panicles)
1913/17 / Ziegler
470
Block printed / 21.2:17 cm / 15

946
Tantalus
1913/17 / Ziegler
515
Block printed / 17.8:17.8 cm / 8

947
Tanagra
1916 / Ziegler, Neumann,
Teltscher
517
Block printed / 46.5:30.5 cm / 17
Wien 1929 (exhib. cat.), p. 120
(lampshade)
MBF XXX, 1931, p. 71 (up-
holstery of a chair)
Tokyo 1989 (exhib. cat.), p. 351
179

948
Vesuv (Vesuvius)
1913/15 / Bujatti, Alpenländische
Druckfabrik, WW, Teltscher
523
Block printed / 2.5:1 cm / 18

949
Parfüm (Perfume)
1913/19 / Albouts, Finkh & Co,
Ziegler
628, 628a
Block printed / 29.3:36.8 cm / 8

950
Teehaus (Teahouse)
1919 / Ziegler, Clavel & Lindenmeyer
641
Block printed / 1.2:42 cm / 8
Kleiner 1927, p. 65 (length of
fabric)

951
Ombré
1919 / Ziegler
655
Block printed / variable
repeats / 17
ID XXXIV, 1923, p. 188 (lampshade)
Wien 1923 Peche (exhib. cat.),
fig. 25 (lampshade)
Baroni/D'Auria 1981, p. 145,
fig. 362, 363; p. 146, fig. 364
Völker 1984, p. 223, fig. 313, 314;
p. 224, fig. 315; p. 226, fig. 317;
p. 281

952
Libanon (Chitra)
1919 / Ziegler
668
Block printed / repeats not
ascertainable / 6
Schweiger 1984, p. 234

953
Donnerwetter (Thunderstorm)
1919 / Ziegler, Teltscher
669
Block printed / 43:43 cm / 9
334

954
Lobau
1919 / Teltscher, Ziegler
670
Block printed / 56:44 cm / 3

955
Nachtvogel (Night Bird)
1919 / Ziegler
671
Block printed / repeats not
ascertainable / 1

956
Cabaret
1919 (blocks produced 26 Nov.
1919) / Ziegler, WW ('Haus')
711
Block printed / repeats not
ascertainable

957
China
1920 / Ziegler
745
Block printed / 172:172 cm

958
Parmaveilchen (Parma Violet)
1920 / Ziegler
783
Block printed / 49.5:44 cm / 10

959
Alpenveilchen (Cyclamen)
1920/21 / Ziegler
797
Block printed / 33:20.7 cm / 13

960
Sumpfreiher (Marsh Heron)
1921 (21 Sep. 1921) / Ziegler
800
Block printed / 20.3:23 cm / 7

961
Kirschgarten (Cherry Garden)
1922 / Ziegler, Teltscher
803
Block printed / 23.2:14.8 cm / 16

962
Waldblume (Forest Flower)
1922 / Ziegler
807
Block printed / 74:46.5 cm / 6
Koch 1923, pl. between pp. 26,
27 (length of fabric)

963
Hutfeder (Feather on a Hat)
1922
808
Block printed / 55:94 cm / 9
Koch 1923, pl. between pp. 26,
27 (length of fabric)
Tokyo 1989 (exhib. cat.), pp. 350,
no. 473

964
Japanland (The Land of Japan)
1923 (blocks produced 27 Mar.
1923) / Ziegler, Teltscher
811
Block printed / 47:47 cm / 9
329

965
Brillenschlange (Spectacled
Snake)
1922 (31 July 1922) / Ziegler,
Teltscher
812
Block printed / width of stripes
24.5 cm / 11
Wichmann 1990 (stock cat.),
p. 124

966
Sommerwinde
1922 (13 Sep. 1922) / Ziegler,
Teltscher
820
Block printed / 54:32 cm / 15
Völker 1984, p. 216, fig. 307;
p. 280
Wien 1985 (exhib. cat.), p. 398,
no. 13/11/43

967
Frühlingswiese (Spring Meadow)
1922 (13 Nov. 1922) / Teltscher,
Ama, Ziegler
821
Block printed / 45:37.5 cm / 12
Wichmann 1990 (stock cat.),
pp. 122f.

968
Ziergras (Ornamental Grass)
1922 / Neumann, Ziegler
822
Block printed / 23.5:24 cm / 29

969
Stiefmütterchen (Pansy)
1922 / Ziegler, WW ('Haus')
823
Block printed / 33:30.5 cm / 15
DKD LXI, 1927/28, p. 458
(lampshade)
Wien 1929 (exhib. cat.), p. 111
(lampshade)

970
Bengal
1922 / Haendel, Teltscher
824
Block printed / 16:24 cm,
pattern staggered / 4

971
Korngold (Corn Gold)
1922 / Ziegler
825
Block printed / 64.5:92 cm / 12
Kleiner 1927, p. 65 (length of
fabric)

972
Juniblumen (Flowers of June)
1923 (10 Jan. 1923) / Ziegler,
Teltscher
830
Block printed / 27.5:31.5 cm / 12
ID XXXVIII, 1927, pp. 64f.
(lampshade)
Kleiner 1927, p. 48 (lampshade)
Studio Yearbook, 1928, p. 141
(lampshade)

973
Feldfrüchte (Produce of the
Fields)
1923 / Ziegler, Haendel
831
Block printed / 50:23.5 cm / 17

974
Jussuf
1923 / Neumann, Haendel
834
Block printed / 29.5:47.5 cm / 19
Wien 1929 (exhib. cat.), p. 136
(length of fabric)
Wiener Mode XLIII, 1930, WW
special number (length of
fabric)
Wichmann 1990 (stock cat.),
p. 148

975
Marsblume
1923 / Ziegler
838
Block printed / 57:34 cm / 10

976
Himmelobst (Fruits of Heaven)
1923
839
Block printed / 47.5:45.5 cm / 12

977
Schweden (Sweden)
1924 (16 Jan. 1924) / Ziegler,
Teltscher, Ama
852
Block printed / 31.5:45.5 cm / 9
Wiener Mode XLIII, 1930, WW
special number (cushion)

978
Gartenstrauß
1924 (16 Jan. 1924) / Ziegler
854
Block printed / repeats not
ascertainable / 12

979
Tokio (Tokyo)
1924 (10 Jan. 1924) / Ziegler,
Teltscher
857, 857a
Block printed / 40.8:30 cm / 18
Kleiner 1927, p. 65 (cushion),
p. 79 (lampshade)
Steinoel 1929, fig. X (cushion)
Wien 1929 (exhib. cat.), p. 128
(length of fabric)
SSR XXX, 1929/30, p. 164
(cushion)
Wien 1967 (exhib. cat.), p. 83,
no. 421
Tokyo 1989 (exhib. cat.), p. 358,
no. 492
Wichmann 1990 (stock cat.), p. 125
272

980
Gespann (Team)
1924 (5 Mar. 1924) / Ziegler
859
Block printed / 35:31 cm / 4
Wichmann 1990 (stock cat.), p. 148

981
Gespinst (Thread)
1924 (5 Mar. 1924) / Ziegler
859
Block printed / 35:31 cm / 14
Wichmann 1990 (stock cat.), p. 149
267, 268

982
Mandarin
1924 (May) / Ziegler, Teltscher
866
Block printed / 22.5:31 cm / 12
Kleiner 1927, p. 65 (length of
fabric)

983
Ouverture
1924 (blocks produced 2 May
1924) / Ziegler
867
Block printed / 30:30 cm / 16
365

984
Sylvester
1924 (blocks produced 1924) /
Ziegler
868
Block printed / 10.2:10 cm / 10
335

985
Moosblumen (Moss Flowers)
1924 (blocks produced 30 Aug.
1924) / Ziegler, Teltscher
873
Block printed / 49.5 cm:repeat
width not ascertainable / 14
250

986
Holland
1924 (blocks produced 30 Aug.
1924) / Teltscher, Ziegler
875
Block printed / 29.6:30.8 cm / 14
Koch 1926, p. 37 (cushion)
MBF XXVII, 1929, p. 421 (curtain)

987
Purpurnelke (Purple Pink)
1924 (August) / Ziegler,
Teltscher
876
Block printed / 34.5:90 cm / 12
MBF XXIV, 1925, p. 283 (lamp-
shade)
Kleiner 1927, p. 65 (length of
fabric)
Wien 1929 (exhib. cat.), p. 97
(length of fabric)
Weiser 1930, p. 23 (length of
fabric)

988
Double-Fox
1924 (blocks produced 8 Oct.
1924) / Ziegler, Teltscher
877
Block printed / 25.8:30 cm / 16
MW 1925, no. 19, p. 27 (dress)
Wien 1928 (sales cat.), p. 301
(cushion)
Völker in WKK 1984, p. 46,
fig. 11
Völker 1984, p. 210, fig. 298;
p. 280
Trad. u. Exper. 1988, p. 67

989
Biarritz
1924 (blocks produced 6 Dec.
1924) / Ziegler, Teltscher
883
Block printed / 10:10 cm / 15

990
Laxenburg
1924 / Ziegler
884
Block printed / repeats not
ascertainable

991
Nanking
1924/25 (blocks produced 18
Mar. 1925) / Ziegler, Teltscher
892
Block printed / 39.5:30 cm / 6

992
Murray
1924/25 (blocks produced 25
Feb. 1925) / Teltscher, Mailand
894
Block printed / 27.4:30 cm / 24

993
Palamos
1925 (blocks produced 29 Apr.
1925) / Ziegler, Teltscher
896
Block printed / 40:30 cm / 11
Völker in WKK 1984, p. 47,
fig. 12

994
Sommerfalter (Summer
Butterfly)
1925 (blocks produced 1 July
1925) / Ziegler, Teltscher
915
Block printed / 47.8:30 cm / 11
Völker 1984, p. 216, fig. 308;
p. 280

995
Kobra (Cobra)
1925 (blocks produced 28 July
1925) / Ziegler, Haendel
917
Block printed / 34.5:30 cm / 12
367

996
Malta
1925 (blocks produced 3 July
1925) / Ziegler
921
Block printed / 43:30 cm / 13
Weiser 1930, p. 23 (length of
fabric)

997
Tramino
1925 (blocks produced 28 July
1925) / Ziegler, Teltscher
924
Block printed / 49.2 cm:repeat
width not ascertainable / 17

998
Burano
1925 (15 Nov. 1925) / Ziegler
927
Block printed / 44.5:43.5 cm / 9
Wien 1929 (exhib. cat.), p. 100
(cushion)
Steinoel 1929, fig. X (cushion)

999
Blumenduft (Scent of Flowers)
1925 (15 Nov. 1925) / Ziegler
938
Block printed / 31.8:29.8 cm / 12
ID XL, 1929, p. 345 (curtain),
p. 346 (curtain, bedspread),
p. 347 (curtain, bedspread)
SSR XXXI, 1930/31, p. 120 (neck
cushion)

1000
Vogelhain (Bird's Grove)
1925 (15 Nov. 1925) / Ziegler
940
Block printed / 29.5:30.5 cm / 10

1001
Dnjestr (Dniester)
1926 (July) / Ziegler, Teltscher
944
Block printed / 12:30.5 cm / 20

1002
Sargans
1926 (August) / Ziegler, Teltscher
949
Block printed / 30.5:28.5 cm / 22
367

1003
Reuss
1926 (August) / Ziegler
950
Block printed / 15:10.4 cm / 20

1004
Simme
1926 (August) / Teltscher, Ziegler
952
Block printed / 10:32 cm / 13

1005
Kirschblüte (Cherry Blossom)
1926 (July) / Teltscher, Ziegler
953
Block printed / 30:30 cm / 19
Wien 1929 (exhib. cat.), pp. 96f.
(length of fabric)

1006
Kiuschiu (Kyushyu)
1927 (March) / Ziegler
959
Block printed / 35.5:31 cm / 7

1007
Sues
1927 (March) / Ziegler, Teltscher
960
Block printed / 35.5:31 cm / 9
Wien 1929 BiR (exhib. cat.), p. 59
(length of fabric)
MW 1929, issue 13, p. 8 (length
of fabric)
SSR XXX, 1929/30, pp. 12f.
(cushion)

1008
Engadin
1927 (April) / Ziegler, Teltscher,
Bruggmann
964
Block printed / 44.5:31 cm / 10
ÖBWK VI, 1929/30, p. 67
(cushion)

1009
Rosenhain (Rose Grove)
1927 (April) / Ziegler, Teltscher
965
Block printed / 65:45.5 cm / 12
Wien 1929 (exhib. cat.), p. 137
(length of fabric)
SSR XXX, 1929/30, p. 12
(cushion)
DKD LXV, 1930 I, p. 330 (length
of fabric)
Wiener Mode XLIII, 1930, WW
special number (length of fabric)
273

1010
Teerose (Tea-Rose)
1927 (April) / Ziegler
966
Block printed / 39:30.5 cm / 8

1011
Nelkenduft (Scent of Pinks)
1927 (March) / Ziegler
967
Block printed / 15.2:15.7 cm / 10

1012
Blütenblätter (Flower Petals)
1927 (March) / Ziegler
968
Block printed / 32:16 cm / 8

1013
Buschmann (Bushman)
1927 (October) / Ziegler
980
Block printed / 34:30.5 cm / 14
Wien 1928 (sales cat.), p. 302
(neck cushion), p. 304 (cushion)
Steinoel 1929, fig. X (neck cushion)

1014
Anemone
1927 (October) / Ziegler,
Teltscher, FAG
982
Block printed / 33:60.5 cm / 12
Wien 1928 (sales cat.), p. 1002
(length of fabric)
Wien 1929 (exhib. cat.), p. 67
(length of fabric)

1015
Morgentau (Morning Dew)
1927 (November) / Ziegler,
Ama, Teltscher
983
Block printed / 32:30.5 cm / 14

1016
Polo
1927 (November) / Clavel &
Lindenmeyer
993
Block printed / 36:30 cm / 13

1017
Rhapsodie (Rhapsody)
1928 (April) / Ziegler
1010
Block printed / 28.7:31.7 cm / 9

1018
Dschong
1929 (24 Jan. 1929) / Ziegler
1093
Block printed / 30.5:30.5 cm / 11
Brussels 1987 (exhib. cat.), p. 184,
no. 9.21

1019
Nikon
1929 (12 Feb. 1929) / Ziegler
1097
Block printed / 30.5:30.5 cm / 12

1020
Arizona
1929 (21 Feb. 1929) / Ziegler
1098
Block printed / 39:35 cm / 5

1021
Dreiblatt (Trefoil)
1929 (20 Mar. 1929) / Ziegler
1101
Block printed / 36:30.5 cm / 18

1022
Tarantella
1929 (25 Apr. 1929) / Ziegler, Sax
1109
Block printed / 30.2:30.8 cm / 15

1023
Krasnojarsk
1929 (12 May 1929) / Ziegler,
Teltscher, FAG
1118
Block printed / repeat height
not ascertainable:32 cm / 11
333

1024
Mohn (Poppy)
1929 (19 June 1929) / Ziegler
1123
Block printed / 13:16 cm / 17

1025
Kicku
1929 (25 June 1929) / Ziegler,
Ama
1128
Block printed / 32:32 cm / 12
Völker 1984, p. 247, figs. 342, 343
Wien 1985 (exhib. cat.), p. 398,
no. 13/11/57

1026
Geranie (Geranium)
1929 (28 June 1929) / Ziegler
1132
Block printed / 30:65 cm / 9
331

1027
Camille (Chamomile)
1929 (26 July 1929) / FAG
1133
Block printed /39:32 cm / 12
327

1028
Kreml
1929 (26 July 1929) / Teltscher,
Ziegler
1136
Block printed / 18:31.8 cm / 13

1029
Almira
1929 (26 July 1929) / Ziegler,
FAG
1139
Block printed / 33.5:35 cm / 10

1030
Mirza
1929 (2 Nov. 1929) / Ama,
Teltscher, Ziegler
1157
Block printed / 45:35 cm / 10

1031
Ogi
1930 (November) / FAG
1185
Block printed / 43:32 cm / 14
Fanelli 1976, fig. 731

1032
Akelei (Honeysuckle)
1930
1187
Block printed / repeats not
ascertainable

1033
Fuchsie (Fuchsia)
1930 (November) / Clavel &
Lindenmeyer
1195
Block printed / 17:31 cm / 10

1034
Tilupi
1930 (December) / FAG
1203
Block printed / 9:10.5 cm / 14

1035
Lyon
1927 (12 Sep. 1927) / Schenk
5163
Spray printed / repeats not
ascertainable / 3

1036
Silberblatt (Silver Leaf)
1927 (October) / Teufel
5212
Spray printed / repeats not
ascertainable / 7

1037
Francisco
1929
5226
Spray printed / repeats not
ascertainable

1038
Touring
1929 (29 Apr. 1929) / Posnanski
5240
Spray printed / repeats not
ascertainable / 7

1039
Brasilien (Brazil)
1929 (29 Apr. 1929) / Presser
5241
Spray printed / repeats not
ascertainable / 9

1040
Rahat
1930/31
5268
Spray printed / repeats not
ascertainable

1041
Jalapa
1930
5269
Spray printed / repeats not
ascertainable

1042
Almata
1927 (August) / Vogel
0162
Woven fabric / repeats not
ascertainable / 2

1043
Wellen (Waves)
1927 (October) / Vogel
0173
Woven fabric / 27.2 cm:repeat
width not ascertainable / 6
ÖBWK VI, 1929/30, p. 262
(upholstery)
MBF XXXI, 1932, p. 168 (upholstery of an armchair)
Wien 1980 NW (exhib. cat.),
pp. 48f., fig. 53
208

1044
Eiland (Isle)
1923 (blocks produced 15 June
1923)
Block printed / repeats not
ascertainable / 11

1045
Glastraube (Glass Grape)
1913/22
Block printed / repeats not
ascertainable / 9

1046
Raptus
1921

1047
Waldveilchen (Hedge Violet)
1925

1048
Wetterleuchten (Sheet Lightning)
1913/22
Block printed / repeats not
ascertainable / 8

1049
Zackenband (Zigzag Braid)
1922
Roller printed / repeats not
ascertainable / 12

Juliana RYSAVY (1893–   )

1050
Leonie
1916/18 / Ziegler
600
Block printed / 11:10 cm / 4

1051
Annie
1916/18 / Ziegler
601
Block printed / 11:14.8 cm / 8

1052
Funke (Spark)
1916/18 / Ziegler
605
Block printed / 11.5:10 cm / 6

1053
Blumenteppich (Carpet of Flowers)
1916/19 / Ziegler
656
Block printed / 25.5:12 cm / 5

Arthur SCHARRISCH (1888–   )

1054
Blumenwiese (Flowery Meadow)
1910/12 / Bremges & G.,
Albouts, Finkh & Co
3
Block printed / 22:25.5 cm / 8
TKI VI, 1913, p. 250 (length of
fabric)
ID XXIV, 1913, p. 115 (lampshade)
DKD XXXII, 1913, p. 61 (trimming)
126

Irene (Reni) SCHASCHL-SCHUSTER (1895–1979)

1055
Zaunkönig (Wren)
1912/17 / Ziegler, Neumann,
Alpenländische Druckfabrik
82
Block printed / 20.3:13.5 cm / 10
ID XXXII, 1921, p. 159 (lampshade)

1056
Troja (Troy)
1912/17 / Ziegler, Neumann,
Teltscher
87
Block printed / 12.7:10.3 cm / 19
232

1057
Gitterblume
1912/17 / Alpenländische
Druckfabrik
102
Block printed / 19.6:10 cm / 5
217

1058
Boston
1912/17 / Ziegler
182
Block printed / 49.5:29.5 cm / 2
Berlin 1977 (exhib. cat.), pp. 48,
144
Florence 1978 (exhib. cat.),
p. 146, fig. 120; p. 162
198

1059
Cäsar (Caesar)
1912/17 / Ziegler
188
Block printed / 42:30.5 cm / 3

1060
Iselberg
1912/17 / Albouts, Finkh & Co
189
Block printed / 41:29.7 cm / 4

1061
Columbia
1912/17 / Ziegler
191
Block printed / 33:15 cm / 2
MBF XXIV, 1925, p. 283 (lampshade)
Tokyo 1989 (exhib. cat.), p. 351
186, 187

1062
Miki
1912/17 / Ziegler
192
Block printed / 46:30 cm / 5

1063
Ilus
1912/17
196
Block printed / 7.5:7.5 cm / 2

1064
Dubno
1912/18 / Ziegler, Blumenegg
250, 250a
Block printed / 14:10 cm / 15

1065
Luftschloß (Castle in the Air)
1916/18 / Ziegler
549
Block printed / 16:22.5 cm / 8
Tokyo 1989 (exhib. cat.), p. 351
177

1066
Fingerhut (Thimble)
1916/18 / Ziegler
557
Block printed / 10:9.9 cm / 7

1067
Wurzelsepp
1916/18 / Ziegler
560
Block printed / 10:5 cm / 4

1068
Malve (Mallow)
1916/18 / Ziegler
565
Block printed / 13.6:5 cm / 4

1069
Tropenblume (Tropical Flower)
1916/18 / Ziegler
633
Block printed / 81:23.5 cm / 2
MBF XXIV, 1925, p. 294 (upholstery)
ÖBWK II, 1925/26, pp. 46, 47
(upholstery)
Kleiner 1927, p. 38 (upholstery)
Baroni/D'Auria 1981, p. 176,
fig. 449
184, 185

1070
Hexentanz (Witches' Dance)
1919
687
Block printed / 19:11 cm / 8

1071
Lachtaube (Ring Dove)
1919 / Ziegler
688
Block printed / repeats not
ascertainable / 2

1072
Unschuld (Innocence)
1919 / Ziegler
689, 689a
Block printed / 20:11 cm / 7

1073
Ringelblume (Marigold)
1920/21 / Ziegler
753
Block printed / 7.5:9 cm / 1

1074
Strohröschen (Everlasting
Flower)
1920/21 / Ziegler
758
Block printed / 10.5:4 cm / 8

1075
Menuett (Minuet)
1920/21 / Ziegler
759
Block printed / 4:6 cm / 1

1076
Nok
1920/21 / Ziegler
760
Block printed / 9:9.8 cm / 7

1077
Siena
1920/21 / Ziegler
761
Block printed / 10:8.8 cm / 7

1078
Windröschen (Anemone)
1920/21 / Alpenländische
Druckfabrik, Ziegler
781
Block printed / 8.8:17.2 cm / 8

1079
Klotildis
1912/21
Block printed / repeats not
ascertainable / 8

SCHENK

1080
Peter
1928 / Schenk
5171
Spray printed / repeats not
ascertainable / 8

SCHINKO

1081
Osmond
1910/17 / Bujatti
199
Block printed / 11.2:14.8 cm / 4

1082
Brüssel (Brussels)
1910/17 / Ziegler
263
Block printed / 8.2:5.2 cm / 2
Brussels 1987 (exhib. cat.), p. 183,
no. 9.20

1083
Sternblume (Starflower)
1910/17 / Ziegler
499
Block printed / repeats not
ascertainable / 2

Anny SCHRÖDER-EHRENFEST (1898–1972)

1084
Grindlwald
1913
239
Block printed / 6:6 cm / 15

1085
Edelweiß (Edelweiss, Lion's Foot)
1916/18 / Ziegler
555
Block printed / 13.5:7.3 cm / 5

1086
Feldblume (Wild Flower)
1916/18 / Ziegler
562
Block printed / 7.5:7.5 cm / 6
Völker 1984, p. 118, fig. 161;
p. 276

1087
Kokospalme (Coconut Palm)
1916/18 / Ziegler
566
Block printed / 9:7.5 cm / 3

1088
Steinnelke
1916/18 / Ziegler
567
Block printed / 6:6 cm / 4

1089
Wasserblüten
1916/18 / Ziegler
579
Block printed / 4:5 cm / 3
Koch 1926, pp. 44f. (covering of
a showcase)

1090
Ranken (Tendrils)
1918 / Ziegler, Neumann,
Teltscher
580
Block printed / 12:7.3 cm / 8

1091
Laube (Summerhouse)
1918 / Teltscher, Ziegler,
Neumann
582
Block printed / 10.9:2.5 cm / 9

1092
Zaun (Fence)
1918 / Ziegler, Neumann,
Neunkirchner Druckfabrik
584
Block printed / 7.3:5 cm / 11

1093
Gitter (Lattice)
1918 / Teltscher, Ziegler,
Neumann
585
Block printed / 4.5:3.5 cm / 8

1094
Kaplan (Curate)
1918 / Ziegler
594
Block printed / 6:6 cm / 7

1095
Lusthaus (Pleasure House)
1919 / Ziegler
645
Block printed / 20:15 cm / 4

1096
Türkenbund (Turk's Cap)
1919 / Ziegler, Alpenländische
Druckfabrik
672
Block printed / 20.2:11 cm / 10

1097
Tobias
1919 / Ziegler
704
Block printed / 3:5.5 cm / 1

1098
Lukas
1919 / Ziegler
705
Block printed / 3.5:7.4 cm / 15

1099
Arabeske (Arabesque)
1920/21 / Ziegler
719
Block printed / 25.5:14.5 cm,
pattern staggered/ 4
Berlin 1977 (exhib. cat.), p. 101
195, 196

1100
Chi-ki
1920/21 / Ziegler
720
Block printed / 68:29 cm / 5

1101
Kerker (Dungeon)
1921/22 / Ziegler
796
Block printed / 7.5:7.5 cm / 7

1102
Aida
1921/22 / Ziegler
798
Block printed / 7.2:7.5 cm / 7

1103
Rapallo
1921/22 / WW, Ziegler
802
Block printed / repeats not
ascertainable

SCHWABEL

1104
Moschee (Mosque)
1912/22
Block printed / repeats not
ascertainable / 10

Susanne (Susi) SINGER-SCHINNERL (1891–1965)

1105
Sterngucker (Stargazer)
1916/18 / Ziegler
563, 563a
Block printed / 35:23 cm / 16

1106
Staniol (Tinfoil)
1923 (27 Mar. 1923) / Ziegler,
Teltscher
836
Block printed / 16.5:11.5 cm / 11
228

1107
Wipfel (Treetop)
1923 / Ziegler
846
Block printed / repeats not
ascertainable / 4

Max SNISCHEK (1891–1968)

1108
Märchen (Fairy Tale)
1912/17 / Ziegler, Bremges & G.,
Albouts, Finkh & Co
408
Block printed / 51.5:29.5 cm / 2

1109
Berggeist (Mountain Sprite)
1924 (5 Mar. 1924) / Ziegler,
Teltscher
860
Block printed / 41:30 cm / 22
Wichmann 1990 (stock cat.),
p. 147
373

1110
Phantom
1924 (blocks produced 5 Nov.
1924) / Ziegler, Teltscher
879
Block printed / repeat height
not ascertainable:30 cm / 17
SSR XXIX, 1928/29, p. 75
(cushion)
Wichmann 1990 (stock cat.),
p. 146
376

1111
Zyprian
1924 (blocks produced 5 Nov.
1924) / Ziegler, Teltscher, FAG
880
Block printed / 27:30 cm / 17
379

1112
Missouri
1925 (blocks produced 28 July
1925) / Ziegler, Teltscher
914
Block printed / repeats not
ascertainable / 9
339

1113
Manissa
1925/26 (blocks produced 8 Feb.
1926) / Ziegler, Teltscher
925
Block printed / 37:45 cm / 12
DKD LXV, 1929/30, p. 330
(cushion)
Leipzig 1930 (exhib. cat.), p. 155
(cushion)
273, 303, 304

1114
Rhodos
1926 (31 Dec. 1926) / Ziegler,
Teltscher
956
Block printed / 30:30.5 cm / 11

1115
Enos
1926 (31 Dec. 1926) / Ziegler
957
Block printed / 41:30.5 cm / 9
SSR XXIX, 1928/29, p. 15
(cushion)
378

1116
Exeter
1927 (March) / Ziegler, J. M.
Müller's Erben
962
Block printed / 30.5:19.5 cm / 10

1117
Schwan (Swan)
1927 (March) / Ziegler,
Teltscher
971
Block printed / 31:31 cm / 15

1118
Lenglen
1927 (October) / Ziegler,
Teltscher
976
Block printed / 30.5:31 cm / 14
Pichler 1992 (stock cat.), p. 58,
fig. 104; p. 109, no. 32
249, 336

1119
Elfenbein (Ivory)
1927 (December) / Ziegler,
Teltscher, FAG, Ama
985
Block printed / 38.8:32.5 cm / 9
Leipzig 1930 (exhib. cat.), p. 157
(length of fabric)
MBF XXXI, 1932, p. 355
(cushion)
DSH III, 1931/32, pp. 159, 193
(cushion)
Völker 1984, p. 232, fig. 324;
p. 281
Neuwirth 1984, pp. 209f.

1120
Turf
1927 (October) / Ziegler
989
Block printed / 31:31 cm / 8

1121
City
1927 (October) / Ziegler,
Teltscher
990
Block printed / 30.5:30 cm / 11

1122
Samoa
1928 (1 Feb. 1928) / Ziegler,
Teltscher
996
Block printed / repeat height
not ascertainable:61 cm / 12
338

1123
Laubgewinde (Garland of Leaves)
1928 (April) / Ziegler
1002
Block printed / 30:15.2 cm / 7
Völker 1984, p. 222, fig. 312;
p. 281

1124
Syrakus (Syracuse)
1928 (blocks produced 29 Mar.
1928) / Ziegler, Ama, Teltscher
1003
Block printed / 29.2:31.5 cm / 20

1125
Pux
1928 / Ziegler
1004
Block printed / 32.5:34 cm / 7

1128
Biel
1928 (21 Apr. 1928) / Teltscher,
Clavel & Lindenmeyer
1015
Roller printed / 38.7:62 cm / 12
374

1127
Votum
1928 (blocks produced 10 July
1928) / Ziegler
1017
Block printed / 29:32 cm / 15

1128
Flims
1928 (20 June 1928) / Ziegler,
Alpenländische Druckfabrik,
Teltscher
1023
Block printed / 16.4:15.2 cm / 10

1129
Moldau
1928 (blocks produced 30 June
1928) / Teltscher, Ziegler
1025
Block printed / 48:31.5 cm / 6
341

1130
Yen
1928 (July) / Ziegler, Teltscher
1027
Block printed / 26:30.5 cm / 12
Neuwirth 1984, p. 223, fig. 175

1131
Dilly
1928 (20 June 1928) / Teltscher,
Wasservogel, Ziegler
1028
Block printed / 22.5:33 cm / 17

1132
Pucker
1928 (20 June 1928) / Teltscher
1029
Block printed / 43:66.5 cm / 14

1133
Quelle (Spring)
1928 (July) / Teltscher, Clavel &
Lindenmeyer
1032
Block printed / 35.5:60 cm / 17

1134
Hyazinthe (Hyacinth)
1928 (July) / Ziegler, Teltscher
1033
Block printed / 38:30.5 cm / 8

1135
Corona
1928 (July) / Ziegler, Sax
1035
Block printed / 44:30.5 cm / 15

1136
Idyll
1928 (July) / Teltscher, Ziegler
1038
Block printed / 39.5:31 cm / 12
ÖBWK VI, 1929/39, p. 64

(wallpaper), p. 67 (curtain,
upholstery), p. 69 (mattress
cover)
DSH I, 1930, pp. 226f.
(upholstery of a chair)

1137
Piacenza
1928 (July) / Ziegler
1042
Block printed / 41.2:30.5 cm / 13

1138
Kasuar
1928 (21 Aug. 1928) / Ziegler
1047
Block printed / 40:30 cm / 15
SSR XXXII, 1931/32, pp. 62, 149
(cushion)
DKD LXV, 1929/30, p. 44
(length of fabric)
MBF XXX, 1931, p. 44 (cushion)
Völker in WKK 1984, p. 48,
fig. 14

1139
Münster
1928 (19 Sep. 1928) / Teltscher,
Ziegler
1053
Block printed / 31:30.5 cm / 8

1140
Vorau
1928 (September) / Ziegler
1055
Block printed / 35:31.5 cm / 8
375

1141
Danubius
1928 (4 Oct. 1928) / Ziegler
1060
Block printed / 26:15.2 cm / 7

1142
Trinidad
1928 (2 Oct. 1928) / Ziegler
1061
Block printed / 39:30 cm / 7
SSR XXXII, 1931/32, p. 62
(cushion)

1143
Melodie (Melody)
1928 (2 Oct. 1928) / Ziegler
1062
Block printed / 30:30.5 cm / 11

1144
Philadelphia
1928 (8 Oct. 1928) / Ziegler
1063
Roller printed / 38:30.5 cm / 11

1145
Horizont (Horizon)
1928 (9 Oct. 1928) / Teltscher,
Ziegler
1064
Block printed / 38:29.5 cm / 13

1146
Ossiach
1928 (10 Oct. 1928) / Ziegler
1066
Block printed / 34:29.3 cm / 10

1147
Abbazia (Abbey)
1928 (13 Oct. 1928) / Ziegler
1067
Block printed / repeat height
not ascertainable:32 cm / 12

1148
Retz
1928 (12 Oct. 1928) / Ziegler
1068
Block printed / 46:30.5 cm / 8

1149
Lothar
1928 (26 Oct. 1928) / Ziegler
1073
Block printed / 30:15 cm / 12

1150
Cartago (Carthago) (Carthage)
1929 (blocks produced 10 Jan.
1929) / Ziegler
1087
Block printed / 36:30.5 cm / 13
DKD XLVI, 1930, p. 308
(cushion)
SSR XXXI, 1930/31, p. 129
(cushion)
DKD LXVII, 1930/32, p. 207
(cushion)
ID XLII, 1931, p. 33 (cushion)

1151
Ybbs
1929 (31 Jan. 1929) / Teltscher,
Ziegler
1095
Block printed / 36:30.5 cm / 11

1152
Elbasan
1929 (4 Feb. 1929) / Ziegler
1096
Block printed / 35:30.5 cm / 8
337

1153
Fernando
1929 (6 May 1929) / Teltscher,
Ziegler
1111
Block printed / 37:31.5 cm / 11

1154
Othmar
1929 (7 May 1929) / Teltscher
1114
Block printed / 40:31.5 cm / 11

1155
Carlos
1929 (13 May 1929) / Teltscher,
Ziegler
1120
Block printed / 36:31.5 cm / 8

1156
Darling
1929 (September) / Teltscher,
Ziegler
1129
Block printed / 32:36 cm / 22

1157
Celebes
1929 (June) / Ziegler, Teltscher
1130
Block printed / 40:32 cm / 13
340

1158
Spoleto
1929 (blocks produced 15 July
1929) / Teltscher
1131
Block printed / 32:40 cm / 9
DKD XXV, 1929/30, p. 420
(cushion)
Leipzig 1930 (exhib. cat.), p. 193
(cushion)
Völker 1984, p. 232, fig. 325;
p. 281

1159
Bilbao
1929 (July) / Teltscher, Ziegler
1134
Block printed / 32:32 cm / 12
ID XLII, 1932, p. 127 (curtain,
upholstery for a living room and
dining room)
MBF XXX, 1931, p. 72 (curtain,
upholstery for a living room and
dining room)

1160
Dolores
1929 (26 July 1929) / Teltscher,
Ziegler
1135
Block printed / 27:32.5 cm / 12

1161
Klepper
1929 (July) / Ziegler
1137
Block printed / 32:32 cm / 14

1162
Zelenika
1929 (26 July 1929) / Teltscher,
FAG
1138
Block printed / 32:30 cm / 18
Völker 1984, p. 245, fig. 339;
p. 281
Trad. u. Exper. 1989, p. 74

1163
Arina
1929 (26 Aug. 1929) / Teltscher,
Ziegler
1141
Block printed / repeats not
ascertainable / 17

1164
Miri
1929 (July) / Sax, Ziegler
1144
Block printed / 32:36 cm / 10

1165
Togo
1929 (July) / Sax
1145
Block printed / 32:32 cm / 10

1166
Niagara
1929 (2 Sep. 1929) / Sax
1148
Block printed / 32:32 cm / 9

1167
Sirocco
1929 (26 Oct. 1929) / Ziegler
1152
Block printed / 42:34 cm / 13

1168
Monsun (Monsoon)
1929 (26 Oct. 1929) / Ziegler,
Ama
1153
Block printed / 29.5:32 cm / 10
DKD LXVI, 1930, p. 308 (length
of fabric)
DSH III, 1931/32, p. 16 (lamp-
shade)

1169
Origan (Origon) (Oregano)
1929 (26 Oct. 1929) / Sax, Ama,
Teltscher
1154
Block printed / 40:30 cm / 13

1170
Taifun (Typhoon)
1929 (28 Oct. 1929) / Ama, FAG
1155
Block printed / 40:32 cm / 12

1171
Pelly
1930 (January) / Ziegler, FAG
1167
Block printed / 32:32 cm / 12
Völker 1984, p. 221, fig. XXX;
p. 270

1172
Seeboden
1930 (January) / Ziegler
1171
Block printed / 32:32 cm / 16

1173
Rauten (Rhombs)
1930 (February) / Ziegler
1175
Block printed / 15.5:33 cm / 13

1174
Eden
1930 (December) / FAG
1202
Block printed / 33:33 cm / 9

1175
Colette
1928 (4 Jan. 1928) / Posnanski,
Schenk
5012
Spray printed / repeats not
ascertainable / 12

1176
Olinda
1927 (September) / Posnanski
5050
Spray printed / 24.3 cm: repeat
width not ascertainable / 8

1177
Sofia
1927 (November) / Vetter,
Posnanski
5072
Spray printed / 12:15.5 cm / 6
Wien 1929 (exhib. cat.), p. 135
(length of fabric)

1178
New York
1928 (21 Apr. 1928) / Vetter
5134
Spray printed / 50 cm:repeat
width not ascertainable / 12
377

1179
Sport
1928 (March) / Vetter
5142
Spray printed / 38.5:43 cm / 8
244

1180
Sahara
1927 (November) / Schenk
5179
Spray printed / repeat height
not ascertainable:14.5 cm / 5

1181
Sesam (Sesame)
1927 (November) / Schenk
5182
Spray printed / 14.5:14.8 cm / 9

1182
Inka (Inca)
1928 (25 Sep. 1928) / Neumann,
Hämmerle
5192
Spray printed / repeat height
not ascertainable:41.5 cm / 9

1183
Colombo
1929 (20 Feb. 1929) / Posnanski
5223
Spray printed / repeats not
ascertainable / 6

1184
Australia
1929
5224
Spray printed / repeats not
ascertainable

1185
Bosporus
1929 (27 Feb. 1929) / Schenk
5231
Spray printed / repeats not
ascertainable / 7

1186
Dempsey
1929 (29 Apr. 1929) / Presser
5239
Spray printed / repeats not
ascertainable / 7

**Maria Lucia STADL-
MAYER (1906–   )**

1187
Helium
1928 (July) / Ziegler, Teltscher
1085, 5157
Block printed, spray printed /
30.5:30.5 cm / 14
SSR XXX, 1929/30, p. 12 (length
of fabric)

1188
Hongkong
1928 (July) / Posnanski, Schenk,
Wasservogel, Vetter, WW
('Haus')
5028
Spray printed / repeat height
not ascertainable:30 cm / 31

1189
Rigi
1928 (10 July 1928) / Anderegg
14607 (archive no.)
Woven fabric / stripes with
different repeats/ 12

Luise STOLL

1190
Bisamberg
1910/16
267
Block printed / 31.8:45.8 cm / 9
Kleiner 1927, p. 33 (upholstery)
116

1191
Meran
1910/17 / Bremges & G.,
Albouts, Finkh & Co, Ziegler
423
Block printed / 51.5:44 cm / 1

1192
Nippon
1910/17 / Bujatti, Ziegler
437
Block printed / repeats not
ascertainable / 2

Maria TRINKL (1896–   )

1193
Cook
1913/18 / Ziegler
629, 629a
Block printed / 10.5:7.5 cm / 9

Guido UXA (1895–   )

1194
Nürnberg (Nuremberg)
1912/17 / Ziegler
433
Block printed / repeats not
ascertainable / 1

**Marie VOGEL
(1892–   )**

1195
Edelkoralle (Precious Coral)
1910/11 / Ziegler
291
Block printed / 6.6:6 cm / 9
TKI VII, 1914, p. 52 (length of
fabric)
Völker 1984, p. 30, fig. 33;
p. 271

1196
Edelmarder (Beech Marten)
1910/11 / WW, Neumann,
Ziegler, Neunkirchner Druckfabrik
292
Block printed / 13:8.2 cm / 2
Völker 1984, p. 12, fig. 5;
p. 271
45

1197
Kanarienvogel (Canary)
1910/11 / Ziegler
375, 375a
Block printed / 7.5:10 cm / 3
TKI VI, 1913, p. 242 (length of
fabric)
TKI VII, 1914, p. 55 (length of
fabric)
27, 98

**Emma WABAK
(1902–   )**

1198
Germania
1916/17 / Ziegler
249
Block printed / 47.5:30 cm / 8

**Gertrude WEINBERGER
(1897–   )**

1199
Alpenkönig (King of the Alps)
1916/18 / Ziegler
604, 604a
Block printed / 16.5:14.8 cm / 9

1200
Sternschnuppen (Shooting Stars)
1919 / Ziegler, Neumann
648
Block printed / 9:7.2 cm / 10

Maria WEISSENBERG

1201
Benares
1919 / Ziegler
696
Block printed / 9.7:11.5 cm / 8
118

1202
Hannover (Hanover)
1914/19
Block printed / repeats not
ascertainable / 11

241

Valerie (Vally) WIESEL-THIER (1895–1945)

1203
Schlingpflanze (Creeping Plant)
1914/17 / Ziegler
64
Block printed / 28.1:15 cm / 16

1204
Federwölkchen (Cirrus Cloud)
1914/17 / Ziegler
65, 65a
Block printed / 17.5:25 cm / 17

1205
Federball (Badminton)
1914/17 / Ziegler, Klinger,
Bujatti
66
Block printed / 6.2:3.8 cm / 3

1206
Passionsblume (Passionflower)
1914/17
68
Block printed / 19:21.2 cm / 3

1207
Himmelbrand (Velvet Dock)
1914/18
128
Block printed / 57.5:44.5 cm / 9

1208
Meerblume (Sea Flower)
1914/18 / Ziegler, Klinger,
Bujatti
130
Block printed / 20:15.2 cm / 3

1209
Gundula
1914/18
164
Block printed / 15:12.4 cm / 7

1210
Fruchtstamm (Fruit-stalk)
1914/18 / Ziegler, Alpen-
ländische Druckfabrik
166
Block printed / 51:30 cm / 3
Tokyo 1989 (exhib. cat.), p. 351

1211
Meerqualle (Sea Nettle)
1914/19 / Ziegler, Klinger,
Bujatti
197
Block printed / 12:7.5 cm / 2

1212
Fruchtkätzchen (Fruit Catkin)
1914/19 / Bujatti, Ziegler
202
Block printed / 10:7.5 cm / 10

1213
Salpinx
1914/19 / Bujatti, Ziegler
203
Block printed / 10:15 cm / 13
131

1214
Reigen (Round Dance)
1914/19 / Ziegler, Klinger,
Bujatti
204
Block printed / 16:10 cm / 1

1215
Sent Mahese
1914/19 / Ziegler
213, 213a
Block printed / 16:14.7 cm / 2

1216
Aesthet (Aesthete)
1914/19 / Ziegler
234
Block printed / 20:15 cm / 5

1217
Delft
1914/19 / Ziegler, Teltscher
242
Block printed / 9.8:9.8 cm / 8

1218
Pfeil (Arrow)
1916/19 / Ziegler
578
Block printed / 8:5 cm / 3

1219
Himmelhof (Heavenly Court)
1916/19
610
Block printed / 10:10 cm / 3

1220
Ursula
1916/19 / Ziegler
613
Block printed / 14.3:14 cm / 9

1221
Quadern (Ashlars)
1916/19 / Teltscher, Ziegler
617
Block printed / 28.5:15.2 cm / 9
215

1222
Anitra
1919 / Ziegler
690
Block printed / repeat width
11 cm / 10

1223
Peer Gynt
1919 / Ziegler, Alpenländische
Druckfabrik, Teltscher
691, 691a
Block printed / repeat width
11 cm / 9

1224
Andromache
1919 / Ziegler, Blumenegg
692
Block printed / repeat width
17 cm / 10
Wichmann 1990 (stock cat.),
pp. 124f.
222, 223

1225
Aloe
1919 / Haendel, Ama, Ziegler
695
Block printed / repeat width
30 cm / 8
Wichmann 1990 (stock cat.),
p. 124

1226
Spieldose (Music Box)
1920/21 / Teltscher, Ziegler
718
Block printed / 82:44 cm / 6

1227
Soldanellen
1920/21 / Ziegler, Alpen-
ländische Druckfabrik
780
Block printed / 12.5:9.5 cm / 7

Eduard Josef WIMMER-WISGRILL (1882–1961)

1228
Ameise (klein und groß) (Ant,
small and large)
1910/11 / Bremges & G.,
Albouts, Finkh & Co, Ziegler,
Teltscher, Neumann
33, 33a
Block printed / 17.9:12.2 cm and
35:24.5 cm / 20
KKHW XIV, 1911, p. 618 (upholstery of a chair), pp. 621, 631,
687 (length of fabric)
DKD XXIX, 1911/12, p. 396
(curtain, upholstery)
DI XII, 1911, p. 96 (upholstery of
a chair), pl. 92 (curtain, upholstery), pl. 93 (upholstery of a
chair)
Rome 1911 I (exhib. cat.), p. 113
(covering of an showcase)
Rome 1911 II (exhib. cat.), pl.
Room VII (covering of a
showcase)
TKI V, 1912, pp. 51, 53 (length of
fabric)
ID XXIII, 1912, p. 37 (curtain,
upholstery), p. 97 (upholstery of
a chair)
ID XXIV, 1913, pp. 480, 481, 483
(wall-coverings)
DKD XXXI, 1912/13, p. 341
(upholstery)
MBF XII; 1913, p. 2 (upholstery
of a chair)
DKD XXXIV, 1914, p. 369 (tablecloth, upholstery of a chair,
floor-covering, curtain)
DK XVII, 1914, p. 476 (tablecloth,
upholstery of a chair, floor-
covering, curtain)
DKD XXXV, 1914/15, p. 384
(wall-covering)
ID XXVI, 1915, p. 190 (curtain),
p. 240 (wall-covering)
JDW 1915, p. 7 (tablecloth,
upholstery of a chair, floor-
covering, curtain)
Koch 1916, p. 39 (tablecloth,
upholstery of a chair, floor-
covering, curtain)

Eisler 1916, p. 214 (length of
fabric)
DKD XXXIX, 1916/17, p. 407
(wall-covering)
ID XXVIII, 1917, p. 125 (wall-
covering), p. 164 (floor-covering)
DKD XL, 1917, p. 183 (length of
fabric)
Nebehay 1976, fig. 149
Fanelli 1976, fig. 586, 587, 588
Baroni/D'Auria 1981, p. 132,
fig. 323
Wien 1983 (exhib. cat.), p. 24,
no. 23
Völker 1984, p. 13, fig. 6; p. 77,
fig. 98; pp. 272, 274
Hansen 1984, p. 54
Schweiger 1984, p. 133; pp. 73,
95, 133, 220 (figs.).
Venice 1984 (exhib. cat.), p. 249,
fig. 1; p. 516, fig. 1
Gmeiner/Pirhofer 1985, p. 34,
fig. 18
Wien 1986 (exhib. cat.), p. 65,
no. 35.1; cat. no. 37.6
Trad. u. Exper. 1988, p. 66
New York 1992/93, p. 17
55, 56, 57, 58, 59, 257, 258

1229
Aurelia
1910/12
154
Block printed / 84.5:65 cm / 3

1230
Albanien (Albania)
1910/12 / Ziegler, Neumann,
Teltscher
157
Block printed / repeat width
14.5 cm / 2

1231
Bajazzo (Buffoon)
1910/12
257
Silk brocade / repeats not
ascertainable / 3

1232
Carmen
1910/11 / Bremges & G.,
Albouts, Finkh & Co, Neunkirchner Druckfabrik; Neumann
272
Block printed / 24.5 cm:repeat
width not ascertainable / 10

1233
Goldblatt (Gold Leaf)
1910/11 / Ziegler
318
Block printed / 5.5:5 cm / 3
DKD XLVII, 1920/21, p. 341
(length of fabric)
Pichler 1992 (stock cat.), p. 92,
fig. 170
19

1234
Heimchen (House Cricket)
1910/11
340
Block printed / 38.5:66 cm / 1
DI XII, 1911, p. 74 (curtain), p. 76

(curtain, wallpaper)
JDW 1912, p. 89 (fashion drawing)
ID XXIV, 1913, p. 115 (upholstery of a chair)
DKD XXXI, 1912/13, p. 340 (upholstery)
DKD XXXIV, 1914, p. 301 (lampshade)
TKI VIII, 1915, p. 201 (length of fabric)
DKD XXXVII, 1915/16, p. 410 (wallpaper, curtain, upholstery)
ID XXXII, 1921, p. 302 (wallpaper, curtain, lampshade), p. 303 (wallpaper, curtain, lampshade, upholstery)
ID XXXVII, 1926, p. 22 (wallpaper, curtain, upholstery)
Brussels 1927 (stock cat.), p. 385, no. 452 (length of fabric)
Kleiner 1927, p. 13 (wallpaper, curtain, upholstery of a chair)
Völker 1984, p. 119, fig. 162; p. 276

1235
Herbstsonne (Autumn Sun)
1910/12
343
Block printed / 22.5:27 cm / 10
DKD XXXII, 1913, p. 367 (upholstery of a chair)
DI XIV, 1913, pl. 70 (upholstery of a chair, curtain)
TKI VI, 1913, p. 445 (floor-covering)
Fanelli 1976, fig. 631
Brussels 1987 (exhib. cat.), no. 9.22; p. 184
70, 104

1236
Kuckuck (Cuckoo)
1910/12 / Bremges & G., Albouts, Finkh & Co, Ziegler
370
Block printed / 14.6:14 cm / 9
Fanelli 1976, fig. 629
16

1237
Kaschmierziege (Kashmir Goat)
1910/12 / Bremges & G., Albouts, Finkh & Co
378
Block printed / repeat height not ascertainable:18 cm / 2
Fanelli 1976, fig. 212

1238
Lachs (Sachs)
1910/12 / Ziegler
391
Block printed / repeat height not ascertainable:13 cm / 1

1239
Leopard
1910/11 / Bremges & G., Albouts, Finkh & Co
393
Block printed / repeat height not ascertainable:8.7 cm / 1
Brussels 1927 (stock cat.), p. 386, no. 453 (length of fabric)

Fanelli 1976, fig. 630
Neuwirth 1984, pp. 22, 23
Brussels 1989 (exhib. cat.), p. 154, no. 26
16

1240
Maikäfer (Cockchafer)
1910/11 / Ziegler
416, 416a
Block printed / 26.7:30 cm / 2
TKI VII, 1914, p. 62 (length of fabric)
DKD XXXVII, 1915/16, p. 85 (costume)
Fanelli 1976, fig. 135
94

1241
Seerose (Water Lily)
1910/12 / WW, Ziegler
472, 472a
Block printed / 8.5:9.5 cm / 9
Fanelli 1976, fig. 213
307

1242
St. Veit
1910/12 / Ziegler
494
Block printed / repeats not ascertainable / 3
TKI VIII, 1915, p. 200 (length of fabric)
Eisler 1916, p. 116 (upholstery of a chair)
Baroni/D'Auria 1981, p. 130, fig. 320

1243
Turandot
1910/12 / Bremges & G., Albouts, Finkh & Co
509
Block printed / repeats not ascertainable / 1

1244
Mandelkrähe (Roller)
1910/11 / Ziegler
518
Block printed / 14.4:22.8 cm / 3
DKD XXXI, 1912/13, p. 102 (corsage)
DI XIV, 1913, pl. 2 (lampshade, tablecloth, upholstery of a chair, curtain), pl. 70 (lampshade)
DA XX, 1914/15, pl. 3 (curtain)
Eisler 1916, p. 116 (lampshade, tablecloth, upholstery of a chair, curtain)
DA XXI, 1916/18, p. 95 (lampshade, tablecloth, upholstery of a chair, curtain)
DKD XXXIX, 1916/17, p. 110 (bag)
Neuwirth 1984, p. 120, fig. 84; p. 121, fig. 85
Schweiger 1984, p. 241
Neuwirth 1985, cat. no. 66
52

1245
Warschau (Warsaw)
1910/12 / Bremges & G., Albouts, Finkh & Co

532
Block printed / repeats not ascertainable / 1

1246
Bachus (Bacchus)
1910/17
Silk brocade/ repeats not ascertainable / 6

1247
Caballero (Knight, Horseman)
1910/17
Silk brocade/ repeats not ascertainable / 7

1248
Lord Corinc
1910/17
Silk brocade/ repeats not ascertainable / 11

Johanna (Hanna) WINTER-STEINER-PULITZER (1904–)

1249
Mexiko (Mexico)
1923 (3 May 1923) / Ziegler, Teltscher
848
Block printed / 11.5:10.8 cm / 20
Wichmann 1990 (stock cat.), pp. 148f.
213

Anny WIRTH

1250
Persien (Persia)
1910/11 / Ziegler, Alpenländische Druckfabrik
455, 455a
Block printed / 26:31 cm / 5
Tokyo 1989 (exhib. cat.), p. 351
291

Marianne ZELS (1876–)

1251
Alpengipfel (Alpine Peak)
1910/25 / Ziegler, Alpenländische Druckfabrik, Teltscher
111
Block printed / 24.9:11.5 cm / 4

Julius ZIMPEL (1896–1925)

1252
Sold (Salary)
1911/17 / Ziegler
224
Block printed / repeat height not ascertainable:21.7 cm / 1

1253
Meanon
1911/18 / Ziegler
588
Block printed / 17.8:22 cm / 9

1254
Orient
1911/19 / Ziegler
659
Block printed / 24.5:22 cm / 2

1255
Litaipo
1919 / Ziegler, Teltscher
663
Block printed / 12.5:21.8 cm / 17

1256
Triton
1919 / Ziegler
683
Block printed / 15.3:22 cm / 5

1257
Ruth
1919 / Teltscher, Ziegler
684
Block printed / 30:22 cm / 6

1258
Schiwa (Shiva)
1919 / Ziegler
685
Block printed / 32.5:21.8 cm / 9

1259
Buddha
1919 / Ziegler
686
Block printed / 7.5:10 cm / 3

1260
Orplid
1919/21
712
Block printed / repeats not ascertainable / 1

1261
Pax
1919/21 / Teltscher, Ziegler
714
Block printed / repeats not ascertainable / 5

1262
Laurenz
1919/22 / Ziegler
814
Block printed / 4:3 cm / 5

1263
Email (Enamel)
1919/23 / Ziegler, Clavel & Lindenmeyer, Rodauner Druckfabrik
841, 841a
Block printed / 11.5:8.6 cm / 15

1264
Batavia
1925 (blocks produced 1 July 1925) / Ziegler, Teltscher
912
Block printed / 37.3:29.8 cm / 10
Wien 1929 (exhib. cat.), p. 96 (cushion)
SSR XXXII, 1931/32, p. 149 (cushion)
237

1265
Peru
1925 (blocks produced 28 July
1925) / Ziegler
913
Block printed / 8:6 cm / 9

1266
Bahia
1925 (blocks produced 1 July
1925) / Teltscher, Ziegler
919
Block printed / 14.3:15.2 cm / 10
Neuwirth 1985, pp. 38f.

1267
Valencia
1925 (blocks produced 28 July
1925) / Ziegler, Teltscher
920
Block printed / 24:30 cm / 15
221

1268
Rimini (Bimini)
1927 (block produced in
October) / Ziegler
979
Block printed / 35.5:30.5 cm / 12
234

1269
Zwergpalme (Dwarf Palm)
1928 (blocks produced 19 Mar.
1928) / Ziegler, Teltscher
991
Block printed / 37:30 cm / 15
Leipzig 1930 (exhib. cat.), p. 155
(cushion)
235

1270
Guinea
1928 (blocks produced in
April) / Ziegler, Teltscher,
Alpenländische Druckfabrik
1013
Block printed / 32:30.5 cm / 6
Neuwirth 1985, p. 38
236

1271
Rafael
1930 (blocks produced in
January) / Ama, Telstscher
1168
Block printed / 32:32 cm / 10

1272
Farina
1924 (September) / Vetter
5124
Spray printed / repeat height
not ascertainable:61 cm / 8
DK XXXVII, 1929, p. 43
(tablecloth)

1273
Kanton (Canton)
1927 (produced in October) /
Vogel
6165
Woven fabric / 14.8:8 cm / 6

1274
Orient
1925 / Vogel
9624
Woven fabric / 40:31.5 cm / 3

1275
Marabu
1923 / Vogel(?)
9642
Woven fabric / repeat height not
ascertainable:65 cm / 12

1276
Arizona
1925 / Vogel
9682
Woven fabric / 29 cm:repeat
width not ascertainable / 6

1277
Obst (Fruit)
1925 / Vogel
9684
Woven fabric / repeats not
ascertainable / 1

1278
Stockrose (Hollyhock)
1925 / Vogel
9702
Woven fabric / repeats not
ascertainable / 24

1279
Flamme (Flame)
1928
51W (archive no.)
Woven fabric / 74.5 cm:repeat
width not ascertainable

1280
Amoy
1925 (26 Oct. 1925) / Backhausen
58W (archive no.)
Woven fabric / repeats not
ascertainable

1281
Mocca
1925
10130 (archive no.)
Woven fabric / repeats not
ascertainable

1282
Florida
1925 / Backhausen
Woven fabric / repeats not
ascertainable / 1

1283
Kleo
1925 / Backhausen
Woven fabric / repeats not
ascertainable / 2

Ugo ZOVETTI (1879–)

1284
Adrianopel (Adrianople)
1910/11
25
Block printed / repeats not
ascertainable / 4
Fanelli 1976, fig. 619
97

1285
Arbe
1910/11 / Ziegler, Ströbel

26
Block printed / 36.5:38 cm / 4
Eisler 1916, p. 122 (upholstery)
DBK 1916/17 in DA XXI,
1916/18, pl. 15 (upholstery)
DKD XLI, 1917/18, p. 122
(upholstery)
Venice 1984 (exhib. cat.), p. 511
97, 174

1286
Benz
1910/11
259
Block printed / 11.3:5.5 cm / 4

1287
Daimler
1910/11 / Bujatti
278, 278a
Block printed / 10:5 cm / 7
TKI VII, 1914, p. 58 (length of
fabric)
DK XXIV, January 1916, p. 330
(length of fabric)
Fanelli 1976, fig. 627

1288
Eisblume (Frost Flower)
1910/11 / Ziegler
293
Block printed / 44:22 cm / 9
Fanelli 1976, fig. 625

1289
Federbusch (Plume)
1910/12 / Ziegler
305
Block printed / repeat height
not ascertainable:19.5 cm / 9
TKI VII, 1914, p. 58 (length of
fabric)
Fanelli 1976, fig. 622

1290
Fiat
1910/12 / WW
313
Block printed / 22:22 cm / 2
TKI VII, 1914, p. 58 (length of
fabric)

1291
Ikarus (Icarus)
1910/12
351
Block printed / 48.5:23.7 cm / 2
TKI VIII, 1915, p. 203 (length of
fabric)

1292
Ibikus
1910/12
352
Block printed / repeats not
ascertainable / 2

1293
Iris
1910/12
353
Block printed / 38:18.8 cm / 2
TKI VIII, 1915, p. 204 (length of
fabric)
DK XXIV, 1916, p. 330 (length of
fabric)

1294
Ilona
1910/12 / Bremges & G.,
Albouts, Finkh & Co, Ziegler
354
Block printed / 15.4:7.3 cm / 4

1295
Itala
1910/12
355
Block printed / 22:10 cm / 3

1296
Konstantinopel (Constantinople)
1910/12 / Bremges & G.,
Albouts, Finkh & Co, Ziegler
381
Block printed / 35.5:31.3 cm / 1
109

1297
Linsa (Sinsa)
1910/12 / Ziegler, Alpen-
ländische Druckfabrik
396
Block printed / 24:11 cm / 5
Fanelli 1976, fig. 624

1298
Mikado
1910/12 / WW, Teltscher
413
Block printed / 9.3:11 cm / 6
Fanelli 1976, fig. 621

1299
Marokko (Morocco)
1910/12 / Ziegler, Klinger,
Bujatti
415
Block printed / 19.5:14.5 cm / 2
TKI VII, 1914, p. 56 (length of
fabric)

1300
Mercedes
1910/12 / Bremges & G.,
Albouts, Finkh & Co, Ziegler
421
Block printed / repeats not
ascertainable / 1

1301
Messina
1910/12 / Ziegler
428
Block printed / repeats not
ascertainable / 3

1302
Montenegro
1910/12 / Ziegler
429
Block printed / repeats not
ascertainable / 1
Sekler 1985, p. 130, fig. 162
Paris 1986 (exhib. cat.), p. 187
Wien 1990 (exhib. cat.), pp. 88f.,
no. 10.36

1303
Pfauenauge (Peacock's Eye)
1910/12 / Bremges & G.,
Albouts, Fink & Co, Ziegler
446
Block printed / 57:32.5 cm / 1

1304
Puch
1910/12 / Klinger, Bujatti,
Teltscher
450
Block printed / 24.3:11.2 cm / 2

1305
Pfingstrose (Peony)
1910/12 / Ziegler
459
Block printed / repeat height
not ascertainable:19 cm / 1
TKI VIII, 1915, p. 203 (wall
paper)
ID XXXII, 1921, p. 297 (curtain)

1306
Seetang (Seaweed)
1910/21 / Bremges & G.,
Albouts, Finkh & Co, Ziegler
476
Block printed / 50.5:23.5 cm / 4
Neuwirth 1985, p. 23

1307
Schigatze
1910/12 / Ziegler
492
Block printed / 34.2:26.7 cm / 1

1308
Stichblatt (Coquille)
1910/11 / Bremges & G.,
Albouts, Finkh & Co, Ziegler
497
Block printed / 12:13.5 cm / 11
DK XXIII, 1915, p. 234 (bed-
spread, upholstery of a chair)
DKD XXXVIII, 1916, p. 224
(lampshade, bedspread)
Baldass 1925, photo Atelier Irene
Messner (costume)
Völker amk, p. 5
Kessler-Aurisch 1983, p. 225;
p. 344, fig. 422
Hansen 1984, p. 142
Schweiger 1984, p. 221, fig.
Sekler 1985, p. 130, fig. 162
Paris 1986 (exhib. cat.), p. 187
Tokyo 1989 (exhib. cat.), p. 351
16, 261, 262

1309
Tripolis
1910/12 / Neunkirchner Druckfabrik, Ziegler, Ströbel
508
Block printed / 35.5:19 cm / 2
Florence 1978 (exhib. cat.), vol. 1,
p. 146, fig. 121; p. 162
23

1310
Wanderer
1910/12 / Bujatti, Ziegler
527
Block printed / 11:11 cm / 3

1311
Zauberflöte (Magic Flute)
1910/12 / Albouts, Finkh & Co.,
Bremges & G., Ziegler
542
Block printed / 11:11 cm / 3

1312
Zierpflanze (Ornamental Plant)
1910/12 / Ziegler
543
Block printed / 13.7:repeat
width not ascertainable / 1
Fanelli 1976, fig. 620

**Eleonore ZUCKERKANDL
(1898–)**

1313
Fürchtegott
1918 / Clavel & Lindenmeyer
602
Block printed / 9.5:10 cm / 6

1314
Konfuzius (Confucius)
1918/19 / Ziegler
694
Block printed / 15:14.7 cm / 9

**Franz von ZÜLOW
(1883–1963)**

1315
Oberösterreich (Upper Austria)
1910/11
46
Block printed / 23: 45 cm / 3
TKI VII, 1914, p. 56 (length of
fabric)
TKI VIII, 1915, p. 200 (length of
fabric)
Trad. u. Exper. 1988, p. 68

1316
Dorfrose (Village Rose)
1910/11 / Ziegler
280, 280a
Block printed / 44:45 cm / 9
DKD XXXVIII, 1916, p. 218
(lampshade)
Völker 1984, p. 43, fig. 47; p. 272
86, 87

1317
Dolde (Umbel)
1910/11 / Ziegler
286
Block printed / 22.7:22.5 cm / 9
TKI VII, 1914, p. 61 (length of
fabric)

1318
Eva
1910/11 / Bremges & G.,
Albouts, Finkh & Co, Ziegler
294
Block printed / 45:43.7 cm / 1

1319
Flieder (Lilac)
1910/12 / Ziegler
302
Block printed / 22.3:22.8 cm / 19

1320
Galizien (Galicia)
1910/12 / Ziegler, Neumann,
Teltscher
325
Block printed / 44:69 cm / 5
ID XXIV, 1913, p. 353 (length of
fabric)
Wien 1929 (exhib. cat.), p. 138
(length of fabric)
Wiener Mode XLIII, 1930, WW
special number (length of fabric)

1321
Goldregen (Golden Rain)
1910/12 / Bujatti
332
Block printed / 30:30 cm / 5
TKI VII, 1914, p. 61 (length of
fabric)

1322
Haugsdorf
1910/12
348
Block printed / 44:45.5 cm / 7

1323
Kakadu (Cockatoo)
1910/12 / Ziegler
380
Block printed / repeats not
ascertainable / 1

1324
Lianen (Liane)
1910/12 / Ziegler
380
Block printed / 21.5:22.5 cm / 2
TKI VII, 1914, p. 61
Wien 1967 (exhib. cat.), p. 77,
no. 362
Florence 1978 (exhib. cat.),
p. 162, no. 126
25

1325
Melk
1910/12 / Bremges & G.,
Albouts, Finkh & Co, Ziegler,
Teltscher
406
Block printed / 22.2:22.2 cm / 4

1326
Osterglocken (Narcissus)
1910/12 / Teltscher, Ziegler
441
Block printed / 45:22.5 cm / 11
ID XXXI, 1920, p. 226 (curtain)

1327
Pulkau
1910/12 / Bujatti, Ziegler

458
Block printed / 45:44 cm / 2
Eisler 1916, p. 126 (upholstery)
Neuwirth 1984, p. 144, cat. no.
106
Trad. u. Exper. 1988, p. 68

1328
Reichenau
1910/16 / Bremges & G.,
Albouts, Finkh & Co
467
Block printed / repeats not
ascertainable / 1
10

1329
Süden (South)
1910/16 / Ziegler
478
Block printed / repeats not
ascertainable / 1

1330
Sommerabend (Summer Evening)
1910/16 / Bremges & G.,
Albouts, Finkh & Co, Ziegler
481
Block printed / 44:44 cm / 12
125

1331
Sonnenblume (Sunflower)
1910/16 / Bremges & G.,
Albouts, Finkh & Co, Ziegler
482
Block printed / 11.3:11.3 cm / 6

1332
Passion
1924 (blocks produced 9 May
1924) /Ziegler
858
Block printed / 26.5:30 cm / 15
211

1333
Bergwald (Mountain Forest)
1924 (blocks produced 30 Aug.
1924) / Ziegler
869
Block printed / 15.5:24 cm / 8
212

1334
Algier
1925 (blocks produced 28 July
1925) / Società Italiana Angeli,
Ziegler
910
Block printed / 38.3:30 cm / 8
214

1335
Lucca
1927 / Vogel
9534
Woven fabric / repeats not
ascertainable / 4

Biographies of Artists

A comprehensive list of biographies of artists associated with every aspect of the Wiener Werkstätte's varied activities appears in Werner J. Schweiger, *Wiener Werkstätte. Design in Vienna 1903–1932* (1984). The selection of some of the leading names associated with the textile department which appears below has been adapted, by agreement with the author, from the details first published in 1984. In the case of some individuals such as Wilhelm Jonasch or Clara Posnanski, so little information is available that no useful listing is possible here.

Alber, Martha Born at Rumburg, Bohemia, 15 January 1893. Studied at the Kunstgewerbeschule in Prague and from 1918 at the Kunstgewerbeschule in Vienna (under Strnad and Hoffmann). Her work included postcards, fabrics and textile patterns.

Baudisch-Wittke, Gudrun Born at Pols, Styria, 17 March 1906. Studied in Graz, 1921–5, and was a member of the Wiener Werkstätte from 1926 to 1930. Her work included ceramics, bookbinding and textiles.

Berger, Arthur Born in Vienna, 27 May 1892; died in Moscow, 11 January 1981. After studies at the Kunstgewerbeschule, Vienna (under Strnad and Hoffmann), he worked for the City of Vienna (municipal building works) and designed over 30 film sets between 1920 and 1936, when he emigrated to Moscow. His work for the Wiener Werkstätte included textiles, silver bowls and boxes. His sister Fritzi produced postcard and textile designs.

Blonder, Leopold Born in Vienna, 1 July 1893, and studied at the Kunstgewerbeschule there from 1911 (under Strnad and Hoffmann). His work at the Wiener Werkstätte covered a wide variety of media in addition to textiles, and he was responsible for the reliefs on the wall of the Wiener Werkstätte room at the Werkbund Exhibition in Cologne, 1914.

Calm-Wierink, Lotte Born in Prague, 1 October 1897. Studied in Vienna at the Kunstgewerbeschule (under Strnad and Hoffmann), 1914–19, and became a member of the Wiener Werkstätte in 1918. She designed ceramics, jewellery and wooden objects, as well as textile patterns.

Czeschka, Carl Otto Born in Vienna, 22 October 1878; died in Hamburg, 10 July 1960. He taught at the Kunstgewerbeschule, Vienna 1902–7, before becoming a professor at the Hamburg Kunstgewerbeschule, 1907–43. His association with the Wiener Werkstätte dated from 1905 and continued after his move to Hamburg. His work, which ranged from calenders to theatre designs, stained glass and commercial graphics, was widely exhibited. Designs for the Wiener Werkstätte included jewellery, metalwork, furniture and wooden toys and boxes.

Flögl, Mathilde Born in Brünn (Brno), 9 September 1893; died in Salzburg, 1950. Studied in Vienna at the Kunst-gewerbeschule and became a member of the Wiener Werkstätte. She also ran her own workshop 1931–5, and exhibited at fashion and interior design shows mostly in the late 1920s. Her work for the Wiener Werkstätte, which featured a large number of textile patterns, also included graphics, fashion and accessories, lace and embroidery.

Friedmann-Otten, Marie Rosali (Mitzi) Born in Vienna, 28 November 1884; died in New York, 5 May 1955. A versatile artist, she studied in Vienna and designed metalwork and jewellery, as well as fashions, and from 1920 specialized in enamelwork.

Frömel-Fochler, Lotte Born in Vienna, 1 May 1884. After studying in Vienna at the Kunstgewerbeschule under Hoffmann (1904–8), she designed numerous textile patterns for the Wiener Werkstätte from 1910; her work also included fashion accessories, lace and embroidery.

Häusler, Philipp Born in Hungary at Panczowa on 7 November 1887; died in Frankfurt am Main, 18 February 1966. His association with the Wiener Werkstätte, 1920–5, was principally in an organizational role, but his designs ranged from metalwork and jewellery to textiles and leatherwork, and also included postcards and stationery.

Hoffmann, Josef Born in Pirnitz, Moravia, 15 December 1870; died in Vienna, 7 May 1956. After studying in Brünn (Brno) until 1895, he entered the drawing office of Otto Wagner and taught in Vienna at the Kunstgewerbeschule from 1898. A joint founder of the Wiener Werkstätte, he was its artistic director, 1903–31, during which time he also exhibited widely in various European cities. Within the Wiener Werkstätte his designs, which were versatile and wide-ranging, included a large number of textile patterns. His artistic output has been the subject of numerous articles and books.

Jesser-Schmid, Hilda Born at Marburg an der Drau, 21 May 1894. She studied at the Kunstgewerbeschule in Vienna 1912–17, and was a member of the Wiener Werkstätte, 1916–21. Her work included postcards, graphics, glass, metalwork, toys and painted flower boxes, as well as embroidery and textile patterns.

Jungnickel, Ludwig Heinrich Born at Wunsiedel, Upper Franconia, 22 July 1881; died in Vienna, 14 February 1965. Studied in Munich and Vienna, and from 1911 taught at the Kunstgewerbeschule in Frankfurt am Main. His work for the Wiener Werkstätte included postcards and textiles.

Kalhammer, Gustav Born in Vienna, 16 June 1886; presumed dead after being reported missing since 23 August 1919. He studied in Vienna at the Kunstgewerbeschule 1905–10. He designed wallpapers, textiles and graphics and, for the Wiener Werkstätte, postcards and broadsheets, as well as textiles.

Köhler-Broman, Melanie Leopoldina Born in Vienna, 18 November 1885; died in Stockholm, 15 December 1960. She achieved early success while still a student at the Kunstgewerbeschule, 1905–10. Her work for the Wiener Werkstätte included postcards, advertising graphics and textile designs.

Krenek, Karl Born in Vienna, 7 September 1880, and died there on 15 December 1948. He was a painter and graphic artist and designed ceramics. His designs for the Wiener Werkstätte were for postcards and textiles.

Likarz-Strauss, Maria Born in Przemyal, 28 March 1893. She studied in Vienna at the Kunstgewerbeschule, 1911–15, and worked at the Wiener Werkstätte first from 1912 to 1914 and later from 1920 mainly on graphic design and wallpaper. In addition to her many textile designs, she produced postcards, ceramics and glass, embroidery and lace etc.

Löw-Lazar, Friederike (Fritzi) Born in Vienna, 23 October 1891, and died there, 19 May 1975. After studying at the Kunstgewerbeschule, she worked as a book illustrator, especially for the publisher Anton Schroll, 1917–23. Here designs for the Wiener Werkstätte covered a wide range, including postcards, jewellery, ceramics, glass, fashion and fashion accessories, textiles, lace, embroidery etc.

Moser, Kolo(man) Born in Vienna, 30 March 1868, and died there on 18 October 1918. After studying in Vienna at the Akademie, 1888–92, and the Kunstgewerbeschule, 1893–5, he taught at the latter. He was a co-founder of the Vienna Secession and of the Wiener Werkstätte, with which he was associated until 1928. He then designed stage sets, postage stamps, stained-glass windows etc, as well as furniture, carpets and textiles for commercial organizations. His work for the Wiener Werkstätte was similarly varied, including metalwork, jewellery, furniture and posters, as well as bookbindings, stationery and textiles.

Nechansky, Arnold Born in Vienna, 17 March 1888; died at Kitzbühel in the Tyrol, 25 March 1938. Studied at the Kunstgewerbeschule, Vienna, 1909–13, and subsequently taught in Berlin, 1919–33. His first work for the Wiener Werkstätte dates from 1912, and he exhibited widely in the following years. His designs for the Wiener Werkstätte included postcards, wallpaper, ceramics, jewellery, silver and textiles.

Peche, Dagobert Born at St Michael im Lungau, Salzburg, 3 April 1886; died at Mödling bei Wien, 16 April 1923. Studied in Vienna at the Technische Hochschule and the Akademie until 1911. From 1913 he was a leading member of the Wiener Werkstätte and took charge of its Zurich branch in 1917–18. His work was wide-ranging and he provided designs for a variety of commercial clients. Within the Wiener Werkstätte his versatile talents extended to metalwork, jewellery, glass, ceramics, ivory and tortoiseshell, leather and bookbinding, wallpaper, stationery and postcards, painted Easter eggs, stage designs, fashion and textiles.

Rix-Ueno, Felice Born in Vienna, 1 June (or July) 1893; died in Kyoto, Japan, 15 October 1967. Studied at the Kunstgewerbeschule, 1913–17. After becoming a member of the Wiener Werkstätte, he visited Japan several times, and eventually settled in Kyoto in 1935. In addition to his textile designs for the Wiener Werkstätte, he also worked in ceramics, glass painting, painted boxes and enamel.

Schaschl-Schuster, Reni Born in Pula (formerly Pola, Istria), 26 April 1895. She studied in Vienna at the Kunstgewerbeschule, 1912–16. In addition to her textile patterns for the Wiener Werkstätte, she designed ceramics, glass, graphics, painted boxes, lace etc.

Schröder-Ehrenfest, Anny Born in Vienna, 16 May 1898; died at Bad Segeberg, near Lübeck (Schleswig-Holstein), 11 April 1972. She studied at the Kunstgewerbeschule, 1913–16. Her designs for the Wiener Werkstätte included enamel and metalwork, jewellery, ceramics and glass, textiles, covered boxes and playing cards decorated with national costumes.

Snischek, Max Born at Dürnkrut, Lower Austria, 24 August 1891; died at Hinterbrühl, 17 November 1968. Studied in Vienna at the Kunstgewerbeschule, 1912–14. His principal activity within the Wiener Werkstätte was in the fashion department, of which he was director from 1922; in addition to his numerous textile patterns, his designs included graphics, enamel, jewellery and wallpaper.

Wieselthier, Valerie (Vally) Born in Vienna, 25 May 1985; died in New York, 1 September 1945. After studying at the Kunstgewerbeschule, she worked within the Wiener Werkstätte and at her own studio in Vienna. Her activities ranged over ceramics and glass, graphics for posters, wallpaper and textiles.

Wimmer-Wisgrill, Eduard Josef Born in Vienna, 2 April 1882, and died there, 25 December 1961. After studying at the Kunstgewerbeschule until 1907, he later taught there, both before the First World War and afterwards, with an interval during which he taught at the Art Institute of Chicago, 1923–25. He was director of the fashion department at the Wiener Werkstätte, 1910–22, and was succeeded by Max Snischek. In addition to fashion and stage designs, his other work there included textiles, postcards, metalwork, jewellery and bookbinding.

Zovetti, Ugo Born in Curzola (Korčula), Dalmatia. Studied in Vienna at the Kunstgewerbeschule, 1898–1901. Apart from his textile designs for the Wiener Werkstätte, he worked independently in his own studio from 1911. He also designed fashion accessories and haberdashery items.

Zülow, Franz von, Born in Vienna, 15 March 1883, and died there, 26 February 1963. After studies at the Akademie der bildenden Künste and at the Kunstgewerbeschule, 1903–6, he exhibited widely in the years preceding and following the First World War. His prints and graphics were sold by the Wiener Werkstätte, and were supplemented by a portfolio of original lithographs, published by the Wiener Werkstätte c. 1912; in addition to fabric patterns, he also designed fans and screens.

Pattern name	Designer	Cat. no.	Fig. no(s).	Pattern name	Designer	Cat. no.	Fig. no(s).	Pattern name	Designer	Cat. no.	Fig. no(s).
Aare	Likarz(-Strauß)	512		Ariadne	Peche	819	244	Blues	Flögl	163	371
Abbadie	Flögl	176		Ariano	Likarz(-Strauß)	632		Blütenblätter	Rix(-Ueno)	1012	
Abbazia	Snischek	1147		Ariel	Peche	752	315	Blütenflocken	Löw(-Lazar)	693	
Abendröte	Jesser(-Schmid)	391		Arina	Snischek	1163		Blütenstaub	Jacobsen	362	
Abisag	Löw(-Lazar)	670		Arizona	Rix(-Ueno)	1020		Blütenzweig	Peche	740	
Abruzzen	Jesser(-Schmid)	389		Arizona	Zimpel	1276		Blumenblitz	Friedmann(-Otten)	222	
Adelgunde	Paradeiser	736		Arlberg	Likarz(-Strauß)	629		Blumenduft	Rix(-Ueno)	999	
Adler	Hoffmann	292	98, 147	Ascher-mittwoch	Friedmann(-Otten)	212	114	Blumenhorn	Peche	738	
Adonis	Likarz(-Strauß)	568	323	(Carneval)				Blumenkorb	Nechansky	727	
Adria	Kalhammer	414		Asta	Friedmann(-Otten)	207	112	Blumenregen	Peche	770	
Adrianopel	Zovetti	1284	97	Asunta	Likarz(-Strauß)	555		Blumensockel	Jesser(-Schmid)	392	
Adventstern	Löw(-Lazar)	677		Athos	Hoffmann	332		Blumenspitze	Jesser(-Schmid)	385	
Aesthet	Wieselthier	1216		Ätna	Flögl	189		Blumenstrauß	Peche	737	
Ägypten	Blonder	24	270	Aulus	Likarz(-Strauß)	587		Blumenteppich	Rysavy	1053	
Ähre	Löw(-Lazar)	665		Aurelia	Wimmer-Wisgrill	1229		Blumenwiese	Scharrisch	1054	126
Aida	Schröder (-Ehrenfest)	1102		Aussee	Blonder	23		Blumenzaun	Flögl	101	
Ajax	Likarz(-Strauß)	504		Australia	Snischek	1184		Bonifaz	Möschl(-Lagus)	711	
Akelei	Rix(Ueno)	1032		Ava	Likarz(-Strauß)	623		Bonn	Liepmann	453	
Akita	Likarz(-Strauß)	591		Azania	Flögl	185		Bora	Likarz(-Strauß)	563	
Akka	Posnanski	860		Azoren	Likarz(-Strauß)	540		Borneo	Likarz(-Strauß)	477	319
Akropolis	Frömel-Fochler	229		Azur	Flögl	180		Bosporus	Snischek	1185	
Akustik	Calm(-Wierink)	66		Bacchus	Hoffmann	343		Boston	Schaschl (-Schuster)	1058	198
Alarich	Möschl(-Lagus)	715		Bachstelze	Moser	720					
Alaun	Peche	841		Bachus	Wimmer-Wisgrill	1246		Bouquet	Peche	764	
Albanien	Wimmer-Wisgrill	1230		Backfisch	Krenn	444		Bozen	Likarz(-Strauß)	531	273, 361
Alexander	Flögl	173		Baden	Löw(-Lazar)	656	218	Brasilien	Rix(-Ueno)	1039	
Algier	Zülow	1334	214	(Alland,				Bremen	Hoffmann	331	
Ali	Likarz(-Strauß)	566	324	Vöslau)				Bridge	Likarz(-Strauß)	529	359
Alland	Löw(-Lazar)	656	218	Bagita	Flögl	182		Brillenschlange	Rix(-Ueno)	965	
(Baden, Vöslau)				(Bedonia)				Brindisi	Likarz(-Strauß)	503	320
Allegro	Flögl	90		Bahia	Zimpel	1266		Brioni	Posnanski	863	210
Almata	Rix(-Ueno)	1042		Baja	Flögl	188		Brüssel	Schinko	1082	
Almira	Rix(-Ueno)	1029		Bajazzo	Wimmer-Wisgrill	1231		Buchenwald	Flögl	105	
Aloe	Wieselthier	1225		Baker	Likarz(-Strauß)	528		Buddha	Zimpel	1259	
Alpenfalter	Hoffmann	291	98	Balaton	Hoffmann	354		BuenosAires	Frömel-Fochler	231	
Alpengipfel	Zels	1251		Balkan	Likarz(-Strauß)	456		Bukarest	Kalhammer	415	
Alpenkönig	Weinberger	1199		Ballade	Flögl	91		Burano	Rix(-Ueno)	998	
Alpenveilchen	Rix(-Ueno)	959		Bambi	Flögl	120	369	Burgenland	Flögl	111	
Alpenweide	Pospischil	930		Bantu	Hoffmann	347		Buschmann	Rix(-Ueno)	1013	
Alzette	Likarz(-Strauß)	549		Basel	Likarz(-Strauß)	454		Byzanz	Flögl	145	
Amanda	Löw(-Lazar)	661		Basra	Höchsmann	285	298	Caballero	Wimmer-Wisgrill	1247	
Amanullah	Flögl	133		Batavia	Zimpel	1264	237	Cabaret	Rix(-Ueno)	956	
Amaro	Likarz(-Strauß)	517		Bauerngarten	Jesser(-Schmid)	380	178	Cadillac	Flögl	175	
Amazonas	Flögl	151		Baumblüten	Flögl	108		Caliopsis	Flögl	156	
Ambrass	Likarz(-Strauß)	595		Baumfalke	Moser	721	103	Camille	Rix(-Ueno)	1027	327
Ameise	Wimmer-Wisgrill	1228	55–59, 257, 258	Baummarder	Moser	719	297	Cannes	Flögl	128	332
				Bavaria	Czeschka	70	77, 138, 139	Capri	Peche	755	
Amely	Posnanski	861						Carlos	Snischek	1155	
Amoy	Zimpel	1280		Bedonia	Flögl	182		Carlton	Likarz(-Strauß)	541	
Amsel	Moser	722	48, 49	(Bagita)				Carmen	Wimmer-Wisgrill	1232	
Amur	Peche	741		Benares	Weissenberg	1201	118	Carneval	Friedmann(-Otten)	212	115
Anastasius	Piotrovska (-Wittmann)	859	110	Bengal	Rix(-Ueno)	970		(Ascher-mittwoch)			
				Benz	Zovetti	1286		Cart(h)ago	Snischek	1150	
Andante	Flögl	119		Bergen	Perlmutter	850		Carus	Hoffmann	340	381
Andorra	Likarz(-Strauß)	510		Bergfalter	Moser	718	50, 51	Cäsar	Schaschl-Schuster	1059	
Andromache	Wieselthier	1224	222, 223	Bergfink	Frömel-Fochler	228		Castello	Likarz(-Strauß)	644	
Andros	Posnanski	862		Berggeist	Snischek	1109	373	Celebes	Snischek	1157	340
Anemone	Rix(-Ueno)	1014		Bergkristall	Hirsch (-Landesmann)	279		Ceylon	Obermann	731	
Angela	Möschl(-Lagus)	713						Chiki	Schröder (-Ehrenfest)	1100	
Anilin	Kovacic	433		Bergwald	Zülow	1333	212				
Anitra	Wieselthier	1222		Bermuda	Likarz(-Strauß)	539		China	Rix(-Ueno)	957	
Annie	Rysavy	1051		Berna	Likarz(-Strauß)	640		Ching-Chang	Flögl	95	
Anninger	Häusler	272	279	Bethlehem	Friedmann(-Otten)	227	233	Chios	Posnanski	864	
Antonio	Posnanski	918		Biarritz	Rix(-Ueno)	989		Chitra	Rix(-Ueno)	952	
Apfel	Czeschka	71	134	Biel	Snischek	1126	374	(Libanon)			
Apistin(o)	Likarz(-Strauß)	551		Biene	Hoffmann	290	13, 14	Chypre	Flögl	139	330
Apollo	Hoffmann	293	3–5, 71	Bilbao	Snischek	1159		Chytera	Peche	812	345
Apollonia	Likarz(-Strauß)	575		Bimini (Rimini)	Zimpel	1268	234	Cinta	Likarz(-Strauß)	625	
April	Pospischil	929		Birma	Löw(-Lazar)	683		Cinzano	Likarz(-Strauß)	620	
Arabeske	Schröder (-Ehrenfest)	1099	195, 196	Bisamberg	Stoll	1190	116	(Ginzano)			
				Blätter	Alber	1	263, 264	Cirkus	Birke(-Eber)	22	231
Aras	Likarz(-Strauß)	585		Blattpflanze	Foltin	194		Citronenfalter	Frömel-Fochler	232	
Arbe	Zovetti	1285	97, 174	Blattwinde	Peche	739	244	City	Snischek	1121	
Arbino	Likarz(-Strauß)	633		Blitz	Krenek	437	122	Clan	Flögl	135	
Archibald	Rix(-Ueno)	938	366	Bluefox	Likarz(-Strauß)	628		Claudia	Peche	838	

Pattern name	Designer	Cat. no.	Fig. no(s).	Pattern name	Designer	Cat. no.	Fig. no(s).	Pattern name	Designer	Cat. no.	Fig. no(s).
Cloe	Peche	810		Eiderente	Frömel-Fochler	233		Florentina	Flögl	112	
Cobenzl	Jonasch	396		Eiland	Rix(-Ueno)	1044		Florenz	Likarz(-Strauß)	518	
Colette	Snischek	1175		Eilido	Jesser(-Schmid)	379		Florestan	Likarz(-Strauß)	475	
Colombo	Snischek	1183		Einfalt	Flögl	94		Florian	Möschl(-Lagus)	717	
Columbia	Schaschl(-Schuster)	1061	186, 187	Einsame	Peche	774		Florida	Zimpel	1282	
Cook	Trinkl	1193		Blume(n)				Florio	Likarz(-Strauß)	583	
Coriandoli	Friedman-Otten	225		Eisbär	Falkenstein	89		Fluchthorn	Posnanski	871	
Corinth	Likarz(-Strauß)	550		Eisblume	Zovetti	1288		Flut	Peche	777	158
(Korinth)				Eisfigur	Foltin	200		Forelle	Frömel-Fochler	237	
Corona	Snischek	1135		Eisfuchs	Frömel-Fochler	234		Forsitie	Flögl	166	
Croatien	Friedmann(-Otten)	215		Eismeer	Frömel-Fochler	230		Fox	Flögl	167	
Csikos	Hoffmann	344	252, 310	Elbasan	Snischek	1152	337	Francisco	Rix(-Ueno)	1037	
Curzola	Flögl	116	370	Elbe	Höchsmann	286		Frascati	Likarz(-Strauß)	621	
Cyan	Peche	842		Elfenbein	Snischek	1119		Frass (Dillon,	Peche	744	
Cyma	Likarz(-Strauß)	584		Ellen	Hackl	267		Dilon, Trass)			
Cypern	Hoffmann	296	254	Ellen Petz	Müllner	725		Fregoli	Angerer	5	
Dachstein	Posnanski	865		Email	Zimpel	1263		Freimaurer	Löw(-Lazar)	678	
Daimler	Zovetti	1287		Endigung	Peche	821	347	Freude	Krenn	449	
Dammhirsch	Friedmann(-Otten)	216		(Die Endi-				Freude	Peche	814	311
Danaeblume	Peche	772		gung)				Freudenau	Peche	775	
Danubius	Snischek	1141		Engadin	Rix(-Ueno)	1008		Fritz	Likarz(-Strauß)	544	
Daphne	Peche	767	180	Enos	Snischek	1115	378	Frohsinn	Jacobsen	367	
Darling	Snischek	1156		Epinglé	Flögl	181		Fruchtkätzchen	Wieselthier	1212	
Davos	Rix(-Ueno)	942		Epirus	Posnanski	869	348	Fruchtstamm	Wieselthier	1210	
Delft	Wieselthier	1217		Epos	Peche	756		Frühling	Peche	776	
Delia	Angerer	8		Erlau	Hoffmann	355		Frühlings-	Jacobsen	372	
Delos	Likarz(-Strauß)	580		Erlenzeisig	Hoffmann	298	18	himmel			
Delphinen	Peche	771		Ernestine	Kopriva	426		Frühlingslied	Krenn	450	
Dempsey	Snischek	1186		Erzerum	Flögl	93		Frühlingswiese	Rix(-Ueno)	967	
Der Garten	Flögl	104		Escali	Likarz(-Strauß)	635		Fuchs	Frömel-Fochler	238	
Erde				Ethik	Likarz(-Strauß)	488		Fuchsie	Rix(-Ueno)	1033	
(Gartenerde)				Eva	Zülow	1318		Funke	Rysavy	1052	
Dezember	Peche	768		Evian	Likarz(-Strauß)	534		Fürchtegott	Zuckerkandl	1313	
Diabolo	Krenek	438		Exeter	Snischek	1116		Gabriel	Jungwirth	408	265, 266
Diana	Peche	761		Fabeltier	Likarz(-Strauß)	648		Galizien	Zülow	1320	
Die Endigung	Peche	821	347	Falte	Peche	828	342, 343	Gallia	Likarz(-Strauß)	536	
(Endigung)				Falter	Flögl	114		Gallus	Likarz(-Strauß)	491	
Die Ranke	Peche	831		Fano	Likarz(-Strauß)	519		Ganges	Peche	779	
Die Tulpen	Peche	835		Fantasie	Peche	765		Gardasee	Likarz(-Strauß)	464	
Dillon (Dilon,	Peche	744		Farina	Zimpel	1272		Gartenerde	Flögl	104	
Frass, Trass)				Fasching	Frömel-Fochler	239	105	(Der Garten			
Dilly	Snischek	1131		Faser	Peche	840		Erde)			
Dilon (Dillon,	Peche	744		Fatima	Likarz(-Strauß)	572		Gartenstadt	Friedmann(-Otten)	208	
Frass, Trass)				Fayal	Likarz(-Strauß)	586		Gartenstrauß	Rix(-Ueno)	978	
Diomedes	Peche	762	191	Federball	Wieselthier	1205		Gartenwinde	Peche	778	
Diskus	Blonder	32		Federbusch	Zovetti	1289		Gavotte	Jesser(-Schmid)	377	
Distel	Flögl	96		Federgans	Blonder	34		Gazelle	Frömel-Fochler	241	
Dnjestr	Rix(-Ueno)	1001		Federwölkchen	Wieselthier	1204		Geier	Frömel-Fochler	244	
Dolde	Zülow	1317		Federwisch	Peche	843		Geisha	Köhler(-Broman)	423	11
Dolomiten	Peche	837		Feiertag	Hoffmann	299	95	Gemse	Frömel-Fochler	240	
Dolores	Snischek	1160		Feldblume	Schröder	1086		Georgine	Blonder	25	
Domingo	Flögl	152			(-Ehrenfest)			Geranie	Rix(-Ueno)	1026	331
Don	Flögl	164		Feldfrüchte	Rix(-Ueno)	973		Germania	Wabak	1198	
Donau	Perlmutter	856		Feldlerche	Czeschka	72	98	Gespann	Rix(-Ueno)	980	
Donauwellen	Perlmutter	855		Feldpost	Friedmann(-Otten)	213	115	Gespinst	Rix(-Ueno)	981	267, 268
Donnerwetter	Rix(-Ueno)	953	334	Felix	Flögl	165		Gewitter	Foltin	198	
Dorfrose	Zülow	1316	86, 87	Fels	Flögl	193		Ginefra	Kopriva	425	
Dorfschwalbe	Hoffmann	297	246	Felsenhuhn	Martens	699		Ginzano	Likarz(-Strauß)	620	
Doris	Peche	833	316	Fernando	Snischek	1153		(Cinzano)			
Dornbach	Posnanski	866		Ferro	Posnanski	919		Girl	Likarz(-Strauß)	562	
Dornegg	Flögl	184	209	Festschmuck	Jacobsen	368		Gitter	Schröder	1093	
Dornier	Hoffmann	350		Feuerwerk	Frömel-Fochler	265			(-Ehrenfest)		
Dornröschen	Kalhammer	416		Fiat	Zovetti	1290		Gitterblume	Schaschl(-Schuster)	1057	217
Double-Fox	Rix(-Ueno)	988		Fidelio	Likarz(-Strauß)	497	360	Gitterstern	Friedmann(-Otten)	226	
Draperie	Peche	773		Fingerhut	Schaschl(-Schuster)	1066		Glacis	Löw(-Lazar)	662	
Dreiblatt	Rix(-Ueno)	1021		Finis	Posnanski	870		Glastraube	Rix(-Ueno)	1045	
Dronte	Krenn	448		Fiori	Likarz(-Strauß)	574		Gletscherblume	Peche	749	299, 301
Dschong	Rix(-Ueno)	1018		Firming	Flögl	186		Globus	Freund	203	
Dschungel	Pranke	932		Fischotter	Kovacic	434		Glockenblume	Prutscher	934	
Dubary	Likarz(-Strauß)	469		Fischreiher	Czeschka	73	132	Gloggnitz	Kalhammer	417	
Dubno	Schaschl	1064		Fixstern	Likarz(-Strauß)	485		Glückspilz	Peche	809	
Ebenholz	Müllner	726		Flagge	Blonder	35		Goldblatt	Wimmer-Wisgrill	1233	19
Ebro	Likarz(-Strauß)	511	206, 207	Flamingo	Frömel-Fochler	236		Goldfasan	Frömel-Fochler	246	
Edelkoralle	Vogel	1195		Flamme	Hackl	268		Goldfisch	Blonder	38	
Edelmarder	Vogel	1196	45	Flamme	Zimpel	1279		Goldregen	Zülow	1321	
Edelweiß	Schröder	1085		Flandern	Likarz(-Strauß)	646		Gorilla	Frömel-Fochler	245	
	(-Ehrenfest)			Fledermaus	Frömel-Fochler	235		Gorlicze	Piotrovska	858	124
Eden	Snischek	1174		Flieder	Zülow	1319			(-Wittmann)		
Edfu	Posnanski	867		Flims	Snischek	1128		Gotemba	Hoffmann	329	
Edison	Peche	759	346	Flitter	Berger, A.	16		Gotland	Rix(-Ueno)	937	
Edlach	Posnanski	868		Flockentanz	Jesser(-Schmid)	395	229	Gracilis	Hoffmann	356	
Ehrenpreis	Löw(-Lazar)	668		Flora	Blonder	36		Grado	Blonder	37	

Pattern name	Designer	Cat. no.	Fig. no(s).	Pattern name	Designer	Cat. no.	Fig. no(s).	Pattern name	Designer	Cat. no.	Fig. no(s).
Granatblüte	Flögl	106		Indigo	Brunner	61	292, 300	Klein Zaches			
Granate	Krenek	439	121		(-Frieberger)			(Klein Zack)	Löw(-Lazar)	659	21
Granit	Flögl	99		Indus	Likarz(-Strauß)	560		Kleo	Zimpel	1283	
Gräser	Likarz(-Strauß)	479		Inka	Snischek	1182		Klepper	Snischek	1161	
Grasmücke	Frömel-Fochler	242		Inn	Flögl	125		Klotildis	Schaschl(-Schuster)	1079	
Gratianus	Flögl	110		Intarso	Blonder	54		Knabenkraut	Likarz(-Strauß)	472	
Grindlwald	Schröder			Iris	Zovetti	1293		Kobra	Rix(-Ueno)	995	367
	(-Ehrenfest)	1084		Irland (Irrland,	Likarz(-Strauß)	458	99–102,	Königskerze	Manfreda	698	
Grinzing	Posnanski	872		Schottland)			172, 251	Körmend	Peche	758	
Grönland	Likarz(-Strauß)	650		Irrgarten	Peche	781	189, 190	Kohleule	Hoffmann	307	309
Große Blätter	Peche	829		Irrland (Irland,	Likarz(-Strauß)	458	99–102,	Kohlmeise	Frömel-Fochler	249	
Großvesir	Lichtblau	452	230	Schottland)			172, 251	Kokoro	Foltin	201	
Grünfink	Frömel-Fochler	243	393	Irrlicht	Hackl	269		Kokos	Dostal	86	
Grünspecht	Hoffmann	300		Irrweg	Peche	844		Kokospalme	Schröder	1087	
Guido	Hoffmann	341	385	Isabella	Likarz(-Strauß)	552			(-Ehrenfest)		
Guinea	Zimpel	1270	236	Ischl	Krenek	443		Kolibri	Frömel-Fochler	250	
Gundula	Wieselthier	1209		Ischl	Posnanski	879		Komet	Jungwirth	405	
Haag	Baudisch(-Wittke)	12		Iselberg	Schaschl(-Schuster)	1060		Kommers	Likarz(-Strauß)	490	
Habana	Likarz(-Strauß)	642		Isis	Hoffmann	357		Konfuzius	Zuckerkandl	1314	
Habsburg	Friedmann(-Otten)	206		Isonzo	Hoffmann	304		Kongo	Blonder	33	
Halbmond	Friedmann(-Otten)	219		Isphahan	Blonder	52	15	Kongreß	Löw(-Lazar)	680	
Halifax	Likarz(-Strauß)	645		Itala	Zovetti	1295		Konstantinopel	Zovetti	1296	109
Hall	Likarz(-Strauß)	598		Jagdfalke	Hoffmann	305	60–63	Korfu	Flögl	190	
Hallensee	Jesser(-Schmid)	375		Jaguar	Peche	751		Korinth	Likarz(-Strauß)	550	
Hallstadt	Posnanski	873		Jalapa	Rix(-Ueno)	1041		(Corinth)			
Hameau	Jonasch	397	129	Jamaika	Kovacic	431		Kornblume	Löw(-Lazar)	686	
Hannover	Weissenberg	1202		Jansa	Berger, F.	19		Korngold	Rix(-Ueno)	971	
Harlekin	Peche	780		Jap (Yap)	Höchsmans	289	226	Kosmos	Flögl	168	
Harlem	Kovacic	435		Japanland	Rix(-Ueno)	964	329	Kram(m)et(s)-	Frömel-Fochler	251	42, 164
Hase	Czeschka	74		Java	Blonder	39		vogel			
Hatasu	Posnanski	874		Jena	Posnanski	877		Kranich	Martens	701	
Haugsdorf	Zülow	1322		Jonny	Posnanski	917		Kranichgeier	Martens	702	127
Haushund	Czeschka	75	96	Jordan	Hoffmann	333		Krasnojarsk	Rix(-Ueno)	1023	333
Hecht	Czeschka	76		Josta	Posnanski	878		Krassin	Blumberger	57	
Hedin	Hoffmann	334		Jugend	Jacobsen	364		Krebs	Frömel-Fochler	252	106
Heimchen	Wimmer-Wisgrill	1234		Julia	Möschl(-Lagus)	712		Kreml	Rix(-Ueno)	1028	
Hekla	Posnanski	875		Juniblumen	Rix(-Ueno)	972		Kresse	Flögl	159	
Helena	Likarz(-Strauß)	502		Junker (Junka)	Rix(-Ueno)	944		Kreuzband	Jungwirth	411	219
Helenental	Alber	2		Juno	Friedmann(-Otten)	210	113	Krieau (Kriau)	Jonasch	398	72-74
Helis	Flögl	179		Jupiter	Paradeiser	734		Krim	Flögl	130	
Helium	Stadlmayer	1187		Jussuf	Rix(-Ueno)	974		Kristall	Peche	815	
Hellbrunn	Perlmutter	854		Juvelle	Peche	760		Kristiania	Calm	67	
Herbst	Czeschka	77		Kab	Flögl	149		Krokus	Flögl	118	
Herbstsonne	Wimmer-Wisgrill	1235	70, 104	Kahlenberg	Alber	3	69	Krone	Peche	818	275, 314
Herbstwind	Kovacic	432		Kairo	Nechansky	730		Kropftaube	Czeschka	78	92, 280
Hermada	Blonder	51		Kaisergarten	Kalhammer	418		Kubin	Kaestner	412	
Hermelin	Frömel-Fochler	247		Kakadu	Zülow	1323		Kuckuck	Wimmer-Wisgrill	1236	16
Herzblatt	Hoffmann	301		Kaktus	Löw(-Lazar)	685		Kultur	Berger, F.	18	
Herzblüten	Kopriva	424		Kalkutta	Angerer	9		Kursk	Pamberger	732	
Herzegowina	Frömel-Fochler	248		Kama	Posnanski	920		Küste	Möschl(-Lagus)	706	
Hesperiden-	Peche	827	197	Kamilla	Blonder	26		Labyrinth	Peche	782	161
frucht				Kanarienvogel	Vogel	1197	27, 98	Lachs (Sachs)	Wimmer-Wisgrill	1238	
Hexentanz	Schaschl(-Schuster)	1070		Kandidus	Calm(-Wierink)	68		Lachtaube	Schaschl-Schuster	1071	
Hiaz	Kopriva	427		Kaninchen	Czeschka	79		Lady	Hoffmann	353	
Himmelbrand	Wieselthier	1207		Kansas	Flögl	191		Lakme	Likarz(-Strauß)	599	
Himmelhof	Wieselthier	1219		Kanton	Posnanski	880		Lama	Martens	703	
Himmelobst	Rix(-Ueno)	976		Kanton	Zimpel	1273		Laube	Schröder	1091	
Himmel-	Löw(-Lazar)	660		Kaplan	Schröder				(-Ehrenfest)		
schlüssel					(-Ehrenfest)	1094		Laubfrosch	Häusler	273	
Hirschenzunge	Hoffmann	302	151, 296	Kardinal	Peche	750	192, 256	Laubgewinde	Snischek	1123	
Hobby	Flögl	143		Karmen(i)a	Flögl	174		Laura	Likarz(-Strauß)	460	
Hochwald	Jungnickel	401	24, 80	Karo	Foltin	196		Laurenz	Zimpel	1262	
Hockey	Likarz(-Strauß)	559		Karst	Friedmann(-Otten)	214	117	Lava	Hirsch	281	220
Höflein	Posnanski	876	349	Kaschmier-	Wimmer-Wisgrill	1237			(-Landesmann)		
Holland	Rix(-Ueno)	986		ziege				Lawine	Blonder	40	
Holztaube	Martens	700		Kassandra	Likarz(-Strauß)	553		Laxenburg	Rix(-Ueno)	990	
Hongkong	Stadlmayer	1188		Kassiopäa	Löw(-Lazar)	684		Leda	Likarz(-Strauß)	516	
Hopfen	Hoffmann	303	143, 244	Kasuar	Snischek	1138		Leila	Flögl	154	
Horizont	Snischek	1145		Kayala	Likarz(-Strauß)	581	317	Lemberg	Foltin	195	
Hortensie	Flögl	138	326	Kentucky	Flögl	137		Lenglen	Snischek	1118	249, 336
Hutfeder	Rix(-Ueno)	963		Kerker	Schröder	1101		Lenz	Hudec	361	
Hyazinthe	Snischek	1134			(-Ehrenfest)			Leonardo	Brunner(-Frieberger)	64	
Hymen	Peche	823	277, 278	Kernbeißer	Hoffmann	308	17	Leonie	Rysavy	1050	
Ibera	Hoffmann	337		Kicku	Rix(-Ueno)	1025		Leopard	Wimmer-Wisgrill	1239	16
Ibikus	Zovetti	1292		Kiebitz	Hoffmann	306		Leopold	Likarz(-Strauß)	643	
Idyll	Snischek	1136		Kieneck	Posnanski	881		Lerche	Hoffmann	310	142
Ikarus	Zovetti	1291		Kioto	Flögl	177		Lese	Angerer	6	
Ilona	Zovetti	1294		Kirschblüte	Rix(-Ueno)	1005		Levante	Likarz(-Strauß)	610	
Ilonka	Blonder	29		Kirschgarten	Rix(-Ueno)	961	275	Lhasa	Likarz(-Strauß)	506	11, 248
Iltis	Flögl	134		Kitty	Müllner	724		Lianen	Zülow	1324	25
Ilus	Schaschl(-Schuster)	1063		Kiuschiu	Rix(-Ueno)	1006		Libanon	Rix(-Ueno)	952	
Indien	Frömel-Fochler	266		Klatschrose	Riedel	936	69, 70	(Chitra)			

Pattern name	Designer	Cat. no.	Fig. no(s).	Pattern name	Designer	Cat. no.	Fig. no(s).	Pattern name	Designer	Cat. no.	Fig. no(s).
Libelle	Löw(-Lazar)	679		Mauer-blümchen	Frömel-Fochler	254	64, 65	Nachthimmel	Likarz(-Strauß)	476	362
Liebesgarten	Jacobsen	373		Mauerwerk	Blonder	53	119	Nachtvogel	Rix(-Ueno)	955	
Liliom	Likarz(-Strauß)	515	358	Mauritius	Likarz(-Strauß)	537		Nanking	Rix(-Ueno)	991	
Lillith	Likarz(-Strauß)	467		Meanon	Zimpel	1253		Narcyssus	Peche	789	
Lima	Likarz(-Strauß)	614		Medea	Friedmann(-Otten)	209		Narew	Kovacic	430	
Limanova	Löw(-Lazar)	687		Medina	Peche	787		Narwal	Likarz(-Strauß)	465	
Lindbergh	Likarz(-Strauß)	522		Meerblume	Wieselthier	1208		Natter	Flögl	115	
Linsa (Sinsa)	Zovetti	1297		Meerqualle	Wieselthier	1211		Nayade	Likarz(-Strauß)	463	
Linz	Posnanski	882		Mekka	Berger, A.	14	22,59,75, 165, 166, 167–171	Neapel	Flögl	172	
Lipiti	Likarz(-Strauß)	651						Nebelstreifen	Jacobsen	363	
Lissy	Likarz(-Strauß)	600		Mela	Berger, A.	15		Neckar	Löw(-Lazar)	671	
Liszt	Peche	753		Meleda	Likarz(-Strauß)	542		Nedschibe	Hirsch (-Landesmann)	282	
Li-tai-po	Zimpel	1255		Meledek	Likarz(-Strauß)	605					
Liverpool	Krenn	445		Melk	Zülow	1325		Nelke	Jesser(-Schmid)	381	
Loanda	Höchsmann	284		Melodie	Snischek	1143		Nelkenduft	Rix(-Ueno)	1011	
Loanda	Posnanski	921		Melodram	Likarz(-Strauß)	578		Nelson	Likarz(-Strauß)	533	
Lobau	Rix(-Ueno)	954		Mengo	Angerer	10		Nepal	Likarz(-Strauß)	594	
Löwe	Czeschka	80	96	Menorea	Likarz(-Strauß)	527		Nephrit	Likarz(-Strauß)	554	
Lohengrin	Löw(-Lazar)	688		Menuett	Schaschl(-Schuster)	1075		Neptun	Friedmann(-Otten)	224	
Loja	Likarz(-Strauß)	631		Meran	Stoll	1191		Nero	Blonder	31	
Lorbeer	Jesser(-Schmid)	382		Mercedes	Zovetti	1300		New York	Snischek	1178	377
Lord Corinc	Wimmer-Wisgrill	1248		Mercedes	Likarz(-Strauß)	639		Niagara	Snischek	1166	
Lothar	Snischek	1149		Merkur	Peche	763		Niger	Posnanski	924	
Lucano	Posnanski	922		Messina	Zovetti	1301		Nihilit	Jungwirth	409	
Lucca	Zülow	1335		Mexiko	Wintersteiner	1249	213	Nikon	Rix(-Ueno)	1019	
Lucca (Lugo)	Likarz(-Strauß)	514		Miami	Flögl	192		Nil	Hoffmann	315	152
Luchs	Hoffmann	309	144	Mignon	Frömel-Fochler	255	300	Ninon	Krenn	446	
Luftschloß	Schaschl(-Schuster)	1065	177	Mikado	Zovetti	1298		Nippon	Stoll	1192	
Lugo (Lucca)	Likarz(-Strauß)	514		Miki	Schaschl(-Schuster)	1062		Nizza	Frömel-Fochler	256	
Lukas	Schröder (-Ehrenfest)	1098		Milchstraße	Jacobsen	366		Nok	Schaschl(-Schuster)	1076	
Lurko	Peche	754		Mill(es)fleur(s)	Löw(-Lazar)	689		Norden	Peche	790	
Lusthaus	Schröder (-Ehrenfest)	1095		Milos	Posnanski	883		Nordkap	Frömel(-Fochler)	257	
Luther	Likarz(-Strauß)	601	353	Minsk	Likarz(-Strauß)	597		Novelle	Likarz(-Strauß)	489	
Luxemburg	Frömel-Fochler	253		Mira	Hoffmann	338	380	Nuance	Peche	845	
Luzia	Likarz(-Strauß)	481		Miramar	Hoffmann	314	150	Nürnberg	Uxa	1194	
Lymphe	Hirsch (-Landesmann)	283		Miri	Snischek	1164		Nussdorf	Likarz(-Strauß)	603	
Lyon	Hoffmann	311		Mirza	Rix(-Ueno)	1030		Nyitra	Likarz(-Strauß)	558	
Lyon	Rix(-Ueno)	1035		Missouri	Snischek	1112	339	Oase	Krenn	451	
Mäander	Peche	783		Mitsu	Flögl	136		Ob	Flögl	123	
Macedonien	Blonder	42		Mittagstee	Flögl	100		Oberösterreich	Zülow	1315	
Magig	Likarz(-Strauß)	577		Mocca	Zimpel	1281		Obst	Zimpel	1277	
Magnus	Likarz(-Strauß)	652		Mohn	Rix(-Ueno)	1024		Oder	Hoffmann	336	382
Magnus	Posnanski	923		Moldau	Snischek	1129		Odessa	Flögl	171	
Maharadscha	Likarz(-Strauß)	636	205	Molia	Likarz(-Strauß)	647		Ogi	Rix(-Ueno)	1031	
Mai	Likarz(-Strauß)	466		Mombasa	Likarz(-Strauß)	538	354	Olinda	Snischek	1176	
Maikäfer	Wimmer-Wisgrill	1240	94	Monaco	Flögl	121		Oliven	Flögl	109	
Malacca	Brunner (-Frieberger)	60		Mondschein-blume	Rix(-Ueno)	940		Olympia	Peche	788	
Malmö	Ehrlich	87		Monos	Flögl	169		Ombré	Rix(-Ueno)	951	
Maloja	Likarz(-Strauß)	630		Monsun	Snischek	1168		Onix	Likarz(-Strauß)	576	363
Malta	Rix(-Ueno)	996		Montblanc	Likarz(-Strauß)	526		Opal	Kaestner	413	
Malve	Schaschl (-Schuster)	1068		Monte Carlo	Krenek	441	16	Opium	Jesser(-Schmid)	388	
				Montenegro	Zovetti	1302		Oporto	Likarz(-Strauß)	626	
Mandarin	Rix(-Ueno)	982		Montezuma (Monte Zuma)	Hoffmann	312	22, 68, 245	Orakel	Likarz(-Strauß)	495	
Mandelkrähe	Wimmer-Wisgrill	1244						Oran	Likarz(-Strauß)	606	
Manissa	Snischek	1113	273, 303, 304	Moorland	Birke(-Eber)		241	Orient	Zimpel	1254	
				Moosblumen	Rix(-Ueno)	985	250	Orient	Zimpel	1274	
Mantua	Likarz(-Strauß)	520		Morelia	Ehrlich	88		Origan (Origon)	Snischek	1169	
Maorie	Likarz(-Strauß)	604		Morena	Hahn	275					
Marabu	Zimpel	1275		Morgentau	Rix(-Ueno)	1015		Orina	Flögl	187	
Märchen	Snischek	1108		Morphium	Likarz(-Strauß)	508		Orleans	Peche	846	
Marchesa	Flögl	144		Morrer	Likarz(-Strauß)	482		Orlow	Blonder	30	
Marelli	Likarz(-Strauß)	545	355	Morris	Likarz(-Strauß)	619		Orpheus	Peche	757	
Margerith	Likarz(-Strauß)	521		Mosaik	Krenek	440	120	Orplid	Zimpel	1260	
Marina	Peche	785	22, 88–92, 169	Moschee	Schwabel	1104		Osiris	Löw(-Lazar)	663	199
				Mosel	Flögl	122		Osmond	Schinko	1081	
Marius	Likarz(-Strauß)	638		Möven	Peche	745	22	Ossiach	Snischek	1146	
Marizza	Likarz(-Strauß)	530		Mozart	Likarz(-Strauß)	602		Osten	Peche	791	157
Markus	Möschl(-Lagus)	710		München	Blonder	41	22	Ostende	Likarz(-Strauß)	622	
Marmon	Likarz(-Strauß)	523		Münchhausen	Hirsch (-Landesmann)	278		Osterglocken	Zülow	1326	
Marmor	Peche	786						Othello	Peche	792	
Marokko	Zovetti	1299		Mur	Flögl	124		Othmar	Snischek	1154	
Marsblume	Rix(-Ueno)	975		Münster	Snischek	1139		Ottilie	Likarz(-Strauß)	567	
Martha	Hoffmann	313		Mungo	Likarz(-Strauß)	592		Ouverture	Rix(-Ueno)	983	365
Martin	Likarz(-Strauß)	525	357	Muratti	Likarz(-Strauß)	524		Ozon	Hoffmann	328	308
Martina	Möschl(-Lagus)	714		Murray	Rix(-Ueno)	992		P	Posnanski	887	
März	Hackl	270		Mürz	Peche	839		Pacific	Flögl	129	
Maskat	Likarz(-Strauß)	618		Muttler	Posnanski	884		Page	Likarz(-Strauß)	596	
Maskenzauber	Kovacic	436		Nachtfalter	Jungnickel	402		Palamos	Rix(-Ueno)	993	
								Palatin	Peche	847	
								Paleika	Likarz(-Strauß)	570	
								Paliuri	Posnanski		350
								Palme	Peche	746	

251

Pattern name	Designer	Cat. no.	Fig. no(s).
Pamina	Löw(-Lazar)	674	
Pan	Peche	826	193, 194
Panama	Flögl	127	
Panath	Likarz(-Strauß)	565	
Panay	Likarz(-Strauß)	589	
Pandora	Peche	816	
Papageienwald	Jungnickel	403	76
Papagena	Flögl	141	269, 271
Pappelrose	Peche	795	183
Paradiesvogel	Peche	794	78
Parasit	Peche	825	276
Parfüm	Rix(-Ueno)	949	
Parmaveilchen	Rix(-Ueno)	958	
Parsifal	Blonder	43	
Passion	Zülow	1332	211
Passionsblume	Wieselthier	1206	
Passo	Likarz(-Strauß)	615	
Patria	Dostal	84	
Paul	Posnanski	885	351
Paulus	Posnanski	886	
Pax	Zimpel	1261	
Peer Gynt	Wieselthier	1223	
Pegasus (Thalia)	Posnanski	888	
Peking	Frömel-Fochler	132	
Peking	Flögl	132	
Pelargonie	Rix(-Ueno)	943	172
Pelly	Snischek	1171	
Pelusium	Posnanski	889	
Pepita	Kalhammer	419	
Pergola	Flögl	148	
Perlen	Flögl	142	
Perlis	Flögl	126	
Persien	Wirth	1250	291
Peru	Zimpel	1265	
Pest	Posnanski	890	
Peter	Schenk	1080	
Petrograd	Flögl	117	
Pfau	Likarz(-Strauß)	468	
Pfauenauge	Zovetti	1303	
Pfeil	Wieselthier	1218	
Pfingstrose	Zovetti	1305	
Phantast	Likarz(-Strauß)	493	
Phantom	Snischek	1110	376
Philadelphia	Snischek	1144	
Philipp	Kopriva	428	224
Piacenza	Snischek	1137	
Picino (Ticino)	Likarz(-Strauß)	513	
Pierre	Posnanski	891	
Pierrot	Peche	793	96
Pilot	Jungwirth	406	
Pintus	Posnanski	892	
Planei	Posnanski	925	
Plato	Posnanski	893	
Po-Ho	Czeschka	81	135
Pola	Posnanski	894	
Polo	Rix(-Ueno)	1016	
Pompadour	Hoffmann	349	
Pompeji	Nechansky	728	26
Portepee	Likarz(-Strauß)	486	238-240
Portici	Likarz(-Strauß)	556	
Portorose	Löw(-Lazar)	682	
Poseidon	Hoffmann	358	255
Pram	Posnanski	895	
Prater	Likarz(-Strauß)	507	11
Preblau	Posnanski	896	
Priel	Flögl	147	
Primula	Jesser(-Schmid)	393	
Prisma	Peche	848	
Prix	Posnanski	897	
Prolog	Likarz(-Strauß)	484	
Prosa	Posnanski	898	
Puch	Zovetti	1304	
Pucker	Snischek	1132	
Pulkau	Zülow	1327	
Purpurnelke	Rix(-Ueno)	987	
Pux	Snischek	1125	
Quadern	Wieselthier	1221	215
Quartett	Blumberger	58	227
Quaste	Flögl	155	328
Quelle	Snischek	1133	
Quodlibet	Löw(-Lazar)	690	

Pattern name	Designer	Cat. no.	Fig. no(s).
Radio	Likarz(-Strauß)	573	8
Rafael	Zimpel	1271	
Ragaz	Likarz(-Strauß)	637	
Ragusa	Hoffmann	319	247, 259, 260
Rahat	Rix(-Ueno)	1040	
Raket(t)en	Krenek	442	10
Ramona	Likarz(-Strauß)	561	
Rana	Likarz(-Strauß)	593	
Ranken	Schröder (-Ehrenfest)	1090	
Rapallo	Schröder (-Ehrenfest)	1103	
Rappelkopf	Löw(-Lazar)	673	
Raps	Likarz(-Strauß)	653	
Raptus	Rix(-Ueno)	1046	
Rauten	Snischek	1173	
Rax	Peche	798	10, 163
Rebhuhn	Likarz(-Strauß)	498	
Refrain	Hoffmann	342	6
Regenbogen	Peche	822	256
Regia	Flögl	170	
Reichenau	Zülow	1328	10
Reifen	Hoffmann	339	383
Reigen	Wieselthier	1214	
Rengo	Likarz(-Strauß)	611	
Retz	Snischek	1148	
Reuss	Rix(-Ueno)	1003	
Revue	Likarz(-Strauß)	492	
Rhapsodie	Rix(-Ueno)	1017	
Rhodos	Snischek	1114	
Rhomben	Peche	834	
Rhombus	Hoffmann	318	7
Rialto	Angerer	4	
Riedgras	Jesser(-Schmid)	387	
Riesenblatt	Flögl	102	
Rigi	Stadlmayer	1189	
Rimini (Bimini)	Zimpel	1268	234
Ringelblume	Schaschl(-Schuster)	1073	
Risa	Höchsmann	287	
Rispen	Rix(-Ueno)	945	
Riva	Hoffmann	316	10, 140, 141
Riva-See	Berger, A.	17	
Riviera	Peche	797	10
Robinson	Likarz(-Strauß)	478	
Rogate	Flögl	183	
Roland	Jacobsen	371	
Rollschnecke	Hoffmann	317	9, 71
Rom	Peche	849	174, 176
Roma	Likarz(-Strauß)	500	
Romana	Likarz(-Strauß)	654	
Romeo	Friedmann(-Otten)	223	
Romulus	Likarz(-Strauß)	535	364
Rosanna	Likarz(-Strauß)	455	
Rosengarten	Peche	747	79, 159
Rosenhain	Rix(-Ueno)	1009	273
Rosenkavalier	Peche	796	10
Rosita	Hoffmann	359	
Rosmarin	Luzatto	696	
Royal	Likarz(-Strauß)	543	
Rübezahl	Friedmann(-Otten)	217	
Rubin	Hoffmann	360	
Rummy	Likarz(-Strauß)	607	
Ruth	Zimpel	1257	
Rütli	Posnanski	899	
Sabino	Likarz(-Strauß)	634	
Sachs (Lachs)	Wimmer-Wisgrill	1238	
Sachsen	Jacobsen	369	
Sada Jacco	Frömel-Fochler	261	20
Saffi	Posnanski	926	
Säge	Perlmutter	852	
Sahara	Snischek	1180	
Sakatali	Hoffmann	345	
Salambo	Hoffmann	295	203, 204
Salpinx	Wieselthier	1213	131
Salzburg	Posnanski	900	
Sambesi	Flögl	140	
Samnaun	Posnanski	901	
Samoa	Snischek	1122	338
Samtente	Frömel-Fochler	259	53, 54
Samun	Likarz(-Strauß)	564	

Pattern name	Designer	Cat. no.	Fig. no(s).
San Sebastian	Likarz(-Strauß)	509	
Sandy	Likarz(-Strauß)	582	
Santa Sophia (Santa Sofia)	Hoffmann	320	70, 296
Santos	Likarz(-Strauß)	616	
Saragossa	Prutscher	933	
Sargans	Rix(-Ueno)	1002	367
Saturn	Möschl(-Lagus)	709	
Säule	Peche	824	344
Save	Hoffmann	335	
Savonarola	Reinold	935	
Schatten	Peche	808	274
Schattenriß	Jesser(-Schmid)	378	
Schiene(n)	Möschl(-Lagus)	705	
Schigatze	Zovetti	1307	
Schilfblüte	Friedmann(-Otten)	211	
Schiras	Flögl	103	
Schiwa	Zimpel	1258	
Schlinge	Foltin	199	
Schlingpflanze	Wieselthier	1203	
Schönau	Kalhammer	420	130
Schönbrunn	Likarz(-Strauß)	931	
Schönbrunn	Pospischil	501	98
Schöpfl	Posnanski	902	
Schöpfung	Frank	202	
Schottland	Kovacic	429	
Schottland (Irland, Irrland)	Likarz(Strauß)	458	99–102, 172, 251
Schraube	Foltin	197	
Schuppen	Peche	801	
Schwalbenschwanz	Peche	800	153–155
Schwan	Snischek	1117	
Schwarzblatt	Hoffmann	322	306
Schweden	Rix(-Ueno)	977	
Schwertlilie	Jungwirth	410	
Seeboden	Snischek	1172	
Seekoralle	Friedmann(-Otten)	221	
Seerose	Wimmer-Wisgrill	1241	307
Seestern	Friedmann(-Otten)	220	
Seetang	Zovetti	1306	
Segelstangen	Jesser(-Schmid)	394	
Semiramis	Peche	748	312
Sent Mahese	Wieselthier	1215	
Seraphin	Jacobsen	370	
Serpentin	Hoffmann	321	145
Sesam	Snischek	1181	
Sevilla	Flögl	92	
Sibu	Likarz(-Strauß)	588	
Sieg	Peche	766	
Siena	Schaschl(-Schuster)	1077	
Sievering	Posnanski	903	
Silberblatt	Rix(-Ueno)	1036	
Silvretta	Posnanski	904	
Simme	Rix(-Ueno)	1004	
Simplicius	Blonder	56	
Sinaia	Blumberger	59	
Sining	Likarz(-Strauß)	547	
Sinsa (Linsa)	Zovetti	1297	
Sirene	Likarz(-Strauß)	627	
Sirocco	Snischek	1167	
Sitter	Flögl	161	
Sizilien	Peche	799	
Skorpion	Likarz(-Strauß)	461	321
Smyrna	Blonder	27	
Sofia	Snischek	1177	
Sold	Zimpel	1252	
Soldanellen	Wieselthier	1227	
Sommer	Likarz(-Strauß)	608	
Sommerabend	Zülow	1330	125
Sommerblume	Löw(-Lazar)	666	
Sommerfalter	Rix(-Ueno)	994	
Sommerlust	Jesser(-Schmid)	390	
Sommerwinde	Rix(-Ueno)	966	
Sondervogel	Flögl	107	
Sonja	Angerer	11	
Sonnenblume	Zülow	1331	
Sonnenglanz	Löw(-Lazar)	681	
Soslon	Posnanski	905	
Spätsommer	Häusler	274	
Spalato	Likarz(-Strauß)	457	

Pattern name	Designer	Cat. no.	Fig. no(s).
Sparta	Likarz(-Strauß)	462	
Speda	Hoffmann	348	
Spieldose	Wieselthier	1226	
Spinne	Peche	784	160, 162
Spoleto	Snischek	1158	
Sport	Snischek	1179	244
Spree	Posnanski	906	
St. Andrä	Blonder	45	
St. Veit	Wimmer-Wisgrill	1242	
Stabilo	Likarz(-Strauß)	532	
Stachelrose	Hirsch (-Landesmann)	277	
Staket(t)e	Peche	802	
Staniol	Singer(-Schinnerl)	1106	228
Stanley	Hoffmann	351	
Starling	Müllner	723	
Steinbrecher	Brunner (-Frieberger)	62	
Steinnelke	Schröder (-Ehrenfest)	1088	
Steppe	Möschl(-Lagus)	704	
Sternblume	Schinko	1083	
Sterngucker	Singer(-Schinnerl)	1105	
Sternhimmel	Blonder	55	
Sternschnuppen	Weinberger	1200	
Sternwarte	Blonder	44	
Stettin	Posnanski	907	
Stichblatt	Zovetti	1308	16, 261, 262
Stiefmütterchen	Rix(-Ueno)	969	
Stockrose	Likarz(-Strauß)	496	
Stockrose	Zimpel	1278	
Storch(en)schnabel	Peche	803	
Strauss	Posnanski	908	
Streifen	Likarz(-Strauß)	471	
Strohblume(n)	Friedmann(-Otten)	218	
Strohröschen	Schaschl(-Schuster)	1074	
Styx	Hoffmann	346	
Sudan	Flögl	131	
Süden	Zülow	1329	
Südfrucht	Likarz(-Strauß)	649	
Sues	Rix(-Ueno)	1007	
Sumatra	Frömel-Fochler	260	107
Sumba	Flögl	158	
Sumpfreiher	Rix(-Ueno)	960	
Sünde	Flögl	113	
Susanna	Jungwirth	407	
Sylvester	Rix(-Ueno)	984	335
Syrakus	Snischek	1124	
Tahiti	Birke(-Eber)	20	200
Taifun	Snischek	1170	
Tamara	Likarz(-Strauß)	473	318
Tamaris	Likarz(-Strauß)	579	
Tami	Likarz(-Strauß)	641	
Tamia	Likarz(-Strauß)	655	
Tanagra	Rix(-Ueno)	947	
Tanne	Calm(-Wierink)	69	
Tantalus	Rix(-Ueno)	946	
Tanz	Brunner (-Frieberger)	65	
Tanzpaar	Hirsch (-Landesmann)	280	
Tarantella	Rix(-Ueno)	1022	
Tatra	Friedl	205	
Tausendblumen	Peche	830	
Teehaus	Rix(-Ueno)	950	
Teerose	Rix(-Ueno)	1010	
Teheran	Blonder	46	
Tennis	Flögl	97	
Tenor	Hoffmann	330	384
Terzett	Likarz(-Strauß)	487	
Thalia (Pegasus)	Posnanski	888	
Theba	Angerer	7	
Theben	Hoffmann	294	149
Theiss	Möschl(-Lagus)	707	
Thun	Friedl	204	
Thur	Flögl	162	
Thymian	Peche	804	
Tibet	Birke(-Eber)	21	
Ticino (Picino)	Likarz(-Strauß)	513	
Tientsin	Flögl	146	
Tigris	Posnanski	927	
Tilupi	Rix(-Ueno)	1034	
Timur	Likarz(-Strauß)	569	
Tinos	Posnanski	909	
Titania	Jesser(-Schmid)	374	
Titus	Likarz(-Strauß)	480	
Tizi	Posnanski	928	
Tobias	Schröder (-Ehrenfest)	1097	
Togo	Snischek	1165	
Tokio	Rix(-Ueno)	979	272
Torpedo	Löw(-Lazar)	691	
Toska	Nechansky	729	
Touring	Rix(-Ueno)	1038	
Tramino	Rix(-Ueno)	997	
Trass (Dillon, Dilon, Frass)	Peche	744	
Traumblume	Jesser(-Schmid)	383	
Traun	Posnanski	916	
Traviata	Rix(-Ueno)	939	
Treppe	Likarz(-Strauß)	474	
Treuherz	Löw(-Lazar)	675	
Triangel	Hoffmann	324	146
Triglav	Flögl	153	
Trinidad	Snischek	1142	
Tripolis	Zovetti	1309	23
Triton	Zimpel	1256	
Trocadero	Frömel-Fochler	262	
Troja	Schaschl(-Schuster)	1056	
Tropen	Peche	813	
Tropenblume	Schaschl(-Schuster)	1069	184, 185
Tua	Likarz(-Strauß)	624	
Tulipan	Brunner (-Frieberger)	63	
Tulln	Posnanski	910	
Tulpe	Hoffmann	323	
Tunis	Frömel-Fochler	264	
Tunnel	Luzatto	697	
Turandot	Wimmer-Wisgrill	1243	
Turf	Snischek	1120	
Türkenbund	Schröder (-Ehrenfest)	1096	
Tylli	Jesser(-Schmid)	376	
Tyrol	Posnanski	911	
Ulm	Posnanski	912	
Umbra	Likarz(-Strauß)	483	
Unschuld	Schaschl(-Schuster)	1072	
Unterwelt	Blonder	50	
Uranus	Flögl	178	
Ursula	Wieselthier	1220	
Uruguay	Likarz(-Strauß)	505	11
Urwald	Jungnickel	404	
Valencia	Zimpel	1267	221
Valentin	Möschl(-Lagus)	716	
Vanity	Likarz(-Strauß)	571	
Vase	Peche	743	
Veilchen	Flögl	98	
Velden	Peche	742	
Venedig	Kalhammer	421	
Venusgärtchen	Peche	805	
Venusschuh	Likarz(-Strauß)	459	
Vergißmeinnicht	Peche	769	313
Verona	Likarz(-Strauß)	499	
Vesuv	Rix(-Ueno)	948	
Vielblatt	Likarz(-Strauß)	612	
Viola	Peche	832	188
Violantha	Flögl	160	
Violetta	Hackl	271	
Vöslau (Alland, Baden)	Löw(-Lazar)	656	218
Vogelhain	Rix(-Ueno)	1000	
Vogelkönig	Blonder	47	
Vogelweide	Löw(-Lazar)	657	
Vorau	Snischek	1140	375
Vorfrühling	Löw(-Lazar)	669	
Vorgarten	Löw(Lazar)	658	
Vorgarten	Jonasch	399	95
Vorwitz	Likarz(-Strauß)	494	
Votum	Snischek	1127	
Wachau	Kalhammer	422	
Wadin	Löw(-Lazar)	694	
Waikiki	Likarz(-Strauß)	590	
Waldblume	Rix(-Ueno)	962	
Waldfee	Rix(-Uneo)	941	
Waldidyll	Czeschka	82	81–84, 133
Waldkapelle	Frömel-Fochler	263	85
Waldrand	Hoffmann	327	
Waldveilchen	Rix(-Ueno)	1047	
Waldwiese	Heigl	276	
Walpurga	Möschl(-Lagus)	708	
Wanderer	Zovetti	1310	
Warschau	Wimmer-Wisgrill	1245	
Wasserblüten	Schröder (-Ehrenfest)	1089	
Wasserfall	Hoffmann	325	148
Wasserorgel	Czeschka	83	136, 137
Wasservogel	Krenn	447	
Weekend	Likarz(-Strauß)	557	
Wein	Peche	817	
Weingartl	Löw(-Lazar)	664	
Wellen	Rix(-Ueno)	1043	208
Weltkugel	Likarz(-Strauß)	470	
Wetterleuchten	Rix(-Ueno)	1048	
Whisky	Likarz(-Strauß)	546	356
Wicken	Peche	820	156
Wiedehopf	Blonder	48	
Wien	Peche	836	
Wienerwald	Jonasch	400	281
Wiese	Flögl	150	
Wiesenglocke	Jesser(-Schmid)	386	
Wildling	Dostal	85	
Windblume	Perlmutter	853	
Winde	Löw(-Lazar)	695	
Windling	Löw(-Lazar)	692	
Windröschen	Schaschl(-Schuster)	1078	
Winkel	Likarz(-Strauß)	617	352
Wintergarten	Peyrer	857	
Wipfel	Singer(-Schinnerl)	1107	
Wolga	Höchsmann	288	
Wolkenkratzer	Likarz(-Strauß)	613	
Wolkenstern	Berger, A.	13	
Wörthersee	Peche	807	
Wunderbaum	Peche	806	295
Wundervogel	Peche	811	
Wurzelsepp	Schaschl(-Schuster)	1067	
Yap (Jap)	Höchsmann	289	226
Ybbs	Snischek	1151	
Yen	Snischek	1130	
Yokohama	Likarz(-Strauß)	548	
Zackenband	Rix(Ueno)	1049	
Zaglul	Pamberger	733	
Zakopane	Perlmutter	851	108
Zara	Posnanski	913	
Zarte Bänder	Löw(-Lazar)	667	
Zauberflöte	Zovetti	1311	
Zaun	Schröder (-Ehrenfest)	1092	
Zaunkönig	Schaschl(-Schuster)	1055	
Zebra	Hoffmann	326	
Zelenika	Snischek	1162	
Zell	Hoffmann	352	
Zephir	Jacobsen	365	
Zerbinetta	Löw(-Lazar)	676	
Zeus	Paradeiser	735	
Zickzack (Zick-Zack)	Jesser(-Schmid)	384	
Ziergras	Rix(-Ueno)	968	
Ziermücke	Likarz(-Strauß)	609	
Zierpflanze	Zovetti	1312	
Zinnia (Zimnia)	Flögl	157	
Zugspitze	Blonder	49	
Zuidersee	Löw(-Lazar)	672	
Zwergpalme	Zimpel	1269	235
Zyprian	Snischek	1111	379
2002	Posnanski	914	
2005	Posnanski	915	

Bibliographical Sources

AeD
Art et Décoration. Revue Mensuelle d'Art Moderne
Paris, 1897 *et seq.*

amk
alte und moderne kunst. Öster-reichische Fachzeitschrift des Marktes für Antiquitäten, Bilder, Kunstgegenstände alter und moderner Kunst
Vienna, 1956–85

Amour de l'Art
Amour de l'Art. Art Ancien, Art Moderne, Architecture, Arts Appliqués.
New series, Paris, 1920 *et seq.*

Baldass 1925
Baldass, Alfred von
Wien. Ein Führer durch die Stadt und ihre Umgebung, ihre Kunst und ihr Wirtschaftsleben.
Vienna, 1925

Barcelona 1993 (exhib. cat.)
Elisanda Vives (ed.)
Delicte i Somni. Viena 1900–1930. Interiors mobles objectes
Barcelona, 1993

Baroni/D'Auria 1981
Baroni, Daniele and D'Auria, Antonio
Josef Hoffmann e la Wiener Werkstätte
Milan, 1981

Berlin 1977 (exhib. cat.)
Mundt, Barbara (ed.)
Metropolen machen Mode. Haute Couture der Zwanziger Jahre
Berlin, 1977

Berlin 1987 (exhib. cat.)
Droste, Magdalena (ed.)
Gunta Stölzl. Weberei am Bauhaus aus eigener Werkstatt
Berlin, 1987

Bouillon 1989
Bouillon, Jean-Paul
Art Déco in Wort und Bild 1903–1940
Geneva, 1989

Bowman 1985
Bowman, Sarah
A Fashion for Extravagance
London, 1985

Brussels 1927 (stock cat.)
Errera, Isabelle
Musées Royaux du Cinquantenaire. Catalogue d'Etoffes anciennes et modernes
Brussels, 1927

Brussels 1987 (exhib. cat.)
Schmuttermeier, Elisabeth (ed.)
Wiener Werkstätte. Atelier Viennois 1903–1932
Brussels, 1987

Brussels 1989 (exhib. cat.)
Lambrechts, Marc (ed.)
L'art déco en Europe. Tendances décoratives dans les arts appliqués vers 1925
Brussels, 1989

Buddensieg/Rogge 1979
Buddensieg, Tilmann and Rogge, Henning
Industriekultur. Peter Behrens und die AEG 1907–1914
Berlin, 1979

Buxbaum 1986
Buxbaum, Gerda
Mode aus Wien 1815–1938
Salzburg/Vienna, 1986

Crispolti 1986
Crispolti, Enrico
Il futurismo e la moda
Venice, 1986

DA
Der Architekt. Wiener Monatshefte für Bauwesen und dekorative Kunst
Vienna, 1895 *et seq.*

DBK
Die Bildenden Künste. Wiener Monatshefte
Vienna, 1916 *et seq.*

DI
Das Interieur. Wiener Monatshefte für Wohnungsausstattung und angewandte Kunst
Vienna, 1900 *et seq.*

Die Form
Die Form. Zeitschrift für gestaltende Arbeit
Berlin/Leipzig, 1922 *et seq.*

DK
Dekorative Kunst. Eine illustrierte Zeitschrift für angewandte Kunst
Munich, 1922 *et seq.*

DKD
Deutsche Kunst und Dekoration. Illustrierte Monatshefte für moderne Malerei, Plastik, Architektur, Wohnungskunst und künstlerische Frauenarbeiten
Darmstadt, 1897 *et seq.*

DSH
Das schöne Heim. Illustrierte Zeit-schrift für angewandte Kunst
Munich, 1930 *et seq.*

Düsseldorf 1991 (exhib. cat.)
Svestka, Jiri, Vlček, T., and Liška, P. (eds.)
1909–1925 Kubismus in Prag, Malerei, Skulptur, Kunstgewerbe, Architektur
Düsseldorf, 1991

DW
Die Damenwelt
Vienna, 1917 *et seq.*

Eisler 1916
Eisler, Max
Österreichische Werkkultur
Vienna, 1916

Eisler 1925
Eisler, Max
Dagobert Peche
Vienna/Leipzig, 1925

Fanelli 1976
Fanelli, Giovanni and Rosalia
Il Tessuto moderno: Disegno, Moda, Architettura 1890–1940
Florence, 1976

Fanelli/Godoli 1981
Fanelli, Giovanni and Godoli, Ezio
La Vienna di Hoffmann architetto della qualità
Rome/Bari, 1981

Fenz 1984
Fenz, Werner
Koloman Moser
Salzburg, 1984

Fischer 1987
Fischer, Wolfgang Georg
Gustav Klimt und Emilie Flöge. Genie und Talent, Freundschaft und Besessenheit
Vienna, 1987

Florence 1978 (exhib. cat.)
6.a. Biennale internazionale della grafica d'arte, vol. 1
Florence, 1978

FMR
Ricci, Franco Maria (ed.)
FMR. Mensile culturale di Franco Maria Ricci
Milan, 1981 *et seq.*

Gmeiner/Pirhofer 1985
Gmeiner, Astrid and Pirhofer, Gottfried
Der österreichische Werkbund. Alternative zur klassischen Moderne in Architektur, Raum- und Produktgestaltung
Salzburg/Vienna, 1985

Graz 1972 (exhib. cat.)
Wiener Werkstätte. Art nouveau – Art deco 1903–1932
Graz, 1972

Hansen 1982
Hansen, Traude
Die Postkarten der Wiener Werk-stätte
Munich, 1982

Hansen 1984
Hansen, Traude (in collaboration with Gino Wimmer)
Wiener Werkstätte Mode. Stoffe Schmuck Accessoires
Vienna/Munich, 1984

ID
Innendekoration. Die gesamte Wohnungskunst in Bild und Wort
Darmstadt/Stuttgart, 1890 *et seq.*

JDW
Jahrbuch des Deutschen Werk-bundes
Jena, 1912 *et seq.*

KesslerAurisch 1983
KesslerAurisch, Helga
Mode und Malerei in Wien vom Wiener Kongreß bis zum Ersten Weltkrieg
Bonn, 1983

KKHW
Kunst und Kunsthandwerk. Monatsschrift des k.k. Öster-reichischen Museums für Kunst und Industrie
Vienna, 1897 *et seq.*

Kleiner 1927
Kleiner, Leopold
Josef Hoffmann
Berlin/Leipzig/Vienna, 1927

Koch 1916
Koch, Alexander
Deutsche Werkkunst. Arbeiten deutscher und österreichischer Künstler auf der Werkbund-Ausstellung Köln a. Rhein
Darmstadt/Leipzig, 1916

Koch 1923
Koch, Alexander
Das neue Kunsthandwerk in Deutschland und Österreich unter Berücksichtigung der Deutschen Gewerbeschau München 1923
Darmstadt, 1923

Koch 1926
Koch, Alexander
1000 Ideen zur künstlerischen Ausgestaltung der Wohnung
Darmstadt, 1926

Krefeld 1984 (exhib. cat.)
Der westdeutsche Impuls 1900–1914. Kunst und Umwelt-gestaltung im Industriegebiet. Von der Künstlerseide zur Industrie-fotografie. Das Museum zwischen Jugendstil und Werkbund
Krefeld, 1984

Langenthal 1986 (exhib. cat.)
Stoffe und Räume. Eine textile Wohngeschichte der Schweiz
Langenthal, 1986

Le Corbusier (1925)
Dunnet, James I. (introduction)
Le Corbusier. The Decorative Art of Today (1925)
Cambridge, Mass., 1987

Leipzig 1927 (exhib. cat.)
Ausstellung Europäisches Kunstgewerbe 1927
Leipzig, 1927

Leipzig 1930 (exhib. cat.)
Rochowanski, Leopold Wolfgang (ed.)
Ein Führer durch das österreichische Kunstgewerbe
Leipzig/Vienna/Troppau, 1930

Lesak 1988
Lesak, Barbara
Die Kulisse explodiert. Friedrich Kieslers Theaterexperimente und Architekturprojekte 1923–1925
Vienna, 1988

Lucerne 1974 (exhib. cat.)
Kunst in Österreich 1900–1930
Lucerne, 1974

Malochet 1984
Malochet, Annette
Atelier Simultané de Sonia Delaunay 1923–1934
Milan, 1984

MBF
Moderne Bauformen. Monatshefte für Architektur und Raumkunst
Stuttgart, 1902 *et seq.*

Melbourne 1984 (exhib. cat.)
Lane, Terence (ed.)
Vienna 1913. Josef Hoffmann's Gallia Apartment
Melbourne, 1984

Munich 1922 (exhib. cat.)
Deutsche Gewerbeschau München 1922
Munich, 1922

Munich 1986/87 (exhib. cat.)
Ley, Andreas (ed.)
Anziehungskräfte. Variété de la mode 1786–1986
Munich, 1986

MW
Moderne Welt. Kultur und Gesellschaft. Österreichische Revue
Vienna, 1918 *et seq.*

Nebehay 1976
Nebehay, Christian Michael
Gustav Klimt. Sein Leben nach zeitgenössischen Berichten und Quellen
Munich, 1976

Neuwirth 1981
Neuwirth, Waltraud
Die Keramiken der Wiener Werkstätte Vol. I: Original-Keramiken 1920–1931
Vienna, 1981

Neuwirth 1984
Neuwirth, Waltraud
Wiener Werkstätte. Avantgarde, Art Deco, Industrial Design.
Vienna, 1984

Neuwirth 1985
Neuwirth, Waltraud
Wiener Werkstätte. Die Schutzmarken. Vol. I: Rosenmarke und Wortmarke
Vienna, 1985

New York 1980 (exhib. cat.)
The Imperial Style: Fashions of the Hapsburg Era
New York, 1980

New York 1986 (exhib. cat.)
Kallir, Jane
Viennese Design and the Wiener Werkstätte
New York, 1986

New York 1992/93 (exhib. cat.)
Josef Hoffmann Design
New York, 1992

ÖBWK
Österreichs Bau- und Werkkunst. Illustrierte Monatsschrift
Vienna, 1924 *et seq.*

ÖK
Österreichische Kunst. Monatsschrift für Bildende und Darstellende Kunst, Architektur und Kunsthandwerk
Vienna, 1926 *et seq.*

Paris 1925 (exhib. cat.)
L'Autriche à l'Exposition Internationale des Arts Décoratifs et Industriels Modernes
Paris, 1925

Paris 1986 (exhib. cat.)
Vienne 1880–1938. L'Apocalypse joyeuse
Paris, 1986

Parry 1983
Parry, Linda
William Morris Textiles
London, 1983

Pesaro 1985 (exhib. cat.)
La tessitura del Bauhaus 1919–1933 nelle collezioni della Repubblica Democratica Tedesca
Pesaro, 1985

Pesaro 1987 (exhib. cat.)
Zaletova, Lidija / Ciofi degli Alti, Fabio / Panzini, Franco (eds.)
L'abito della rivoluzione
Pesaro, 1987

Pfabigan 1985
Pfabigan, Alfred (ed.)
Ornament und Askese im Zeitgeist des Wien der Jahrhundertwende
Vienna, 1985

Pichler 1992 (stock cat.)
Pichler, Ruperta (ed.)
Wiener Werkstätte Lederobjekte aus den Sammlungen des österreichischen Museums für angewandte Kunst
Vienna, 1992

Quelle
Moser, Koloman and Gerlach, Martin (eds.)
Flächenschmuck. Die Quelle (3)
Vienna/Leipzig, 1901

Reiter 1987
Reiter, Cornelia
Dagobert Peche und seine Bedeutung für die Wiener Werkstätte
Innsbruck, 1987

Ritter 1933
Ritter, Josef (ed.)
Kunst in österreich. Österreichischer Almanach und Künstler-Adreßbuch
Leoben, 1933

Rome 1911 I (exhib. cat.)
Internationale Kunstausstellung Rom 1911. Österreichischer Pavillon
Rome, 1911

Rome 1911 II (exhib. cat.)
Internationale Kunstausstellung Rom 1911. Österreichischer Pavillon nach Plänen von Architekt Josef Hoffmann
Rome, 1911

St Petersburg 1991 (exhib. cat.)
Josef Hoffmann 1870–1956
Moscow, 1991

Salzburg 1987 (exhib. cat.)
Schaffer, Nikolaus
Dagobert Peche 1887–1923. In seinen Zeichnungen
Salzburg, 1987

Schweiger 1984
Schweiger, Werner J. (with introduction by W. G. Fischer)
Wiener Werkstätte. Design in Vienna 1903–1932
(translated from the German)
London/New York, 1984;
reprinted 1990

Sekler 1982
Sekler, Eduard F.
Josef Hoffmann. Das architektonische Werk. Monographie und Werkverzeichnis
Salzburg/Vienna, 1982

Sekler 1985
Sekler, Eduard F.
Josef Hoffmann. The Architectural Work
Princeton, N.J., 1985

SSR
Stickerei- und Spitzenrundschau. Illustrierte Monatshefte zur Förderung der deutschen Stickerei- und Spitzen-Industrie. Zentral-Organ für die Hebung der künstlerischen Frauen-Handarbeiten
Berlin, 1900 *et seq.*

Steinoel 1929
Steinoel, Theo
Stoffmalerei mit Stempel, Schablonen- und Spritztechnik. Eine Einführung in ihre Praxis
Ravensburg, 1929

Studio Yearbook
The Studio. Yearbook of Decorative Art
London, 1906 *et seq.*

Stuttgart 1980 (exhib. cat.)
Grönwoldt, Ruth (ed.)
Art Nouveau-Textildekor um 1900
Stuttgart, 1980

The Studio
The Studio. An Illustrated Magazine of Fine and Applied Art
London, 1893 *et seq.*

TKI
Textile Kunst und Industrie
Dresden, 1908 et seq.

Tokyo 1989 (exhib. cat.)
Wien um 1900. Klimt, Schiele und ihre Zeit
Tokyo, 1989

Trad. u. Exper. 1988
Noever, Peter (ed.)
Tradition und Experiment. Das österreichische Museum für angewandte Kunst, Wien
Salzburg/Vienna, 1988

Varnedoe 1986 (exhib. cat.)
Varnedoe, Kirk (ed.)
Vienna 1900. Art, Architecture & Design
New York, 1986

Venice 1984 (exhib. cat.)
Le arti a Vienna. Dalla Secessione alla caduta dell'Impero Asburgico
Venice, 1984

Venice 1986 (exhib. cat.)
Hulten, Pontus (ed.)
Futurismo & Futurismi
Venice, 1986

Ver Sacrum
Ver Sacrum. Organ der Vereinigung bildender Künstler Österreichs
Vienna, 1898 *et seq.*

Völker 1984
Völker, Angela
Wiener Mode + Modefotografie. Die Modeabteilung der Wiener Werkstätte 1911–1932
Munich/Paris, 1984

Völker *amk*
Völker, Angela
'Österreichische Textilien des frühen 20. Jahrhunderts' in *amk*,
1980, no. 171, pp. 1ff.
Vienna, 1980

255

Völker WKK 1983 and 1984
Völker, Angela
'Die Mode der Wiener Werk-
stätte. Von den Anfängen bis zum
Ende des ersten Weltkrieges' in
WKK, 1983, no. 2, pp. 121ff.; 'Die
Mode der Wiener Werkstätte. II,
Von 1919 bis 1932' in *WKK*, 1984,
no. 1, pp. 37ff.

Völker/Pichler 1989
Völker, Angela and Pichler,
Ruperta
*Wallpaper Designs of the Wiener
Werkstätte in the Österreichisches
Museum für angewandte Kunst,
Vienna. Vol. I: The First Decade –
1913 to 1922. Vol. II: Designs by
M. Likarz, F. Rix and M. Flögl
before 1925 to 1931*
Tokyo, 1989

Weiser 1930
Weiser, Armand
Josef Hoffmann
Geneva, 1930

Wichmann 1990 (stock cat.)
Wichmann, Hans
*Von Morris bis Memphis. Textilien
der Neuen Sammlung, Ende 19. bis
Ende 20. Jahrhundert*
Munich, 1990

Wien 1909/10 (exhib. cat.)
*Ausstellung österreichischer Kunst-
gewerbe 1909–1910. K.k. Öster-
reichisches Museum für Kunst und
Industrie*
Vienna, 1909

Wien 1911 (exhib. cat.)
*Ausstellung österreichischer Kunst-
gewerbe 1911–1912. K.k. öster-
reichisches Museum für Kunst und
Industrie*
Vienna, 1911

Wien 1912 (exhib. cat.)
*Frühjahrsausstellung öster-
reichischer Kunstgewerbe ver-
bunden mit einer Ausstellung der
k.k. Kunstgewerbeschule Wien*
Vienna, 1912

Wien 1915/16 (exhib. cat.)
*Mode-Ausstellung 1915/16 im
k.k. oesterreichischen Museum für
Kunst und Industrie, Wien I,
Stubenring 5.*
Vienna, 1915

Wien 1923 (sales cat.)
*Wiener Werkstätte G.m.b.H, Wien
I, Graben 15, und Kärntnerstraße
32*
Vienna, 1923

Wien 1923 Peche (exhib. cat.)
*Ausstellung von Arbeiten des
modernen österreichischen
Kunsthandwerks. Dagobert Peche
Gedächtnisausstellung*
Vienna, 1923

Wien 1924
Kiesler, Friedrich (ed.)
*Internationale Ausstellung neuer
Theatertechnik*
Vienna, 1924

Wien 1924 (exhib. cat.)
*Wiener Kunstgewerbe-Verein.
Jubiläumsausstellung 1884–1924*
Vienna, 1924

Wien 1928 (sales cat.)
*Wiener Werkstätte. Wien VII,
Döblergasse 4; Detailgeschäfte:
I, Kärntner Straße 32 und 41.*
Vienna, 1928

Wien 1929 (exhib. cat.)
*Wiener Werkstätte 1903–1928.
Modernes Kunstgewerbe und sein
Weg*
Vienna, 1929

Wien 1929 BiR (exhib. cat.)
*Das Bild im Raum. 11. Ausstellung
des Verbandes Bildender
Künstlerinnen und Kunsthand-
werkerinnen in Berlin*
Vienna, 1929

Wien 1929/30 (exhib. cat.)
Wiener Raumkünstler
Vienna, 1929

Wien 1930 (exhib. cat.)
Werkbundausstellung 1930
Vienna, 1930

Wien 1931/32 (exhib. cat.)
Der gute und billige Gegenstand
Vienna, 1931

Wien 1934 (exhib. cat.)
Kotas, Robert (ed.)
*Carl Witzmann. Anläßlich seines
50. Geburtstags*
Vienna, 1934

Wien 1964 (exhib. cat.)
Wien um 1900
Vienna, 1964

Wien 1967 (exhib. cat.)
Mrazek, Wilhelm (ed.)
*Die Wiener Werkstätte. Modernes
Kunsthandwerk von 1903–1932*
Vienna, 1967

Wien 1978
Oswald Haerdtl (1889–1959)
Vienna, 1978

Wien 1979 (exhib. cat.)
Oberhuber, Oswald and
Hummel, Julius (eds.)
Koloman Moser. 1868–1918
Vienna, 1979

Wien 1980 Kaffeehaus (exhib.
cat.)
*Das Wiener Kaffeehaus. Von den
Anfängen bis zur Zwischenkriegs-
zeit*
Vienna, 1980

Wien 1980 NW (exhib. cat.)
*Neues Wohnen. Wiener Innen-
raumgestaltung 1918–1938*
Vienna, 1980

Wien 1981 (exhib. cat.)
Wawerka, Peter (ed.)
*Moderne Vergangenheit
1800–1900*
Vienna, 1981

Wien 1983 (exhib. cat.)
*Eduard Josef Wimmer-Wisgrill.
Modeentwürfe 1912–1927 aus dem
Besitz der Hochschule für
angewandte Kunst in Wien*
Vienna, 1983

Wien 1985 (exhib. cat.)
*Traum und Wirklichkeit. Wien
1870–1930*
Vienna, 1985

Wien 1985 Cizek (exhib. cat.)
*Franz Cizek. Pionier der Kunst-
erziehung (1865–1946)*
Vienna, 1985

Wien 1985 WW (exhib. cat.)
Neuwirth, Waltraud (ed.)
Die Wiener Werkstätte 1903–1932
Vienna, 1985

Wien 1986 (exhib. cat.)
Lunzer, Heinz and Lunzer-
Talos, Victoria (eds.)
*Kunst in Wien um 1900. Aus-
stellung des Bundesministeriums
für Auswärtige Angelegenheiten*
Vienna, 1986

Wien 1986/87 (exhib. and stock
cat.)
Noever, Peter and Oberhuber,
Oswald (eds.)
*Josef Hoffmann 1870–1956.
Ornament zwischen Hoffnung und
Verbrechen*
Vienna, 1986

Wien 1987 Hoffmann (exhib.
and stock cat.)
Amanshauser, Hildegund
Josef Hoffmann. Variationen
Vienna, 1987

Wien 1987 Peche (exhib. cat.)
Dagobert Peche 1887–1923
Vienna, 1987

Wien 1988 (exhib. cat.)
Bogner, Dietrich (ed.)
*Friedrich Kiesler 1890–1965.
Architekt Maler Bildhauer*
Vienna, 1988

Wien 1990 (exhib. cat.)
*Egon Schiele. Frühe Reife, ewige
Kindheit*
Vienna, 1990

Wien 1990 Japonisme (exhib.
cat.)
Pantzer, Peter and Wieninger,
Johannes (eds.)
*Hidden Impressions. Japonisme in
Vienna 1870–1930.*
Vienna, 1990

Wien 1992 (exhib. cat.)
Völker, Angela and Pichler,
Ruperta (eds.)
*Abstraktes Textildesign in Wien
1899 bis 1912. Beispiele aus dem
Archiv der Firma Backhausen &
Söhne*
Vienna, 1992

Wien/Brtnice 1992 (exhib. cat.)
The Baroque Hoffmann
Vienna, 1992

Wiener Mode
Wiener Mode
Vienna, 1886 *et seq.*

WKK
*Waffen- und Kostümkunde.
Zeitschrift der Gesellschaft für
historische Waffen- und
Kostümkunde*
Berlin/Munich, 1959 *et seq.*

WMB
*Wasmuths Monatshefte für Bau-
kunst*
Berlin, 1914 et seq.

Yasinskaya/Bowlt 1983
Yasinskaya, I. and Bowlt, John E.
(introduction)
*Revolutionary Textile Design.
Russia in the 1920's and 1930's*
New York, 1983

Zurich 1983 (exhib. cat.)
Barten, Sigrid (ed.)
*Josef Hoffmann Wien. Jugendstil
und Zwanziger Jahre*
Zurich, 1983

Zurich 1987 (exhib. cat.)
Barten, Sigrid (ed.)
*rhythmen und farben. sonia
delaunay*
Zurich, 1987

Zurich/Salzburg 1989 (exhib.
cat.)
*Das Leben zur Kunst machen.
Arbeiten auf Papier von Frauen der
russischen Avantgarde. Stoffe und
Porzellan aus der jungen Sowjet-
union.*
Zurich/Salzburg, 1989